Policing: a short history

Policing and Society Series

Series editors: Les Johnston, Frank Leishman, Tim Newburn

Published titles

Policing, Ethics and Human Rights, by Peter Neyroud and Alan Beckley
Policing: a short history, by Philip Rawlings

Policing
A short history

Philip Rawlings

WILLAN
PUBLISHING

Published by

Willan Publishing
Culmcott House
Mill Street, Uffculme
Cullompton, Devon
EX15 3AT, UK
Tel: +44(0)1884 840337
Fax: +44(0)1884 840251
e-mail: info@willanpublishing.co.uk
website: www.willanpublishing.co.uk

Published simultaneously in the USA and Canada by

Willan Publishing
c/o ISBS, 5824 N.E. Hassalo St,
Portland, Oregon 97213-3644, USA
Tel: +001(0)503 287 3093
Fax: +001(0)503 280 8832
e-mail: info@isbs.com
website: www.isbs.com

First published 2002

ISBN 1-903240-26-3 Paperback
ISBN 1-903240-27-1 Hardback

British Library Cataloguing-in-Publication Data

A catalogue record for this book is available from the British Library

Printed and bound by T.J. International Ltd, Padstow, Cornwall PL28 8RW

Contents

Chapter 1

Introduction

The 'man in blue', as the policeman is often called, is one of our best friends. His job is to take care of us, and of our houses, gardens, parks, factories, schools and everything that belongs to each of us or to all of us.[1]

Police history

The establishment of the Metropolitan Police in 1829 has transfixed historians of the police. For some the new police emerged as a means of restoring the social cohesion that was claimed to have been lost through urbanization and industrialization. The police was, therefore, depicted as one of the nineteenth-century inventions which underpinned modern civilization and democracy: Critchley[2] wrote that the purpose of the police was to bring 'the security without which civilisation is impossible'; Melville Lee[3] thought 'the restraining influence exerted by a good police system is as necessary to the welfare of society as are self-imposed moral and physical restraints to the health of the individual'.

Discussion of the period before 1829 has, therefore, been dominated by that date. People and events only acquire importance in so far as they can be linked to the establishment of the new police and earlier models of police are set up to be unfavourably compared with what comes later. Critchley promised *A History of Police in England and Wales 900–1966*,[4] but sped through the first 929 years in 57 pages, while dallying over the next 137 years in the remaining 265 pages. His purpose in writing about the first period is made clear at the outset where he talks about finding the 'origins of the English police system' in the law and customs of the Danes and Anglo-Saxons and claims that 'the nearest equivalent to the modern policeman is the Saxon tythingman':[5]

> The history of the first 1,000 years of police in England, up to, say 1729, is mainly the story of how the tythingman changed into the parish constable, and latterly of the constable's slow decline; that of the next 100 years, in London at least, is the story of the way in which a medley of local parish officers and watchmen came to be replaced by a single body of constables embodied into a police *force*, the governing principles of which were unity of control and professional excellence.[6]

The old system, according to Critchley, was too corrupt and too inefficient to cope with the growth of population and wealth in the eighteenth century that brought criminality of an extent which 'defies description'.[7] Shakespeare's Dogberry, Verges, Elbow and Dull are assumed to be fair representations of the quality of watchmen and constables and the contempt in which they were held: constables 'were at best illiterate fools, and at worst as corrupt as the criminal classes from which not a few sprang'.[8] Since contemporaries found the existing system ineffective or worse, it stands to reason that people must have been casting about for an alternative. Some far-sighted individuals, such as Henry and John Fielding in the eighteenth century, launched experiments in which Critchley detects the first stirrings of the Metropolitan Police. However, these efforts were thwarted by 'apathy'.[9] Yet, although he acknowledges this apathy to be widespread, the nature of the opposition is largely dismissed as a wrongheaded fear of the importation of continental models of police. His view is clear. There is little need to waste time on the opponents of the new police or other forms of policing because both were wrong and doomed: doomed because they were eventually and inevitably abandoned, wrong because their ideas were doomed.

The dawn suddenly breaks and the opposition largely vanishes: the 1829 Act is passed 'without opposition and with scarcely any debate'.[10] There then follows the inevitable spread of this new idea and its rapid acceptance elsewhere. Other measures that inconveniently crop up to spoil the neat arrangement, such as the forces established under the Lighting and Watching Act 1833, are 'stop-gap' measures.[11]

By the 1960s the ideological bias of these histories was being noted by various writers.[12] The traditional histories certainly often seemed to have been prompted by a concern that the public failed to appreciate the police. Melville Lee was saddened that 'the general public has shewn

2

itself somewhat slow to acknowledge the debt which it owes to the men who undertake what is by common consent a thankless task' and hoped that his history would contribute to an 'increase in the tribute of public goodwill, that has been so well earned, and so long awaited, by the police forces of England.'[13]

Alas, fifty years on and Charles Reith still felt the lesson had not been learnt. He was prompted to write *A New Study of Police History* in 1956 by his exasperation with the general public and politicians who failed 'to understand the peculiar values of our police'.[14] In spite of its title, the aim of Reith's book was to urge a return to the principles of preventive policing promoted by the first Commissioners of the Metropolitan Police. He argued that their neglect 'accounts for much that is amiss in police administration in Britain today.'[15]

Those who, from the 1960s, sought to rewrite the history of the police tended also to focus on the establishment of the Metropolitan Police, to present it as inevitable and the police as social engineers. They believed, however, that industrialization and urbanization had led to a society divided along class lines and that the police reinforced those divisions and played an important role in the project of reducing working people to the discipline of industrial capitalism. Allan Silver agreed with the traditional historians that crime was rising in the eighteenth century, but he added a telling adjective to his description: 'Peaceful and *propertied* people in eighteenth-century London … confronted a level of daily danger to which they and their spokesmen reacted indignantly.'[16] He detects this class dimension as pervading eighteenth- and nineteenth-century discussion of crime: 'even where the term is not explicitly invoked, the image persists – one of an unmanageable, volatile, and convulsively criminal class at the base of society.' He adopts many of the arguments of the earlier historians, such as the view that before 1829 the police were 'inefficient'.

The traditional historians saw the connection between the police and the public as the key to its success and popularity, whereas Silver believed that, although the police acquired 'the moral assent of the general population', this was a form of false consciousness slyly manufactured by the police: 'even the earliest policemen were elaborately instructed in the demeanour and behavior required to evoke, establish, and sustain that assent.'[17] The police were, for him, a valuable weapon in the class war: they 'represented the penetration and continual presence of central political authority throughout daily life.'[18]

It is no coincidence that this first wave of revisionist history came in the 1960s during a broader assault on the notion of the benevolent welfare state by the civil rights movement and protesters against nuclear weapons and the Vietnam war. Revisionist historians saw engagement with contemporary issues as underpinning their work. Marxism's concern to analyze the class relations produced by capitalism directed them to the institutions of industrialization and the modern state, such as the factory, the prison and the police. This also meant that, like the traditional historians of the police, the revisionists did not have much interest in policing before 1829. Their task was to subject the institutions of the modern state to critical examination, so raw data about earlier policing and the origins of the new police were readily adopted from conservative historians.

Undoubtedly, the legislation that established the new police in the period between 1829 and 1856 is of great importance, but the focus on this period has led to a number of gaps in our knowledge. One has been the relative neglect of the history of police in the late nineteenth century and the twentieth century. For both the traditional and revisionist historians, once the new police were established, the history of the police largely came to an end.[19] On the other hand, by making explicit and challenging the theoretical framework of conservative history, the revisionists led others to look more closely at the latter's assumptions and factual data. The argument that the police emerged as an instrument of class oppression led to work which purported to demonstrate that this directed their practice and that, contrary to the assertions of the conservatives, there was strong resistance to the police from the working class.[20]

This still tended to leave the creation of the new police as decisive and as largely unexplained. Historians, therefore, began to turn their attention to the knotty problem of why the idea of radical police reform was suddenly accepted in 1829 when it appeared to have been so roundly rejected by a select committee in 1822.[21] The immediate context was subjected to closer examination and, for instance, the influence of the changes in policing in Ireland were made explicit.[22] There was also a re-examination of earlier policing institutions. This disputed the image of constables and watchmen as so many bumbling Dogberrys and revealed major reforms in the watch in London in the eighteenth century.[23] Historians began to look at these institutions within the context of contemporary expectations, and challenged the notion that early policing was corrupt and inefficient merely because it may not have met modern standards.[24]

Working the other way, historians have begun to unravel the nineteenth- and twentieth-century history of the police. Moreover, they have spread out from London and started to examine police history in other parts of the country. There is, in fact, a tradition of local police history. Most forces, past and present, have their historian, although many of the books and essays are in the nature of hagiographies or laments for a lost police force (a lot were written in the late 1960s when about two-thirds of the forces were abolished). Their approach is indicated by the tendency to break chapters at the changing of chief constables. However, they contain much interesting information and provide a useful glimpse into the archival material that is available. Since the 1970s there has been a flow of more critical studies of local police history which have broken out of the straightjacket of the new police and have examined, for instance, the alternative models of police established in the 1830s and 1840s.[25]

The history of the police that is emerging is one of diversity, both before and after 1829, and of slow, evolutionary change. Although the model used by the Metropolitan Police was influential, it was not exactly reproduced elsewhere. The diversity of types of police that existed in the early nineteenth century did not vanish. For instance, the railway police, security guards employed in warehouses and even private watchmen employed by householders did not only survive the establishment of the new police, they flourished. Furthermore, the establishment of the new police was not the end of its development.

Policing history

Recognizing that policing is not just what the police do shifts the focus from the 1829 act. Policing is an aspect of social control. Stan Cohen has defined social control as part of 'the organised ways in which society responds to behaviour and people it regards as deviant, problematic, worrying, threatening, troublesome or undesirable'.[26] This element of directed action has been incorporated into definitions of policing by Reiner:

> The concept of policing connotes efforts to provide security through surveillance and the threat of sanctioning…. Policing is the set of activities *directed* at preserving the security of a particular social order (although the effectiveness of any form of policing is a moot point). Policing does not encompass all activities intended to produce order. It excludes *post hoc* punishment, as well as activities intended to create the conditions of social order (for example socialization, measures to secure family stability, encouragement of religion, or other forms of internalized ethical controls).[27]

This opens an intriguing but frightening possibility for a broad history of

5

policing which recognizes its diversity. This book does not undertake that task. It is, instead, an attempt to use the idea of policing as a route into the state's involvement in policing; to consider questions such as, what shaped that involvement, its objectives and methods, and how these have changed? I do not apologize for the focus on the state police in the last three chapters since one of the main reasons for writing this book was to take a longer view of the question of what it is that the modern police are meant to be doing.

* * *

I have received help and support from a number of people: as always from my parents, Allen and Kay Rawlings, and from my colleagues at Warwick and, previously, at Brunel, in particular, John Lowry. I am a little nervous about acknowledging Richard Ireland's help in case it is taken to implicate him in some way in what follows and his career suffers as a result. I used a number of libraries, but would particularly single out the Rare Books Room at the British Library, whose staff only have themselves to blame for the fact that I spent more time there than at home. Part of this book was written in a flat in Berkeley, for which I must thank Simon Halliday and Sharon Cowan. Brian Willan tore his hair out quietly. Sharon was understanding and reassuring and there.

Notes

1 Adams (1962) *Policemen and the Police Force*, 6.
2 Critchley (1978) *A History of Police*, 321.
3 Lee (1901) *A History of Police*, xi.
4 Critchley (1967) *A History of Police*.
5 Critchley (1978) *A History of Police*, 1.
6 Critchley (1978) *A History of Police*, 29. Also Lee (1901) *A History of Police*, 176.
7 Critchley (1978) *A History of Police*, 21.
8 Critchley (1978) *A History of Police*, 19. Also Lee (1901) *A History of Police*, 108.
9 Critchley (1978) *A History of Police*, 34.
10 Critchley (1978) *A History of Police*, 50.
11 Critchley (1978) *A History of Police*, 60.
12 Robinson (1979) 'Ideology as history'.
13 Lee (1901) *A History of Police*, 409.
14 Reith (1956) *A New Study of Police History*, 246.
15 Reith (1956) *A New Study of Police History*, 135.
16 Silver (1967) 'The demand for order in civil society', 1. Emphasis supplied.
17 Silver (1967) 'The demand for order in civil society', 14.

18 Silver (1967) 'The demand for order in civil society', 12–13.
19 But see Critchley (1978) *A History of Police*.
20 Storch (1975) 'The plague of blue locusts'; Storch (1976) 'The policeman as domestic missionary'.
21 Select Committee (1822) *Report … on the Police of the Metropolis*, 9. See chapter 5.
22 Palmer (1988) *Police and Protest*.
23 Kent (1986) *The English Village Constable*; Reynolds (1998) *Before the Bobbies*.
24 See, for instance, Wrightson (1980) 'Two concepts of order'.
25 Davey (1983) *Lawless and Immoral*; Storch (1989) 'Policing in rural Southern England before the police'; Philips and Storch (1999) *Policing Provincial England*.
26 Cohen (1985) *Visions of Social Control*, 1. Also Johnston (2000) *Policing Britain*, 7–10; Reiner (1997) 'Policing and the police', 1003.
27 Reiner (1997) 'Policing and the police', 1005.

Chapter 2

From the blood feud to the justice of the peace: 600–1400

The blood feud

The reliance we in the twenty-first century appear to place on the modern police to deal with a mixed bag of wrongs rather arbitrarily labelled as crimes would seem very odd to our ancestors. If someone steals from me or attacks me, they might have said, it is up to me to decide on my response, if any. I might take back the stolen property or exact physical revenge or agree compensation or do nothing. I might ask for – and expect to receive – help from my kin and neighbours. Of course, the strong or well-connected thief is more easily able to escape any retribution. Then again, the action by the victim might lead the alleged offender to retaliate, perhaps because the 'thief' claimed the goods were her or his property or because the action taken was considered excessive.[1] Sir William Holdsworth suggested that, 'Physical force is the natural method of redressing wrongs, and, when men are grouped in small families or communities, this leads naturally to the blood feud.'[2] But he recognized that the long-term existence of any community[3] depends on its ability to resolve disputes. In his study of the Franks, Wallace-Hadrill noted that communities seem rarely to have been torn apart by the blood feud:

> Feuding, in the sense of incessant private war, is a myth; feuding in the sense of very widespread and frequent procedures to reach composition and settlements necessarily hovering on the edge of bloodshed, is not. The marvel of early medieval society is not war but peace.[4]

The organization of pre-literate societies is difficult to piece together, but the evidence of anthropologists gives some useful clues. People join together in a community for a variety of reasons – love, friendship, co-operation, safety, prosperity. In an essay on these issues which shifts between the Anglo-Saxons in the early medieval period and the Nuer in Africa in the twentieth century, Gluckman argued that individuals 'obtain their rights by virtue of membership of groups, and they can only maintain themselves by virtue of this membership.'[5] This is most easily seen in a pre-technological, agricultural community in which planting, reaping and so forth require the co-operation of one's neighbours. This interdependence does not remove the individual's personal motivations – revenge, jealousy, greed – for action, but it does empower the community. Paradoxically, where a community rests on the need for co-operation the potential for disputes is likely to be high, but so is the damage which can be caused by those disputes which cannot be resolved between the parties. For these reasons it is in the interests of the community to develop methods for resolving disputes, and for these methods to gain support it is likely that they will be grounded in religion or ritual or some sense of community opinion, or placed in the hands of community leaders.

Gluckman also described how tensions between different sets of loyalties worked to resolve disputes. He argued that people were typically members of more than one community and this established different – and often conflicting – sets of loyalties. Marriage between two people connects each spouse to the kin of the other and sets up conflicts of loyalties: there is conflict between loyalty to one's blood-kin and loyalty to the kin of one's spouse, and both sets of kin, now joined through the marriage, have similarly conflicting loyalties. Because these loyalties pull in different directions, they increase the likelihood that disputes between the two sets of kin will be resolved by peaceful means.

> A man's blood-kin are not always his neighbours: the ties of kinship and locality conflict. And all these ties, I repeat, are elaborately set in custom and backed with ritual beliefs … Over longer periods of time and wider ranges of society the conflicts between these relationships become cohesion … Feud is waged and vengeance taken when the parties live sufficiently far apart, or are too weakly related by diverse ties. Even when they are close together, hot-headedness and desire for prestige may lead to vengeance and constant fighting. But where they are close together, many institutions and ties operate to exert pressure on the quarrellers to reach a settlement.… A man's several loyalties strike at the strength of his

loyalty to any one group or set of relationships, which is thus divided. Hence the whole system depends for its cohesion on the existence of conflicts in smaller sub-systems.[6]

This would suggest that distinctions are made between members of the community and strangers. Since in relation to the latter the concern to maintain harmony is absent, there is little need for mediation. Indeed, the stranger may be feared as a threat and treated accordingly. On the other hand, once a community develops relationships with the world beyond its borders through, perhaps, marriage or trade, those relationships will influence the way 'strangers' who have connections with the village are likely to be treated.

In a cross-cultural study of 51 societies, Schwartz and Miller found that only the simplest societies lack a mechanism for non-kin, third-party mediation in disputes. That deficiency, they argued, might be because these societies are so small that there are fewer disputes and, therefore, less opportunity to develop such mechanisms; they may also have more effective informal controls which prevent disputes from arising; the struggle for survival may reduce internal disputes; or the lack of money and substantial property may reduce the likelihood of disputes because 'property provides something to quarrel about' and 'seems to provide something to mediate with as well.'[7] Yet the development of a mechanism for the mediation of a dispute does not necessarily imply the existence of a means of enforcement, so that, unless there is a mutually acceptable settlement, the implicit threat of the resort to the blood feud may become a reality:[8] as the English proverb put it, 'Buy off the spear or bear it'.[9]

The function of the Anglo-Saxon laws: 600–1066

The most immediate legal impact of the conversion to Christianity in 597 of the Kentish king Æthelberht (died 616) was the adoption of the Christian-Roman practice of writing down laws.[10] The Church also played an important role in sanctifying the king and proclaiming to the people that law, order and justice were key aspects of his responsibilities. Moreover, the political significance of the king owning the laws through the act of having them written down is obvious. The influence of Christianity on the substance of the laws was more gradual and, initially at least, the codes reflected existing custom. Wormald detects a significant shift 'from codified *lex* to royal *edicta*'[11] as early as the laws of Ine (*c.* 690), and he demonstrates that the transition is clear by the late ninth century. Under Alfred (871–99) the law became 'the aggressive weapon of a new state',[12] one of the tools used by the Anglo-Saxon kings to fuse England into a single nation under a single set of laws. Alfred's 'comparison of English law with what God gave Moses implied dramatic new ambitions for his people. Crime could now be perceived as an outrage against God, punishment as his expression of this anger.'[13] The law drew legitimacy and authority from its roots in custom and Christian teaching, but it was now an instrument of state: 'law was at once the vehicle of accepted "popular" tradition and a tool of aggressive royal policy'.[14]

The law reflected the feud-centred nature of Anglo-Saxon society by acknowledging that enforcement was legitimately a matter for the victim and their kin. The codes do refer to compensation,[15] but it seems reasonable to suppose that compensation and the feud had long been interdependent. Compensation was another method of pursuing the feud and people might drift between the two during the course of a dispute.[16] On the other hand, the tariff of payments set out in the Anglo-Saxon laws may have eased the process of settlement,[17] and formalizing the practice of compensation may also have facilitated the extraction of money in a broader range of cases than laid down in the laws.

Of course, it is not possible to tell how often the tariffs were used, or whether they were set at levels which allowed the rich to escape and condemned the poor to debt slavery, or whether the parties agreed to payments which were lower than the tariff figure.[18] While the existence of procedures for compensation did not guarantee payment, the threat of the blood feud as well as custom, the opinion of neighbours, religious belief and fealty provided pressure to settle, although, presumably, the more powerful individuals were better able either to enforce or to resist a settlement.[19]

Anglo-Saxon society was not just organized around the kindred relationships upon which the blood feud rested, loyalty to one's lord – and, therefore, to the king – was of central importance. A wrong injured not just the victim but also the lord or king within whose territory it occurred because it offended against that person's sovereignty. The Anglo-Saxon codes of law sought to break open the kindred relationship and turn it into a mechanism which supported the state under the king rather than competed with it. The requirement that local communities pursue offenders and deliver them to the royal courts rearticulated the notion of self-help inherent in the feud into an obligation owed to the king.[20] Placing the obligation to respond to an offence on a community as defined by the law rather than by consanguinity meant that the right of retaliation began to be conceptualized as an aspect of every person's public duty, not as a right of revenge or as a duty owed to the victim through a kindred relationship. According to the laws of Athelstan (925–39) if a thief fled:

> [he] shall be pursued to his death by all men who are willing to carry out the king's wishes, and whoever shall meet him shall kill him. And he who spares or harbours him shall forfeit his life and all that he has as if he were a thief himself, unless he can prove that he was not aware of any theft or crime for which his [the fugitive's] life was forfeit.[21]

Generally, the laws asserted the pre-eminence of formal justice over private revenge and restricted the circumstances in which the victim could inflict summary punishment. For instance, the laws of Æthelberht required anyone who 'take revenge before he demand justice' to relinquish what had been taken and pay for any damage as well as compensate the invasion of the other's rights.[22] A hundred years later, the laws of Ine stated that, 'If a thief is taken he shall die the death, or his life shall be redeemed by the payment' of a fixed amount. However,

> He who kills a thief shall be allowed to declare with an oath that he whom he killed was a thief trying to escape, and the kinsman of the dead then shall swear an oath to carry on no feud against him. If however he keeps it secret, and it afterwards comes to light, then he shall pay for it.[23]

The laws of Edward the Elder (899–925), Athelstan (925–39) and Edmund (939–46) stated that certain types of offenders could be summarily executed – that is, without having been put through a formal trial – only if they had fled or had ignored a summons to appear in court. Increasingly, the laws acknowledged the need to atone to the king, as well as the victim, through the payment of a fine, and even declaring that certain offences could not be settled by compensation but only by execution or mutilation.

Yet, in spite of the shifts away from the blood-feud and towards a more formal system of justice, the dependence on private prosecution left the key decision to initiate proceedings with the victim. This enabled the pursuit of different agendas, such as concealing an offence to protect a relative. Depending on the objectives of the royal justice system, this need not have been a problem. However, as will be seen during the course of this book, what emerged over a long period was a tension between the state's conceptions of justice and those subscribed to by the community and the individual. While the state continued to rely on the community and the individual, it eventually sought to control their involvement by, for instance, limiting further and eventually criminalizing non-judicial forms of justice, such as direct violence against an offender and even settlements between the offender and the victim. This subordination of the community and the individual only became properly explicit – although never fully realized – with the rise of professional state-police forces in the nineteenth century; nevertheless it was inherent in the formation of the state.

Law enforcement after the Conquest

The legal and administrative systems that emerged after the Conquest in 1066 were built upon foundations laid by the Anglo-Saxons. The duty to uphold law, order and justice throughout the kingdom was at the core of the medieval concept of kingship.[24] In the eleventh century, Bishop Wulfstan claimed that one object of kingship was to promote the spiritual welfare of the people through, among other things, the use of force against evildoers,[25] and the preamble to a statute of 1284 claimed that Edward I wished to,

> promote pleasantness and ease and quiet for our subjects dwelling in our realm, for in their quiet we have rest, and in their tranquillity we are inwardly cherished with the scent of satisfaction amidst the flowers of hoped-for peace.[26]

At the same time, the justice system provided a valuable source of revenue through fines and the confiscation of property from felons. Moreover, while the king could only fulfil his duty by placing obligations on others to maintain the peace and arrest offenders, this opened up the possibility of boosting the royal revenues through fines imposed on people who neglected these duties.

The connection with the personal and communal elements of the blood-feud in the Anglo-Saxon codes of law remained after the Conquest, but the process by which these elements were being rearticulated within a judicial context and a set of obligations owed to the king also continued. The most obvious manifestation of the survival of the blood feud was the summary execution of felons caught in the act or 'beheaded as a thief in flight'.[27] As Richard Ireland has shown, 'proof by fact of capture in circumstances of evident guilt, is an integral part of the twelfth-century legal system, though its use is restricted to cases where the evidence is so strong as to be equivalent to confession'.[28] At Northampton in 1329 the royal justices heard how Simon Vyel of Cranford had escaped from custody when two of the men guarding him on the journey to Northampton castle went into a church to attend divine service. Simon was pursued and, refusing to surrender, had his head cut off by one of his pursuers, Robert Aldif of Wolweston. The judges declared that Aldiff – who died before the hearing – should have been arrested and arraigned 'because he had made himself judge. But if the facts were found to be described above he would be acquitted'.[29]

Prosecution through the appeal of felony was introduced after the Conquest,[30] but it also demonstrated the continued focus on the victim. It carried echoes of the blood-feud in the personal nature of the accusation by the appellor, the way proof was offered 'by his body' (that is, by battle), and in leaving the victim the choice about whether to pursue an appeal. Indeed, it is unclear if there was a formal mechanism by which the king could prosecute offenders. This issue was tackled under Henry II (1154–89), who was keen to address problems of law and order through a more powerful central government machine.

By the mid-twelfth century the jury of presentment, composed of men from the hundred and the vills, was required to present any felons who lived in the local community to the royal justices.[31] By this means the king could bring offenders into court. The problem was that the appeal took precedence so the presentment could only be used if there had been no appeal. Henry II and his successors, therefore, encouraged those who had brought appeals not to abandon them by, for instance, imposing fines for doing so, and in the early thirteenth century by passing abandoned appeals on to a jury. Under Henry III, the king became ' "a shadow appellor" who stepped in and prosecuted to protect his peace when an appellor abandoned an appeal'.[32] This empowered the crown and largely sealed the fate of the appeal.

The other method introduced under Henry II to take control of the prosecution process was the approver's appeal. The basis of this was described in the 1170s:

> But when some notorious criminal is apprehended by the King's officers of the peace, crime being so rife, the justices sometimes consent, as an extreme measure to purge the country of criminals, that if such a man confesses and turns King's evidence against his associates, and succeeds in proving by battle a charge against one or more of them, he may escape the death he has deserved, and save his skin by losing his civil rights and abjuring the realm.[33]

Henry II also used 'King's approvers' and hired 'crown approvers' to accuse people of crimes against the crown, even though the appellors had not been either injured or associated with the appellees.

The crown's growing interest in crime can also be seen in the law enforcement system as it emerged in the thirteenth century. Greater emphasis was placed on the role of the community and its accountability to the king through the system of frankpledge, the watch, the hue and cry and the judgment of outlawry. The origins of frankpledge lie in obligations to pursue offenders and to ensure the good behaviour of other members of the community which first appeared before the Conquest.[34] By, at the latest, the early twelfth century these two facets merged into the system of frankpledge, which appeared across most of the south of England. Each frankpledge unit was based upon a vill or township, which was then split into tithings. All men – free and servile – were required to be members of a tithing, although clergy and wealthy freemen were exempted. On being received into frankpledge, an oath of loyalty to the king was sworn, indicating that the roots of communal policing lay in obligations owed to the crown and in the crown's overall responsibility for law and its enforcement. Each member also promised, 'I … will not be a thief nor the fellow of a thief, nor will I conceal a theft nor a thief but will reveal it to those to whom it should be revealed.'[35]

In charge of the tithing were one or two chief pledges, who were elected, although the sheriff had overall responsibility for regulating the frankpledge and ensuring that all eligible males were in tithings. The chief pledges were meant to lead the tithing in pursuit of offenders and to represent it at the view of frankpledge held once or twice a year. Strangers to a village had to find pledges from among the tithing members who were willing to guarantee their good behaviour; those receiving strangers who were not bonded or harbouring local residents who were not in frankpledge were liable to be fined and held responsible for their good behaviour.[36] In 1279 jurors sitting at Little Stukeley found,

> that William Salathiel received a stranger, Robert of Coldmorton by name, who is an iron-smith; therefore he is mercy [fined], 6d.; pledge, Hugh Thomas's son. And the said Robert found pledges, namely William Salathiel, Ralph of Stowe, that he will behave as a faithful subject in his going and coming in the vill of Stukeley without occasioning harm to any.[37]

The tithing was also required to keep in custody offenders until they could be handed over to the sheriff, prevent those felons who had reached sanctuary from escaping (a felon who reached asylum under the protection of the Church was, under certain conditions, able to abjure the realm),[38] and secure any evidence and witnesses.[39]

The watch reinforced the idea of inclusion-exclusion which was at the core of the system of frankpledge.[40] The Assizes of the Watch of 1233, 1242 and 1253 (also the Statute of Winchester 1285, below) obliged every town, borough and city to set a watch each night during the summer, which was when, the roads being drier, travel was easiest and vagrants thought more likely to seek entry. The watch was to arrest strangers and pursue those who sought to flee. The escape of a felon or the failure to set a watch would result in a fine.[41] Although the enthusiasm with which the watchmen undertook their duties doubtless varied, some appear to have been determined, like those from Northumbria who chased a group of offenders for almost 50 miles in 1287, while others were little short of heroic, such as the watchmen in Oxford in 1300 who, having arrested an armed man, lost him when they were attacked by a gang of his comrades, so gave chase and managed to arrest two men. The watch was probably better kept when the townspeople felt themselves to be in danger, such as during an outbreak of the plague or at market-time when strangers were attracted to a town.[42]

The pursuit of an offender was not just a matter for the watch. Victims varied in their enthusiasm for the chase: while many doubtless did nothing, Given notes one thirteenth-century case where the victim chased three burglars through Buckinghamshire into Oxfordshire and eventually took them in Northamptonshire.[43] Neighbours might also join in, prompted, as Vinogradoff put it, by 'the natural cry for help of the victim of an assault'.[44] Whether or not there was a formal duty to follow the hue and cry before the Conquest,[45] it certainly existed by the late twelfth century. The victim, or, following a homicide, the person who found the body raised the hue and cry 'with horn and mouth'.[46] The hue was carried into neighbouring communities, which then had a responsibility for raising the hue locally and, if necessary, passing it to the next community. An illustration of how the watch and the hue operated comes from Northamptonshire:

At Heyford on 30 May 1317, Robert fitz Bartholomew of Heyford received certain unknown thieves as guests in his house. The watchmen of the town saw that those thieves were staying up suspiciously late in the night and therefore went to enter the house; when they came to one door Robert and the rest of the thieves went out the other door. The hue and cry were raised at once and the men of the town came to pursue and arrest the aforesaid felons. Among the men of the town came a certain John of Bannebury, who has now died, who pursued the felons, calling upon them to surrender to the king's peace. They would by no means surrender or permit themselves to be judged by the law, nor could those who were pursuing them take them alive. A general fight ensued between the felons and their pursuers, and John of Bannebury cut off the head of the aforesaid Robert. The chattels of the aforesaid Robert are confiscated for flight.[47]

Finally, if a felon did escape, then he or she could have the protection of the law withdrawn by the judgment of outlawry. The felon was summoned before four sittings of the county court and would be declared an outlaw at the fifth:[48] according to the late thirteenth-century text, *The Mirror of Justice*,[49] '[the outlaw] shall be accounted a wolf … for that a wolf is a beast hated of all folk; and from that time forward it is lawful for anyone to slay him like a wolf.'

While this system seemed based on the responsibilities of the whole community, it quickly acquired a profusion of officials with overlapping duties and mechanisms of review to check and re-check whether appropriate actions had been taken. What was being constructed was not just a means of apprehending offenders, but also a way of rendering the community and particular individuals accountable for their actions. For instance, the case from Northampton quoted above shows that the hue was not simply a way of pursuing offenders, it was also a means of rendering the local community accountable for its policing work since every raising of the hue was inquired into by the hundred court and by the royal judges. If it was improperly raised or not properly pursued, fines were imposed.

In the counties the key official was the sheriff,[50] who was, among other things, responsible for the custody of offenders handed over to him and for regulating the system of frankpledge. The sheriff could also call out the *posse comitatus*, which consisted of all adult males, against vagabonds and malefactors. However, from the late twelfth century the sheriffs began to lose their authority. They were regarded as too powerful and too independent to be trusted with the pursuit of the crown's interests to the exclusion of their own. Their authority was slowly undermined by the creation of new officials to whom power was delegated by the crown. From 1194 coroners were appointed by the crown, apparently as a result of Richard II's financial difficulties. One of their tasks was to track the progress of crown pleas and, thereby, protect the crown's interest in any fines that might be due and any property that might be confiscated from felons. Their other duties included, holding inquests upon dead bodies, receiving abjurations of the realm made by felons in sanctuary, hearing appeals, confessions of felons and appeals of approvers, and attending and sometimes organizing exactions and outlawries promulgated in the county court.[51]

The coroner could also attach or arrest witnesses and suspects.

Other officials had principally executive roles. Some of these offices were more or less permanent features of the justice system, others were short-term experiments. Keepers of the peace were appointed for relatively short periods to meet particular exigencies and undertake specific tasks. The first appointments may have followed the edict of 1195 which had been intended to reinforce the obligation of communities to pursue offenders.[52] They were appointed at various times in the thirteenth century to assist the sheriffs in maintaining order and to organize military defence, particularly during times of crisis, such as in the wake of the Baron's War in the 1260s. Serjeants of the peace were appointed in places where there was no system of frankpledge, such as in Wales, on the English side of the Welsh borders and in the north of England.[53] They undertook to arrest and keep in custody offenders, secure evidence and witnesses, make presentments about offences and offenders to courts, and secure the chattels of felons. In Shropshire about a dozen professional serjeants of the peace were appointed in the late twelfth century, but they were abolished in the 1220s following complaints that they were a source of oppression.[54] In 1223 John of Thornton led eight serjeants to Yorkshire in pursuit of 'brigands and malefactors who were wandering' the county and a similar commission was issued to Walter, son of Robert, to keep the roads of Bedfordshire, Cambridgeshire and Huntingdonshire safe.[55] Serjeants of the peace were appointed in some twenty English counties in 1241,[56] but the office had largely vanished by the next century.

In England there was also a variety of lesser officials with responsibilities for law enforcement.[57] Serjeants of the hundred or the wapentake[58] were responsible to the sheriff and performed some of the functions later acquired by the coroner, such as supervising the progress of pleas of the crown. The constables of castles or castellans were appointed by, and took their instructions from, the crown and worked in co-operation with the sheriff. Constables of the hundred and the vill or township were elected annually from and by members of those communities. They had a range of military, policing and revenue functions: for example, they were required to ensure that individuals possessed arms (Statute of Winchester 1285, c. 6) and that the hue and cry was properly pursued. The constable also arrested people on the instructions of the sheriff or coroner and guarded both offenders and the property of those accused of felony. Bailiffs itinerant or errant travelled across designated parts of the county executing royal writs on the instructions of the sheriff. Bailiffs of the hundred were, among other things, expected to pursue those whom the hue failed to catch, to carry out administrative orders for the sheriff and, most importantly, to empanel juries, a role which opened them to the accusation of providing favourable juries for those willing to pay. The hundred bailiff was assisted by sub-bailiffs, bedels (beadles), constables and so forth. These minor officials were vital in connecting the micro-community of the vill or the manor to the macro-community of the shire. They were not confined to one function within the legal system and might, for instance, also sit as members of a presenting jury.[59] Their work and the degree of autonomy they enjoyed depended on the county, their own characters, the energy and attitude of their immediate superiors, and their relationship with the communities in which they operated. In the boroughs a similar network of officials existed, including, at its summit, the mayor, the borough coroner and the bailiffs.[60]

Local officers reported to other officials and to courts in a system designed to allow multiple opportunities for supervision. Overseeing that entire structure was the general eyre, which was conducted by royal justices. They tried felons, but, most importantly, they reviewed the system of law enforcement and punished any neglect. By the mid-twelfth century a structured system of county-by-county visitations was under way, apparently as part of Henry II's initiative on law and order.[61] While Henry laid emphasis on the responsibility of the community, he also sought to facilitate broader and more effective royal supervision: as Hudson puts it, 'Judicial activity and law continued to be characterized by a considerable degree of local self-government, but in important aspects it was self-government at the king's command.'[62]

From the crown's point of view, the eyre served four main purposes: it asserted royal authority and provided an opportunity to disseminate among the county's élite the government's views on a range of issues through the opening speech of the presiding judge; it ensured that local law enforcement systems were working efficiently; it enhanced royal revenues by imposing fines on those who had not performed their duties and by ensuring that the fines and property taken from felons were rendered to the crown; and it imposed a degree of uniformity on government throughout the country. Some idea of the depth of the inquiry undertaken and the possibilities it opened up for raising revenue can be gathered from a case before the eyre of Northampton in 1329:

The jurors [of Brackley] present that Geoffrey le Saltere of Yorlauston and Agnes wife of Richard le Saltere of Wouminton, who were from Staffordshire, killed the aforesaid Richard le Saltere by night in the house of Denise Crabbe in Brackley. The aforesaid Agnes and Denise were arrested after the deed and conducted to the gaol in Northampton castle. Robert le Baud was sheriff at that time. Therefore the holders of the lands belonging to the aforesaid Robert are to answer what became of the prisoners. The aforesaid Geoffrey fled immediately after the deed, and the jurors suspect that he is guilty of the aforesaid killing; therefore let him be *exacted* and *outlawed*. He had no chattels, and because he was a vagabond he was not in tithing.... By judgment the township is charged with a murder. And the township of Brackley is in *mercy* [i.e. fined] because when the hue was raised it did not pursue it to the next township, as is customary. And the jurors are in mercy because they report nothing concerning the neighbours. No one appears for the aforesaid holders of lands to answer what became of the aforesaid Agnes and Denise. Therefore an *escape* by the said Agnes and Denise is adjudged against the aforesaid tenants. And after Agnes and Denise escaped they fled, and it is suspected that they are guilty; therefore let them be *exacted* and *waived*. They had no chattels.[63]

The eyre was a victim of its own success as the expansion of its terms of reference dragged out the proceedings and reduced the frequency of visits. This meant it became less useful as an instrument for supervising local administration, raising revenue and, because it was unlikely that the eyre would return for a long time, improving the future behaviour of officials. That the limited value of the eyre was recognized long before its final demise in the fourteenth century is indicated by the development of more precise instruments of royal supervision in the counties. As has been mentioned, the first coroners were appointed in 1194 to supervise crown pleas, then in the early thirteenth century commissions of gaol delivery were issued for the conduct of felony trials and by the end of that century there was a network of circuits of assize and gaol delivery (these circuits were linked in 1299) staffed by serjeants and officials from the royal courts, supplemented in the early fourteenth century by royal justices and members of the local gentry.[64]

While those who had obligations in connection with law enforcement were doubtless encouraged to fulfil them by the penalties that might be imposed, this also encouraged them to take greater care in concealing offences where, perhaps, they had failed, or did not wish, to apprehend a criminal. There was a variety of reasons why individuals or whole communities might avoid their obligations: fear, a simple desire not to get involved, sympathy for someone who had accidentally killed during a quarrel,[65] or a preference for the use of extra-judicial methods, such as reprisal or settlement. The villagers of Cleaving in Yorkshire seem to have been sympathetic to the plight of John of Cleaving, for when he returned to his home in the early thirteenth century having been outlawed for the death of his wife's brother, not only did the villagers fail to surrender him to the authorities, they attended a party which he gave to celebrate his homecoming.[66]

The most notorious case of a community closing ranks to protect offenders occurred in 1248 after some Brabantine merchants had been robbed as they were passing through Alton in Hampshire. The local people were only induced to bring any accusations against the offenders by the intervention of Henry III, who was concerned at the impact the crime might have on trade.[67] People may not have wished to expose themselves to the risk of being killed during a pursuit, as was the fate of the constable of Brackley in the early fourteenth century.[68] There was also the danger of retaliation: Simon, son of Edward of Ardsley, may have been murdered in 1218 because as serjeant of the wapentake he had been involved in the arrest of Adam de Almele, who had been hanged for robbery;[69] Henry Bobbe, who had been involved in the execution of Robert le Bole in 1303, was shortly afterwards ambushed and killed; the enthusiastic pursuit of criminal gangs in Rutland by Sir John Wittlebury, who was a keeper of the peace, seems to have led to his murder in 1336; and in the 1330s one royal justice, Richard de Willoughby, was kidnapped and another, Roger Bellers, murdered by gangs.[70]

Although the system of law enforcement continued to draw on traditions of the blood-feud in its focus on the victim, by the thirteenth century the crown had both asserted its right and recognized its obligation to intervene in the delivery of justice. It sought to fill gaps in the policing system and hold people to the duties which were imposed on them by appointing officials, such as the keepers of the peace and serjeants of the peace, by establishing mechanisms through which the crown could initiate inquiries into offences, and by creating processes to enable the operation of the law enforcement system to be reviewed. Yet, it is also clear that this strategy of greater royal intervention and greater accountability to the crown could be met by resistance: from the silence of the victim and the concealment of the villagers to the corrupt practices through which the more powerful could distort the law enforcement system to their own ends.

The law-and-order crises in the thirteenth and fourteenth centuries

The period from the late thirteenth century through to the middle of the fourteenth century saw a good deal of experimentation in methods of law enforcement. The preamble of the Statute of Winchester 1285 (13 Edw. I, c. 1) lamented that, 'Robberies, Murthers, Burnings and Theft, be more often used than they have been heretofore', and blamed this on the poor state of law enforcement. Forty years later the situation seemed not to have improved. The chief justice, Sir Geoffrey Scrope, told those present at the opening of the general eyre of Northampton in 1329:

> In the last parliament at Northampton complaints were brought to our lord the king from all parts of the kingdom that the people were suffering severely under manifold oppressions of magnates and from the extortions of maintainers, the petty tyranny of bailiffs, and homicides and thefts committed throughout the kingdom, and many from all parts who were troubled asked that measures be taken to deal with these problems.[71]

Concern about law and order during this period was a symptom of a range of problems. Some of these were associated with war and civil unrest: Edward I's enthusiasm for fighting his neighbours; the overthrow of Edward II by Queen Isabella and Mortimer; Edward III's *coup d'état* of 1330, his struggle to establish his authority, and then the continuation of wars begun by his grandfather. There were also social and economic upheavals. By the end of the thirteenth century the population had risen rapidly, but the economy was beginning to stagnate, partly as a result of the enormous cost of war. Food production declined causing prices to rise and there was a devastating famine between 1315 and 1318 which killed large numbers of people. This was followed by the plague in 1348 during which perhaps as many as half the population died.[72]

The crown's policies exacerbated these problems. While Edward I and his successors initiated various campaigns to deal with crime (see below), their insatiable demand for soldiers led them to grant pardons to those felons who agreed to join the army.[73] Legislation apparently ending this practice was enacted in 1328 (2 Edw. III, c. 2) and re-enacted in 1330 (4 Edw. III, c. 13), 1336 (10 Edw. III, c. 2) and 1340 (14 Edw. III, c. 15), but as each new period of fighting approached, the demand for fresh recruits overwhelmed other considerations. People who lived on the Scottish and Welsh borders and in those coastal counties facing France grew to fear the English troops garrisoned on them almost as much as an invasion. Moreover, as fighting ended and the army was rapidly demobilized to save the crown money, men, who had been brutalized by their experiences, were discharged with little prospect of work and were met by crown policies which treated them as criminals to be swept up. In the 1290s Edward I established commissions of inquiry into vagrancy and in 1361 justices of the peace were instructed to deal with 'all those who have been pillagers and robbers in parts beyond the sea, and have now returned and go wandering and will not labour as they were wont to do in times past'.[74] But these law-and-order policies ran up against the earlier strategy of recruiting by pardoning felons; so, for instance, when Edward I sent out special commissions of royal justices (the trailbaston commissions) in the early fourteenth century to tackle crime, they were regularly confronted by serious offenders waving royal pardons.[75]

Finally, the policing mechanisms based on kinship and neighbourliness, such as frankpledge and the hue, were undermined because village populations became less stable as a result of the increased mobility which accompanied the expansion and contraction of the economy and the rise and fall in the general population during the thirteenth and fourteenth centuries. While there were attempts to reinforce communal responsibilities for policing, these were made in ways which in fact increased the tendency for law enforcement functions to pass to local officials acting as representatives for the community. This not only offered the possibility of more effective accountability (although not necessarily the means), it also gave a continuity to functions by attaching them to an office rather than an individual or community.

The Statute of Winchester 1285 (13 Edw. I)[76] seems to confirm many of the key features of the communal policing system. It required all felonies to be publicized and felons actively pursued (c.1):

> Cries shall be solemnly made in all Counties, Hundreds, Markets, Fairs, and all other Places where great Resort of People is, so that none shall excuse himself by Ignorance, that from henceforth every County be so well kept, that immediately, upon such Robberies and Felonies committed, fresh Suit shall be made from Town to Town, and from Country to Country.

The hundred in which an unsolved robbery was committed was to compensate the victim (c. 2).[77] The gates of towns were to be closed from sunset to sunrise and a watch posted during the summer months to arrest strangers where 'they find Cause for Suspicion' and deliver them to the sheriff. If a stranger fled, the watch was 'to levy Hue and Cry upon them … from Town to Town'. Strangers were not forbidden entry into a town, but the bailiffs were to ensure that any resident who gave lodging to a stranger was to 'answer for him' (c. 4). The obligation to pursue the hue and cry was reinforced by the requirement that adult males maintained arms (c. 5. The Assize of Arms 1253 required the vill to pay for a communal store of arms for the watch). Each side of the highway was to be cleared to reduce the hiding places for robbers (c. 5). Some aspects of the statute seem to have had an immediate impact, such as the provisions on the watch, while others were resented and obstructed – claims for compensation by robbery victims could take years.[78] By 1300 government was complaining that crime had risen because the statute was not being observed; in 1306, as Edward I was about to set out on a campaign against Robert the Bruce, the sheriffs were instructed to read the statute at their county courts;[79] and again in 1354 people were urged to pursue robbers 'according to the form contained in the Statute late made at Winchester'.[80]

The statute rapidly became a symbol of communal self-policing such that the leaders of the Peasants' Revolt of 1381 rebuffed government intervention in local affairs with a demand that there should be 'no law but the law of Winchester'.[81] Yet the existence of the statute suggests that communal policing had already begun to lose its connection to an instinctive common self-interest. Moreover, by the late thirteenth century a substantial body of local officials existed on whom duties connected with law enforcement had been devolved and this continued: for instance, although the Statute of Winchester required the community to pursue and arrest felons by means of the hue and cry, legislation in 1331, while not abolishing this role and while maintaining the liability of the hundred to compensate victims, specified that the primary responsibility for raising the hue lay with the constable.[82]

There remained something of a problem in ensuring that local officials undertook their duties as defined by the crown, and it was only with the creation in the mid-fourteenth century of the justice of the peace that something approaching a solution to this was hit upon.[83] The plague in 1348 created a shortage of labour which encouraged higher wages and mobility among workers. This threatened the final collapse of a political structure built on land and there seems to have emerged an acceptance that the nature of the problem required a national solution and, therefore, greater intervention by the crown supported by a more cohesive ruling élite. What occurred in the mid-fourteenth century was an intensification of the crown's interest in local government executed by means of law and through local officials.

> Authority throughout society, came more thoroughly to be exercised not by virtue of innate individual power but by virtue of state mandate, and the government took responsibility for the

regulation and direction of the whole of society: it became a government of inherent authority. Vigorous action to preserve the status quo in fact transformed both governance and law.[84]

The principal manifestations of this transformation were the Ordinance of Labourers 1349 and the Statute of Labourers 1351,[85] which empowered justices of the peace to regulate wages, prices and vagrancy.

The justices were appointed by the crown from among the local élite. They combined the administrative and inquisitorial roles of the keeper of the peace with judicial functions, reflecting the growing demand created by the expansion of royal justice from the late twelfth century and the decline of the local courts (the sheriff's tourn and the manorial and county courts). The number of justices of the peace grew rapidly as their powers were extended: there were two in Wiltshire in 1327, five in 1364, twelve in 1427, seventeen in 1478 and thirty-five in 1529.[86] Since the sort of people who sat as members of parliament were appointed as justices of the peace, it is not surprising to find the Commons supporting the extension of this office. At the same time, the crown was keen to ensure its control over the justices through appointment and dismissal, through the assertion by the King's Bench of its right to supervise their work,[87] and through the appointment of assize judges to the commissions of the peace from 1350.[88]

The creation of the justice of the peace enabled the crown to have officials in the counties who were more dependent on royal patronage than the sheriffs had been and sealed the decline in importance of that office, although the sheriff did not finally lose the power to try offences at his court until 1461 and continued to perform various duties connected with the administration of justice. The justices were certainly not mere puppets of the crown and appointments had to reflect the balance of local politics. Nevertheless, by the end of the fourteenth century, the justice of the peace had become a key part of an 'elaborate and co-ordinated system which for the first time provided the crown with a permanent judicial presence in the localities.'[89] They were a means of reconciling the crown's wish to influence local justice with the distaste in the shires for intervention by commissions sent down by government.[90]

The early fifteenth century

While the crown did struggle with issues of domestic government and law enforcement at various points in the middle ages, it was commonly a concern driven by the need to assert political authority. Once the crisis had passed attention drifted on to other issues, typically war. As has been seen, this pattern was repeated in the reigns of Edward I and Edward III, and it surfaced again in the early fifteenth century.

The usurpation of the throne from Richard II by Henry IV in 1399 was followed by a period of widespread disorder with which Henry was unwilling or unable to deal. This may have been because after 1405 he was repeatedly ill or because he was reluctant to intervene in the illegal activities of his supporters out of loyalty to them or out of recognition of their power.[91] On his accession in 1413 Henry V (1413–22) set about restoring order as a precursor to his main objective of regaining possessions in France. He was faced not just by the general disorder inherited from the reign of Henry IV and the challenges from supporters of Richard II, but also the threat from the Lollards, who rose up under Sir John Oldcastle in 1414. The Leicester Parliament of 1414 enacted various measures to improve law and order, many of which continued the expansion of the role of the justice of the peace (e.g. 2 Henry V, st. I, c. 8). Henry V also sent commissioners to Wales to ensure that the Glendower rebellion, which his father had suppressed, would not flare up again while he was in France. The King's Bench was despatched to tackle feuding among the gentry in the North and the Midlands. Yet, although it acted swiftly and with a good degree of effectiveness in terms of ensuring that those who had been summoned put in an appearance, relatively few were convicted. This was because juries acquitted, probably as a result of concern about the disruption a conviction might cause to the region, and also because offenders brought an early end to proceedings by paying a fine or buying a pardon. Henry seems to have seen the fiscal possibilities in allowing people to buy their way out of trouble, but preferred in any case to tackle disorder among the gentry through reconciliation rather than punishment.[92]

Henry's interest in law enforcement had primarily been to secure his position by subduing and reconciling the magnates and gentry, rather than deal with crime *per se*. He had learnt from the opportunity that Richard II's absence campaigning in Ireland in 1399 had given Bolingbrooke (the future Henry IV) to usurp the throne, that it was crucial to ensure order among the ruling classes before he went to France. Once his authority was secure in 1415, his interest in issues of law enforcement waned. Other aspects of crime were left to the gentry, who served as justices of the peace, and the yeomen, who acted as constables and jurors. After 1415 the assize circuits do not seem to have been held regularly, except in the Midlands, although the royal justices continued to take part in local administration as members of the bench of justices of the peace.

*   *   *   *   *

Changes in the formal institutions of law enforcement reflected not only the aspirations of the king and the county élite, but also the shifts in the community. It was difficult for a system of policing based on frankpledge to survive in the face of the decay of the feudal system and the demographic changes of the fourteenth century. The remnants of an approach based on the engagement of the whole community in policing were still evident, but there was a significant, long-term shift towards a more structured system based on a network of officials. On the other hand, the victim remained central and the lower officials were drawn from the community. Both of these factors facilitated flexibility. There was space for formal processes to be ignored or subverted, if they were seen as inappropriate to a particular case or as working against the interests of a powerful member of the community: so, for instance, the victim might still be able to settle with a thief for the return of stolen property or compensation. Yet, even though officials, including justices of the peace, might collude in these actions, they were not part of the law enforcement process. This was not, however, an issue in the medieval period: law was only one among a number of tools which might be used to settle a dispute or further an interest.[93]

Notes

1 Bohannan (1968) *Justice and Judgement Among the Tiv*, 139.
2 Holdsworth (1923) *A History of English Law*, vol II, 43.
3 Hidden in this simple word 'community' is a library-full of issues with which I have neither the space nor the inclination to deal. As a result, I use the word rather flexibly in this book to mean various things: in one place, a group of people defined geographically (such as a village or a town); in another, a group defined by the views of its most powerful members; and in another, a group whose members share particular characteristics (such as gender, sexuality or race). My use of the term does not ignore the issues of diversity or volatility within such communities since I typically use it in situations where someone is distinguished from her or his neighbours. The reader who is concerned to explore this further could start by looking at Cowan (2001) *Identity, Community, Difference* and the literature cited therein.
4 Wallace-Hadrill (1958–9) 'The blood-feud of the Franks', 487.
5 Gluckman (1970) *Custom and Conflict*, 17.
6 Gluckman (1970) *Custom and Conflict*, 18–20.
7 Schwartz and Miller (1964) 'Legal evolution and societal complexity', 165.
8 Evans-Pritchard (1940) *The Nuer*, 169; Wallace-Hadrill (1958–9) 'The blood-feud of the Franks', 467.
9 Holdsworth (1923) *A History of English Law*, vol II, 45.
10 Wallace-Hadrill (1971) *Early Germanic Kingship*, 32; Wormald (1997) 'Frederic

William Maitland and the earliest English law'; Wormald (1999) *The Making of English Law*.

11 Wormald (1999) *The Making of English Law*, 105–6.
12 Wormald (1999) *The Making of English Law*, 429.
13 Wormald (1999) *The Making of English Law*, 106, 429.
14 Wormald (1999) *The Making of English Law*, 109.
15 Rubin (1996) 'The *bot*, or composition in Anglo-Saxon law'.
16 Wallace-Hadrill, (1958–9) 'The blood-feud of the Franks'.
17 Simpson (1981) 'The laws of Ethelbert'.
18 Riggs (1963) *Criminal Asylum in Anglo-Saxon Law*, 20; Simpson (1981) 'The laws of Ethelbert', 15.
19 Evans-Pritchard (1940) *The Nuer*, 169; Wallace-Hadrill, (1958–9) 'The blood-feud of the Franks', 467).
20 'Community' refers to a place defined by a combination of geography and the needs of state organization: see note 3, *supra*.
21 Riggs (1963) *Criminal Asylum in Anglo-Saxon Law*, 46.
22 Thorpe (1840) *Ancient Laws*, 109.
23 Simpson (1981) 'The laws of Ethelbert', 14.
24 Hudson (1996) *The Formation of the English Common Law*, 27.
25 Loyn (1984) *The Governance of Anglo-Saxon England*, 86.
26 Prestwich (1988) *Edward I*, 287.
27 Hopkinson (2000) *The Rolls of the 1281 Derbyshire Eyre*, 120; Stenton (1937) *Rolls of the Justices in Eyre*, 214–5, 281.
28 Ireland (1986) 'The presumption of guilt'.
29 Sutherland (1983) *The Eyre of Northamptonshire*, vol I, 212 (also, vol I, 168–9). See, Stenton (1953–67) *Pleas before the King*, vol III, 71–2.
30 Kerr (1995) 'Angevin reform of the appeal of felony'.
31 Hurnard (1941) 'The jury of presentment'.
32 Kerr (1995) 'Angevin reform of the appeal of felony', 353.
33 *Dialogue of Exchequer* in Kerr (1995) 'Angevin reform of the appeal of felony', 353.
34 Crowley (1975) 'The later history of frankpledge'; O'Brien (1990) 'Studies of the "Leges Edwardi Confessoris" ', 194–7.
35 Maitland and Baildon (1891) *The Court Baron*, 76.
36 See the Assize of Clarendon 1166, cl. 15 and the Assize of Northampton 1176, cl. 2, in Douglas and Greenaway (1981) *English Historical Documents*, 440–6.
37 Maitland (1888) *Select Pleas of the Crown*, 96. Also, Sutherland (1983) *The Eyre of Northamptonshire*, vol I, 177, 197.
38 Riggs (1963) *Criminal Asylum in Anglo-Saxon Law*.
39 Crowley (1975) 'The later history of frankpledge'; Hudson (1996) *The Formation of the English Common Law*, 63–7; Maitland and Baildon (1891) *The Court Baron*; Morris (1910) *The Frankpledge System*; Robertson (1925) *The Laws of the Kings of England*, 241; Schofield (1996) 'The late medieval view of frankpledge'; Summerson (1979) 'The structure of law enforcement'; Summerson (1986) 'Maitland and the criminal law in the age of *Bracton*'.

40 Summerson (1979) 'The structure of law enforcement'.

41 Rothwell (1975) *English Historical Documents Volume III*, 357–9; Summerson (1979) 'The structure of law enforcement', 316–7; Sutherland (1983) *The Eyre of Northamptonshire*, vol I, 152.

42 Summerson (1992) 'The enforcement of the Statute of Winchester', 237, 241–2.

43 Given (1977) *Society and Homicide in Thirteenth-Century England*, 132–3.

44 Vinogradoff (1920) *Outlines of Historical Jurisprudence*, vol I, 355.

45 Jewell (1972) *English Local Administration*, 162, 165.

46 Maitland and Baildon (1891) *The Court Baron*, 88; Sutherland (1983) *The Eyre of Northamptonshire*, vol I, 163; Whittaker (1895) *The Mirror of Justices*, 39, 48–9; Statute of Winchester 1285, 13 Edw. I, c. 1.

47 Sutherland (1983) *The Eyre of Northamptonshire*, vol I, 168–9.

48 Richardson and Sayles (1955) *Fleta Volume II*, 68–76; Stenton (1937) *Rolls of the Justices in Eyre*, 313 (but see, 319–20); Summerson (1979) 'The structure of law enforcement'; Summerson (1986) 'Maitland and the criminal law in the age of *Bracton*'.

49 Whittaker (1895) *The Mirror of Justices*, 125.

50 Boroughs and ecclesiastical liberties had their own official whose authority paralleled that of the sheriff: Cam (1950) 'Shire officials, coroners, constables and bailiffs'.

51 Hunnisett (1961) *The Medieval Coroner*, 1.

52 Harding (1960) 'The origins and early history of the keeper of the peace'.

53 Jewell (1972) *English Local Administration*, 167; Stewart-Brown (1936) *The Serjeants of the Peace*.

54 Cox (1975–6) 'Peace-keeping without frankpledge', 92.

55 Given (1977) *Society and Homicide in Thirteenth-Century England*, 132.

56 Harding (1960) 'The origins and early history of the keeper of the peace', 8.

57 Cam (1950) 'Shire officials, coroners, constables and bailiffs', 8.

58 An administrative unit which, like the hundred, was the tier below the shire.

59 Musson (1995) *Public Order and Law Enforcement*, 31.

60 Meyer (1950) 'Boroughs'.

61 Van Caenegem (1990–1) *English Lawsuits*, vol II, 466. Also, Crooks (1982a) *Records of the General Eyre*; Crooks (1982b) 'The later eyres'; Douglas and Greenaway, (1981) *English Historical Documents*, 440–3; Turner (1985) *The English Judiciary*.

62 Hudson (1996) *The Formation of the English Common Law*, 141.

63 Sutherland (1983) *The Eyre of Northamptonshire*, vol I, 151.

64 Musson (1995) *Public Order and Law Enforcement*, 85–122; Taylor (1950) 'The justices of assize'.

65 Hurnard (1969) *The King's Pardon for Homicide*.

66 Stenton (1937) *Rolls of the Justices in Eyre*, 311–12.

67 Clanchy (1978) 'Highway robbery and trial by battle'; Given (1977) *Society and Homicide in Thirteenth-Century England*, 113. See also the fear and support

engendered by a criminal gang in the Midlands in the 1330s: Bellamy (1964) 'The Coterel gang'.

68 Sutherland (1983) *The Eyre of Northamptonshire*, vol I, 198. Also, Cox (1975–6) 'Peace-keeping without frankpledge'; Pugh (1978) *Calendar of London Trailbaston Trials*, 125.
69 Stenton (1937) *Rolls of the Justices in Eyre*, 214–15.
70 Given (1977) *Society and Homicide in Thirteenth-Century England*, 89; Stones (1957) 'The Folvilles of Ashby Folville'.
71 Sutherland (1983) *The Eyre of Northamptonshire*, vol I, 5–6. Also, Cam (1944) *Liberties and Communities in Medieval England*, 150–62.
72 Campbell (1991) *Before the Black Death*.
73 Hurnard (1969) *The King's Pardon for Homicide*. But see Musson and Ormrod (1999) *The Evolution of English Justice*, 82. Also, Powell (1987) 'The administration of criminal justice in late-medieval England', 84–5.
74 Musson (1995) *Public Order and Law Enforcement*, 19–20; Musson and Ormrod (1999) *The Evolution of English Justice*, 84.
75 Lugard (1933) *Trailbaston*, vol I, 4.
76 See also Statute of Westminster 1275, 3 Edw. I.
77 Pollock and Maitland (1968) *The History of the English Law*, vol I, 181. See also, 28 Edw. III, c. 11 (1354).
78 Summerson (1996) 'The criminal underworld of medieval England'.
79 Rothwell (1975) *English Historical Documents Volume III*, 522–3.
80 Harding (1984) 'The revolt against the justices', 166–7.
81 Harding (1984) 'The revolt against the justices', 166. Nineteenth-century police reformers, and some modern police historians, treated it as a symbol of obsolete localism: Critchley (1978) *A History of Police*, 29, 34.
82 Crowley (1975) 'The later history of frankpledge'.
83 Musson (1995) *Public Order and Law Enforcement*; Musson and Ormrod (1999) *The Evolution of English Justice*; Powell (1987) 'The administration of criminal justice in late-medieval England'; Putnam (1908) *The Enforcement of the Statute of Labourers*; Putnam (1929) 'The transformation of the keepers of the peace'; Putnam (1938) *Proceedings before the Justices of the Peace*.
84 Palmer (1993) *English Law in the Age of the Black Death*, 295. For a critique, see Musson and Ormrod (1999) *The Evolution of English Justice*.
85 Putnam (1908) *The Enforcement of the Statute of Labourers*.
86 Jewell (1972) *English Local Administration*, 146.
87 Putnam (1938) *Proceedings before the Justices of the Peace*, lxiii–lxxvi.
88 Musson and Ormrod (1999) *The Evolution of English Justice*, 45–50, 54, 109–13; Powell (1987) 'The administration of criminal justice in late-medieval England'.
89 Musson and Ormrod (1999) *The Evolution of English Justice*, 74.
90 Musson (1995) *Public Order and Law Enforcement*.
91 This section is based on Powell (1989) *Kingship, Law and Society*.
92 Powell (1984) 'Settlement by disputes by arbitration'.
93 Maddern (1992) *Violence and Social Order*.

Chapter 3

Policing the poor and the bureaucratization of policing: 1400–1660

Communal policing in the early modern period

During the late medieval and early modern periods the main institutions of communal policing lost their importance. Most of the tithing's functions vanished or passed to the parish constable and the presentation of offences at the view of frankpledge largely passed to the justices of the peace.[1] The judgment of outlawry also lost its force.[2]

The hue and cry did survive and, indeed, it was occasionally extended, as, for instance, in 1444 (23 Hen. VI, c. 5). In the 1580s Sir Thomas Smith declared that the hue and cry meant that 'everie English man is a sergiant to take the theefe'.[3] Yet, while formally this was true, there is evidence that Smith was not describing contemporary practice. The raising of the neighbourhood had been replaced by a warrant sworn by the victim before a justice of the peace or coroner and issued to an official, usually a constable.[4] After a murder in York in 1575,

> the baylyfs were sent forth to prosecute Hew and Crye, and for that the offender ys not found or knowne therfore it is agreed that wardens, Aldermen in ther severell wards shall goe aboute to everye inne, great and little, and knowe the names and state of all the guests that loged within this Cittie the last night.[5]

The hue allowed the constable to effect an arrest without waiting for an indictment and to pursue offenders across jurisdictional boundaries, and it placed a duty to assist on officials in those areas into which it was carried. In 1580 the authorities in York noted that the hue and cry 'is commed to this Cyttie' to apprehend three men and so they ordered a search and placed a watch at the entrances to the city;[6] and in 1626 the constables of Manchester made a search upon the hue and cry being brought from Newton for John Wynterbourne, a sailor wanted for a felony, and then 'delyvered the hewe & Crye' to the constable in the next parish.[7]

In spite of this change in practice, there remained concern about the failure of the community to pursue the hue. In 1578 the government was complaining that the failure to raise the neighbourhood had undermined good order and crime detection.[8] Then, in 1585 legislation (27 Eliz. I, c. 14)[9] reinforced the obligation on places to which the hue had been brought by requiring them to contribute towards the damages obtained by a victim if the inhabitants did not join in the pursuit. This may have increased the use of warrants issued by justices, but seems not to have improved the likelihood of the community being drawn into the pursuit. Indeed, although the act required the hue to be 'made by horsemen and footmen', there was no (and there had never been any) precise definition of what was involved.

Soon after the statute Sir Francis Bacon complained that 'now hues and cries are of no consequence, only a little paper is sent up and down with a soft pace, whereas they should be prosecuted with horse and foot and hunted as a thief.'[10] Although, around this time, a disgruntled victim of crime gives a slightly different impression of the process, his view of its effectiveness is no more approving, 'though a Hue and crye make a great noyse, t'is no dangerous business and a man hath ill luck that is caught with them for they creepe too slowlye to overtake a man that walks afore them'.[11]

It is difficult to assess the efficiency of the warrant system in apprehending offenders.[12] The records of the constables of Manchester in the early seventeenth century certainly suggest that it was used a good deal: for instance, they noted eight hue and cries, which they either initiated or passed on, between 2 and 21 October 1613, including three cases of horse stealing, one theft of cloth, a murder and two woundings.[13] Yet, the enthusiasm with which the Manchester constables undertook their task is not recorded. When the hue arrived at Dallwood in Dorset in 1640 it 'rested about eight howers without prosecution, by reason whereof the theeves were not apprehended'.[14] In West Riding in 1641 a constable, Thomas Lister, was fined for failing to assist the hue,[15] but such prosecutions seem to have been rare, and, unsurprisingly, the present-ments made by constables to the quarter sessions typically claimed, like that of the constable of Brigstocke in Northamptonshire in 1657, 'We haue not anie hue and cries that come to our towne butt wee speedily pursue them either by horsemen or footmen.'[16] The reliance on an active official led to complaints that constables routinely dismissed victims who required them to pursue the hue with a curt, 'God restore your losse! I have other businesse at this time.'[17] The inhabitants of Bilham in Yorkshire complained in 1598 that, 'they are forced to goe a myle beyonde Hooton Pannell [the parish in which Bilham was located] with Hue & Crie & other her [majesty's] Service, for want of a Constable'[18] Even if the hue was actively pursued, householders sometimes refused to co-operate: in Essex in 1584 an alehousekeeper's wife assaulted a constable with a lump of wood when he came to search the house for suspects,[19] and in 1634 a pursuit led by constables in Ilminster was refused entry to an inn owned by John and Margaret Burrowe, who, as a result, lost their licence.[20]

Victims did have an interest in raising the hue since this allowed them to bring an appeal of felony, which, in turn, meant they could claim back stolen property found on the offender. However, this motive was extinguished by legislation in 1529 (21 Hen. VIII, c. 11) which enabled the recovery of property where the prosecution was by indictment and the victim had contributed to the conviction of the thief. Robbery victims wishing to claim compensation under the Statute of Winchester 1285 had to show that they had raised the hue.[21] Finally, some attempt to revive this approach to crime detection occurred in the early eighteenth century with legislation such as the Waltham Black Act 1722. This established new grounds on which a victim could make a claim for compensation where an offender had not been apprehended.[22]

The watch was active into the sixteenth and seventeenth centuries, although how active is difficult to assess. It is certainly not difficult to find evidence of communities that failed to appoint watchmen or house-holders who refused to serve,[23] but considering the number of watchmen these complaints are remarkably few. This may be because people did serve, or because the constables had little enthusiasm for presenting people who failed to do so. Some householders certainly seem to have taken violent exception to being required to undertake the duty: in 1665 John Callin attacked William Child, a wardsman in Aldborough, for telling him that it was his turn to serve.[24] Others hired substitutes, although sporadic attempts were made to combat this practice, as, for instance, at the height of a panic over vagrancy in 1597, when the West Riding Quarter Sessions, apparently concerned at the quality of those hired, directed all householders to perform the task in person rather than pay substitutes 'as heretofore hath bene accustomed.'[25]

General calls by the justices for people to perform their duty were not uncommon,[26] but seem often to have been linked with a crisis: for instance, the outbreak of the plague in London in 1665 led Surrey justices to insist on improvements in the keeping of watch and to have prompted a batch of presentments for its neglect.[27]

Evidence as to the activities of watchmen is also variable, but some seem to have been particularly diligent. In 1637 the inhabitants of Wootton Courtney in Somerset were ordered to reimburse William Woollcott for expenses incurred in apprehending and prosecuting various vagrants and felons in 1637.[28] There is evidence of watchmen arresting suspicious persons, such as Roger Styll who was put in the stocks by the watchmen of Devizes in 1583 because 'at nyght [he] did suspiciously walk about the Towne in the nyght'.[29] In Essex one summer's night in 1586, the watch saw lights in an alehouse but, 'hearing no stir', walked away. However, the keeper, William Hyls, took objection to what he regarded as eavesdropping and, for good measure, also accused one of the watchmen, Joshua Waylande, of stealing poultry. Hyls and another man proceeded to set about Waylande. The noise roused the village, including the constable's deputy who advised the watchmen to leave the area to avoid further trouble.[30]

At the core of the law enforcement system as it emerged in the early modern period was the parish constable. Although the origins of this office are somewhat obscure, it seems to have originated in the duties placed on the tithing.[31] As has been seen, the tithing appointed a chief pledge or tithingman (also called a borsholder, headborough or reeve) to appear at the hundred court and the sheriff's tourn or court to answer for the community's performance of its policing tasks. This official acquired powers by virtue of his position as representative of the local community, but, in addition, although the community remained responsible for various functions and liable for their non-performance, duties began to be devolved onto these officials – commonly known as constables – by the state. Initially these seem to have been military responsibilities, such as mustering armed men and ensuring that the villagers maintained arms. Later, the duties which were formally laid on the community began to be shared with or placed in the hands of the constable: in 1328 the constable was empowered to enforce the provision of a statute on affrays, in 1330 'constables and townships' were responsible for apprehending thieves,[32] and, generally, the constable could require assistance from other members of the community to assist in making an arrest or conveying a prisoner to gaol.

In addition, the constable was given responsibility for, among other things, the collection and assessment of taxes, weights and measures, apprehending vagrants, regulating alehouses, dealing with drunkenness and swearing, and enforcing environmental regulations. He was also obliged to make presentments on a range of issues, including policing matters, to the sheriffs tourn, the court leet and the hundred court, although increasingly in the sixteenth century they were required to report to the justices of the peace. These duties were extended further by the obligation to execute the orders of superior officials, most notably the justice of the peace, but also the coroner, the sheriff and the lord lieutenant. The parish constable was supervised by the constable for the hundred.

Yet, although their powers and responsibilities were being extended by the state, the constables were still selected by their village. Moreover, they relied on the co-operation of other villagers, and they still lived in the village and would do so once their term expired. It seems likely that the constable in making presentments and returns to the justices of the peace was seen as representing the community. How much of the community he represented is another matter. In villages where there was a marked social division between the relatively wealthy villagers, from whom the constable was likely to come, and their poorer neighbours he was likely to have less sympathy for the opinions of the latter. Where such divisions were less evident, his reaction to an unlicensed alehouse or drunkenness might be influenced by local opinion about whether that person's general conduct had 'exceeded the bounds of neighbourly tolerance'.[33]

On the other hand, as central government under the later Tudors and the Stuarts and particularly under Charles I, sought to intervene more in local affairs, so the justices, themselves under scrutiny, bore down on the constables. While constables did continue to return presentments to the quarter sessions reporting 'all well', this was becoming less common.[34] The pressure was ratcheted up a notch by the Book of Orders in 1631, which expressed concern about the quality of those chosen as parish constables and claimed 'that the remissenesse and negligence of petty-Constables is a greate cause of the swarming of Rogues and Beggars'.[35] To combat this and other defects the high constables were charged to report defaults by the parish constables to the quarter sessions. The constable must have often found himself trapped between, on the one hand, the justice of the peace, who had the power to fine him, and, on the other hand, the community of which he was a part and whose help was essential to the performance of his functions:[36]

> The Justices will set us by the heels
> If we do not as we should
> Which if we perform, the townsmen will storm
> Some of them hang 's if they could.[37]

In many counties the constable was selected in the leet court by the more prosperous villagers,[38] although in the sixteenth century many leet courts were in decline and, when the Tudors adopted the parish rather than the manor or the township as the basic unit of local government, the parish vestries often took over the selection process. In a few places the justices were appointing constables by the seventeenth century, but this was not common, although in 1662 they did acquire this power where the leet court had not met, or where the office was vacant because the holder had died or moved from the area; there is little evidence that they intervened to remove negligent constables. The social class of constables varied, although most were from the more prosperous or, at least, middle-ranking families, and they would expect to undertake various offices during their lives.[39]

Since the office did not pay (other than expenses and fees), only lasted for a year, and could be time-consuming, dangerous and put the constable at odds with his neighbours or the justices or both, it is not surprising to find some householders were reluctant to take on the office,[40] or that there were disputes about the obligation to serve – one in Felton, Somerset, dragged on for more than twenty-five years in the early seventeenth century.[41] What is remarkable, then, is that only a small minority seem to have attempted to avoid service or to have hired substitutes.[42] There do seem to have been more disputes about serving and substitutions in the 1630s when the responsibilities were greater and when, in particular, constables were faced with collecting – and having financial responsibility for – the enormously unpopular taxes and military levies imposed by Charles I. In general, however, service may have been seen by the wealthier villagers as an incidence of their social position; a few may have seen it as a means of pressing forward a moral agenda; for some it may have been an opportunity to pursue vendettas.

Shakespeare's presentation of the constable as ignorant, incompetent, even corrupt is reflected in some contemporary opinion and, until relatively recently, was adopted in a fairly uncritical way by historians:

> Evildoers did not respect them because they were ignorant, timorous, and powerless; the justices did not respect them because they were lazy, disobedient, and negligent.[43]

It is certainly possible to find examples of all these traits and attitudes,[44] but the question is, did such constables represent the generality? In a society with high levels of illiteracy, criticism of the ignorance of constables based on their inability to read and write seems unfair. Anyway, it is clear that people were able to function effectively without these skills. While some constables were no doubt lazy and negligent, what is remarkable is the amount of work they did and the effort they were prepared to put in. Complaints by justices about the efficiency of constables were uncommon, and the number indicted for failing to appear before the justices when required seems also to have been low.[45] Indeed, the apparent inefficiency of a constable may sometimes have had more to do with uncertainty about his powers to arrest or to search premises. On the whole, Joan Kent, in her history of the constable in the late sixteenth and early seventeenth centuries, was 'impressed by the time, effort, and even financial sacrifice that was expected, and so often given, by the yeomen, husbandmen, and craftsmen who filled the constableship.'[46]

Constables were not expected to be particularly active in the detection of offenders; their role was really seen as to support the efforts of the victim by, for instance, effecting an arrest of someone identified by the victim and conveying the suspect to prison, or executing a search warrant. Occasionally they refused to make an arrest or allowed an escape.[47] Accusations were made that certain officers were corrupt, or used their powers to extract money or to pursue their own vendettas or to protect friends or relatives, and that they broke the laws they were meant to enforce. In 1598 William Dicconson, an innkeeper, was brought before the West Riding Quarter Sessions for being 'a receiptor of Rouges suspicious [persons] & others of badd Demeanour', and accused with him was William Ramscarr, the constable, for failing to take action because, it was alleged, of 'some favour wch he specially carryeth towards the said Dicconson'.[48]

The sympathy felt by a constable for the actions of his neighbour might derive from friendship or, perhaps, from having committed similar offences himself.[49] In 1665 Robert Doughty, a Norfolk justice of the peace, did uncover a conspiracy by which constables extracted money from people they arrested,[50] but the evidence of widespread corruption is not strong and partiality may often have been an expression of the role the constable was expected to play by the community.[51] Indeed, many took a good deal of trouble over these duties. Constables seem to have expected the assistance of their neighbours and that assistance seems, generally, to have been given – and often given very generously.[52] They occasionally hired assistance: in the early seventeenth century, the constables of Manchester hired a deputy on a regular basis, and they also paid people to do various specific tasks, such as watch two murder suspects, 'make dilliegent Seairche in the ffeaire tyme to apprehend Suspictieouse pickepcokets', or 'goe about the Towne to see good order'.[53]

Contemporary court records are full of prosecutions for the abuse of constables. Some people were merely colourful in their language, like

William Shepheard who, in the late seventeenth century, confronted Thomas Webb, a constable in Sheringham, Norfolk, and asked: 'I wonder what rogues made you a constable. I could shit a better constable, the devil take you … You Goodman Jackanapes, what will you do to me Goodman Constable, Goodman Turd'.[54] Others were more physical. Sir Richard Mawliverer, a justice, issued a warrant ordering the constable to arrest a runaway servant of Sir Robert Gibson whom, it was believed, was being harboured by a Mrs Ramsden. She turned out to be rather unco-operative, telling the constable 'in most scornefull maner she cared not, for Sr Richard, nor Sr Robte' and encouraging her servants to assault him.[55] Katherine Black was prosecuted in Scarborough in 1631 for 'an assalt against Richard Farthing constable in taking him by the beard and geveng him reviling words for doying his office'.[56] Friends of an arrested person might gather as when four men attacked the two constables who had arrested Robert Stowe in Colchester in 1583 and obtained his release.[57] It was also not uncommon to retaliate against a constable by litigation, which, even if vexatious, could involve him in time and expense and might land him in front of the Court of Star Chamber.[58]

Attacks on the constable sometimes reflected a dislike of the law he was enforcing, as was the case when constables met local resistance to the collection of ship-money and military levies in the 1630s.[59] But this might be coupled with a sense of disgust at his enthusiasm. At Wells in 1607 when John Hole attempted to suppress games, morris dancing and pageants which contravened the proclamation against the profaning of the Sabbath, he encountered opposition from most of the town, including many of its leading citizens. He became a target for ridicule during the pageants and those whom he arrested were either rescued or released by the mayor and burgesses.[60] Such divisions became more common in the early seventeenth century as campaigns by the 'godly' against popular festivities gathered ground.[61] Anger at such actions by the constable may have been intensified by the expectation that, as a leader of the com-munity, he should represent its interests and wishes. Certainly, constables can be found refusing to carry out their duties or leading protests, and this expectation may lie behind the attack on a constable who failed to join a rising in 1398 in western Oxfordshire.[62]

The other key official in the policing system as it emerged from the late medieval period was the justice of the peace. As the justices grew in importance, the sheriff and the manorial courts declined, so that by the seventeenth century many manorial courts had become 'nothing more than registries of land transactions … meeting very irregularly'.[63] Under the Tudors and the Stuarts the justices became 'rulers of the countryside' and 'the chief administrators of royal policy in domestic affairs.'[64] Aside from their role in local administration, the continuous presence of the justices of the peace in the shires was expected to deter crime and encourage order in a way that the assize judges could not because, awesome though the appearances of the judges were, they were too infrequent and were confined to the county towns. The price of this was an increase in the burden of work the justices had to bear. Although by the end of the sixteenth century they had virtually lost the power to try felonies, there had been an enormous increase in the number and range of misdemeanours, which they tried, 'to the overburthening of all the Justices', as one sympathetic contemporary put it.[65] The greater interest taken by the Tudors and early Stuarts in domestic issues required more powers to be given to the justices and, as a result, there was a more intense scrutiny of their work.[66]

As before, the assize judges provided the connection between these local 'rulers' and central government in the form of the Privy Council at Westminster. The judges advised the justices, were the conduit through which the crown passed directions on policy to the justices and provided a vital source of information for the crown about the mood in the counties, particularly during the eleven years of personal rule under Charles I when Parliament did not sit.

The detection of crime

From the early modern period, the work of the justices was also extended in the area of pre-trial investigation. The Marian legislation of 1554–5 required them to make decisions about bail and to gather evidence for the prosecution by examining the victim, the offender and the witnesses.[67] These techniques evolved from earlier legislation, principally concerned with minor offences, and, probably, reflected existing practice in felony cases.[68] Where a felony had been committed and a suspect was brought before the justice, he was required to remand that person to prison or allow bail, although the latter option was not available in certain offences and could only be granted by two justices. The justice could only discharge the suspect if it appeared to him that no felony had been committed.[69] It was also provided that the justice,

> shall take the examination of the said prisoner, and information from them that bring him, of the fact and circumstances thereof, and the same, or as much thereof as shall be material to prove the felony shall put in writing before they make the same bailment (s. 4).

The statute was intended to tackle the problem of justices corruptly granting bail and the provision about the examination appears to have been designed to enable the royal judges at gaol delivery to supervise the bailment decision.[70] The committal statute extended the limited function which the examination had under the bail statute (2 & 3 Ph. & Mar., c. 10 [1555]). It stated that such an examination was 'as necessary, or rather more' where the suspect has not been admitted to bail (s. 2). Although the act does not reveal why it is 'necessary', the justice is instructed to 'take the examination of such prisoner, and information of those that bring him'. He was also authorized to bind over witnesses to appear at the trial, but under neither of these statutes was the justice obliged to seek out evidence, his only duty being to question the suspect, who was not obliged to answer,[71] and the people – usually, the constable and the victim – who brought him. He then recorded such circumstances 'as shall be material to prove the felony'; in other words, he was seeking, primarily, inculpatory evidence.

There was some incentive to look more broadly than just at the evidence against the prisoner, if only to establish that a felony had occurred and that the 'right' person had been arrested for it: when John Davies was taken on suspicion of stealing at Lewes fair in 1614, Richard Amherst, the justice before whom he was brought, checked his claim to be a respectable shoemaker from London and found it was false.[72] Although the framework described in the Marian statutes applied only to felonies, Barnes has shown that Somerset justices also certified examinations in misdemeanour cases to the quarter sessions.[73]

Langbein argues that, while the event which triggered these statutes cannot be discovered, the general context was the gradual shift away from the medieval jury trial, in which local jurors had been expected to bring their knowledge of the circumstances of the crime, to a situation in which the jury decided guilt or innocence on the basis of evidence brought before them (a shift which was not completed for more than two hundred years).[74] This meant there was more emphasis on the role of the victim. What the Marian statutes did was to designate the justice of the peace as the person who pushed forward the prosecution by bringing the evidence together and taking steps to ensure the attendance of the suspect, the prosecutor and any witnesses. The statutes did not seek to replace the system of private prosecution, and, in general, the justice was binding over victims to prosecute. Rarely did justices undertake any investigation. The justice was usually only required to ensure that once notice of a felony had been brought to his attention, the criminal justice system was engaged in a process that would lead to a trial and from which the victim could not disengage.

Yet on occasions some justices were willing to be drawn into a more active role: for instance, where there had been a serious offence, such as murder, and no suspect had been identified by the local community.[75] Indeed, manuals written for justices in the Tudor and early Stuart periods listed 'the pointes that may ingender Suspition': what was the suspect's reputation in the community, with whom did he or she keep company, was there any connection to the crime (for instance, in terms of opportunity), had the suspect lied?[76] William B. Robison has described how Sir John Gaynesford, a Surrey justice, actively pursued the murderer of Robert Grame, a collier, in 1532.[77] Similarly, after the murder and dismemberment of William Trat in 1624, two Somerset justices visited the place where the – at first unidentified – body was found and questioned the neighbours. This caused their suspicions to alight on a servant and, under questioning, she revealed an elaborate plot.[78] Where the justices had produced insufficient evidence to support a prosecution, they might be ordered to take further action. In 1639 Edward Britten was indicted for stealing, but an order issued by the Somerset assizes noted that the 'cause is not prepared and fitt to be tryed att this assizes in regard the felony will not be fully proved by witnesses', and it instructed two justices of the peace to take further examinations.[79]

Sometimes the crown tried to prod local officials, including the justices, into action against offenders, as, for instance, when the Council in the North issued instructions on law enforcement to the justices of the peace in 1557. They directed between two and five people to be appointed as overseers of the poor in each parish and, among their duties, they were required to go:

> to every howse that they shall thincke mete within there charge nightlye or at the leaste ones or twyse in the weke and that as secretlie as they may some tymes after midnighte or in the latter ende of the night and there peruse and viewe any of the same house and yf they shall perceyve any of the same house to be absent and not a sufficient excuse and declaracon maide of his beinge furthe then the same men put in trust assone as the said persons so missinge shall come home to taik him as one suspected for some evil persone and hym to bryng affore the said Justice of peax

After a felony the overseers were to see who was 'found suspeciously absent about the tyme of the fellonye commytted'. Inhabitants were to report to the overseers the presence of any strangers in their houses and the overseers were required to provide the justices with a general report on 'the state and rule' of their parishes. The overseers were also directed to report to the Council any negligence on the part of the justices in carrying out their duty to investigate suspicious persons reported to them.[80]

Typically, however, detection was a matter for the victim, like William Stevenson who, while at Scarborough market in 1637, 'feltt the hand of a man whoe calles himselffe John Wattson very busie aboute his reight pockett'.[81] A victim might hire someone to watch property: for instance, when a farmer in Scarborough had property stolen from his barn in 1634, he hired two people to watch and they duly caught a woman and her son stealing.[82] Third parties might become involved in the detection process. In 1628 Francis Pellat, a yeoman from Hartfield, became suspicious when he saw a 'meanly dressed' man, John Burt, walk by with a freshly-killed pig on his back. He forced Burt to go with him to the nearest head-borough, where it was discovered that the pig had been stolen.

A victim might also hire someone to undertake inquiries. In 1630 William Lankester, a labourer from Cullworth, was asked by John Price, whose house in Banbury had been broken into, to make inquiries for a woman whom Price suspected. Lankester caught up with her in Cullworth and asked the constable, Thomas Webb, to hold her while he fetched Price. Price seems to have been too busy to come himself and so hired someone to go with his wife and Lankester to see the woman. However, by the time they returned, Webb told them that she had gone, although what had happened is unclear. Lankester then went to see John Tew the elder, who had been watchman at the relevant time, 'and desired to know of him where certaine thinges weare which the said woman did offer to sell in the said towne'. Tew sent his daughter with Lankester to the house of 'Cresent Iremonger' where it was discovered that the woman had sold some clothes stolen from Price.[83]

People continued to help their neighbours and the local officials: late one night in May 1546 John Boldy returned to his house and on entering his bedroom found John Wynscott asleep on his bed; he fetched Symon Logg, the tithingman, for assistance and several neighbours came with Logg.[84] Where a suspect was not immediately obvious, the victim might follow clues, such as tracks across a field, or might light on someone whose behaviour, reputation or indiscrete conversation rendered them suspicious, although mere suspicion or suspicious behaviour was typically not enough to support a conviction.

Victims might also resort to cunning men and women to assist in the search: at the end of the sixteenth century in Yorkshire, Christopher Slater was ordered to find sureties for his good behaviour on the grounds of 'suspicon of Witchcrafte & telling what was becomed of goods lost or stollen &c.'[85] When in 1649 in North Yorkshire, John Dickinson had ten sheep stolen, his suspicions fell on Thomas Elvard. He found that a man called Charles Huntres had bought some sheepskins from Francis Gamble who had them from Elvard. Elvard then came and begged forgiveness. Dickinson took 'some satisfaction ... because as he said it was a dangerous tyme and Elvard was a soldier and may been hee and his partners might have done the said Dickinson some harme.'[86] At key points the aid of the constable could be sought, such as to undertake the search of premises, to arrest, or to add weight to the suspicions of the victim by witnessing the discovery of stolen property or the confrontation with a suspect.[87]

For the victim prosecution was not necessarily the main aim: catching the suspect, obtaining an apology and the return of stolen goods or a settlement might have been enough. In early fifteenth-century Shropshire, the alleged perpetrator of an attempted rape, Adam Osborne, a parson, was taken by the victim and three men to a house where he was held until he paid them 40 pence.[88] Often it was the victim who had to pay: Mr Baker paid pirates £20 for the return of his hoy captured off the Norfolk coast in 1576, presumably because there was little expectation of recovering his property any other way.[89] Of course, the victim might resort to direct action, as may have happened when a woman and her two daughters waylaid Roger de Pulesdon early in the fifteenth century in Shropshire. They proceeded to tie him up and – in what may have been a symbolic act of revenge – cut off his testicles, and then rode away on his horse.

Neighbours and officials, who became involved, might have been motivated by a desire to maintain local harmony. Indeed, in 1591 William Lambarde emphasized the need for his fellow justices of the peace to 'step in betwixt those that be at variance'.[90] This could mean seeking to reconcile parties to reach a settlement, even though an offence had apparently occurred or the offender had confessed, and the justice could bind someone to keep the peace as a means of enforcing the settlement. The reaction of Robert Doughty, a Norfolk justice of the peace, to some petty offenders in 1665 seems to have been fairly common:

> the 3 pease stealers were before me. One confessed a handful, the other[s] each a peck apiece. Elizabeth Swan offered for satisfaction a day's work in harvest & Mary Beare to make full satisfaction for her handful & Susan Dickthorne the 3rd being a poor silly lame wench he forgave.[91]

Such actions were not necessarily disapproved by the assize judges. In Somerset in 1616 William Newborne was discharged after the assizes were told he had confessed to a charge of poaching and given satisfaction to the landowner, presumably in the form of a public apology;[92] while in 1639 the assize judges ordered those involved in a riot at Beckington church to make a humble submission to the Bishop of Bath and Wells in a form of words prescribed by the court, with the threat that failing to do so would lead to imprisonment.[93]

Finally, in the fourteenth century government began to encourage private individuals who were not victims to prosecute certain statutory misdemeanours by allowing them a share of the fine imposed. By the early seventeenth century the offences included profane swearing, running an unlicensed alehouse and forestalling.[94] Some common informers proved particularly industrious. Thomas Warrie brought informations before the Somerset Quarter Sessions against 27 people in July 1628, another five in September and seventeen in April 1629, and he followed these up with further batches in September 1630 and 1631.[95] Most notorious was the Hilton gang which operated in the early 1680s.[96] The gang consisted of more than 40 members led by John Hilton, who even published a newspaper containing stories of his exploits, *The Conventicle Courant*. As the title suggests, the target of the gang were those dissenters whose method of worship broke the provisions of the Conventicle Act 1670. Hilton was involved in Tory politics and revelled in forcing Whig constables, who tended to be more sympathetic to the dissenters or reluctant to disturb parish harmony, to do their duty under the act. Hilton's power only declined after James II came to the throne and pursued a policy of religious toleration.

Such common informers were disliked. Edward Coke, a chief justice under James I, called them 'viperous vermin';[97] mobs attacked those who prosecuted breaches of the Gin Act 1736, and the Bow Street magistrate, Thomas De Veil, allegedly denounced the way that the act had 'let loose a crew of desperate and wicked people who turn'd informers merely for bread'.[98] Sometimes the courts seem to have shared this distaste for informers. Warrie was ordered in 1637 to pay the enormous sum of £3 6s 8d – or be imprisoned until he did – to cover the costs incurred by a Mr Coggan in connection with an information brought under an obsolete penal statute. It was alleged that Warrie's motive was 'to molest and trouble' Coggan, although quite why is not made clear and one is left to wonder whether he was being punished for his trade rather than his mistake.[99]

The criminalization of the poor

While there were some important changes in the law enforcement system during the late medieval and early modern periods, the most significant shift in policing was initiated by the attempts to regulate working people in the wake of the plague of 1348 and the incursions of moral policing.

These were legitimized by the belief that poverty, vagrancy, the spread of the plague, idleness, immorality, irreligion and crime were linked together. Before the mid-fourteenth century it was not uncommon to argue that public policy should reflect the Christian duty to relieve all poor people, but afterwards there developed a stark separation between the 'deserving' and the 'undeserving' and a tendency to conclude that a pauper came within the latter category until it was shown otherwise. Christ's blessing of the poor had been replaced by St Paul's warning that idleness disqualified them from eating; and, while the former advice might continue to guide private behaviour, the latter became more influential in terms of public policy.[100]

People had been instructed by the Statute of Labourers 1351 not to give alms to 'valiant beggars' who, 'as long as they may live off begging, do refuse to labour, giving themselves to idleness and vice, and sometimes to theft and other abominations' (23 Edw. III, c. 7). That statute also characterized the shortage of workers as being connected to problems with the attitudes of labouring people and their mobility: '[some] will not serve unless they may receive excessive wages, and some rather willing to beg in idleness, than by labour to get their living' (preamble). The solution was to require the able-bodied 'to serve him which so shall him require' (c. 1), prohibit servants from leaving their employment early and limit wages (c. 2–5). This legislation was regularly reinforced or tightened.[101]

The plague had demonstrated that the labouring poor were crucial to the economy. Mobility might allow them to exploit that position, and, furthermore, it did not fit a system of government which rested on land. Mobility was, therefore, wrapped up in terms of the sin of idleness and the crime of vagrancy. Crucially, it was assumed to be an innate tendency of labouring people. Regulation, therefore, had to encompass the whole of the labouring class, and it was justified in terms of not only the public good, but also the good of the poor who were its subject.

In the sixteenth and early seventeenth centuries concern about vagrants was often expressed in alarming terms: from John Bayker's letter to Henry VIII in the late 1530s claiming that 'the multytude of thayme dothe dayly encreace more and more' to Edward Hext's remarkable letter to Lord Burghley in 1596 ascribing all manner of misfortunes to 'the wandryng Souldiers and other stout roages of England',[102] and the view of the Quarter Sessions at Pontefract in 1612 that there was a 'greate aboundance of wandring rogues and concourse of beggers and strangers … more now of late than att any time heretofore hath beene'.[103] Vagrants were associated with the spread of disease as well as vice and the persistence of dearth. Hext, who was a justice of the peace in Somerset, told Burghley that,

> the Infynyte numbers of the Idle wandrynge people and robbers of the land are the chefest cause of the dearthe, for thowghe they labor not, and yet they spend dobly as myche as the laborer dothe, for they lye Idlely in the ale howses daye and nyght eatinge and drynkynge excessively.[104]

These images were most dramatically and persuasively presented to sixteenth-century readers through the pamphlets describing criminals and vagrants as inhabiting a parallel world. This literature was convincing in its detail of the methods and of the argot of the inhabitants of this underworld. It both arose from, and reinforced, the fears of its prosperous readers about that other world.[105] Paul Slack argues that a new conception of the body politic had emerged which was not seeking to include everyone: 'The simplest way of defending virtue and order was by defining vice and disorder; and the identification of an external menace protected the essence of a body politic threatened with dissolution.'[106] During the sixteenth century the willingness to identify and castigate the undeserving poor became more pronounced, partly as a result of the sweeping away of the idea of holy poverty with the abolition of religious orders during the Reformation, and, partly, because of the economic depression which was hanging over from the previous century and which the vagrant poor seemed to symbolize (and were, in some measure, blamed for).

These attitudes remained influential as the economy revived and were reinforced by the conviction that God's blessing was signified by wealth and God's disapproval by poverty. The vagrant poor symbolized deepening divisions in society. Even within relatively stable village communities divisions between the more and less prosperous began to appear and further break apart such unity as had survived the upheavals of the fourteenth century.[107]

The definition of a vagrant varied. In 1383 it was simply people 'wandering from place to place' (7 Ric. II, c. 5). This proved far too indefinite for the more legalistic Elizabethans who, after a number of attempts, had replaced it in 1597 with a list of people, such as scholars and sailors who begged, gamesters, fortune tellers, people who gathered alms for prisons, hospitals and so forth, 'Players of Enterludes and Minstrelles wandring abroade', jugglers and pedlars. The list was supplemented by a catch-all phrase, 'all wandering persons and common Labourers being persons able in bodye using loytering and refusing to worcke for … reasonable Wages' (39 Eliz. I, c. 4, s. 2).[108] The punishment of vagrants was regularly increased. The Vagrancy Act 1495 (11 Hen. VII, c. 2)[109] condemned vagrants to the stocks, but a perceived increase in vagrancy following three poor harvests in the late 1520s led to the act of 1531 in which the punishment was increased to whipping, after which the vagrant was returned to their place of settlement (22 Hen. VIII, c. 12). Another statute of 1547 condemned vagrants to a period of two years in slavery (1 Edw. VI, c. 3), although this was repealed three years later because no one would take these slaves. In 1572 (14 Eliz. I, c. 5) vagrants were required to be whipped and a hole bored through one ear (to identify them in case of re-offending and, by stigmatizing them, ensure that they had no choice but to re-offend); death was the punishment for a second offence, unless the vagrant could persuade someone to take her or him into service. Under an act of 1576 (18 Eliz. I, c. 3) houses of correction were to be constructed for vagrants. In the midst of the dearth, food riots, risings and general moral panic over vagrancy of the 1590s, the act of 1597 ordered vagrants to be summarily whipped by the constable and returned to their place of settlement (39 Eliz. I, c. 4) – the vagrant was never deemed to be worth a trial.

As well as the legislation, the Tudors and Stuarts routinely lectured local officials about the control of vagrancy. In 1485, shortly after his seizure of the throne, Henry VII issued directions to all local authorities. He noted the 'grete robbries, murdres, manslaughters and othre heynous offenses' committed 'daily', and expressed himself anxious for 'the spedy and effectyall redresse therof' so as to return the kingdom and his subjects 'quietly to live in good rest and peax undre Godds lawes and ours.' Such broad statements were not unusual, but Henry went further and elaborated fairly precise plans he required the authorities to follow:

> youre officers and servants, severally and distinctley in evere place convenient of our said Citie, dividing your self as by your discreccions shalbe thought moost metely, and for evere of the said places to be serched at oone tyme, as well in evere ostery, taverne and suspect house of our said Citie as else where within the precincts of the same, so as noo corner thereof be unsoght, putting this in execuscion the xij day of January next commying, and your said serche to begynne the same day at viij of the clok in the eveneyng and soo to continue til the said citie be through soght and serched, as is above said

He added that 'all vacbunds, idel people, mighty and valiant beggers and othre suspect personnes' found were to be put in prison until inquiry could be made of them and, if appropriate, punishment inflicted. The crown was to be notified of those people who took responsibility for carrying out these commands and who undertook the searches – to which was added the somehow chilling explanation – 'to thentent we may geve

47

you thanke according to your merits', and certainly those who neglected the order were warned 'ye woll answer therefor unto us at your perills'.[110]

Orders from government to local officials requiring them to undertake searches along these lines were by no means unusual. An order in 1575 required a 'previe searche' to be made at least every three weeks for 'masterlesse men', who, it was claimed, roamed the countryside committing felonies.[111] Fear of invasion around the time of the Armada in 1588 led the Privy Council to urge on local authorities punitive measures to deter vagrants whom, it was claimed, spread sedition.[112] Then, as soldiers and sailors were demobilized in the late 1580s, so levels of anxiety once again increased.[113] A proclamation in 1591 cautioned that 'there is a wandering abroad of a multitude of people, the most part pretending that they have served in the wars, though that many have not served at all, or have run away, and therefore ought to be punished instead of relieved'. Justices were directed to control these vagrants, and the lord lieutenant of each county was to appoint itinerant provost marshals to sweep them up.[114] Another proclamation in 1596 required monthly searches for these 'pretended soldiers', some of whom, it was claimed, had 'committed robberies and murders'. Justices of the peace were to be directed on further policing measures by the justices of assize, while the crown would appoint provost marshals to search these people out and 'execute them upon a gallows without delay'.[115]

Yet, alongside this harsh attitude to vagrancy, the Tudors built a state poor relief system which, albeit loosely, recognized the rights of the poor. So, at the same time as vagrants were to be whipped and holes bored through their ears, assistance was to be given to the impotent poor out of a poor rate collected through a compulsory property tax and administered by overseers in each parish (14 Eliz. I, c. 5). The vagrancy statute of 1597 was matched by another on poor relief which recognized the existence of unemployment among the able-bodied by requiring the overseers to provide materials and put them to work (39 Eliz. I, c. 3).[116]

Local regulations introduced by town councils and quarter sessions often anticipated – and sometimes influenced – national policy, and, like national policy, those regulations responded to particular problems.[117] In 1549 Norwich established provision for the poor based on a compulsory poor rate after Kett's Rebellion,[118] and further risings in Norfolk led to schemes in the early 1570s which combined a punitive approach to vagrants with a new poor relief programme.[119] An outbreak of the plague in 1607 led justices at Thirsk to order petty constables to keep day watches 'for the avoyding the danger of infected people, and the suppressing of roagues and vagrant persons'.[120] At times of crisis the security of good order seemed more precious. Those who did not conform to the image of a stable family life, regular work and a connection to a respectable community were likely to be treated as outcasts and dealt with as such, even though, of course, many were simply hapless products of the crisis. In general, those singled out for punishment as vagrants were the people with no trade and no ties to a community, or at least no ties to what was deemed as a respectable community; that they may have fled from an abusive employer, partner or parent seems to have had little influence on their treatment, particularly if they exhibited traits of what was regarded as an immoral lifestyle. When Margaret Cheecke and Martin Drake arrived in Salisbury in 1620, it was noted that they 'lived together lewdly for about three years'. They were swiftly whipped and returned to their places of birth, thereby ending a relationship which had survived the rigours of homelessness.[121]

Discovering the place of settlement (birth or residence for a year) was potentially an enormous problem, but, since most authorities just wished to rid themselves of vagrants, they were content to rely on information supplied by the vagrant. Amy Moore was arrested three times in Salisbury for vagrancy: in 1603 she was sent to Wareham in Dorset where she said she was born; in 1605 she told the authorities she had been born in Chesselbury in Somerset and so was sent there; and in 1607 she was sent to Dorchester where she said she had last resided.[122] Not surprisingly, some vagrants were immediately returned by the authorities in the places to which they had been sent.[123]

Control of vagrants, even if it could be achieved, did not address the problems of the resident poor who 'as their numbers rose, were themselves disorderly as well as increasingly able'.[124] It was normal to allow resident paupers to beg since this reduced the cost of relief,[125] and this also fitted in with notions of Christian charity, but it created problems in discriminating between licensed and unlicensed beggars. In York in 1541 resident paupers were licensed as beggars, but required to wear badges and only to beg on Sundays and Fridays in the presence of a master of beggars appointed by the city. In 1567 a scheme was devised under which all resident paupers, including the old and the young, were required to be put to work and those who refused were to be punished. During a crime panic in the 1580s all begging was again prohibited and four new sets of stocks were installed around the city.[126]

The decentralized administration meant that parishes were liable only for their own poor. This encouraged expensive disputes between parishes, and meant that the poor were likely to be moved on before they could acquire settlement, thereby exposing them to punishment as vagrants. Indeed, it was this concern not to allow someone who might become a charge on the parish to acquire settlement that seems to have been an important factor in the minds of local administrators. Edward Hext believed in the need for firmness and criticized what he saw as a regrettably sympathetic attitude to the plight of vagrants: he complained 'of Constables and Tythingmen that suffer them to wander, and of inhabitants that releve them contrary to the lawe'.[127] The balance drawn by local officials – the constable and the overseer of the poor – between relieving, moving on and punishing the mobile poor was constantly changing: it was dictated by the personal views of the official, or the pauper's circumstances, or a general downturn in the economy, or the dependence of some parts of the economy on the circulation of casual labour at particular times of the year, such as during harvest, or by panics about the plague or crime, and always there was the consideration of cost. Local officials realized that in times of crisis, such as the mid-1590s and the 1620s, it was both pointless and cruel to inflict punishment on those who could not find work.[128] Writing in 1596, the same year as Hext's letter, William Lambarde recognized the dilemmas that faced officials in dealing with the wandering bands of demobilized soldiers. He noted that many had been drawn from the prisons and from the poorest sections of society, so they had nothing to which they could return:

> what marvel is it if after their return from the wars they do either lead their lives in begging or end them by hanging. Nevertheless we are by many duties most bounden to help and relieve them, considering that they fight for the truth of God and defense of their country; yea, they fight our own war and do serve in our places, enduring cold and hunger when we live at ease and fare well.[129]

On the other hand, in his practice Lambarde was ready to use the whip against vagrants, and, almost imitating the excellent Mr Hext, he warned:

> Yea, such is the inundation of wickedness in this last and worst age that if speedier help and hand of justice be not applied, we are justly to fear that we shall every one be overwhelmed thereby.[130]

While local policy was typically driven by the concerns of the more prosperous villagers, the impact of Kett's Rebellion in Norwich shows that the poor themselves sometimes had an influence. Moreover, other villagers did not necessarily welcome a harsh policy on mobility. Innkeepers and others earned part of their livelihood from lodging strangers. John Austen, an innkeeper in Yorkshire, was prosecuted repeatedly between 1598 and 1622 for lodging people whom the court termed vagrants, but who were for Austen, presumably, simply customers. Several of Austen's male neighbours were cited for allowing women to lodge with them: whether their actions in doing so were motivated by money, sexual gratification or love appears not to have concerned the court.[131] Local authorities were routinely ordering people not to take in poor lodgers, instructing constables to search for them and criticizing constables for failing to present these offences.[132]

Moral policing

The poor were also hemmed in by laws on morality which worked to constrain their lives. Crime, illegitimacy, idleness, irreligion, poaching, drinking, dancing, the playing of games and so forth were believed to be linked. These activities were, therefore, criminalized, as were the places, such as alehouses, in which the poor engaged in them.[133] Drunkenness was denounced in 1606 as,

> the root and foundation of many other enormous sins, as bloodshed, stabbing, murder, swearing, fornication, adultery, and such like, to the great dishonour of God, and of our nation, the overthrow of many good arts and manual trades, the disabling of divers workmen, and the general impoverishing of many good subjects, abusively wasting the good creatures of God' (4 Jac. I, c. 5).

Poaching was associated, according to an act of 1389, with irreligion and 'assemblies, conferences, and conspiracies' (13 Ric. II, st. 1, c. 13). The connections were sometimes made even more explicit by wrapping these different issues up in one statute: for instance, an act of 1494 (11 Hen. VII, c. 2) covered vagrancy, begging, unlawful games and alehouse regulation. The laws on illegitimacy were rooted in various concerns, but as the Tudors constructed rights to poor relief the issue of cost became uppermost: 'the great burden' of the parish, 'defrauding of the relief of the impotent and aged true poor … and … the evil example and encouragement of lewd life' (18 Eliz. I, c. 3, s. 2 [1576]). While this led to measures designed to make fathers maintain their children,[134] under James I attention also swung to the mothers who were to be imprisoned in the house of correction (7 Jac. I, c. 4, s. 7 [1609]), while the brutal Infanticide Act of 1623 (21 Jac. I, c. 27), which, on its face, made conceal-ment by the mother of the birth of an illegitimate child, who died before or after birth, a capital offence.

Although the late Tudor and early Stuart period saw great activity among moral reformers, this was not just a matter of concern to the

Puritans nor was it a new phenomenon. Legislation to restrict the playing of games had been associated with the concern to maintain archery skills (see 12 Ric. II, c. 6 [1388]), but later became linked to poverty and so to crime (also 17 Ed. IV, c. 3 [1477]). Under the Tudors increasingly strong powers to regulate alehouses were placed in the hands of the justices of the peace.[135] In 1578 the crown issued an order concerning the regulation of inns. These 'nurseries of naughtiness'[136] were suspected of harbouring vagrants and criminals, so innkeepers were ordered to keep records of all guests, the dates of their stay, and 'of the intencon of there jorney, from what plaice they came, and wheather they saie they mind to travile [work] or goe'.[137] Parliament considered 25 bills on the regulation of alehouses in the sessions of 1601, 1604 and 1606.[138] In 1604 an attempt was made to return inns and alehouses to what was said to be their original purpose of providing accommodation for travellers and to stamp out the practice of local people just going for a drink, referring to them as 'lewd and idle people [who] spend and consume their money and their time in lewd and drunken manner' (1 Jac. I, c. 9 [1604]).

Governments periodically prodded justices to enforce laws on morality. This reached a peak with the Book of Orders in 1631, which was issued by the Privy Council after a period of economic depression and food rioting that had raised fears over crime and vagrancy. Local authorities were required to enforce laws 'tending to the reliefe of the poore, and the reformation of disorders and disordered persons'. The emphasis, however, was on the latter rather than the former: relieving the poor was seen mainly in terms of dissuading them from engaging in those immoral actions which led to poverty. The focus was on the laws on vagrancy, drunkenness, idleness and alehouses, and, to prevent the movement of vagrants, the keeping of the watch: 'the due execution of [these laws] ... would preuent and cut off many offences and crimes'.[139] The blame for their non-enforcement was placed on the 'neglect of duetie in some of Our Justices of the Peace and other Officers'.[140] This, in turn, was put down to the lack of appropriate penalties and the burdens placed on assize judges which made it difficult for them to supervise inferior officers. Members of the Privy Council were personally assigned to ensure the enforcement of the laws, and the threat for justices of the peace was removal from the commission and prosecution in the Star Chamber.[141] The supervision over inferior officers was increased by requiring them to report to a justice each month. The justices were, in their turn, required to report every three months on their work.[142]

Manorial and church courts records indicate that local interest in morality went back to the fourteenth century.[143] This means that, while part of the explanation for the zeal behind the prosecutions in the sixteenth century can be traced to the development of the Tudor poor relief system and its cost, this is not the only reason. Patterns in the enforcement of law on morality do seem linked to social and economic crises and with the growing divisions between rich and poor, in the same way as can the laws on vagrancy. Nevertheless, both religious zeal and the effects of socio-economic divisions were at their most powerful in the late sixteenth and early seventeenth centuries. In the 1590s the Puritan, Philip Stubbes, asked, 'Are not unlawful games, plays, interludes and the like every-where frequented? … Was there ever seen less obedience in youth of all sorts, both menkind and womenkind, towards their superiors, parents, masters and governors?'[144]

The lack of a strong Puritan presence did not necessarily inhibit the drive for moral reformation. There was a broader concern over the growth of irreligion, the effect of immorality on village harmony, the polarization between rich and poor villagers, and the belief that poverty was growing.[145] While Puritanism may have given some shape to the response to the problems of the late Tudors and the Stuarts, it was the depth and chronic nature of those problems which led to the search for a response. Even so, enthusiasm for moral campaigns varied.[146] In places the magistracy, supported by many of the middling people – the more prosperous farmers, craftsmen and tradesmen – pressed harder for moral reformation, but, as has been seen in the case of John Hole of Wells, the local élite were not always sympathetic to the efforts of a 'godly' reformer.[147] Of course, that case also shows how local popular culture might resist change. In Shropshire, during the Easter celebrations of 1621, one man rounded on the parson, who had tried to stop dancing and sports in the churchyard, and scoffed at the threat of punishment in the church court as 'but the wearing [of] sheet' (as an act of public penance).[148]

Moral policing was not exclusively a concern of the village élite. The maintenance of social harmony depended on the existence of a broad consensus between neighbours on appropriate behaviour. The openness of medieval and early modern society, the lack of a clear division between public and private meant both that privacy was important (hence, the protection of reputation from slanderous gossip and the denunciation of eavesdroppers)[149] and that neighbours scrutinized, as well as helped, their neighbours.[150] Acts of private immorality, such as adultery, might be marked out by public displays of disapproval in the form of rough music: 'to make soe notorious an abuse exemplarye whereby others evill disposed might be discoraged from committinge the like'.[151] Rough music drew on traditions of intra-communal justice which determined the bounds of morality and the penalties for their breach without recourse to external intervention, although it is not uncommon to find the parish constable taking a role which both reflected his standing as a community leader and acknowledged the ideological function of the law and its institutions. Such displays often concealed complex village politics and neighbourhood disputes. Moreover, it cannot be assumed to have represented a consensus; indeed, the need for such a display would suggest otherwise.

Resort to the law was, perhaps, more likely during times of crisis, such as a period of dearth or economic decline, when a community came under pressure. It might be used to resolve disputes between individual protagonists. In York in 1485 Hugh Glover was ordered to pay a fine of twenty shillings if he repeated his accusation that Alex Ambler was a 'Scot'.[152] The spread of justices of the peace and their ability to bind someone to keep the peace without the tiresome need to prove an offence was valuable:[153] Thomas Fisher was imprisoned until he found 'sufficiant suretie from hensfurth of his gude berying' in 1480 because he had used 'unfittying language' when talking about the mayor and the sheriff of York in a tavern,[154] while in 1583 in Devizes Roger Styll was ordered to find sureties to keep the peace after three men gave evidence to the magistrates that they 'stand in dedely feare' of him.[155]

The courts were also used by the community more generally to restore social harmony. In 1577 the manorial court of Acomb in Yorkshire ordered Elizabeth Banks 'not to chide or scold with her neighbours and to kepe hir house in the neight season and not be an esinge droper under mens' windows'.[156] In the 1590s the inhabitants of Little Onn presented a petition to the Staffordshire quarter sessions requesting that William Alcocke be bound over.[157] They complained of his failure to repair his fences and of his habit of tearing lumps out of the hedges of his neighbours to use as fuel. Alcocke was accused of being a thief:

> the manner of his lyffe ys so suspicious as wee greatlie doubt hym for he goeth gallantlie and hath to supplye his wantes that which men of farre greater lyveing have not. And howe he cometh unto yt no man knoweth … [He] thinketh hym selfe a man Lawlesse and therefore lyvethe without the compasse of all good order.

Attempts to remonstrate with Alcocke had failed: 'no curteyse or neighbourlie perswacions will reforme the same', and 'he ys so stout and prodigall that he may in no wyse be reprehended for any of these his manifest faultes and suspiciouse lyffe but he thereupon threateneth to kill'. Similarly, the villagers of Henton in Somerset petitioned the quarter sessions in 1612 about Elizabeth Busher who, they alleged, was:

the mother of divers basse children, the suspected maintainer of incontinencie in her owne house, the continuall Disturber of her neighbors quietnes and threatninge of mischieffe against them, And lastlie both reputed and feared to be a dangerous witch thorow the untimely Death of men, women and children wch she hath hated, threatned and handled.[158]

William Lambarde in Kent, 'sent to the house of correction Jane Cowper of Shorne at the complaint of the better sort of the parish' in 1584.[159] At times we get a glimpse of the rifts within a community that were concealed by the one-sided nature of many of these petitions: a petition presented to the Somerset quarter sessions in 1608 about John Newman led to a response signed by twenty-six of his fellow villagers that 'he liveth very honestly and with his handy labour as is fitting for a man of his sort'.[160]

*   *   *   *

During the late medieval and early modern periods government's interest in law enforcement and order maintenance grew, although its enthusiasm tended to fluctuate in accordance with the ebb and flow of social, political and economic events. The community retained various roles in policing, but increasingly these tasks were being passed to officials, in particular, the parish constable and the justice of the peace. Moreover, communities became accustomed to using legal or quasi-legal mechanisms and officials for resolving problems. All of which made possible the more detailed regulation which was introduced by the Tudors and early Stuarts. The restructuring of the economy following the collapse of feudalism led to enormous disruption in the lives of the labouring classes in the fifteenth and sixteenth centuries and opened up divisions between them and the prosperous. This led to pressure for greater regulation of the poor and of popular culture. For men like Edward Hext and, to a lesser extent, William Lambarde, the vagrant symbolized the threat to social order posed by an unregulated labouring population and justified a severe and wide-ranging response. The whole of the labouring class was targeted by the laws on labour, vagrancy, morality and poor relief, and these laws operated outside the constraints imposed by the criminal justice system and increased the summary authority of officials. This structure was legitimized by the provision of relief. Yet, while the local officials on whom this system depended might have subscribed to the views of Hext and Lambarde, in practice other considerations impinged on their implementation of the laws, such as the time and inconvenience involved in a particular course of action, or sympathy for the plight of an individual. Nevertheless, the agenda of state policing of the labouring poor was firmly established.

Notes

1 Crowley (1975) 'The later history of frankpledge'; Schofield (1996) 'The late medieval view of frankpledge'.
2 Powell (1989) *Kingship, Law, and Society*, 75–6.
3 Smith (1982) *De Republica Anglorum*, 107.
4 For example, Ashcroft (1991) *Scarborough Records 1600–1640*, 158.
5 Raine (1939–53) *York Civic Records*, vol VII, 112.
6 Raine (1939–53) *York Civic Records*, vol VIII, 39.
7 Earwaker (1891–2) *The Constables' Accounts*, vol I, 161.
8 Raine (1939–53) *York Civic Records*, vol VII, 173.
9 Read (1962) *William Lambarde and Local Government*, 40.
10 Herrup (1987) *The Common Peace*, 71.
11 Bettey (1982) *Calendar of the Correspondence of the Smyth Family*, 181.
12 For some successes, see Gaskill (2000) *Crime and Mentalities in Early Modern England*, 248–9. For a wrongful arrest, see Ashcroft (1991) *Scarborough Records 1600–1640*, 227.
13 Earwaker (1891–2) *The Constables' Accounts*, vol I, 8–9.
14 Barnes (1959) *Somerset Assize Orders*, 48–9.
15 Lister (1888–1915) *West Riding Sessions Rolls*, vol II, 355–6. Also, Emmison (1970) *Elizabethan Life*, 306–7.
16 Wake (1924) *Quarter Sessions Records of the County of Northampton*, 125.
17 Kent (1986) *The English Village Constable*, 264.
18 Lister (1888–1915) *West Riding Sessions Rolls*, vol I, 25.
19 Emmison (1970) *Elizabethan Life*, 175.
20 Barnes (1959) *Somerset Assize Orders*, 23–4.
21 Lister (1888–1915) *West Riding Sessions Rolls*, vol II, 301–2; Powell and Jenkinson (1934) *Surrey Quarter Sessions … 1659–1661*, 5–6 and 53.
22 But see chapter 4.
23 Atkinson (1884) *The North Riding Record Society … Quarter Sessions*, 196; Emmison (1970) *Elizabethan Life*, 306.
24 Rosenheim (1991) *The Notebook of Robert Doughty*, 59.
25 Lister (1888–1915) *West Riding Sessions Rolls*, vol I, 125–6.
26 Raine (1939–53) *York Civic Records*, vol VII, 108–9, 116.
27 Powell and Jenkinson (1938) *Surrey Quarter Sessions … Easter 1663–Epiphany 1666*, 69, 71, 245–6. See also Lister (1888–1915) *West Riding Sessions Rolls*, vol II, 7–8, 10–11, 23–4.
28 Barnes (1959) *Somerset Assize Orders*, 25–6.
29 Cunnington (1925) *Some Annals of the Borough of Devizes*, part II, 1.
30 Emmison (1970) *Elizabethan Life*, 176–7.

31 Kent (1986) *The English Village Constable*, 14–56.

32 Kent (1986) *The English Village Constable*, 17.

33 Kent (1986) *The English Village Constable*, 270.

34 Wrightson and Levine (1995) *Poverty and Piety*, 115–16.

35 Anon (1940) *The Book of Orders of 1630/1*, sig. G3 and see below.

36 Herrup (1987) *The Common Peace*, 69–70; Sharpe (1977) 'Crime and delinquency'; Sharpe (1980) 'Enforcing the law'; Wrightston (1980) 'Two concepts of order'.

37 James Gyffon, 'The song of the constable' (1626), in Wrightson and Levine (1995) *Poverty and Piety*, 115.

38 Kent (1986) *The English Village Constable*, 57–79.

39 Kent (1986) *The English Village Constable*, 80–151; Powell and Jenkinson (1938) *Surrey Quarter Sessions … Easter 1663–Epiphany 1666*, 20; Wrightson and Levine (1995) *Poverty and Piety*, 104.

40 Cunnington (1932) *Records of the County of Wilts*, 60.

41 Barnes (1959) *Somerset Assize Orders*, 35. Also Bates Harbin (1907–8) *Quarter Sessions Records for the County of Somerset*, vol I, 87, 94–5, 106–7, 111.

42 Kent (1986) *The English Village Constable*, 72–9.

43 Barnes (1961) *Somerset 1525–1640*, 77.

44 For example, Hassell Smith, Baker, and Kenny (1979) *The Papers of Nathaniel Baker*, 232, 234–5.

45 Kent (1986) *The English Village Constable*, 152–221.

46 Kent (1986) *The English Village Constable*, 220.

47 Powell and Jenkinson (1938) *Surrey Quarter Sessions … Easter 1663–Epiphany 1666*, 86, 235.

48 Lister (1888–1915) *West Riding Sessions Rolls*, vol I, 118.

49 Reay (1998) *Popular Cultures in England*, 184–5.

50 Rosenheim (1991) *The Notebook of Robert Doughty*, 49–50. Also Bradford (1911) *Proceedings in the Court of the Star Chamber*, 258.

51 Barnes (1959) *Somerset Assize Orders*, 34; Kent (1986) *The English Village Constable*, 205–21; Wrightston (1980) 'Two concepts of order'.

52 Kent (1986) *The English Village Constable*, 235.

53 Earwaker (1891–2) *The Constables' Accounts*, vol II, 9; vol I, 158, 61.

54 Rosenheim (1991) *The Notebook of Robert Doughty*, 65.

55 Lister (1888–1915) *West Riding Sessions Rolls*, vol I, 87. Also Emmison (1970) *Elizabethan Life*, 172–9.

56 Ashcroft (1991) *Scarborough Records*, 216.

57 Emmison (1970) *Elizabethan Life*, 106.

58 Emmison (1970) *Elizabethan Life*, 175–6; Kent (1986) *The English Village Constable*, 261–3.

59 Kent (1986) *The English Village Constable*, 242.

60 Kent (1986) *The English Village Constable*, 258–9.

61 Underdown (1987) *Revel, Riot and Rebellion*.

62 Kimball (1983) *Oxfordshire Sessions of the Peace*, 72–3.

63 Wrightson and Levine (1995) *Poverty and Piety*, 106. But see McIntosh (1998) *Controlling Misbehaviour*.

64 Gleason (1969) *The Justices of the Peace*, 116; Barnes (1959) *Somerset Assize Orders*, xx.
65 Barnes (1961) *Somerset 1525–1640*, 54.
66 Cockburn (1972) *A History of English Assizes*; Herrup (1987) *The Common Peace*, 44–7, 52–3.
67 Barnes (1955) 'Examination before a justice'; Langbein (1974) *Prosecuting Crime*. On the coroner's role in homicide cases, see Langbein (1974) *Prosecuting Crime*, 13–15.
68 Langbein (1974) *Prosecuting Crime*, 63–97.
69 Langbein (1974) *Prosecuting Crime*, 6–10; 3 Edw. I, c. 15; 1 & 2 Ph. & Mar., c. 13 (1554).
70 Herrup (1987) *The Common Peace*, 88–91.
71 Beattie (1986) *Crime and the Courts in England*, 271.
72 Herrup (1987) *The Common Peace*, 81.
73 Barnes (1961) *Somerset 1525–1640*, 56.
74 Langbein (1974) *Prosecuting Crime*, 22–3, 118–25. Also Green (1985) *Verdict According to Conscience*.
75 Barnes (1961) *Somerset 1525–1640*, 56.
76 William Lambarde, 1588, in Langbein (1974) *Prosecuting Crime*, 42. Also Herrup (1987) *The Common Peace*, 86–7.
77 Robison (1988) 'Murder at Crowhurst'.
78 Langbein (1974) *Prosecuting Crime*, 53–4.
79 Barnes (1959) *Somerset Assize Orders*, 45–6.
80 Raine (1939–53) *York Civic Records*, vol V, 154–8; also vol VI, 86–7.
81 Ashcroft (1991) *Scarborough Records 1600–1640*, 299.
82 Ashcroft (1991) *Scarborough Records 1600–1640*, 251–2.
83 Wake (1924) *Quarter Sessions Records of the County of Northampton*, 53–4.
84 Bradford (1911) *Proceedings in the Court of the Star Chamber*, 252.
85 Lister (1888–1915) *West Riding Sessions Rolls*, vol I, 79.
86 Ashcroft (1991) *Scarborough Records 1600–1640*, 196–7.
87 Herrup (1987) *The Common Peace*, 72–85, 114.
88 Kimball (1959) *The Shropshire Peace Roll*, 57, 75.
89 Hassell Smith, Baker, and Kenny (1979) *The Papers of Nathaniel Baker*, 213. William Lambarde, writing in 1582, denounced such practices as an encouragement to crime: Read (1962) *William Lambarde and Local Government*, 71; also 41.
90 Herrup (1987) *The Common Peace*, 54.
91 Rosenheim (1991) *The Notebook of Robert Doughty*, 61; also 39.
92 Bates Harbin (1907–8) *Quarter Sessions Records for the County of Somerset*, vol I, 159.
93 Barnes (1959) *Somerset Assize Orders*, 43, 48.
94 Beresford (1957–8) 'The common informer'; Radzinowicz (1948–68) *A History of English Criminal Law*, vol II.
95 Barnes (1959) *Somerset Assize Orders*, 30, 32; Bates Harbin (1907–8) *Quarter Sessions Records for the County of Somerset*, vol II, 77–8, 84, 98, 139, 143.

96 Goldie (1997) 'The Hilton gang'.
97 Radzinowicz (1948–68) *A History of English Criminal Law*, vol II, 139.
98 Anon (1748) *Memoirs … of Sir Thomas Deveil*, 39.
99 Bates Harbin (1907–8) *Quarter Sessions Records for the County of Somerset*, vol II, 77–8, 84, 98, 139, 143.
100 Slack (1988) *Poverty and Policy*; Summerson (1996) 'The criminal underworld of medieval England', 199.
101 For example, 12 Ric. II (1388), 2 Hen. V, c. 4 (1414), 4 Hen. V, c. 4 (1416), 23 Hen. VI, c. 13 (1444).
102 Tawney and Power (1951) *Tudor Economic Documents*, vol III, 302, 345. Generally, Beier (1985) *Masterless Men*.
103 Lister (1888–1915) *West Riding Sessions Rolls*, vol II, 7.
104 Tawney and Power (1951) *Tudor Economic Documents*, vol III, 341–2.
105 Salgado (1972) *Cony-Catchers and Bawdy Baskets*.
106 Slack (1988) *Poverty and Policy*, 24.
107 Wrightson and Levine (1995) *Poverty and Piety*.
108 Tawney and Power (1951) *Tudor Economic Documents*, vol III, 354–62. See Slack (1974) 'Vagrants and vagrancy'.
109 Slack (1988) *Poverty and Policy*, 113–37.
110 Raine (1939–53) *York Civic Records*, vol I, 139–40.
111 Raine (1939–53) *York Civic Records*, vol VII, 87–8, 110–12.
112 Lemon (1865) *Calendar of State Papers … 1581–1590*, 324, 435. Also Goring and Wake (1975) *Northamptonshire Lieutenancy Papers*, 53–4.
113 Read (1962) *William Lambarde and Local Government*.
114 Green (1867) *Calendar of State Papers … 1591–1594*, 120.
115 Green (1869) *Calendar of State Papers … 1595–1597*, 335–6.
116 See also 43 Eliz. I, c. 2.
117 Raine (1939–53) *York Civic Records*, vol IV, 57, 68, 71, 158.
118 Beer (1982) *Rebellion and Riot*, 82–139.
119 Pound (1971) *The Norwich Census of the Poor 1570*, 8–9.
120 Atkinson (1884) *The North Riding Record Society … Quarter Sessions*, 73. Also Lister (1888–1915) *West Riding Sessions Rolls*, vol I, 125–6.
121 Slack (1975) *Poverty in Early Stuart Salisbury*, 52.
122 Slack (1975) *Poverty in Early Stuart Salisbury*, 33, 36, 40.
123 Slack (1975) *Poverty in Early Stuart Salisbury*, 30. See Hext's more rigorous inquiries in Tawney and Power (1951) *Tudor Economic Documents*, vol III, 343.
124 Slack (1972) 'Poverty and politics in Salisbury', 178.
125 Lister (1888–1915) *West Riding Sessions Rolls*, vol I, 84.
126 Raine (1939–53) *York Civic Records*, vol VIII.
127 Tawney and Power (1951) *Tudor Economic Documents*, vol III, 344. Generally Ashcroft (1991) *Scarborough Records 1600–1640*, 282; Kent (1986) *The English Village Constable*, 200–5.
128 Slack (1975) *Poverty in Early Stuart Salisbury*, 3, 4–7.
129 Read (1962) *William Lambarde and Local Government*, 183–4.
130 Read (1962) *William Lambarde and Local Government*, 143–4.

131 Richardson (1969–78) *Court Rolls of the Manor of Acomb*, vol I, 95, 103, 135.

132 Dennett (1933) *Beverley Borough Records*, 40; Lister (1888–1915) *West Riding Sessions Rolls*, vol II, 7–8, 10–11, 23–4, 118; Richardson (1969–78) *Court Rolls of the Manor of Acomb*, vol I, 93.

133 Clark (1983) *The English Alehouse*.

134 For example, 18 Eliz. I, c. 3, s. 2.

135 For example, 11 Hen VII, c. 2 (1494); 19 Hen. VII, c. 12 (1503).

136 Read (1962) *William Lambarde and Local Government*, 70.

137 Raine (1939–53) *York Civic Records*, vol VII, 174.

138 Underdown (1987) *Revel, Riot and Rebellion*, 49–50.

139 Anon (1940) *The Book of Orders of 1630/1*, 11.

140 Anon (1940) *The Book of Orders of 1630/1*, 11.

141 Anon (1940) *The Book of Orders of 1630/1*, 27.

142 Barnes (1961) *Somerset 1525–1640*, 172–202; Kent (1986) *The English Village Constable*.

143 Ingram (1996) 'Reformation of manners'; McIntosh (1998) *Controlling Misbehaviour*.

144 Underdown (1987) *Revel, Riot and Rebellion*, 48. Also Wrightston (1980) 'Two concepts of order', 41–4.

145 Ingram (1996) 'Reformation of manners'.

146 Underdown (1987) *Revel, Riot and Rebellion*; Underdown (1992) *Fire from Heaven*; Slack (1972) 'Poverty and politics in Salisbury'; Slack (1974) 'Vagrants and vagrancy'; Slack (1975) *Poverty in Early Stuart Salisbury*.

147 Also Hassell Smith and Baker (1984) *The Papers of Nathaniel Baker*, 270–1.

148 Reay (1998) *Popular Cultures in England*, 138.

149 Emmison (1970) *Elizabethan Life*, 176–7; Richardson (1969–78) *Court Rolls of the Manor of Acomb*, vol I, 60.

150 Reay (1998) *Popular Cultures in England*, 12–13.

151 Joan Kent cited in Reay (1998) *Popular Cultures in England*, 160; and generally 155–60. For examples, see Cunnington (1932) *Records of the County of Wilts*, 64, 79. Rough music involved the noisy gathering of people to expose the misbehaviour of their neighbours.

152 Raine (1939–53) *York Civic Records*, vol I, 113–14.

153 Hindle (1996) 'The keeping of the public peace'.

154 Raine (1939–53) *York Civic Records*, vol I, 37.

155 Cunnington (1925) *Some Annals of the Borough of Devizes*, part II, 1.

156 Richardson (1969–78) *Court Rolls of the Manor of Acomb*, vol I, 60. Also Attreed (1991) *The York House Books 1461–1490*, 708, 723.

157 Burne (1932) *The Staffordshire Quarter Sessions Rolls*, 25–7.

158 Bates Harbin (1907–8) *Quarter Sessions Records for the County of Somerset*, vol I, 96.

159 Read (1962) *William Lambarde and Local Government*, 36.

160 Bates Harbin (1907–8) *Quarter Sessions Records for the County of Somerset*, vol I, 16.

Chapter 4

The professionalization of policing: 1660–1800

'The real strength and riches of a country'

By the eighteenth century the labouring classes tended to be discussed in rather different terms from those used in the late Tudor and early Stuart periods. Vagrancy continued to be a problem and the mobile poor still ran the risk of being whipped out of a parish by the constable, but neither commentators nor government saw the country as besieged by armies of vagrants in the way they had in the late sixteenth century. Instead, the focus was on the role of the labouring classes as an economic resource. Charles Davenant, the economist, asserted in 1695, 'People are the real Strength and Riches of a Country',[1] or, as another writer put it in 1722, they '*get* Estates for the *Rich*, and then *Fight* to defend their *Persons* and *Properties*, from becoming a *Prey* to *any Invaders*'.[2] Therefore, 'Our domestic safety and comfort, our private wealth and prosperity, our national riches, strength, and glory, are dependent upon an industrious and well-order'd Poor'.[3] This dependence was turned into a duty owed by the labouring poor because it was argued that 'mankind in general are naturally inclined to ease and indolence, and that nothing but absolute necessity will enforce labour and industry.'[4] This did not affect the gentry, who had enough to live off; on the other hand, the labouring people,

> having nothing but their labour to bestow on the society, if they withhold this from it they become useless members; and having nothing but their labour to procure a support for themselves they must of necessity become burdensome.[5]

This obligation was reinforced by the connection between idleness, poverty, immorality and crime: 'where *Idleness* prevails, it nurses Wantonness, Baseness, and Effeminacy, and almost every Vice';[6] indeed, 'Idleness is the Road to the Gallows'.[7] The printer and novelist Samuel Richardson invited young apprentices to learn the lessons of crime literature:

> Let the *Sessions-Paper* and the *Dying-Speeches* of unhappy Criminals tell the rest: Let them inform the inconsiderate Youth, by the Confessions of the dying malefactors, how naturally, as it were Step by Step, Swearing, Cursing, Profaneness, Drunkenness, Whoredom, Theft, Robbery, Murder, and the Gallows, succeed one another![8]

Even among those who did work, it was claimed, 'That the poor, in general work only for the bare necessaries of life, and for the means of a low debauch, which when obtained they cease to labour, till rounded again by necessity.'[9] The concern in the eighteenth century was, therefore, with labour discipline, and, more specifically, labour discipline among town dwellers. They tended to be compared unfavourably with the rural labouring people: 'in London amongst the lower classes all is anarchy, drunkenness, and thievery; in the country good order, sobriety and honesty.'[10] The effect of this, warned contemporary demographers, was that the population of London was declining, while that of the country-side increased. The difference between the two communities lay in the perception that the labouring people of London were seen as outside government: Henry Fielding famously compared London to 'a vast wood or forest, in which a thief may harbour with as great security as wild beasts do in the deserts of Africa or Arabia'.[11]

In general terms, then, commentators on social policy were interested in ensuring that the poor were kept at work:

> the Poor, who are not able to help themselves, should be maintain'd; and such as are able and willing be employed; and those that are obstinate and unwilling, be compelled to labour.[12]

There was a good deal of criticism of the administration of the Elizabethan poor laws and ideas for reform sought to address this issue. Many put their faith in the effect of workhouses. In 1696 John Cary established a workhouse in Bristol. Here the poor would be taught habits of industry and the institution could derive its funding from the goods they manufactured.[13] However, while some followed his lead,[14] these experiments typically proved uneconomic and their failure led others to propose that workhouses be used as quasi-penal institutions – 'gaols without guilt', as one critic called them – to deter the poor from seeking relief and by that means inculcate habits of industry.[15]

Yet there was a general lack of enthusiasm for workhouses because of their cost; for local officials and ratepayers it was often seen as easier and cheaper to provide relief to the poor in their homes. By the late eighteenth century this debate had tended to shift from concern about the waste of the labouring poor as an economic resource to the issue of the cost to the ratepayers, which was escalating without having any apparent impact on the numbers of the indigent.[16] Unsurprisingly, the blame for this situation was often put down to an inclination to idleness among the poor. One commentator summed up this strand of opinion: 'if the poor have a certain and a liberal provision made by the public, we may bid farewell to industry and frugality among that class of men'.[17] At the same time, it was being argued that the poor quality of administration, which was in the hands of local property owners, was a problem.[18] This drove some to conclude that the poor relief system was bound to fail and to argue for its virtual abolition.[19] While such a radical solution was not adopted, the scheme that emerged as the Poor Law (Amendment) Act 1834 was built on the principle of deterring the poor from claiming relief and on a structure of administration in which central government intervened more directly than had previously been the case.

The other aspect of intervention in the lives of the labouring classes was through prosecution as a means of effecting moral reform. The enthusiasm for promoting reform that was such a feature of the late sixteenth and early seventeenth centuries did not entirely disappear: in 1735 a campaign against gin drinking led to the controversial Gin Act 1736 (and the Gin Act 1751), which was intended to stamp out the trade and which depended for its enforcement on common informers; there were also periodic campaigns led by justices against bawdy houses, gaming houses and street prostitution.

However, the most influential, best-organized and longest lasting of these campaigns involved the societies for the reformation of manners. They were set up in 1690, following an initiative that emerged from the court of William III, and remained fairly active until 1738.[20] They counted among their members justices of the peace and parish officials who were able to promote enforcement of laws on prostitution, swearing, Sabbath-breaking and 'lewd and disorderly conduct'. The societies also hired constables and encouraged common informers. There was criticism of their concentration on the poorer classes: 'Your Annual Lists of Criminals appeare/ But no Sir *Harry* or Sir *Charles* is there.'[21] Moreover, in London, where the societies were most active, the Middlesex justices sought to have their reforming colleagues removed because of, among other things, their inflexible approach to the enforcement of the law and their interference in the work of their fellow justices. In 1702 and 1709 London crowds murdered two of their constables.[22] The activity of the societies dropped sharply after 1725 and they seem finally to have collapsed as a result of the general hostility towards informers following the Gin Act 1736. However, their longer decline was also attributable to their methods of working. The use of informers was essential to their approach of promoting moral reform through full enforcement of the laws, but it was unpopular and opened up the societies to the same allegations of corruption as were typically laid at the doors of informers. Yet, the remarkable vitality of the societies over a period of almost 50 years does suggest there was a good deal of support for their general aims and, indeed, other societies with similar objectives, although sometimes different methods, appeared later in the century.[23]

The principal features of the regulation of the labouring classes, which had been constructed between the late medieval and early Stuart periods, remained in place, but there was less certainty about the effectiveness of the administrative arrangements. In spite of these problems and even though the problems posed by the poor were characterized differently from how they had been in the sixteenth century, the belief in the need for regulation was well established.

The London watch

While the societies for the reformation of manners showed there was a good deal of support for the effective policing of morality, they also suggested that the existing mechanisms of crime control were regarded by some as ineffective. Watchmen had some responsibility for dealing with drunkenness, soliciting and so forth, and legislation in the eighteenth century broadened their powers to arrest the idle, the disorderly and the homeless,[24] but these tended to be seen as public order issues. Indeed, the criticism of the watch was as much to do with the concerns of householders and the parish vestry about order on the streets as about crime control.

The watch system was built around the idea that householders had an obligation to protect their community, but by the eighteenth century many were reluctant to fulfil this duty. This is unsurprising in view of the nature of the work which kept them out of their beds at night and was often odious, time-consuming and either dangerous or boring. Many sought to excuse themselves on grounds of age or health, others preferred to pay a fine rather than serve or to hire a substitute, and by the 1720s that this had become the accepted position is suggested by the fact that, while refusals to serve did not cease, prosecutions virtually did.[25] This professionalization by default raised some concerns about the quality of these substitutes. Shakespeare's watchman who would 'rather sleep than talk'[26] may be dismissed as merely a dramatic device or a caricature, but successful dramatists nevertheless work with characters who strike a chord with their audiences. A hundred years later, such complaints were still commonplace: for instance, in reporting a burglary in which a large amount of rum and brandy was stolen, *The Daily Journal* commented that this had happened,

> notwithstanding the watchman's box being only over the way, and in full view.[27] This makes the fourth robbery of that kind committed in that neighbourhood within this fortnight; a proof of the great vigilance of the watchman!

Daniel Defoe wrote four pamphlets and a broadsheet on the issue of street crime in which, among other things, he roundly attacked the efficacy of the watch and called for measures to ensure it 'be compos'd of stout, able-body'd Men, and of those a sufficient Number'.[28]

These criticisms have been taken out of context by some historians of the police and held up as evidence of a desire for the sort of radical reform which they find in the Metropolitan Police of 1829. Yet contemporary critics seemed to view the solution in terms of the number and quality of the watchmen rather than the restructuring of the watch system, and, at that time, the idea of taking control out of the hands of the parish authorities, as happened in 1829, was not on the agenda. People like Defoe would have regarded the establishment of a police force controlled by central government as a threat to the liberty enjoyed by 'the freeborn Englishman'. Furthermore, contemporary writers and also historians have, typically, ignored the problems of being a watchman:[29] the routine of assaults by those whom they encountered and the uncertainties of the law which resulted in the threat – probably only occasional but nonetheless real – of expensive litigation over an arrest.

Various reform proposals were put forward. In 1720 the Middlesex magistrates suggested a radical scheme under which they would take control of the watch in Westminster:

> several Persons of Quality, and others, have been lately, and in an unusual manner, attacked in their Coaches and Chairs, and some of them robbed, in the high Streets; and yet none of the Persons

concerned in these Robberies have been taken; which is imputed to the Want of a proper and regulated Watch, except the Statute of *Winchester*, which has made no Provision between *Michaelmas* and *Lady-day*; and the Method now used is, for the Constables to appoint what Persons, and what Number of Watchmen, they think fit, and to raise and levy great Sums on the Inhabitants, under Pretence of paying them, without rendering any Account, there being no Law to compel them thereunto; and yet the Watch, so kept, is found not to be sufficient.[30]

This immediately prompted a petition claiming to come from 'the Inhabitants of the City and Liberties of Westminster', although actually it was subscribed to by only a small minority, and another from the Dean and Chapter of St Peter, Westminster. Both objected that the proposal was an assault on 'their ancient Rights and Privileges' and asserted that 'due Care is taken of the Watch within *Westminster*; and that the Petitioners do not apprehend themselves, or their Houses, to be in any Danger, or to need any further Aid for their Preservation'.[31] Although other petitions supported reform, the idea was killed off when opposition came from the powerful West End vestries which had members in both Houses of Parliament.[32] The main objection was the loss of vestry control, so it cannot have been too much of a surprise that an even bolder attempt in 1729 to reform the watch throughout England disappeared rather more rapidly.[33]

The failure of these schemes was a rejection of the method of reforming the parish watch and, in particular, passing control to the magistrates. It did not mean that parishes discarded reform. In the City of London a mixed professional and amateur system under the control of the City authorities had existed since the sixteenth century.[34] Marshals and their assistants were appointed with jurisdiction across the City. In addition, each of the 26 wards had its own constables and watchmen under the direction of the alderman for that ward. The problem of getting house-holders to serve had only partially been dealt with by the Watch Act 1705, which permitted substitutes to be hired. Under legislation in 1726 and 1737 the obligation to serve was replaced by a duty to pay a rate out of which professional watchmen would be hired, although the requirement for householders to serve as parish constables remained. The size of the watch, wages, hours of duty and how they were to be armed were controlled by the Lord Mayor, Alderman and Common Council, but in other matters the wards regulated their own watchmen.

Outside the City of London, as the 1720 petition from the Middlesex justices indicated, some parishes had already introduced watch reform financed by voluntary contributions gathered by the constables. Parish vestries wanted more control and a more certain source of finance in the form of a compulsory rate. The solution adopted was for individual parishes to apply for a watch act which would give the vestry this authority. In 1735 the wealthy West End parishes of St James, Piccadilly and St George, Hanover Square were moved by concern over street robberies to obtain legislation to establish a professional night watch paid for by a compulsory rate levied on householders; in exchange, the householders were exempted from their obligation to serve under the Statute of Winchester (8 Geo. II, c. 15).[35] Although another attempt at reform across the whole of Westminster failed in 1736,[36] the 1735 act sparked a steady flow of parish schemes. The reasons for reform given in these statutes were always along similar lines:

> Whereas by the laws now in being no effectual provision is made for the establishing, ordering, or well governing of such a nightly watch, or for levying and collecting any sums of money for defraying the necessary charges thereof (10 Geo. II, c. 22 (1737)).

The watchmen were authorized to arrest 'all night walkers, malefactors, rogues, vagabonds, and other disorderly persons whom they shall find disturbing the publick peace, or shall have just cause to suspect of any evil designs' (see 10 Geo. II, c. 22). However, behind the legislation there was, often, a local power struggle and the watch act commonly 'marked the ascendancy of the more well-to-do over smaller property owners and the working poor' with the latter resenting the control acquired by the former.[37] The creation of a compulsory rate also meant the watch system was commonly caught between a desire among the ratepayers to keep spending down and their criticism of any failure to prevent crime or catch criminals. Moreover, parish-by-parish reform left unresolved the issue of parochial boundaries: for instance, in the early hours of 10 March 1741 Stephen Haydon was at his watchstand on the corner of Catherine Street in London when he heard robbers assaulting Arabella Strickland for 'near half an Hour', but 'it being out of my Parish I durst not venture to go' to her aid.[38]

The onset of war in 1739 saw anxiety about crime wane, only to return with peace in 1748.[39] This rhythm of concern over crime had a history which, as has been seen, went back to at least the thirteenth century, and reflected the belief that war took away the young men who committed crime and peace returned them. In the midst of the panic Horace Walpole, who had himself been robbed in Hyde Park by James Maclean, 'the Gentleman Highwayman', complained to a friend, 'One is forced to travel even at noon as if one was going to battle',[40] and George II urged Parliament 'to consider seriously of some effectual Provision to suppress these audacious Crimes of Robbery and Violence, which are now become so frequent, especially about this great capital'.[41] In London, on which most attention was focused, the watchman emerged as a target for blame: they were 'either infirm, old, or indigent People, who serve their Offices for Hire, are often in Fee with the Public-Houses'.[42] A select committee under Sir Richard Lloyd declared the watch in Westminster defective in terms of numbers of watchmen, their quality and pay. Although no legislation followed, many parishes decided it was time to consider the issue again.[43] Some took emergency measures: Islington raised a subscription in March 1749 to supplement its watch by hiring soldiers. The government itself directed soldiers to patrol the roads leading into London during the winter of 1749–50, although the experiment was brief both because of the cost involved and some concern about the constitutional implications of using soldiers in this role. This latter objection was also raised against the use of soldiers by magistrates to raid illegal gaming houses.[44]

Just as this crime panic began Henry Fielding (1707–54) was appointed a justice of the peace for Westminster and Middlesex at Bow Street in 1748 and also became 'court justice', a semi-official post as government advisor on crime and policing matters in the metropolis.[45] In 1751 his stepbrother John joined him on the commission for Westminster and later for Middlesex, and was appointed 'court justice' on Henry's retirement in 1754.[46] Henry launched into the 'poor old decrepit People' employed as watchmen.[47] He submitted a proposal in 1749 to Lord Chancellor Hardwicke for a watch scheme covering the whole of Westminster to be funded from the poor rates and controlled by commissioners. In 1763 the government funded a force, directed by John Fielding, to patrol the highways leading into London. Government support was withdrawn in the following year on the ground that policing was a matter for the local authorities, although the cost of £1,000 and the belief that crime had continued to rise doubtless influenced the decision.[48] However, John Fielding was able to attract funding for a few foot patrols operating from Bow Street across Westminster, which were used proactively to target trouble spots and serious crime, such as robbery.[49]

The efficiency of the parish constables also came under scrutiny. Although constables had jurisdiction across the whole of Westminster, familiar problems remained: the better off avoided service by hiring a deputy or paying a fine, and, indeed, for some parishes these fines represented a valuable source of income. Many of the vestries did try to control the quality of deputies and impose a system of discipline.[50] Some deputies undertook other parish offices and, perhaps, acquired a degree of expertise, although whether they used this to improve their ability to prevent and detect crime or simply to enhance their earnings is difficult to know. In 1756 legislation increased the number of constables for Westminster and formalized the appointment of deputies, leading John Fielding to praise 'the general good Behaviour, Diligence and Activity of the Constables' in Middlesex and Westminster.[51] Nevertheless, in his evidence to a select committee in 1770, James Sayer, the deputy High Steward of Westminster, remained critical of the practice of hiring deputies on the ground that 'many unfit Persons are appointed, who, he is informed, make a Trade of serving the Office'. His suggestions that more constables should be appointed to reduce their workload and a more stringent line be taken with those who neglected to serve were never likely to be popular.[52]

The select committee of 1770 also took evidence on the state of the watch in Westminster from just a handful of witnesses who were highly critical of the system and who seem to have been chosen to appear precisely because the committee wanted support for views that its members had already formed. John Fielding complained, 'The watch is insufficient; their Duty too hard, and Pay too small'.[53] He argued that the watchmen were too old and the parishes too parsimonious; he criticized the failure of neighbouring parishes to co-ordinate their beats which 'leaves the Frontiers of each Parish in a confused State' and the inability of a watchman in one parish to assist a watchman in another parish. Not surprisingly, he recommended that the watch be put under the control of the magistrates. James Sayer agreed, adding that there was often no way to discipline watchmen since the threat of dismissal was difficult to use because parishes found it hard to find replacements. It was also complained before this committee that the constables were inefficient in their supervision of the watch because the householders who did serve were unfamiliar with the task and the abilities of deputies were difficult to test. The committee reported in favour of reform, but their proposals made no headway.

Reform of the watch remained in the hands of the parishes. Some sought to improve efficiency by introducing minimum requirements as to age, height and education as well as better salaries and tougher disciplinary regimes. In some places watchmen were switched between beats to avoid familiarity between them and the communities they policed. Many parishes also hired patrols – often armed – who were not constrained by the beat system. To reduce the cost involved some parishes combined to obtain legislation while retaining parochial separation in the schemes which were constructed. In 1766 the parishes in Southwark empowered commissioners to administer a system which stretched over parochial boundaries. This scheme may, as Reynolds suggests, have been influenced by Southwark's proximity to other unitary policing authorities across the river to the north in the City of London and to the south in Surrey.[54]

Watch reforms spread into outlying parishes and into the counties around London, prompted by the belief that criminals would migrate from an area which had improved the efficiency of its watch to one which had not. In 1785 the residents of Clapham in Surrey obtained legislation to reform the watch on the grounds that the village,

> is become large and populous, and, from its Vicinity to the Metropolis, the Inhabitants thereof, and also all Persons passing to and from the same in the Night Time, are much exposed to Robberies, and other Outrages.[55]

This migration theory was reinforced by the rapid construction of roads by turnpike trusts. These roads seemed to make obsolete the assumption underpinning the Statute of Winchester that the watch was needed only during summer months because the state of the roads in winter made travel very difficult. The turnpike trusts established their own watch systems to protect travellers. For instance, the trustees of the turnpike between Tyburn and Uxbridge obtained a statute in 1769 (7 Geo III, c. 102) allowing lighting and watching on a road which 'is frequently infested in the Night-time with Robbers and other wicked and evil disposed Persons, and Robberies, Outrages and Violences are committed thereon'. The watchmen were empowered 'to apprehend and secure all Rogues, Vagabonds, and other disorderly Persons, who shall be found loitering, wandering, or misbehaving themselves, or committing any Disorders or Offences' on the highway, or whom the watchmen reasonably suspect 'of any evil Designs'. The problem was that, while the turnpikes might be well guarded, the same was not always true of the areas to which they brought travellers. Kingston-upon-Thames, for example, requested the extension of the nightly watch established by the trustees of the turnpike from Southwark because of the fear of criminals moving to an area without a watch and the reluctance to spend money creating one.[56]

Even in those parishes that undertook reform criticisms of the watch continued. Newspapers delighted in reporting cases showing incompetent watchmen, as when the lead was stolen from the roof of a London watch-house in February 1772.[57] The Westminster night watch was again before a select committee in 1772. Its report highlighted the disparities between parishes: 'the present Mode of Watching, and Pay of the Watchmen … is very irregular and various, and ought to be put under proper Regulations.'[58] While some parishes had obtained special legislation, some had not and this meant they could not fund an efficient watch system. St Giles-in-the-Fields and St George, Bloomsbury operated under the 1285 act which meant that the extended watch scheme depended on voluntary contributions collected by the constables, who 'never account for the same':

> above 200 Inhabitants do not pay any Thing; and most of them are so dissatisfied with this Mode of Watching, that they have entered into voluntary Subscriptions to pay other Watchmen than those provided by the Constables.[59]

Staffing levels varied between St Mary-le-Strand with three watchmen and the nearby parish of St Martin-in-the-Fields with 85. Some of the parishes, such as St Andrew's Holborn and St. George the Martyr, employed armed patrolmen as well as the watch; others did not. The differences in expenditure were vast, from £89 to £1497 a year. The committee concluded that 'the Statute of *Winchester* being very obsolete is a very improper Regulation'; that the method of watching and of paying watchmen in Westminster 'is very irregular and various, and ought to be put under proper Regulations'; that 'a regular and uniform Watch, with Patroles … under proper Regulations' would improve 'the Safety of the Inhabitants'; that the watch should be paid from a compulsory rate; that constables of the night need to be appointed; and that the watch in each parish should be placed under Directors of the Watch.[60]

Once again the proposals failed to make headway. However, Sir Charles Whitworth, who chaired the committee, produced a new bill in 1773 and published a pamphlet proposing the creation of patrols in each locality to work alongside the watchmen.[61] The patrols would work only during the winter and would cover a wider area than the watchmen, who only looked after the beat to which they were assigned or remained in the watchstand. While the watch was more concerned with order on the streets – the 'broils and affrays, and the sallies of intemperance' – than with crime, guarded a relatively small area and announced their presence by calling the hours,[62] the patrols would operate with some stealth and unpredictability. The bill specified minimum numbers of watchmen and patrols, minimum pay and tasks, laid out a scale of punishments for watchmen, and enabled watchmen from different parishes to assist their fellows in other parishes. The appointment of deputy constables would be further regulated: a deputy would have to be a resident householder in the parish in which he was to serve and be approved by the vestry. On the face of it these were radical proposals, but Whitworth was careful to argue that they merely built on existing provisions or on experiments that had been successfully tried in some of the parishes of Westminster. He also lobbied the vestries and reassured them by maintaining the principle of parish control.[63] Moreover, by introducing an acceptable level of uniformity and co-operation between parishes he tapped into the growing support for greater efficiency in government. This time the bill succeeded and became the Westminster Night Watch Act 1774 (14 Geo. III, c. 90).

The crime panic of the 1780s was as bad as any in the century. The concerns were familiar: as the American War of Independence wound down, so it was feared 'the reducing of the navy, army, and militia, will cast a number of men adrift, many of whom are idly inclined, and may become obnoxious to the laws'.[64] The situation seemed worse to many because the loss of the North American colonies meant there was no-where convicts could be transported to. The result was that both the number of those hanged and the percentage of convicted felons hanged rose to levels not seen before in that century. The criticism of the watch was renewed, even though many parishes continued to make improvements by, for instance, increasing the number of watchmen,[65] or, as in the parishes of St Margaret and St John the Evangelist in 1782, employing extra patrols.[66]

In 1785 Pitt's government introduced the Police Bill. The idea was that three Commissioners of Police would be appointed by the government to oversee the policing of the metropolis. The bill was subject to criticism about the cost, the loss of parochial authority and the increase in government power and patronage. The *Daily Universal Register* complained, 'Our constitution can admit nothing like a French police; and many foreigners have declared that they would rather lose their money to an English thief, than their liberty to a *Lieutenant de Police*'.[67] However, it was the City of London's resentment at what it regarded as the interference with its privileges which seems to have killed off the proposal.[68] A diluted version of the bill was enacted as the Middlesex Justices Act 1792 (32 Geo. III, c. 53) which, as its title suggests, did not apply to the City. The act established seven police offices, each with three stipendiary magistrates and six police-office constables. Some commentators continued to argue for centralization as the only efficient solution, but it seemed unlikely that this would ever occur in the face of the opposition from the parishes.[69] It does seem likely that the watch in London had become more effective in terms of apprehending offenders,[70] but, as ratepayers saw expenditure increase so their expectations rose, driving many parish authorities to tinker further with the arrangements.

Reform of the watch outside London

Outside London, reform of the watch seems to have been driven by concerns about the migration of criminals and by the expansion of urban areas. There was also a powerful sense of civic pride which saw watch reform as part of a package of measures aimed at the improvement of the urban environment, which included schemes for paving, sewage disposal, lighting and water supplies.[71] Bristol obtained legislation in 1700 (11 & 12 Will. III, c. 23) for cleaning, paving and lighting the streets, but a new act was obtained at the height of the post-war crime panic in 1749 (22 Geo. II, c. 20). According to the preamble:

> for want of erecting and maintaining a competent number of such publick lamps, the citizens and inhabitants of the said city are exposed to the danger of fires, murders, burglaries, robberies, and many other outrages and inconveniences

This was followed in 1755 (28 Geo. II, c. 32. Also, 29 Geo. II, c. 47) by a statute 'for establishing, maintaining, and well-governing, a nightly Watch', which, it was claimed, 'would prevent Accidents by Fire, Street-Robberies, Burglaries, and other Outrages, in the Night-time'.[72] The act empowered the justices – the mayor and aldermen – to appoint watchmen, direct their work, determine their wages (subject to a maximum of seven shillings a week) and make orders for their regulation. In addition, there were night constables, appointed by the alderman of each ward but under the direction of the justices. The watchmen and night constables were to arrest nightwalkers and disorderly persons. A mistake in the original act meant the corporation had to return to Parliament the following session. This time it was claimed that the night constables and watchmen who had been appointed were 'very bad characters, who have been guilty of many and great Irregularities, and have even committed a most horrid Murder, with many Circumstances of Cruelty'.[73]

The proposals were opposed from the start by those who, while not disputing the need for reform, argued that it put too much power into the hands of the unelected mayor and aldermen, and who insisted that the watch should be accountable to the ratepayers through the parish vestries:

> that the Inhabitants themselves, as hath ever been the Custom, may be permitted to depute and direct the Persons, who are, at their Expence, to watch and guard their Properties.[74]

73

In fact, the debate over the Bristol watch was as much about party politics as about the reforms themselves. The Whigs, who held power in the city, saw it as a way to extend their authority and the Tories saw it as an opportunity to attack them.[75] Elsewhere, the reorganization of the watch was sometimes accompanied by restructuring of the parish constables: for instance, in eighteenth-century York the constables were, for many purposes, regulated and co-ordinated by a city official.[76]

As the economy grew, places which had barely been villages in the early eighteenth century boomed and pressed for Improvement Acts. In 1735 Newcastle-upon-Tyne petitioned for legislation to provide improved street lighting and a night watch because the town 'is very large and populous, and to which many Strangers resort'.[77] Liverpool grew rapidly in the eighteenth century on the back of trade with America in tobacco, salt, sugar and slaves, and in 1748 legislation authorized the building of a new church and the lighting, cleaning and watching of its streets (21 Geo. II, c. 24). The act created a body of commissioners – the mayor, the recorder, the trustees of the town and eighteen people elected by those paying poor rates – who appointed and regulated a night watch of up to 60 men. A compulsory rate was imposed on householders whose duty to watch was abolished (21 Geo. II, c. 24, s. 59). Liverpool continued to grow and a further statute in 1788 removed the limit on the number of watchmen (28 Geo. III, c. 13, s. 1).[78] Better communications between the burgeoning towns of the industrial North, the Midlands and London brought wealth and higher aspirations to those who lived in the villages in between: well-lit, clean, paved and watched streets became symbols of prosperity. In 1790 the hamlets of Deretend and Bardesley in the parish of Aston sought an Improvement Act because,

> the Great Road, leading from *Birmingham* towards *London*, extends through the High Streets of the said Hamlets; that the Trade and Popularity of the said Hamlets are greatly increased, and several new Streets have been lately laid open and erected therein.[79]

Private and quasi-public watch schemes

The difficulties of obtaining watch reform or the poor quality of cover provided prompted some of the more prosperous urban householders to subscribe to schemes which supplemented the parish watch, while in the countryside some subscription patrols were established where no previous provision existed beyond the parish constable. Often these were responses to a particular crisis, so that once the emergency had passed there was often a reluctance to continue the arrangement.[80] One of the reasons advanced in 1755 by the promoters of the bill to raise a compulsory watch rate in Bristol was that 'many People of Substance having absolutely refused either to watch or pay',[81] and a committee appointed by inhabitants of Woodbridge in 1827 to look into reform concluded that a compulsory rating system would be necessary because a voluntary subscription would sooner or later 'be found utterly inadequate'.[82]

As has been seen, turnpike legislation often included provision for a watch and such schemes were also established under statute by dockyard operators. In London each of the dock companies had its own force.[83] In 1806 the Directors of the Bristol Dock Company were empowered to nominate constables who were then sworn in by magistrates.[84] These officers were paid by the company, but had powers to stop and search persons and boats and, with a magistrate's search warrant, to search premises; they could also arrest thieves and 'all ill-disposed and suspected Persons and reputed *Thieves*' (s. 35). Similarly, the Dock Police Office was established in Liverpool in 1811 with powers to stop and search people and seize goods.[85]

Other commercial undertakings established non-statutory watch schemes to protect their property: John Kemp was apprehended in 1780 by a watchman employed by John Archer Robinson, who had suffered three thefts of carnations in a week from his market garden in Westminster.[86] Country landowners employed large numbers of gamekeepers to protect their hunting privileges. In Yorkshire between 1764 and 1776 the Worsted Committee, an employer's organization, employed two inspectors to enforce the laws on embezzlement and to reduce the industrial power of the spinners.[87]

Merchants on the Thames not only employed their own watchmen,[88] they banded together as early as 1711 to fund joint patrols. In 1797 John Harriott and Patrick Colquhoun established a privately-funded police force, the Thames Police, which was responsible for setting piece-rates and paying wages to those who loaded and unloaded the West India ships. Fifty officers were hired to control the labour force and, among other things, to eradicate the customary practice of taking sweepings and scrapings, that is, 'any article whatsoever, whether sugar, coffee, or anything else, which may drop into the hold from the casks and packages.'[89] Since these perquisites were regarded as a legitimate part of their wages, the workers resented this interference and that resentment exploded into a riot in October 1798, following the conviction of two coal-heavers by Harriott and Colquhoun. The Marine Police Office in Wapping High Street was attacked and in the battle which followed a foreman was shot dead, for which one of the workers was hanged. Two years later the Thames Police Act passed control of, and financial responsibility for, the force to the government. This represented a major innovation since the Thames Police was the first force to be controlled by central government, whereas previous initiatives, such as the Bow Street patrols, had been funded by government but left in the hands of others.[90]

Detecting crime

From the seventeenth century the government regularly employed agents – sometimes supplemented by soldiers – in the detection of smugglers and those who committed offences relating to the coinage,[91] but, for the most part, the detection and prosecution of offenders were matters for the victim, although they were able to draw assistance from the parish constable, the justice of the peace and, in towns, the watch. In addition, the eighteenth century saw the growth of thief-takers who apprehended offenders for reward, particularly in London.

In a study of the detection of larceny in Essex in the second half of the eighteenth century, Peter King has shown that most offenders were caught in the act (26 per cent) or in the area where the offence occurred (13 per cent), or were apprehended by someone to whom they tried to sell the goods (14 per cent).[92] The next most common methods were that an accomplice gave evidence, the accused was seen carrying stolen goods or a suspicious bag, a watch was set to trap the thief, or a vagrant was searched and the goods found. These findings are echoed in the evidence about those brought for trial at the Old Bailey and the Surrey assizes. As he walked through Thames Street in 1817, Henry Cooper found himself in the midst of a large crowd. He became aware of,

> a person pressing against my back, I put my hand to my pocket, as I crossed Botolph-lane, and missed my handkerchief; the prisoner passed me – I told him he had got my handkerchief – he said he had not; a man said he had.[93]

Cooper grabbed the suspect anyway and the handkerchief was later found on him.

A cry of 'Stop thief! Stop highwayman!' might also draw bystanders to help in a chase.[94] Solomon Nichols ran into the *Hampshire Nag*, a public house in Hoxton, after he was robbed in 1722. There he met John Dickman, 'and supposing the Persons who had robb'd him, would rob thereabouts that Night, they both went out in Search after them, and hearing the cry of Murder, made by Mrs Dormy, they came and assisted at the apprehending of the Prisoners.'[95] The assistance which people seemed so ready to provide in these cases may, of course, have been motivated by the desire to help, but the knowledge that there were statutory rewards (see below) may have had some influence. House-holders or their servants sometimes caught burglars in the act: in 1772 a coachman employed by Godfrey Thornton in Aldermanbury, on hearing a noise in the house, discovered burglars and managed to apprehend one of them;[96] while in 1817 Edward Hurry was awoken by the noise of people breaking into his house and, rushing into the backyard, shot William Mitchell.[97] Servants were detected stealing from their employers,[98] and a victim of repeated thefts might set a trap: the farmer might lay in wait for a cattle thief,[99] and the shopkeeper, who suspected an employee, might leave marked money in a shop till.[100]

Sometimes the arrest was the result of a chance encounter. William Holms was identified at the wrestling ring in Moorfield in 1732 by the person he had allegedly robbed some time before.[101] As he was walking along St Martin's Lane, Westminster in 1784, Sir Thomas Davenport spotted two of the men whom he believed had robbed him, although both were later acquitted.[102] In 1829, four months after a theft from the coffee house in which he worked, James Strowger bumped into George Claremont, who had been a lodger there and on whom suspicion had fallen.[103] On occasions victims engaged in a prolonged process of detection. When horses owned by Richard Wallis, a baker, and William Thornton, a tallow chandler, were stolen from a field in Dulwich in June 1769, they received information that the horses had been offered to Samuel Dowker, an innkeeper in Egham. As they were discussing the theft with Dowker, he saw John Dalton and James Griffiths go by the inn. Wallis and Thornton gave chase and apprehended them.[104] In 1784 George Arthur, a shopkeeper on Tower Hill, pursued a former employee to Old Street in London, then Bristol, finally arresting him in Bath.[105]

The wealthy could delegate such tasks to their servants: in 1733 Thomas Smithers, the employee of a warehouse owner, successfully tracked down the person who stole barrels from his employer.[106] Lacking such leads, victims might resort to traditional methods for obtaining information: in 1753 the Old Bailey was told of a victim who 'talk'd of going to the cunning man' about the theft of his silver punch ladle.[107] Information might be bought from among London's prisoners and gaolers. After he was robbed in 1732 George Young went to Newgate prison 'to enquire if no Body there knew such Persons, who commissioned such a Robbery; and they said, they did not doubt, but I might hear of them.'[108] Information might also be gathered at inns where strangers, local people and alcohol mixed, and goods, including stolen property, were traded:[109] John Poulter's account of the activities of his gang in the early 1750s revealed a sophisticated network of inns at which they regularly stayed and where they disposed of goods – the Pack Horse Inn at Bath, William Trinder's inn at Faringdon, the Bell in Chapel Plaster near Box and the Rock Tavern near Stourbridge in Staffordshire.[110]

Third parties who were unaware of a crime might be drawn into the process of detection by the suspicious behaviour of an individual, as, for instance, when someone spent freely,[111] or suddenly acquired valuable property. In 1733 Mary Gakely's landlord rushed off to inform Joseph Staton, the constable, when Gakely came home drunk and in possession of a gold watch, a guinea and some bank notes. Staton identified the owner of the property by a reward advertisement which had been left on file at Goldsmith's Hall.[112] John Felt came across John Cullington as he lay in the highway after having been thrown from his horse in 1733. After putting Cullington's dislocated neck back into place, Felt noticed that some bullets had rolled out of his pocket, 'which made me suspect him for a Highwayman, and therefore I secur'd him.'[113] David Hart, a dealer in chinaware, was offered a silver mug by Ambrose Pearson as the men sheltered from the rain in the doorway of a public house in 1753. Hart grabbed him and called for a constable.[114]

Since capture might lead to the gallows, offenders sometimes offered resistance to a chasing mob. In 1796 when James Sparks, a suspected pickpocket, was chased by several people and caught, a crowd gathered, and tried to free him.[115] The motive of the crowd cannot be determined: they might, perhaps, have been friends of Sparks, or have believed he was being assaulted, or have regarded ducking in the nearest horse trough – the traditional punishment for pickpockets caught in the act – as more appropriate than prosecution for a capital offence. The landlady of John Fox, an Irishman accused of a robbery on London Bridge in 1741, having agreed to give evidence against him, later declined to do so: 'the *Irish* … about *St. Giles*'s have rioted her, and threaten'd her, and she says she would not hang her Countryman for a Pot full of Guineas.'[116]

The constable and the watch might come to the assistance of a victim. At night a cry for help could bring a watchman.[117] Some houses had alarms which could be used by the occupant to alert the watch.[118] Offenders were occasionally caught in the act by a passing watchman,[119] or he might notice a break-in as he checked the doors and windows of properties on his beat:[120] early one morning in 1817 Walter Cross, a watchman, seeing the cellar window of the Half Moon in Stretton

Ground, Westminster, was open, entered the property and took Michael Hollingsworth.[121] Some arrests resulted from a constable or watchman stopping a person in the streets. Walking at night with a bundle or box and being unable to offer a credible explanation was typically the reason later given for the stop.[122] When William Paine was stopped in Bermondsey in 1740, the watchman, Richard Perry, heard a squeak from the sack he had over his shoulder and inside he found a stolen pig.[123]

Very occasionally officers proved active in their pursuit of suspects, as when in 1733 a constable went to the Isle of Man in search of smugglers who were wanted for murder,[124] and in 1741 the beadle of Shoreditch, Thomas Rogers, was sent to Stratford by a magistrate to check on the identification of an alleged highwayman.[125] Doubtless many constables were as unenthusiastic as the one who, when approached by John Atkinson in 1734 and given a description of the men who had robbed him, replied that, 'he should be upon Duty that Night, and would look after such Fellows as I had describ'd'.[126] Yet, this reply did not draw un-favourable comment in the Old Bailey. It was not necessarily that the constables were lazy or inefficient, but that active detection was simply not part of their work.

Generally, unless the constable or watchman came across a crime in progress, officers would usually become involved only if called on to make an arrest or to undertake the search of a suspect[127] or premises.[128] In 1739 Henry Davies, suspecting that Elizabeth Williams, a prostitute, had picked his pocket while he was asleep, discovered where she lived, obtained a warrant from a magistrate, and, in company with a friend and a constable, arrested her.[129] At about seven o'clock one evening in 1733 Ben Johnson met Margaret Webb in St Giles's. She agreed to go to an inn for a drink, and he hired a private room. After a while, Johnson noticed his watch was missing: 'Upon which I call'd the Landlord, and sent for the Constable, who carry'd her to the Watchhouse, and from thence to the Round-House'. There the watch was found after an intimate search had been conducted, and, although Webb claimed he had given her the watch in exchange for sex, she was not believed by the jury.[130]

Effecting an arrest could involve a good deal of danger for the constable. When John Warden, a constable, went to arrest a man at the notorious Black Boy Inn in Lewkener Lane in 1734 he took others to assist him, but they were quickly surrounded by 'about thirty shabby Fellows, who begun to mob us, so that we were glad to get away.'[131] Eighty years later, when John Edmund Wilson, a Bow Street police officer, went to arrest James Frampton in 1817 in *The Angel*, Goswell Street, 'there was nineteen others in the room with him; I was obliged to produce my cutlass to protect myself.'[132] Having made an arrest, the job of taking the prisoners to prison involved further hazards and tales of rescues by armed gangs were not uncommon.[133]

If the victim caught the offender, prosecution was by no means inevitable, rather the reverse. Most victims were content to have their goods back; some extracted compensation from the offender or an apology; an employee might be dismissed; a pickpocket might be ducked in the nearest horse trough. The cost and inconvenience might well deter a victim from prosecuting, so might the penalty that could be inflicted on the offender or the disapproval of neighbours at carrying the matter into court.[134]

Thief-taking

The victim could offer a reward for the arrest of the offender or the recovery of the stolen property or both through a town crier or a handbill distributed to pawnbrokers and dealers in second-hand goods. Societies for the prosecution of felons typically offered rewards for the conviction of those who committed offences against their members:[135] merchants on the river Thames collected £1,100 to fund rewards and prosecutions in the wake of the crime panic of 1748, and between 1749 and 1751 at least 24 people were hanged at Tyburn for crimes committed on the river.[136] Where gold or silver items were stolen victims could leave information at Goldsmith's Hall from where it was distributed to goldsmiths:[137] when Edward Bodenham was tried in 1733 for receiving stolen goods he claimed not to have realized that the goods he had bought were stolen, prompting a juror to ask, 'Had not you one of the Warnings that were given out on this Occasion? – for it's common to send them to Watchmakers, as well as to Goldsmiths.'[138]

Dealers in second-hand goods or pawnbrokers might stop goods offered to them because they suspected that they had been stolen and feared being prosecuted for receiving: Priscilla Davis was arrested in 1753 when she tried to pawn a silver spoon because the answers she gave to questions put by Samuel Prior, the pawnbroker, aroused his suspicions.[139] However, plenty of pawnbrokers did take goods without asking too many questions:[140] Mr Seely, a pawnbroker who was appearing as a witness, was reprimanded at the Surrey Assizes in 1749 'for buying Things so cheap, because it was an Encouragement to Thieves.'[141] Pawnbrokers also fished for rewards: John Ingram advertised in *The Daily Journal* in February 1733: 'stopt … 23 Pounds of Yellow English Bees-Wax, suspected to be Stole. Whoever has lost the said Wax, by applying to Mr Ingram aforesaid, may have it again for paying the Charges.'[142]

The rapid growth of newspapers in the eighteenth century enabled victims to advertise widely for information.[143] The advertisements varied in their objectives. Some were placed by magistrates and noted the arrest of a 'suspicious' person so as to encourage victims to come forward;[144] others offered a reward for the detection of an offender. In February 1733 a series of advertisements appeared in *The Daily Journal* offering 20 guineas for the arrest of a man called Dekiser or Cæsar alleged to have been responsible for a murder and robbery, and a couple of weeks later £200 were offered by a Joseph Smith for the arrest of Henry Gambier who had defrauded several people of 'many Thousand Pounds'.[145] In 1753 Christian Crosby, an innkeeper, advertised a reward of three guineas for the discovery of the person who stole a silver tankard from the Coach and Horses in St James's Street, London.

Obtaining a conviction did not mean a victim of theft would get the stolen property back. A gentleman, who chose to remain anonymous, advertised his gold-decorated cane as 'Lost' in *The Daily Journal* in 1733,[146] but promised that whoever brought it to John's Coffee House 'shall have TWO GUINEAS Reward, and no Questions ask'd.' Many thieves recognized that the return of property was the victim's main concern. In 1750 Horace Walpole, a son of the former prime minister Sir Robert Walpole, negotiated a payment to James Maclean for the return of a watch stolen during a robbery in Hyde Park.[147]

Jonathan Wild established a business in the 1710s and 1720s by organizing thefts in London and then negotiating with the victims for the return of stolen items. While Wild's efforts to present himself as a public-spirited citizen were almost certainly not believed even before his exposure and execution in 1725, the survival of his business for a number of years testifies to the demand for his services: 'The People who had been robb'd, it may be suppos'd were always willing enough to hear of their Goods again, and very thankful to the Discoverer'.[148] Wild was eventually hanged under legislation, supposedly passed to deal with his activities, that made it a capital offence for anyone to take a reward for assisting someone to recover stolen goods.[149] Interestingly, the person who paid the reward or advertised 'no questions asked' was not covered by this act. When Joseph Jennison and Robert Payton were tried in March 1738 for receiving a reward of £5 for the return of goods stolen from a Mr Manners and not producing the thief, the judge remarked to Manners, 'so you offer a Reward, to tempt a man to bring you your Goods, and then you would be so kind as to hang him for it'. He responded, 'I should not come, but I was bound to prosecute', at which the judge commented, 'A wise Man'.[150]

Encouragements to detection were also provided by statute and by the government. The Statute of Winchester 1285 gave certain victims, who had raised the hue, the right to be compensated by the community if the offender was not apprehended and this idea was used in the Waltham Black Act 1722 (9 Geo. I, c. 22, s. 9) which allowed the victim of a range of offences to claim compensation from the hundred.[151] However, in 1735 the procedure for making a claim was tightened (8 Geo. II, c. 16) and the exposure in 1748 of a fraud on the hundred of Sonning in Berkshire by Thomas Chandler, who faked a robbery and almost succeeded in recovering £1000, led to even more rigid requirements which effectively stifled this remedy (22 Geo. II, c. 24),[152] although the action against the hundred was not abolished until 1827 (7 & 8 Geo. IV, c. 31). By the eighteenth century courts were also occasionally encouraging poor prosecutors by awarding them their costs, and this practice was formalized in legislation beginning in 1752.[153]

Rewards were also offered by government. The well established practice of using common informers to enforce a range of statutory misdemeanours continued and was extended.[154] This practice spread to felonies in the late seventeenth century at a time when concern about crime had increased and had led to changes in the law to increase the number of capital offences.[155] An act of 1692 promised £40 for the conviction of a robber (4 Will. & Mar. c. 8, s. 7) and the Offences against the Customs Act 1746 offered the enormous sum of £500 for the conviction of those guilty of certain smuggling offences. Such statutes routinely offered immunity from prosecution to an offender who gave evidence against other gang members: so, under the act of 1692 a robber who gave evidence which led to the conviction of two robbers was pardoned in respect of all previous robberies;[156] and a statute of 1706 (5 Ann. c. 31, s. 4) offered anyone who convicted two other persons of burglary or housebreaking a pardon for any previous felonies with the exception of murder or treason.[157]

It was not uncommon for the government to offer rewards in connection with particular offences or offenders. At various times in the first half of the eighteenth century a reward of £100 was offered for the conviction of anyone who had committed a street robbery in London, and a reward was offered for the conviction of Dick Turpin who had proved particularly troublesome in the 1730s.[158] The Post Office was well known for its determination to detect those who robbed the mails and offered £200 together with the promise of immunity for a gang member who convicted her or his colleagues. This led one highwayman to say of the mails in 1722 that it was 'certain Destruction to any body that rob them. Not one has escaped yet'.[159] Public and private rewards were often combined, as in 1733 when the government offered a pardon and a

Londoner called William Thompson promised £40 for the conviction of the murderer of William Wright in Lincolnshire.[160] Local authorities might also offer rewards when crime levels were believed to be high, such as during the crime panic which began in 1748: the authorities in Bristol offered £50 in 1753 for the conviction of anyone for a capital offence.[161] The Leeds Improvement Act 1815 authorized the justices of the peace to advertise rewards in connection with any offence as thought fit.[162]

The offer of these rewards had long been subject to criticism. Almost from their inception it was asserted that they led to perjury.[163] In 1753 at the Old Bailey Mary Stevens claimed that a watchman had persuaded the prosecutor to pretend he had been robbed so that they might obtain the reward,[164] while Hannah Wilson alleged that a prosecution witness had said, 'I'll hang you for the reward',[165] and Sarah Summers recounted that, 'a great many people came to see me [in prison] and said he'd [the prosecutor] make it up if I would offer him 20l. If not, he'd get the reward money and hang me.'[166] A steady stream of high-profile cases lent some credibility to these claims. Part of Jonathan Wild's technique was to collect the reward for the conviction of thieves and robbers who refused to comply with his orders,[167] which led one of his biographers to remark that 'this willingness of the Government to detect Thieves, seem'd to be a kind of Authority, for *Jonathan* in his vigorous pursuit of those who he thought fit to have Punished.'[168]

Then, in 1730, a street robber called James Dalton, who two years earlier had escaped the gallows and received a large reward by betraying his comrades, was charged with robbing John Waller in Bloomsbury. While Dalton readily admitted that he had 'done many ill Things, and had deserved Death many time', he denied this charge and denounced Waller as 'a man of a vile Character' who informed for the reward. The claim did not save his life. Two years later Waller was himself arrested and convicted following an attempt to secure the conviction of an innocent man for the reward. Put in the pillory at Seven Dials in London, he was beaten to death by the crowd that had gathered. One man was hanged for this murder: Edward Dalton, James's brother.[169] The next major scandal occurred in 1754 when the Macdaniel gang was convicted of falsely accusing young men of robbery in order to collect the reward offered.[170]

The size of the rewards and the fees some victims were prepared to pay for the return of stolen property led some people to become professional thief-takers. Many of the thief-takers enjoyed a close relationship with the more active London magistrates and were often present at the magistrates' public offices which were gradually established after 1737.

They were also familiar faces at the Old Bailey: Jonathan Wild 'was reckoned a very useful Man, and was often call'd upon by the Court to look at the Prisoners, and give them Characters; which seem'd to have great Weight at that time.'[171] Jonathan Wild's public office was a place to which victims of crime knew they could go with some expectation of recovering property,[172] and after his death, they continued to frequent the houses of the thief-takers. When Hugh Comlyn was robbed in Lambeth by two men in 1740, he went to the house of Ralph Mitchell, a famous thief-taker, where he found John Duckett and others to whom he said, according to Duckett, 'if we could find them he would make me and some others who was with us Amends.'[173] The thief-takers fed off information supplied by their contacts with the keepers and turnkeys of the various prisons scattered around London, some of whom were themselves thief-takers: in 1753 a turnkey at Bridewell prison told James Brebrook, the thief-taker, that he had John Brian in the prison and that Brian was willing to provide information about the whereabouts of two fellow burglars, John Harries and Philip Wilson.[174]

Waller and Macdaniel may well represent only an extreme version of the normal practices of thief-takers. If information was sparse, then the choice of someone who fitted a stereotype might be enough. It is likely that thief-takers accused people of felonies and then demanded money to release them: for the suspect the advantage was obvious, for the thief-taker – even if there was justification for the charge – it avoided the possibility of an acquittal or a conviction on a lesser charge for which no reward would be payable.[175] Waller presumably accused James Dalton because he was a self-confessed street robber and because he was already in Newgate on another charge and, therefore, readily available.[176] The Macdaniel gang set up John Ellis and Peter Kelly because they were 'Youths of bad Life and Conversation' and, therefore, unlikely to be believed and unable to produce character witnesses.[177]

Thief-taking was dangerous work and likely to attract dangerous people, but they were quick to assess the risks. One thief-taker recalled how in 1726, having caught up with several men, he found them to be armed and, on being told that 'they had threaten'd to shoot the first Man that follow'd, he declin'd it.'[178] In the early 1740s in spite of having broken the terms of a sentence of transportation, Richard Keble was not arrested: 'All the Thief Catchers well knew where to find him, but he and his Companions were so desperate, that nobody durst attempt to attack their Rendezvous'.[179]

Catching a suspect was only part of the thief-taker's work. Since a reward would only be paid after a conviction, it was important to gather evidence. The thief-takers were aware that the best form of evidence was a confession and were keen both to ensure that any confession made before a justice would suit their aims and to extract as much information as would enable them to pursue other gang members. For these reasons they typically interrogated the suspect before taking them to a magistrate.[180] On occasions the thief-takers doubtless made promises of immunity if the suspect would confess, even though only a magistrate could actually make such an offer.[181] In 1753 Joseph Hall asked Samuel Watts, a thief-taker, 'if I would get him admitted an evidence; I said I would do what lay in my power if he would confess the whole truth to me'.[182] However, Henry Fielding, the Bow Street magistrate, refused to admit Hall because he had been an evidence before. Nevertheless, the thief-taker had obtained a confession from him and he was convicted.

Some suspects seem to have been aware of this possibility and refused to confess to the thief-takers.[183] A range of other techniques were, therefore, also employed to extract a confession. In 1741 Charles Shooter, a child, told the Old Bailey he had been taken to an alehouse by thief-takers where they 'made me fuddled, and I did not know what I said.' The thief-takers involved replied, 'He was very sober – he had some Bread and Cheese, and Small Beer there, and but one Glass of Wine.'[184] The likelihood of obtaining a confession also increased if a competition could be created between suspects; furthermore, the evidence obtained from the loser could be used against her or him. Christopher Johnson was taken in Gray's Inn Lane for the robbery and murder of a postman in 1753. The thief-takers took him to Brentford where they also apprehended John Stockdale. The prisoners were then removed to the Red Lion in Brentford where, according to William Norden, one of the thief-takers:

> when we got the prisoners together they upbraided each other with the murder of the man: *Johnson* wished his eyes might tumble into his hat if *Stockdale* did not shoot the man, *Stockdale* denied it and said it was *Johnson*; I sat between them to keep them from fighting; *Stockdale* owned he took the money from the man, and said *Johnson* held his hat and took the watch, after which *Johnson* shot the man.[185]

Coercion or threats were also used,[186] and, although by the 1730s the judges were insisting that confessions should have been given voluntarily,[187] it was difficult for the accused to demonstrate that this had not been the case. However, George Sutton told the Old Bailey in 1732 that he had been taken by thief-takers to Brogden Poplet's house in Drury Lane 'and there (before I was examin'd by a Justice) *Tom How, Will James*, and *Will Pember* took my Information in writing.' The court condemned the practice:

> Those People ought not to take upon them to prepare and draw up Informations, and to settle among themselves whatever they design the Informist shall swear before a Justice, or in this Court. Informations are to be taken before a proper Magistrate, that the Publick may be satisfied, that no unfair Practices have been made use of.[188]

Thief-takers often took it upon themselves to search people and property and to detain items without a warrant, but the courts rarely challenged their methods.

Identification evidence was important.[189] It is not surprising to find that thief-takers prompted witnesses: when Nicholas Sweetman was asked in court in 1741 how he identified the men who robbed him in spite of it having been a dark night, he replied, 'I was told by a Gentleman who makes it his Business to take up these Sort of People.'[190] One suspects that thief-takers were usually more careful in preparing their witnesses. After William Wade was arrested for a mail robbery in 1721, the post boy and another witness were taken

> to New-Prison to see if they knew the Prisoner, and [the thief-taker] gave them Directions that they should not speak to one another, but give him their Opinion separate: that they both told him the Prisoner was the Man; that he was walking first with one Man, then with another, not alone, but about 12 or 14 People walking; and that he gave them no hint to discover the Prisoner by.[191]

Less common was the experience of Simon Hughes who, after he was robbed in 1751, identified the horse of his attacker from a parade of horses.[192] A positive identification of a defendant was often supported by the discovery of stolen property: John Brooks identified John Crooks at Hertford gaol in 1739 as the man who had robbed him on Banstead Downs and the watch found on him as having been part of the property stolen.[193]

The veniality of the thief-takers caused some to doubt the value of the evidence they produced and the cases of Wild, Waller and Macdaniel reinforced such doubts. Moreover, their reputation was not helped by their involvement in crime.[194] However, the courts do not seem to have regarded the evidence of thief-takers as *prima facie* tainted and, indeed, may have accepted that their work required an association with criminals. Certainly allegations of corruption were commonly made but they were rarely successful: when, in 1732, William Fleming claimed that Jo Williams, the thief-taker, had taken up a further six people who were being tried at the same Old Bailey sessions and another two who appeared at a recent Surrey assize, Williams did not deny this and neither the court nor the jury seemed particularly concerned.[195] Without more accusations that, 'These people will take any man's life away for any thing, they are thief-catchers, and have hanged many a man for the lucre for nothing', typically failed.[196] So, it was in vain that Henry Brian or Bryant launched an attack on thief-takers at the Surrey Assizes in 1751:

> I don't mind my life any more than the fly that flies about my face. These thief-catchers bail out thieves, and take in such wretches as I; then they go upon such a lay, as soon as they can get us to go along with them; they do the fact themselves, and our lives are taken away for the reward. I have never a soul on this side the world I can call to speak in my behalf. God send me to the Old Baily again, where Christians are tried, for there is no more justice here than there is in a common field. Now I see I *will* be hang'd.[197]

A cynic reading reports of trials at the Old Bailey might become a little suspicious about the frequency with which thief-takers were victims of crime,[198] or just happened to be passing as an offence was taking place,[199] but these events seem not to have struck the courts as unusual. Thief-takers might have been disliked and their abuses well known, but there was no mechanism for exposing them, partly because the criminal justice system was constructed around accusations brought by victims and was not designed to deal with the motivations which prompted thief-takers; and partly because they played a useful role for victims and the criminal justice system.[200] Nevertheless, the activities of the thief-takers were constrained, either by rules formed by the judges, such as that a confession should be voluntary and that suspects should only be interrogated by a magistrate, or by expectations as to how the jury might react when, for instance, confronted by evidence that an identification parade had been rigged. Of course, these considerations may have influenced, not so much the way thief-takers worked, but rather the way they presented their cases.

By the end of the century it is possible to detect in the Old Bailey trials a more cautious approach towards the evidence supplied by thief-takers as mechanisms began to emerge by which defendants could probe the strength of the prosecution case. It became normal for anyone involved in a prosecution which might lead to the payment of a reward to be challenged about their motives and their knowledge of the existence of a reward.[201] This may have been, partly, the result of a build up of concern about corruption and, partly, because the increased use of counsel by defendants had sensitized the courts to the issue.

Detection and the magistracy

The commerce in justice stretched to include at least some of the London justices of the peace. The difficulty of getting enough of the gentry to serve as justices of the peace in the eighteenth century was particularly acute in London where the population had been growing rapidly. The solution was to appoint men who, because they were not independently wealthy, earned their living from the office by exploiting the possibilities for charging fees. In spite of the need for such magistrates, they were derided by contemporaries as 'trading justices', not just because of a suspicion that they were corrupt,[202] but because in undertaking the work for profit they represented what was perceived as a general diluting of the principles of civic humanism, according to which men of property undertook duties of governance for noble purposes connected with citizenship and the protection of liberty. Their dependence on fees meant that they encouraged victims to bring cases to them and they were drawn into a relationship with the thief-takers built on mutual advantage.

While justices had always had the power to discharge felony suspects where it was shown that no offence had taken place, by the second quarter of the eighteenth century many had assumed this power where an offence had occurred if there was insufficient evidence before the justice to justify sending for trial, but only in cases where the person was not charged on the oath of the victim.[203] Suspects seem to have been cautioned when they were examined by a London magistrate. In 1753 the clerk at Bow Street – probably, Joshua Brogden – warned John Ayliff as he was about to sign a confession, 'Mind what you do, this may be hurtful to you on your trial'. He refused to sign,[204] although such a refusal did not prevent witnesses – including the thief-takers – being admitted to testify that the defendant had confessed.[205] Some magistrates took confessions on oath, apparently in the belief that this would strengthen the case, but at the Surrey Assizes in 1743 such a confession was rejected:

If it had been voluntarily, it would have been admitted as good Evidence; but the Law supposes that an Oath is a compulsion; and consequently that no Man is obliged to swear against himself in cases where it affects his Life.[206]

As has been seen, most of those who confessed were moved to do so by the hope of being admitted as a witness for the crown by a magistrate. Henry Fielding vigorously defended the practice:

> In Street Robberies the Difficulty of convicting a Criminal is extremely great. The Method of discovering these is generally by means of one of the Gang, who being taken up, perhaps for some other Offense, and, thinking himself in Danger of Punishment, chooses to makes his Peace at the Expense of his Companions.[207]

The judges agreed, declaring in 1775 that, 'it is impossible to get to the bottom of offences committed by divers persons, without having some of the Accomplices admitted to impeach the rest.'[208] The judges, therefore, endorsed the right of the magistrate to grant immunity, arguing that they did not have the time to consider such issues and that gang-breaking required swift action. By 1765 they had also conceded another point for which Henry Fielding had argued, that it should be possible to convict a defendant on the uncorroborated evidence of a crown witness.[209]

Occasionally, offenders sought out a justice in order to offer themselves as witnesses for the crown, doubtless mindful of the problems encountered by those who, having confessed to a thief-taker, were then not admitted by the justice. In 1732, Robert Ward told the Old Bailey how he came to his decision to seek to be admitted as evidence and how, by ensuring the arrest of a fellow robber called John Bumpus, he had tried to secure this role above another possible candidate called Shelton:

> I heard … that *Shelton* was taken up at *Maidstone*, and so to ease my Conscience, and for fear of being hang'd, if he should swear against me, I made my self a voluntary Evidence, as soon as I had an opportunity of taking *Bumpus*, which was on the 29th of *July* last. I met him accidentally in *Newgate-Street*, and asking him to go and drink with me; I took him to the *Sun* Coffee-House, under Sir *William Billers*'s Office. I left him there, and finding Mr. *Taylor* the Constable, at Sir *William*'s door, I Surrender'd my self, and went with him before Sir *William*, and gave my Information, and then we went and took *Bumpus* in the Coffee-House.[210]

When Ralph Wilson was arrested for the robbery of the Bristol mail in 1722, he was taken to see Carteret, the Postmaster General, who showed him a letter from George Simpson, one of the gang who had not been taken, in which he offered to give evidence in exchange for immunity. Wilson immediately confessed, implicating Simpson and John

Hawkins.[211] Thomas Lightowller, while in prison in Wales on a charge of counterfeiting in the 1740s, was cautioned by his friend, Catherine Hawkshaw: 'have a care of the man in prison with you, for he'll hang you before he'll suffer himself, and I hear he is kept in prison for that purpose'.[212]

The need for a suspect to produce fellow gang members in order to have a chance of being admitted as evidence for the crown presumably led to false accusations: the response of William Prew in 1742 to the accusation by James Izzard that they had robbed together was not uncommon: 'I know nothing at all of the Matter. He only swears against me to clear himself.'[213] Where there was competition between two suspects, the justice would usually admit the one who confessed the most joint crimes or implicated the most people: according to William Corbee, Henry Fielding told him 'that if I could make a larger discovery I should receive the King's mercy'.[214] Similarly, after John Westcote was arrested for the burglary of the Earl of Harrington's London home in 1764, he asked to be admitted as evidence for the crown against the other burglars, but John Fielding said 'he could not give him a positive answer, whether his proffer would be accepted, until his accomplices had undergone an examination; but at the same time assured him, that the only means by which he could attain his end, was to be ingenuous and to act with candour and discretion'.[215] Westcote's offer was refused and he was hanged for the robbery because only his colleague Bradley could convict a man called Cooper of receiving the stolen property.

Of course, it was a dangerous gamble to confess because immunity was not granted until after the confession. When in 1741 Thomas Coates heard that his colleague Lilliston had been arrested for a burglary and admitted an evidence, he went to see William Boomer, a constable, and told him 'that he could make the most Discoveries, and would do it if he could be made an Evidence.' It was too late, the choice of Lilliston had already been made and Coates was arrested.[216] John Freelove and Christopher Henley were arrested in 1733 by Brown Linskill, a constable, following a robbery. Linskill recalled later, 'I advised … [Freelove] to discover what he knew, for I told him, if he would not, *Henley* would'. Freelove did confess, but he was not admitted as evidence and was convicted.[217] John Flack complained bitterly at his trial in 1740 that he had made his confession before the justice 'and they told me, I should be admitted an evidence.'[218]

The existence of a reward was an additional inducement to a suspect to turn evidence for the crown.[219] Joseph Whitlock, one of a gang accused in 1733 of a large burglary at Colonel James Romaine's house in Paddington, claimed that 'Justice *Deveil* offer'd *Sutton* a Purse of Guineas to be an

Evidence.' De Veil, the magistrate at Bow Street, said he had simply pointed out that a reward had been offered and the judge commented, 'And any other might have said the same.'[220]

The paradox of the crown witness strategy was that the greater the villain, the more offenders they could implicate and the more likely they would be admitted an evidence. John Macdonald was a member of various gangs in the early 1730s and this meant that his colleagues could not hope to match the amount of information he was able to provide. He was used by the prosecution in a series of cases at the Old Bailey and the Kent Assizes in 1733–5 and also gave information to magistrates in Essex. One of his comrades, William Stickwell, was arrested and did confess before a justice, but, whatever promises he had been made, he was denied immunity because his information was inferior to that provided by Macdonald. His confession was, instead, used against him.[221] Although the number of cases in which Macdonald was involved was unusual, the use of such informers was common and it was in vain that John Sutton launched his attack: '*Macdonald* has been an Evidence three Times before; he makes it his Livelihood and Property to take Men's Lives in this manner; and shall he be admitted to be a Witness again?'[222] There was some concern that giving immunity to a confessed felon simply enabled that person to return to crime: Sutton had been an evidence himself in the case which followed the burglary of Colonel James Romaine's house, and Macdonald was eventually hanged for horse stealing in 1735.[223]

The peril in which suspects were placed by those willing to swear against them and the difficulties involved in denying such allegations can be glimpsed in a letter written from Catherine Hawkshaw to Thomas Lightowller, while he was in Cardiff gaol in 1744:

> as for the man you mention which swore against you, I've made what enquiry I can of the time, but can't hear of any such man living in Burnley, and if he told you he ever was at our house, it was a great story, for I never heard of that name before, but I shall enquire further about it, but as for my part, I don't believe there is any such man.[224]

In a rare occurrence, Henry Simms, who had been admitted as a witness for the crown against five defendants accused of a large-scale burglary in Southwark, withdrew his evidence:

> The Prisoners are all innocent; and the Information I made is wrong. I was persuaded to it by *Will. H——* [Hind?], a Thief-Catcher, who came to see me whilst I was in Prison for an Assault, and he told me

he was sorry to hear that there would be two Warrants of Detainer lodg'd against me, one for robbing a Woman in *Tooley-Street*, and the other for robbing Mr. *Smith* in the Borough. He said the Woman that was robb'd in *Tooley-Street* knew me, and Mrs. *Smith* could swear to me, and I had better make myself an Evidence and discover my Accomplices, and save my own Life. I desired to be carried before Sir *Thomas De Veil*, and there I made a Discovery of some Robberies formerly committed by me and others, *but these were not sufficient*; for *H——* came to me a second Time, and told me that I had done nothing at all, and that I must discover *Smith*'s Robbery, or I should not be sav'd. I then went a second Time before Sir *Thomas*, and made an Information of that Robbery, but it is not true.[225]

Although de Veil's clerk, Joshua Brogden, testified that the confession had been made voluntarily, when asked if it was true, Simms said, 'Not a Word of it. I have perjur'd myself. I did it to save my own Life.'[226]

The certainty of speedy detection

While the trading justices probably derived most of their income from dealing with a high volume of minor cases, Thomas de Veil, Henry Fielding and John Fielding at Bow Street regarded themselves as superior to their comrades by virtue of their appointment as 'court justice'. They sought – and in the cases of de Veil and John Fielding obtained – knighthoods and tried to counter their categorization as trading justices by presenting themselves as successful gang-breakers.[227] The Fielding brothers – in particular John – argued that crime could be reduced by improving the methods of detecting offenders: 'the Certainty … of speedy Detection, must deter some at least'.[228] This represented a shift from an approach that relied on the effect of the public execution of a few offenders and that did not, therefore, need an efficient method of detection.[229] John Fielding contemplated a system in which the unreliable element – the victim – was marginalized. It was his view that effective detection required a professional bureaucracy, headed by a full-time magistrate, through which information would be channelled to professional officers who undertook the pursuit of offenders.

This argument made some headway for a number of reasons. Concern over crime reached a height around the time of Henry's appointment in 1748 and, as old methods such as rewards and executions proved unable to reduce this concern, government became more willing to support new ideas. On the other hand, there was opposition from whose who mistrusted any extension of the civil power because of the threat to liberty it was believed to pose. Moreover, some influential commentators argued that the level of crime was related to a disinclination among people (as victims, witnesses, jurors or judges) to run the risk that offenders might be hanged for minor offences and this led them not to prosecute or convict, so that a reduction in the penalty would, it was assumed, increase the number of prosecutions. Others clung to the idea that the spectacle of the public hanging of a few did deter people from committing offences and that, therefore, an efficient detection system was unnecessary.[230]

Henry Fielding formed the nucleus of a plan to tackle crime as early as 1750 when he authorized a series of raids by constables and placed advertisements in newspapers urging the victims of robberies to attend at Bow Street in order to identify those who had been arrested on suspicion. Publicity was an important part of his strategy. He encouraged news-paper reporters and spectators to came to his office to watch the examination of suspects and witnesses. He also began to feed information and work to certain thief-takers. Yet, in spite of some successes, the crisis over crime in London continued. So, in 1753 he persuaded the govern-ment to fund a strategy that involved paying 'a fellow who had under-taken for a small sum, to betray [the robbers] into the hands of a set of thief-takers whom I had enlisted into the service, all men of known and approved fidelity and intrepidity'.[231] By December 1753 he was boasting that robberies in London had ceased,[232] but the success brought an end to the funding. There was no enthusiasm in government for the sort of long-term plan which Henry favoured, and shortly afterwards, he retired to Lisbon on grounds of health mixed with disappointment at this lack of support. However, the return of the crime crisis provided John Fielding with his opportunity.

Both Henry and John wanted to get rid of rewards and make the thief-takers dependent on them for employment, but the government would not provide the necessary funding. This brought immediate problems for John in the shape of the Macdaniel case which broke shortly after he took over from Henry in 1754. Although in his account of the affair, Joseph Cox, the High Constable of Blackheath who had arrested Macdaniel, praised the Fieldings and cautioned against criticism of 'the *honest Thief-taker*',[233] the pamphlet was a thinly veiled attack on the corruption implicit in thief-taking and included criticism of Henry Fielding's failure to follow up an allegation made well before the scandal broke by Thomas Blee – who eventually proved a key witness against the gang – that Macdaniel had obtained £280 in rewards for hanging two innocent men.[234] By this time Henry was dead and John Fielding, while apparently praising the efforts of his brother, wished to continue to use thief-takers and was, therefore, keen to distance both himself and his men from the case. To do this he laid blame on his brother. He admitted that Blee had given information, but claimed Henry had such a poor opinion of Blee's honesty that he had refused to take any account of it.[235] John also asserted that 'to my knowledge' none of the Macdaniel gang had been employed as thief-takers by Henry Fielding.[236] His caution was wise because gang members had, in fact, been used by Henry, although in 1751–2 he seems to have broken the relationship and recruited a new group of thief-takers.[237] John claimed that most of the thief-takers he used had been constables and were, therefore, householders,[238] and this underpinned his assertion that their main motivation was not the rewards but their sense of public duty. He added that some were also public officials, such as Pentlow, who was the keeper of the New Prison in Clerkenwell, and Hind, who was the deputy governor of Tothill Fields Bridewell, although, in fact, few held such posts and the connection between keepers and criminals was often close. Finally, he referred to the way in which they carried out their duties in the face of danger: Henry had referred to Pentlow as a man of 'Courage and Integrity',[239] and Hind was killed in 1755 while trying to make an arrest.[240] While John acknowledged that rewards encouraged perjury, in the absence of government funding they remained the only means of inducing thief-takers to undertake detection work. Moreover, he regarded the connection between thief-takers and criminals, not as a disadvantage, but as vital to their work.[241]

John Fielding's ability to exercise a degree of control over the thief-takers depended, in part, on his key role in deciding whether to admit an offender as a crown witness, and also on his ability to regulate the flow of information about crime. He envisaged 'the drawing of all Informations of Fraud and Felony into one point [Bow Street], registering Offenders of all Kinds, quick Notice and sudden Pursuit, and keeping up Correspondence with all the active Magistrates in England', and he promised that on notice of a crime he 'would immediately dispatch a Set of brave Fellows in Pursuit, who … are always ready to set out to any Part of this Town or Kingdom, on a Quarter of an Hour's Notice'.[242] The General Preventative Plan of 1772 involved requests being sent to magistrates and gaolers throughout the country to supply information on offences and offenders to Bow Street together with warrants. These could then be sent to the place where a suspect had been apprehended.[243] The use of newspaper reporting and advertisements were key parts of the strategy.[244] Under its title, a notice in *The Public Advertiser* encouraged victims to report offences to Bow Street where they might be either reunited with their property or assisted by the clerks in drawing up an advertisement. It was also claimed that leading pawnbrokers took the newspaper to check for stolen goods.[245]

The publicity needed for this information-gathering process also built up the image of success necessary to encourage government funding.[246] This was reinforced by the criminal literature which was popular at this time. Earlier in the century these pamphlets focused on the life, crimes, trial and execution of an offender, but from the 1750s increasing emphasis was placed on the process of detection and, in particular, the role played by Bow Street.[247] The thieves who broke into the house of the Earl of Harrington in 1764 were, according to one pamphlet, brought to justice by thief-takers from Bow Street and by Fielding's relentless examination of the suspects over a period of twelve days.[248] In 1778 Thomas Hughes, who was suspected of stealing from a fellow servant of Lady Morton's called Alexander Foubister, was pursued by two Bow Street officers to Oxford, then to Worcester, Ludlow, up the English-Welsh borders to Bishop's Castle and Montgomery, eventually arresting him at his mother's house in Keilhull.[249] Fielding was also prepared to make large claims for the success of his plans: in 1770 he claimed that no London street robber had escaped detection in the preceding twenty years.[250]

There were critics, however. *The Gentleman's Magazine*[251] attacked some aspects of Fielding's handling of the Harrington case and Harrington's steward, Bevell, wrote a pamphlet suggesting he had done most of the detection.[252] More forceful was William Miles who was concerned about the effect of the pre-trial proceedings on the trial jury.[253] He attacked Fielding's enthusiasm for publicity and particularly his practice of examining suspects in public. Miles argued that the magistrate should merely take depositions and make decisions about bail, he should not interrogate before 'a motley audience composed of interested individuals, your relations and servants', nor encourage newspaper reporting of the proceedings, nor subject a suspect to 'the torture of repeated examinations',[254] and he should not force the suspect to reveal their defence. He criticized Fielding for concentrating on searching for evidence that tended to show guilt rather than also looking for evidence showing innocence. The practices of the Bow Street thief-takers were also attacked. It was alleged that they nurtured but did not interfere with criminals until they committed crimes which brought them within the statutory rewards, and that the project of detection made the Bow Street justices reluctant to do anything about the places in which their thief-takers obtained information. Finally, he deplored the thief-takers' reliance on a 'too intimate acquaintance with bad men'.[255]

It was John Fielding's fervent hope that he could set up a network of contacts throughout the country whose centre would be at Bow Street. Other magistrates certainly used his services, although few quite matched Alderman John Hewitt of Coventry for the level of his active involvement in the detective process or enthusiasm for telling the world about it.[256] The cases he describes in his somewhat rambling reminiscences do show something of the co-operation that was possible. In 1756 he was involved in a case on counterfeit coins alongside the solicitor of the Mint and the magistrates at Bow Street.[257] In 1758 Hewitt went to London where, with the assistance of one of John Fielding's men, he arrested a member of a gang of robbers, while Fielding assisted by using his men to watch an inn for another gang member and by placing an advertisement in the London newspapers. On Fielding's request Hewitt also arrested some Spitalfields weavers who had been accused of destroying looms as part of an industrial protest in 1769. The peak of their relationship came in the 1760s with the breaking of the Coventry gang, which had operated for a number of years in the Midlands and London.

Few of the Fieldings' ideas were particularly revolutionary. Not only had victims routinely used reward advertisements as a means of acquiring information about crime, so had Sir Thomas de Veil.[258] The Fieldings also echoed the methods of Jonathan Wild who had kept a public office, maintained records, established a network of contacts and used advertisements.[259] The magistrates in the City of London had established a rotation office in 1737 whereby a magistrate was available to the public at set hours, and de Veil had adopted that idea at Bow Street in 1739. But it was Henry and John Fielding who really gave these ideas coherence and, most important, publicity. Although only a fraction of crimes in London was dealt with at Bow Street and, in practice, the victim continued to play the key role, the Fieldings built a public image of their detection system as offering the possibility of a more efficient criminal justice process in which the victim would be subordinated to the detective bureaucracy. Their argument – backed by thirty years of repetition – that crime control could be achieved by a bureaucratic detective system that was national in its outlook, that possessed sufficient legal and financial resources and that utilized skills not available to the ordinary person, acquired an importance beyond its practical impact. The crime panics of the second half of the eighteenth century seemed sufficient proof that the solution to crime was beyond a system which relied on the victim and on the gallows, and the Fieldings offered an alternative vision.

* * * *

The professionalization of the watch was not a new phenomenon, however, during the eighteenth century the process of paying someone to undertake these duties became regularized and institutionalized in many towns as householders exchanged their obligation to turn out at night for a duty to pay a rate. This did not change the key features of the watch system. Although householders complained about the effectiveness of watchmen in detecting offenders or maintaining order on the streets and efforts were made to improve performance in these areas, the watch continued to be, primarily, a system for guarding property. The requirement that they patrol a limited area and cry out their presence was so 'that the Inhabitants may have the Satisfaction of knowing that those Men are Doing their Duty',[260] although, of course, this had obvious advantages for any offenders who might be around the next corner. Nevertheless, many places made regular attempts to improve the quality of the watchmen, and, indeed, the 1828 Select Committee, which endorsed Peel's plan for establishing the Metropolitan Police, included evidence that many parishes were appointing only ex-soldiers who were under forty, fit and had a certificate vouching their character from their commanding officer.[261] The other perceived deficiencies of the watch system – its fragmentation around parishes and beats, and its concentration on night duty – led to the introduction of small day patrols, such as the Bow Street patrols and the parish patrols. To this public provision of policing were added any number of subscription patrols, private watchmen and gamekeepers.

In an entirely separate development, the burgeoning of rewards opened up the possibility of improved detection. The thief-taker depended on information from the victim, from contacts and from offenders. The Fieldings sought to control these thief-takers by monopolizing the sources upon which thief-takers depended.

These separate developments responded to, and reinforced, the tendency to displace the individual – as victim and as householder – and the community from their roles at the centre of policing.[262] Policing – watching, patrolling and detection – was becoming explicitly work for skilled, full-time professionals and people were increasingly willing to pay, even if how much they were willing to pay remained an issue. This can be seen in the spread of professional watchmen, the emergence of thief-takers, the relative success of the Bow Street plans and, indeed, in the criticisms of those watchmen who were too old or too inefficient. The implication of this, which was not fully worked out in the eighteenth century, was that crime work undertaken by householders, victims or the community was regarded as disorganized and unskilled. However, there was no real suggestion that the watch or the patrols should be entirely removed from the parishes: policing was still seen as something that should be controlled locally. Moreover, there was no serious thought given to the idea of combining patrolling and detection.

Notes

1 Davenant (1695) *An Essay Upon Ways and Means*, 144.
2 Anon (1722b) *The Form of a Petition*, 19.
3 Potter (1775) *Observations on the Poor Laws*, 1.
4 Anon (1765b) *Considerations on Taxes*, 6–7.
5 Henry Fielding in 1751, see Fielding (1988) *An Enquiry into the Causes of the Late Increase of Robbers*, 228.
6 Woodward (1697) *Sodom's Vices*, 11.
7 Walker (1728) *The Quaker's Opera*, 16.
8 Richardson (1734) *The Apprentice's Vade Mecum*, 4.
9 Anon (1765b) *Considerations on Taxes*, 6–7.
10 Shebbear, 1776, in Rawlings (1992a) *Drunks, Whores and Idle Apprentices*, 23.
11 Rawlings (1992a) *Drunks, Whores and Idle Apprentices*, 24.
12 Anon (1700) *Proposals for Making Provisions for Setting the Poor on Work*, 1.
13 Cary (1696) *A Proposal Offered to the Committee of the House of Commons*; Poynter (1969) *Society and Pauperism*, 11–12.
14 Marshall (1926) *The English Poor in the Eighteenth Century*, 155–60; Wood (1795) *Some Account of the Shrewsbury House of Industry*.
15 Sir William Young, 1796, cited in Poynter (1969) *Society and Pauperism*, 70. Generally, Marshall (1926) *The English Poor in the Eighteenth Century*, 47–51.
16 Anon (1787b) *A Letter to Thomas Gilbert*, 3.
17 Anon (1787a) 'A letter to the citizens of Glasgow', 88.
18 Gilbert (1786) *A Plan of Police*, 31; Young (1770) *A Six Months' Tour*, vol IV, 329. But see Anon (1773) *Observations on the Present State of the Parochial and Vagrant Poor*, 50–2.
19 Malthus (1798) *An Essay on the Principles of Population*.
20 Shoemaker (1991) *Prosecution and Punishment*, 238–72.
21 Defoe (1709) *Review*.
22 Anon (1732b) *The Tryals of Jeremy Tooley, William Arch, and John Clawson*; Woodward (1702) *A Sermon*.
23 Innes (1990) 'Politics and morals'; Radzinowicz (1948–68) *A History of English Criminal Law*, vol III, 144–6.
24 For example, Westminster Night Watch Act 1774: 14 Geo. III, c. 90; Henderson (1999) *Disorderly Women in Eighteenth-Century London*, 109: 23, 123–7.
25 Shoemaker (1991) *Prosecution and Punishment*, 130.
26 *Much Ado About Nothing*, Act III, Scene iii.
27 *The Daily Journal*, 16 Jan 1733.
28 Rawlings (1983) 'Defoe and street robberies', 25.

29 Although Henderson (1999) *Disorderly Women in Eighteenth-Century London*, 76–103, 112–15.
30 *Journal of the House of Commons*, vol 19, 233, 22 Jan 1719/20.
31 *Journal of the House of Commons*, vol 19, 250, 3 Feb 1719/20. See also vol 19, 296, 9 Mar 1719/20.
32 *Journal of the House of Commons*, vol 19, 255, 8 Feb; 258, 9 Feb; 260, 10 Feb; 276, 23 Feb 1719/20.
33 *Journal of the House of Commons*, vol 21, 313, 10 Apr 1729.
34 Rumbelow (1971) *I Spy Blue*.
35 Reynolds (1998) *Before the Bobbies*, 16–28.
36 *Journal of the House of Commons*, vol 22, 565, 16 Feb 1735/36.
37 Reynolds (1998) *Before the Bobbies*, 43.
38 *OBSP*, Jul 1741, 4.
39 Rawlings (1995) 'The idea of policing'.
40 Rawlings (1992a) *Drunks, Whores and Idle Apprentices*, 139.
41 Torrington (1972–8) *House of Lords Sessional Papers*, sess. 1747–8, 388.
42 Anon (1751a) *Serious Thoughts In Regard to Publick Disorders*, 22.
43 Reynolds (1998) *Before the Bobbies*, 29–44.
44 Anon (1751b) *The Vices of the Cities of London and Westminster*; Anon (1754) *The Right Method of Maintaining Security*, 9; Battestin (1989) *Henry Fielding*, 521, 522. On the use of soldiers in the eighteenth century to quell riots and apprehend smugglers: Hayter (1978) *The Army and the Crowd*; Winslow (1977) 'Sussex smugglers'.
45 Battestin (1989) *Henry Fielding*, 418–585.
46 Leslie-Melville (1934) *The Life and Work of Sir John Fielding*.
47 Battestin (1989) *Henry Fielding*, 477–80, 706–11.
48 Reynolds (1998) *Before the Bobbies*, 47–8.
49 *London Evening-Post*, 24 Mar 1772, 18 Apr 1772; *OBSP*, Dec 1784, 96, 97, 99; Palmer (1988) *Police and Protest in England*, 78–9.
50 Reynolds (1998) *Before the Bobbies*, 62–8.
51 Reynolds (1998) *Before the Bobbies*, 46–7.
52 *Journal of the House of Commons*, vol 32, 880, 10 Apr 1770.
53 *Journal of the House of Commons*, vol 32, 878–83 at 879. Also Fielding (1768) *Extracts from Such of the Penal Laws*, 420.
54 Reynolds (1998) *Before the Bobbies*, 40.
55 *Journal of the House of Commons*, vol 40, 616, 8 Mar 1785.
56 Reynolds (1998) *Before the Bobbies*, 40, 42–3.
57 *London Evening Post*, 29 Feb 1772.
58 Select Committee (1772) *Report*, 6.
59 Select Committee (1772) *Report*, 4.
60 Select Committee (1772) *Report*, 6–7.
61 Whitworth (1773) *The Draught of an Intended Act*.
62 Mainwaring (1821) *Observations on the Present State of the Police*, 49–53.
63 Reynolds (1998) *Before the Bobbies*, 52–7.
64 *Whitehall Evening Post*, 27 Mar 1783; Rawlings (1999) *Crime and Power*, 37–9.

65 Reynolds (1998) *Before the Bobbies*, 78–9.
66 See also *Journal of the House of Commons*, vol 40, 593, 7 Mar 1785; vol 41, 292, 6 Mar 1786.
67 Emsley (1983) *Policing and Its Context*, 28.
68 *Journal of the House of Commons*, vol 40, 1112–13, 29 Jun 1785. For a more radical proposal: Barrett (1786) *An Essay Towards Establishing a System of Police*.
69 Anon (1786) *Outlines of a Plan for Patrolling*; Paley (1989a) '"An imperfect, inadequate and wretched system?"'; Reynolds (1998) *Before the Bobbies*, 73–6.
70 Beattie (1986) *Crime and the Courts*, 71.
71 *The Daily Journal*, 4 Jan 1772. See Municipal Corporations Act 1835, 5 & 6 Will. IV, c. 76, schedule E, for a partial list of these Improvement Acts.
72 *Journal of the House of Commons*, vol 27, 89, 15 Jan 1755.
73 *Journal of the House of Commons*, vol 27, 89, 15 Jan 1755.
74 *Journal of the House of Commons*, vol 27, 128, 29 Jan 1755; Anon (1755a) *Case of the Petitioners*; Anon (1755b) *Reasons in Support of the Bristol Watch Bill*, 3.
75 Anon (1755c) *The Bristol Watch-Bill*.
76 Sharpe (1999) *Crime in Early Modern England*, 262.
77 *Journal of the House of Commons* vol 22, 397, 28 Feb 1734/35.
78 *Journal of the House of Commons*, vol 43, 247, 21 Feb 1788.
79 *Journal of the House of Commons*, vol 45, 185, 25 Feb 1790.
80 See chapter 5.
81 Anon (1755b) *Reasons in Support of the Bristol Watch Bill*, 2.
82 Woodbridge Select Committee (1827) *Report*.
83 Hardwicke (1980) *Keepers of the Door*.
84 46 Geo. III, c. 35 (Local and Personal Acts).
85 51 Geo. III, c. 143 (Local and Personal Acts); Ritchie-Noakes (1984) *Liverpool's Historic Waterfront*; Trustees of Liverpool Dock (1810) *A Statement*, 25.
86 *OBSP*, Jun 1780, 364.
87 Soderlund (1998) ' "Intended as a terror to the idle" '.
88 *Surrey Assizes*, Mar 1741, 12–13.
89 Linebaugh (1991) *The London Hanged*, 431.
90 Colquhoun (1800) *A Treatise on the Commerce and Police of the River Thames*; Linebaugh (1991) *The London Hanged*, 430–5; Radzinowicz (1948–68) *A History of English Criminal Law*, vol II, 353–7; Rawlings (1999) *Crime and Power*, 27, 73.
91 Gaskill (2000) *Crime and Mentalities*, 169–73; Linebaugh (1991) *The London Hanged*, 56–7.
92 King (2000) *Crime, Justice, and Discretion*, 20–2.
93 *OBSP*, Oct 1817, 487.
94 *OBSP*, 18 Jul 1753, 216–17. See also *OBSP*, Dec 1733, 9; Jan 1753, 41; *Home Circuit*, Mar 1739, 21; *Surrey Assizes*, Aug 1739, 7; Mar 1749, 3.
95 *OBSP*, Dec 1722, 2.
96 *The London Evening-Post*, 9 Jan 1772.

97   *OBSP*, Oct 1817, 471–2.
98   *OBSP*, Dec 1733, 22; *OBSP*, 8 Dec 1784, 183–4.
99   *OBSP*, 8 Dec 1784, 150; King (2000) *Crime, Justice, and Discretion*, 63–4.
100 *OBSP*, Dec 1734, pt II, 3; *The London Evening-Post*, 14 Apr 1772; *OBSP*, 8 Dec 1784, 195.
101 *OBSP*, Sep 1732, 190–1.
102 *OBSP*, 8 Dec 1784, 39.
103 *OBSP*, Oct 1829, 891–2.
104 Silverthorne (1978) *Deposition Book of Richard Wyatt*, 13–14.
105 *OSBP*, 8 Dec 1784, 183–4.
106 *OBSP*, Dec 1733, 5. Also Bevell (1765) *An Authentic Narrative*.
107 *OBSP*, 6 Sep 1753, 244.
108 *OBSP*, Oct 1732, 243.
109 Silverthorne (1978) *Deposition Book of Richard Wyatt*, 34, 53–4.
110 Rawlings (1992a) *Drunks, Whores and Idle Apprentices*, 139–77.
111 *OBSP*, Apr 1726, 2.
112 *OBSP*, Dec 1733, 22.
113 *OBSP*, Dec 1733, 10. Also *OBSP*, 6 Sep 1753, 257.
114 *OBSP*, 6 Sep 1753, 257.
115 *OBSP*, 17 Feb 1796, 272–5.
116 *Surrey Assizes*, Aug 1741, 3–4; Linebaugh (1977) 'The Tyburn riot against the surgeons'.
117 *OBSP*, Dec 1722, 2; *OBSP*, 16 Jan 1741, 9–11.
118 *OBSP*, Dec 1828, 118–19. Also *OBSP*, 8 Dec 1784, 125–6.
119 *OBSP*, 6 Oct 1753, 249.
120 *OBSP*, Sep 1732, 177; *OBSP*, 18 Jul 1753, 235; *OBSP*, Jan 1817, 66–7, 109.
121 *OBSP*, Oct 1817, 472–3.
122 *Home Circuit*, Mar 1739, 20; *Surrey Assizes*, Mar 1732, 1; *OBSP*, 24 Oct 1753, 279; *OBSP*, 8 Dec 1784, 109; *OBSP*, Jan 1817, 63; *OBSP*, Jan 1830, 152.
123 *Surrey Assizes*, Jul 1740, 9.
124 *The Daily Journal*, 16 Jan 1733.
125 *OBSP*, 28 Aug 1741, 2–3.
126 *OBSP*, Dec 1734, pt I, 9.
127 *OBSP*, Dec 1733, 1–3; *OBSP*, Dec 1784, 145.
128 *Surrey Assizes*, Mar 1738, 19; *OBSP*, Sep 1732, 192; *OBSP*, 8 Dec 1784, 124.
129 *Surrey Assizes*, Aug 1739, 9.
130 *OBSP*, 5 Dec 1733, 2–3. Similarly *Surrey Assizes*, Mar 1726, 2–3. But *OBSP*, Dec 1734, pt II, 2.
131 *OBSP*, Dec 1734, pt I, 20; *OBSP*, Sep 1732, 193; Linebaugh (1991) *The London Hanged*, 149–50.
132 *OBSP*, Jan 1817, 90.
133 *The Daily Journal*, 13 Feb 1733.
134 King (2000) *Crime, Justice, and Discretion*, 22–35.
135 King (1989) 'Prosecution associations'; King (2000) *Crime, Justice, and Discretion*, 53–7; Philips (1989) 'Good men to associate and bad men to conspire'.

136 Rawlings (1999) *Crime and Power*, 27.
137 *OBSP*, Dec 1724, 8; *OBSP*, Oct 1732, 238.
138 *OBSP*, Dec 1733, 39–40.
139 *OBSP*, 24 Oct 1753, 303. Also *OBSP*, 9 Nov 1747, 12; *OBSP*, 17 Feb 1796, 244.
140 *OBSP*, Dec 1733, 22.
141 *Surrey Assizes*, Mar 1749, 4.
142 *The Daily Journal*, 3 Feb 1733. Also *OBSP*, 6 Sep 1753, 256.
143 Gaskill (2000) *Crime and Mentalities*, 167–9, 266–9; King (2000) *Crime, Justice, and Discretion*, 57–62; Styles (1989) 'Print and policing'; Thomas (1978) *Religion and the Decline of Magic*, 779. For a critique see Anon (1725) *The True and Genuine Account … of the Late Jonathan Wild*, 10–12.
144 *OBSP*, Dec. 1742, 9.
145 *The Daily Journal*, 12 Feb 1733, 1 Mar 1733. See also *Gentleman's Magazine*, vol 23 (1753), 588.
146 *The Daily Journal*, 3 Feb 1733. See also 24 Feb. 1733.
147 Rawlings (1999) *Crime and Power*, 17.
148 Anon (1725) *The True and Genuine Account … of the Late Jonathan Wild*, 8.
149 Howson (1987) *It Takes a Thief*. For an earlier conviction under the statute which only resulted in transportation, *OBSP*, Dec 1724, 7–8.
150 *Surrey Assizes*, Mar 1738, 12.
151 Also Riot Act 1715, 1 Geo I stat. 2, c. 5, s. 6.
152 Wise (1751) *The Remarkable Tryal of Thomas Chandler*.
153 Beattie (1986) *Crime and the Courts*, 41–8, 130.
154 Beresford (1957–8) 'The common informer'; Radzinowicz (1948–68) *A History of English Criminal Law*, vol II.
155 Radzinowicz (1948–68) *A History of English Criminal Law*, vol I.
156 Gurney (1775) *An Account of the Arguments of Counsel*, 30.
157 Radzinowicz (1948–68) *A History of English Criminal Law*, vol II, 33–56.
158 Radzinowicz (1948–68) *A History of English Criminal Law*, vol II, 84–98, 133–7.
159 Wilson (1722) *A Full and Impartial Account*, 18. The reward had been reduced to £50 by 1770: *The London Evening–Post*, 21 Mar 1772.
160 *The Daily Journal*, 15 Jan 1733.
161 *London Daily Advertiser*, 30 Jan 1753; Rawlings (1999) *Crime and Power*, 27.
162 55 Geo. III., c. 42 (Local & Personal), s. 7.
163 Gaskill (2000) *Crime and Mentalities*, 170–1; Wilson (1722) *A Full and Impartial Account*, 15–17.
164 *OBSP*, Jul 1753, 207.
165 *OBSP*, Sep 1753, 245. Also *OBSP*, Sep 1753, 253–4.
166 *OBSP*, Feb 1753, 96. Also *Surrey Assizes*, Mar 1736, 2; Aug 1743, 13.
167 Howson (1987) *It Takes a Thief*.
168 Anon (1725) *The True and Genuine Account … of the Late Jonathan Wild*, 17.
169 *OBSP*, Apr 1730; *The Daily Journal*, 12 May 1730; Anon (1732a) *The Life … of that Perjur'd Villain John Waller*; Rawlings (1992a) *Drunks, Whores and Idle Apprentices*, 79–109.

170 Cox (1756) *A Faithful Narrative … of the Bloody-minded Gang of Thief-takers*; Langbein (1983) 'Shaping the eighteenth-century trial', 109–14.

171 H.D. (1725) *The Life of Jonathan Wild*, 18–19. Also *OBSP*, Dec 1747, 15–16.

172 *OBSP*, Jan 1723, 4.

173 *Surrey Assizes*, Jul 1740, 4; McMullan (1996) 'The new improved monied police'; Paley (1989b) 'Thief-takers in London'. Also *Surrey Assizes*, Aug 1751, 38.

174 *OBSP*, 6–10 Sep 1753, 252. Also *Surrey Assizes*, Aug 1739, 3.

175 Cox (1756) *A Faithful Narrative … of the Bloody-minded Gang of Thief-takers*, 57–67; Paley (1989b) 'Thief-takers in London', 309–10, 322–3.

176 Rawlings (1992a) *Drunks, Whores and Idle Apprentices*, 77–109.

177 Cox (1756) *A Faithful Narrative … of the Bloody-minded Gang of Thief-takers*.

178 *Surrey Assizes*, Mar 1726, 2.

179 Wilson (1743) *A Genuine Account … of the Malefactors*, 5.

180 *OBSP*, 2–7 May 1753, 153; *OBSP*, 18–21 Jul 1753, 227.

181 Jonathan Wild used this strategy without apparent complaint from the judges: *OBSP*, Jan 1723, 4.

182 *OBSP*, 11–15 Jan 1753, 69. Also *OBSP*, Sep 1732, 186.

183 *OBSP*, 24–30 Oct 1753, 313.

184 *OBSP*, Jan 1741. Also *OBSP*, Dec 1733, 21; *Surrey Assizes*, Jul 1740, 3; *Surrey Assizes*, Mar 1742, 4.

185 *OBSP*, 18–21 Jul 1753, 227.

186 *Surrey Assizes*, Aug 1751, 37.

187 *Surrey Assizes*, Mar 1738, 18–19; Jul 1740, 10; Mar 1749, 7; Beattie (1986) *Crime and the Courts*, 364–6, 413–14; Langbein (1983) 'Shaping the eighteenth-century trial', 103–5.

188 *OBSP*, Sep 1732, 186. See chapter 3.

189 *OBSP*, Jan 1753, 41–2.

190 *Surrey Assizes*, Jul 1741, 2–3. Also Wilson (1722) *A Full and Impartial Account*, 27–8.

191 *OBSP*, Jul 1721, 7. Also *OBSP*, 6 Sep 1732, 216; 2 Jul 1735, 90; May 1753, 153; Jun 1753, 90; *Surrey Assizes*, Apr 1752, 7. At the end of the eighteenth century, the Bow Street officers (see below) were conducting their identification parades in the Brown Bear next to the magistrate's office: *OBSP*, 8 Dec 1784, 41–2, 113; Jan 1817, 99; Oct 1817, 483. See Fitzgerald (1888) *Chronicles of Bow Street Police-Office*, vol I, 149–61.

192 *Surrey Assizes*, Aug 1751, 39. Also Anon (1722a) *Tyburn's Worthies*, 20–1; *OBSP*, 8 Dec 1784, 47; Silverthorne (1978) *Deposition Book of Richard Wyatt*, 51–3.

193 *Home Circuit*, Mar 1739, 18. Also *OBSP*, Dec 1722, 2.

194 *OBSP*, Dec 1733, 34.

195 *OBSP*, Sep 1732, 217.

196 *OBSP*, 11–15 Jan 1753, 69. See also *OBSP*, 18–21 Jul 1753, 236.

197 *Surrey Assizes*, Aug 1751, 29–30.

198 See Tom How in *OBSP*, Sep 1732, 202–3.

199 *OBSP*, Feb 1742, 54; Paley (1989b) 'Thief-takers in London'.

200 Rawlings (1999) *Crime and Power*, 21.

201 *OBSP*, 8 Dec 1784, 78, 79.
202 Landau (1984) *The Justices of the Peace*, 184–7.
203 Beattie (1986) *Crime and the Courts*, 274–6; Silverthorne (1978) *Deposition Book of Richard Wyatt*, 23–4.
204 *OBSP*, 7–9 Jun 1753, 168. Also *OBSP*, Feb 1712, 3.
205 *OBSP*, Dec 1722, 2; 11–15 Jan 1753, 69; *Surrey Assizes*, Mar 1738, 19; Mar 1749, 4–5.
206 *Surrey Assizes*, Aug 1743, 13; also Mar 1742, 5.
207 Langbein (1983) 'Shaping the eighteenth-century trial', 63.
208 Mr Justice Gould in Gurney (1775) *An Account of the Arguments of Counsel*, 23; Beattie (1986) *Crime and the Courts*, 367–9; Langbein (1983) 'Shaping the eighteenth-century trial', 91–6.
209 Anon (1765a) *An Account of John Westcote*, 18; Beattie (1986) *Crime and the Courts*, 366–73; Fielding (1988) *An Enquiry into the Causes of the Late Increase of Robbers*; Fielding (1758) *An Account of the Origin and Effects of a Police*; Langbein (1983) 'Shaping the eighteenth-century trial', 96–100.
210 *OBSP*, Sep 1732, 201. Also *OBSP*, Dec 1733, 34; Oct 1753, 313.
211 Anon (1722a) *Tyburn's Worthies*; Wilson (1722) *A Full and Impartial Account*.
212 Hewitt (1783) *The Proceedings of J. Hewitt, Alderman*, 19.
213 *Surrey Assizes*, Mar 1742, 9.
214 *OBSP*, 1–9 Jun 1753, 168.
215 Anon (1765a) *An Account of John Westcote*, 14.
216 *OBSP*, 4 Sep 1741, 5–6.
217 *OBSP*, Dec 1733, 21.
218 *Surrey Assizes*, Mar 1740, 5; also Mar 1742, 12; Rawlings (1992a) *Drunks, Whores and Idle Apprentices*, 139–41.
219 *Surrey Assizes*, Aug 1741, 4.
220 *OBSP*, Dec 1733, 34–5. See also *OBSP*, Dec 1734, pt II, 4; *Surrey Assizes*, Aug 1743, 10–11.
221 *OBSP*, Dec 1733, 8; also Jul 1735, 105.
222 *OBSP*, Dec 1734, pt II: 4. Also *OBSP*, Dec 1733; Apr. 1733.
223 *OBSP*, Jul 1735, 104–5. Also Rawlings (1992a) *Drunks, Whores and Idle Apprentices*, 79–109; Langbein (1983) 'Shaping the eighteenth-century trial', 85.
224 Hewitt (1783) *The Proceedings of J. Hewitt, Alderman*, 13.
225 *Surrey Assizes*, Mar 1745, 7. Also *OBSP*, Feb 1712, 8.
226 *Surrey Assizes*, Mar 1745, 8–10.
227 But see Holloway (1773) *The Rat-Trap*; Langbein (1983) 'Shaping the eighteenth-century trial', 58n.
228 Fielding (1768) *Extracts from Such of the Penal Laws*, vi. Generally Battestin (1989) *Henry Fielding*, 499–502, 576–80; Goddard (1956) *Memoirs of a Bow Street Runner*; Radzinowicz (1948–68) *A History of English Criminal Law*, vol III; Rawlings (1995) 'The idea of policing'; Styles (1983) 'Sir John Fielding and the problem of crime investigation'.
229 Hay (1977) 'Property, authority and the criminal law'.
230 Rawlings (1999) *Crime and Power*, 39–53.

231 Fielding (1754) *The Journal of a Voyage to Lisbon*, 19–23.
232 Battestin (1989) *Henry Fielding*, 580–2.
233 Cox (1756) *A Faithful Narrative … of the Bloody-minded Gang of Thief-takers*, iv.
234 Cox (1756) *A Faithful Narrative … of the Bloody-minded Gang of Thief-takers*, 3–4.
235 Fielding (1755) *A Plan for Preventing Robberies*, 6.
236 Fielding (1755) *A Plan for Preventing Robberies*, 5.
237 Paley (1989b) 'Thief-takers in London'.
238 Neither claim seems to have been true: Paley (1989b) 'Thief-takers in London'.
239 Battestin (1989) *Henry Fielding*, 512.
240 *Gentleman's Magazine*, vol 25 (1755), 138.
241 Fielding (1755) *A Plan for Preventing Robberies*, 10–11.
242 Battestin (1989) *Henry Fielding*, 579; Fielding (1769) *Extracts from Such of the Penal Laws*, v. Generally Anon (1765a) *An Account of John Westcote*; Bevell (1765) *An Authentic Narrative*; Rawlings (1995) 'The idea of policing'; Rawlings (1999) *Crime and Power*; Styles (1983) 'Sir John Fielding and the problem of crime investigation'.
243 *The London Evening-Post*, 31 Mar 1772; Hewitt (1790) *A Journal of the Proceedings of J. Hewitt, Senior Alderman*.
244 Bee (1828) *A Living Picture of London, for 1828*, 288n; Waters (1994) *The Police Gazette*.
245 *The Public Advertiser*, 1 Jan 1753; *OBSP*, Jan 1817, 110–11; *Surrey Assizes*, Mar 1759, 17–18, 20–1.
246 But see Miles (1773) *A Letter to Sir John Fielding*.
247 Hewitt (1783) *The Proceedings of J. Hewitt, Alderman*; Hewitt (1790) *A Journal of the Proceedings of J.Hewitt, Senior Alderman*; Rawlings (1992a) *Drunks, Whores and Idle Apprentices*, 25.
248 Anon (1765a) *An Account of John Westcote*.
249 *OBSP*, Feb 1778, 141–2.
250 *Journal of the House of Commons*, vol 32, 879, 10 Apr 1770.
251 *The Gentleman's Magazine*, vol 35 (1765), 16–19.
252 Bevell (1765) *An Authentic Narrative*.
253 Miles (1773) *A Letter to Sir John Fielding*.
254 Miles (1773) *A Letter to Sir John Fielding*, 21.
255 Miles (1773) *A Letter to Sir John Fielding*. Also Blizzard (1785) *Desultory Reflections on Police*, 4.
256 Hewitt (1790) *A Journal of the Proceedings of J.Hewitt, Senior Alderman*.
257 Hewitt (1783) *The Proceedings of J. Hewitt, Alderman*.
258 *OBSP*, Dec 1742, 9.
259 Anon (1725) *The True and Genuine Account … of the Late Jonathan Wild*, 20–1.
260 Reynolds (1998) *Before the Bobbies*, 78.
261 See chapter 5.
262 See Rawlings (1995) 'The idea of policing'.

Chapter 5

The Jenny Darbies: the New Police

Crime and disorder in the early nineteenth century

From the last quarter of the eighteenth century through to the 1820s problems of crime and order maintenance were regarded as particularly acute: the end of the transportation of convicts to the colonies in North American in the 1770s; the Gordon Riots which paralysed London for five days in 1780; the radicalism generated in England by Wilkes and the American and French Revolutions which combined during the French Wars (1793–1815) with food riots, rising numbers of people claiming poor relief and the disruption of foreign trade to create the fear that a politicized working class might welcome, rather than seek to repel, invaders from France.[1]

In the early nineteenth century, political and industrial disorder proved persistent, creating paranoia among the ruling classes which was stoked up by government spies and sometimes led to bloody consequences: the Luddite disturbances in the Midlands and the North; the demonstrations in 1815 against the Corn Law Bill; the riots in London's Spa Fields and in rural East Anglia in 1816; the march of the Blanketeers from Manchester to demand political reform in 1817; the Peterloo massacre in 1819 when a political demonstration was bloodily broken up; the Cato Street conspiracy to assassinate members of the cabinet and the riots among poor woollen workers in the West Riding in 1820; and the Queen Caroline riots in London in 1820–1.[2] In 1829 the *Quarterly Review* warned, 'if the social plague of poverty and degradation among the peasantry is not stayed … it will inevitably draw after it a strong and dreadful explosion'.[3] During that year and the next there were strikes in the north of England, and in the south rioting, arson and machine-breaking that led to 19 people being hanged and 481 being sent to the penal colonies in Australia.[4] Then in 1831 came widespread demonstrations and riots in support of parliamentary reform.[5]

It is, of course, impossible to determine the 'real' levels of crime at this time. However, policy is driven by opinions and in the second half of the eighteenth century there was a widespread opinion that crime was rising inexorably. Shortly after the end of the American War of Independence, the City of London complained to George III in 1786 of 'the rapid and alarming increase of crimes and depredations in this city and its neighbourhood, especially within the last three years'.[6] The level of panic was registered in the vast numbers carted to the places of execution in the 1780s. The number condemned at the Old Bailey who were later hanged had averaged 29 a year in the quarter of a century up to 1781, while between 1782 and 1787 it rose to 65. The proportion of the condemned who were hanged rose from about 30 per cent to just over 80 per cent in 1787.[7] Although after this the nature of the response became less bloody, the belief that crime was rising seems not to have tailed off during the French Wars, but to have increased, fuelled by the concerns about political radicalism and discontent among impoverished workers.[8] Those fears seemed justified by the first stuttering efforts to collect statistics,[9] and many concluded that crime, disorder and political radicalism were symptoms of a general moral collapse and the decay of authority.

Reform and the watch

This concern about crime levels underpinned the debate over capital punishment, which really got underway in the late 1760s. Opponents of reform, like the moral and political philosopher William Paley, argued that the existing system was better because the 'few actually suffer, while the dread and danger of [death] hang over the crimes of many' and because, even if many were hanged, this was better than a strong police system which would reduce the 'liberties of a free people'.[10] The problem was that Paley failed to address the growing belief that the mere chance of an accused being hanged was deterring prosecutors and that this, in turn, was encouraging people to offend because they never believed they would be punished. Increasingly, it was the efficiency of the criminal justice system in punishing crime that came under scrutiny, but there was no consensus as to how – or even whether – to reform it.[11] In 1785 the Rev. Martin Madan, who opposed a reduction in the number of capital offences, called for a more effective system of enforcement:

Our gangs of thieves are grown too numerous, and the individuals which compose them too desperate and dangerous to be controuled by the comparatively feeble powers of the private magistrate, or of the common parochial constable … [N]othing but active magistrates, who devote their whole time to the one single object of the police – and bands of stout, able, and resolute officers, whose only business is to execute the warrants of those magistrates – can insure any tolerable quiet to the metropolis and its *environs*.[12]

Yet, as has been seen, attempts at general reform of the watch proved difficult and Pitt's Police Bill was defeated in the year Madan wrote.

The London night watchmen at the end of the eighteenth and beginning of the nineteenth century were subject to familiar criticisms: 'the almost useless, decrepid, and inefficient tribe of watchmen with which for the most part, the streets of the metropolis may rather be said to be infested than protected.'[13] Nevertheless, support for the system itself remained strong, not because the criticisms of the watchmen were rejected, but it continued to be the view in the parishes that defects could be remedied within the existing structure.[14] Some did, it is true, express a yearning for the communal policing ideas of 1285, like the Radical MP Sir Francis Burdett,[15] but his opinion smacked of political opportunism and many were content with the existing mix of professionalism and amateurism. The London magistrate, George Mainwaring, acknowledged the value of professionalism because he believed it increased the certainty of detection and spread a beneficial moral influence, but he stoutly defended the role of amateurism in the form of the parish constable:

… though not effective as a regular force, it is, in a constitutional view, entitled to the most sacred preservation. One of the excellencies of our constitution is, that it enlists so many into the various parts of its administration, as thereby to produce a common interest in its preservation, and from the rotation of its official duties identifies a very large portion of the community in the working of the great machinery of the country. A feeling is thence excited, which facilitates and gives vigour to our laws: a graduation of authority is created through the kingdom; a co-operation is produced, which gives a harmony and unity of action more calculated to attach men to the existing establishments of the country than any cause whatever[16]

On the other hand, John Wade complained that the practice of constables hiring deputies meant 'the office has fallen into the hands of the lowest class of retailers and costardmongers, who make up the deficient allowance of their principals by indirect sources of emolument'.[17] But, while critics might exhort householders to serve as constables, none contemplated compelling them, and so some parishes dealt with this problem by swearing in former watchmen as special constables.[18]

In truth in much of London by the early nineteenth century there seems to have been little more than a theoretical concern about pro-fessionalism in policing; indeed, householders were increasingly willing to employ substitute or assistant constables, many of whom became more-or-less permanent, and Westminster had an established system of regulating constables. However, there was a determination among ratepayers to defend local control, which was best expressed in the report of the Select Committee on the Police in 1822. While recognizing that fragmentation caused by the parochial policing system in London did lead to difficulties, the committee rejected a unified system:

It is difficult to reconcile an effective system of police, with that perfect freedom of action and exemption from interference, which are the great privileges and blessings of society in this country; and Your Committee think that the forfeiture or curtailment of such advantages would be too great a sacrifice for improvements in police, or facilities in detection of crime, however desirable in them-selves if abstractedly considered.[19]

The opinions of those, like the police-office magistrate Patrick Colquhoun, who favoured unification and centralization, were largely ignored.[20] Indeed, it was argued that by advocating a strong, government police he was falling into the same trap as the French system, in which policing was detached from the people and, as a result, the people spent all their time evading the police, which meant 'no room was left for conscience, a sense of shame, or the cultivation of moral principles'.[21] Yet the sense of complacency in the 1822 report is fragile. Parliament kept returning to the issue of policing in London in a number of inquiries between 1812 and 1822, and this alone suggests some dissatisfaction. Moreover, the government-funded police were expanded: by 1829 the number of police-office constables, Bow Street Runners and members of the Horse, Foot and Dismounted Bow Street patrols had reached about 400.

There were some general reforms of the watch, such as the acts of 1821 and 1822 (1 & 2 Geo. IV, c. 118; 3 Geo. IV, c. 55) which allowed police-office magistrates (those appointed under the Middlesex Justices Act 1792) to suspend or dismiss incompetent or corrupt parish watchmen and stipulated that no one over the age of forty was to be appointed to the watch or a patrol. The parishes seem not to have objected to these statutes, perhaps because the policies did not interfere with the parishes' right to determine the size or the duties of the watch and because of the precedent in the 1774 act.[22] However, in general, the watch system and its reform continued to be regarded as a matter for the local authorities, and many London parishes did improve the quality of watchmen through changes in recruitment policy, higher wages, pension schemes, disciplinary codes and tougher supervisory systems.

Outside London more towns obtained legislation to establish or improve watch systems. Everywhere the main stumbling block to reform was cost. Householders might complain bitterly about crime and the ineffectiveness of their watchmen, but they were not always keen on paying for improvements. In part this was because parish rates had risen as a result of soaring expenditure on poor relief. As finances eased so objections were relaxed: for instance, in 1812 the London parishes had been reluctant to adopt a proposal which would have extended the hours of the night watch, but their objections faded in the 1820s as finances improved.[23] Sometimes local circumstances overcame funding problems. After the murders of seven people in the Ratcliffe Highway area of Shadwell in December 1811 parishes in the area and local associations for the prosecution of felons stepped up patrols: the thirteen nightwatchmen of St Paul, Shadwell, were replaced by armed patrols consisting of 22 men in spite of a trebling of the cost. The deluge of criticisms and suggestions which flowed into the Home Office following the murders and the frequency of Parliamentary inquiries indicates that, while parishes continued to see themselves as central to the organization of the watch, there was an expectation that the government would play its part in London and, to some extent, it accepted this role.

Public order and detection

Aside from watching and patrolling, the other main policing functions were crime detection and public order policing. The eighteenth and early nineteenth centuries seem to have been high points in the history of riot: food rioting was common and increasingly riots emerged out of labour disputes and politics.[24] Magistrates confronted by a riot could request military assistance, although there was some reluctance to do so. Unless troops were on hand, it was unlikely that they would be able to arrive in time to be of any use, and, even if called in, there was some fear that the soldiers would cause more havoc and resentment than the rioters. The function and legal powers of both the magistrates and the soldiers were also a little unclear and created problems during the Gordon Riots in 1780.[25] There was a fear both of using violent means to disperse the crowd and of failing to disperse it, and there was also concern that the soldiers might sympathize with the rioters. During the Gordon Riots, which began as a protest against Catholic toleration, a visitor to London reported to her family in Wales that:

> the soldiers refused to fire despite orders, then fired over heads, only when officers threatened to shoot them did they fire on [the] mob … It is said that the Soldiers are much on the side of the Populace & tell people that they ought to read Fox's Book of Martyrs, & that then they would see whether the Papists ought to be tolerated[26]

The riots continued for five days and stayed in the collective memory of the ruling class well into the nineteenth century as a symbol of the dangers of an inefficient system for responding to disorder.

A solution to these problems proved hard to find. In urban areas it was possible to swear in the middle classes as special constables to meet temporary exigencies, but this was not really an option in rural or the growing semi-urban districts of the North of England. The government encouraged the formation of Loyal Associations in the 1790s in the expectation that these volunteer organizations would act both against invasion and domestic sedition. Large numbers responded to the call, but they were independent-minded householders and the government found it difficult to guide their actions. Indeed, as the threat of invasion receded, so did the volunteers' enthusiasm. The Yeomanry was established in 1794. Recruited from the middling classes, its various manifestations around the country rapidly built up a total force of 25,000 men.[27] However, after their murderous charge against a peaceful crowd attending a political meeting at St Peter's Field in Manchester – the Peterloo massacre – their appearance was always likely to exacerbate public order problems. In short, the alternatives to the army either never seemed adequate or brought their own difficulties. Using soldiers, therefore, remained the option which both magistrates and government fell back on. The government increased its programme of building barracks, and when the Luddite disturbances broke out in 1811 troops were poured into particularly the Midlands and the North: by 1812 12,000 were stationed in these areas – more than Wellesley took to Portugal.

The uncertainties and weaknesses evident during the Gordon Riots were still present in the 1820s and 1830s. Queen Caroline's triumphant return to England in 1820 on the accession of her estranged husband, George IV, brought opponents of the Tory government on to the streets. To these crowds George symbolized the corruption of the Tories and Caroline its victim. Her entry into London was celebrated in traditional fashion by smashing the windows of a few symbolic Tories. The rioters easily overwhelmed the attendant group of constables so troops had to be called out to restore order. When a little over a year later Caroline died of peritonitis, the Bow Street police and troops were deployed for her funeral. Nevertheless, trouble broke out. This was exacerbated by quarrelling between the civil authorities and the army (and, indeed, between officers in the army) as to the proper course of action. Partly as a result of this, soldiers shot two people dead.

Ten years later in Bristol supporters of the Reform Bill attacked various buildings, including the prisons, the Mansion House and the houses of opponents of the bill. The civil authorities proved impotent once more and the Lord Mayor was later tried for neglect of duty, although acquitted. Troops were called in, but the commanding officer, Thomas Brereton, was sympathetic to the bill and refused to deploy his soldiers against the rioters; he later killed himself while awaiting a court martial. Further troops and yeomanry had to be drafted in to suppress the disorders.[28]

Detective work remained a matter primarily for the victim, although, depending on the location, he or she might be able to call on the assistance of various officials – the constable, the watchman and the justice of the peace – and, particularly in London, might be able to interest a thief-taker or Bow Street Runner if there was a reward or a fee. The adequacy of these arrangements continued to be called into question, particularly after the Ratcliffe Highway murders in 1811, and memories of the Macdaniel gang were revived when a blood-money conspiracy involving police-office constables was uncovered in 1816.[29] However, the idea at the heart of John Fielding's project – that potential criminals could be deterred if the likelihood of detection was increased – was challenged. Instead, it was suggested that the policing system should be designed to prevent crime before it happened. The problem was that there was no incentive for police-office constables to arrest petty offenders before they turned (as it was believed they would) into felons. As one writer put it in 1816, when discussing the difficulties confronted by the police-office constable, 'The fault is in the institution, and not in the agent, for it is clear that the chief employment of the present police establishments is rather in the *detection* than in the *prevention* of crimes'.[30]

An elaboration of the idea of crime prevention had already been presented by Patrick Colquhoun.[31] For a long time his influence on the formation of the new police has been exaggerated by historians, but the recent tendency to dismiss his contribution has also been overdone. His work on the Thames River Police drew a good deal of interest and extracts from his book on the subject were printed in *The Times*,[32] while his *Treatise on the Police of the Metropolis* went through seven editions in nine years.[33] Neither the watch nor the detection system took up much space in his work. He was more interested in the traditional sense of the word 'police' which for him involved the control of working people and the maintenance of the social divisions between the propertied and the propertyless on which he believed national wealth depended. The objective was class control and the victim of crime was of only minor importance. Idleness was the great evil and immorality, poverty and crime its consequences. Colquhoun produced bogus statistics on the number of prostitutes and the depredations committed by various groups of workers as if they were scientific facts. He argued that to eliminate these traits it was necessary to reduce the autonomy of working people through a system of police which regulated all aspects of their lives. The laboratory in which Colquhoun was able to conduct an experiment in policing was the confined, controllable space of the West India Docks where the Thames River Police were established in 1798. He envisaged broadening his scheme to all the working people in London by an integrated approach to crime, prisons, the poor law, moral policing and labour regulation,[34] but this goal was never realized, although there were major reforms in all of these areas in the early nineteenth century.

Robert Peel

In 1822 Robert Peel was appointed Home Secretary. He was a pragmatic conservative who observed with dismay the failure of the civil authorities in London to contain the Queen Caroline Riots in 1820–1. More generally, he was concerned that the perception of crime as spiralling out of control undermined the credibility of the criminal justice system and with it the credibility of the system of government to which he subscribed. For Peel, then, reform was a means of restoring confidence in the basic institutions of government by making them more effective. He believed that there had to be a reduction in the number of capital crimes so that punishments would come more into line with public sentiment; at the same time the mechanisms for enforcing the law could be made more efficient.[35]

Peel's previous experience as Chief Secretary for Ireland between 1812 and 1818 strongly influenced his approach to policing in London. After

Pitt's Police Bill was blocked, it was converted into the Dublin Police Act 1786. It did not prove to be a success, but other experiments followed, including Peel's creation of the Peace Preservation Police in 1814.[36] He seems to have brought with him at least some of the mistrust of local authorities he acquired in Ireland. He believed that a decentralized system of policing lacked the co-ordination and broader vision necessary for efficiency, and he was unenthusiastic about putting the police into the hands of the magistracy. He immediately established a select committee inquiry into the police of the metropolis in 1822.[37] However, while the report acknowledged that there were problems with the existing system and, in particular, the failure in Westminster of 'that unity of action upon which the maintenance of public order so much depends',[38] these considerations were, as has been seen, outweighed by the committee's concern at the threat posed to liberty by greater centralization.

In 1828 Peel set up another Parliamentary inquiry. This time it produced the result he wanted,[39] even though it did so in spite of a lack of evidence: 'the presumption is very strong, even though [the Committee] had no evidence as to particular facts, that the present system of providing by night for the Police … is in principle, defective'.[40] In 1829 he brought the Metropolitan Police Bill before the House of Commons by arguing that the parochial organization of policing had failed and should be replaced by a single police force for London (excluding the City) which would be accountable to the Home Secretary.

First, he endorsed the general belief that crime was increasing rapidly and argued that this was the result, not of poverty, but of the activities of habitual offenders. Second, he pointed out that while parish boundaries confined officers they did not confine criminals. The lack of co-ordination between parishes, therefore, obstructed the task of dealing with crime. Third, he argued that criminals moved from places which had efficient parish watch schemes to those which did not. Fourth, he claimed that the new police would not cost much more than the old methods and that any increase in rates would be offset by the improvements in security that would be enjoyed by householders. Finally, he said that a more effective police system would enable further reforms in the penal codes.[41]

Peel's proposals drew support from John Wade, a radical critic of the corruption and inefficiency inherent in the institutions of government inherited from the previous century. Like Peel, Wade saw no value in trying to repair the old police: 'Any attempt to patch up the present disjecta membra will assuredly fail of success; for there is no foundation either to repair or build on, and recourse must at last be had to an entirely new constitution of the civil force, sanctioned and carried into effect by Government.'[42] Edwin Chadwick, a committed Benthamite, agreed:

Our present police consists of disjointed bodies of men governed separately, under heterogeneous regulations, and acting, for the most part, under the earliest set of expedients: and then only upon being called upon, seizing or receiving in charge an offender and handing him over to the judicature for punishment. A good police would be one well-organised body of men acting upon a system of precautions, to prevent crimes and public calamities; to preserve public peace and order and to perform whatever other useful functions might be comprehended in their duties without hindering the performance of those of the most important nature in the best manner.[43]

Such opposition as there was to the bill in Parliament was muted. In part this was because Peel prepared the ground. By excluding the City from its provisions he had removed a potential source of trouble, even though it hardly fitted in with the logic of his argument.[44] He had good reason to suppose that the City would oppose handing over control of its police because in January 1829 his modest proposal that arrest warrants be enforceable within the City without having to be backed by a City magistrate was firmly rebuffed as an interference with ancient privileges.[45] Peel also avoided controversy by the vague wording used in the bill: while there is an enormous amount of detail about collecting the police rate and accounting procedures, the number of officers and their duties are not specified. To some extent, the broader jurisdiction of the police offices and the gradual increase in the size of the various Bow Street patrols may also have made the idea of officers having a jurisdiction which was not tied to parochial boundaries more acceptable; indeed, Wade went so far as to claim that the new police did not amount to a radical increase in government power, but merely supplemented the Middlesex Justices Act 1792.[46] Finally, Parliament had other things on its mind, most notably the controversy over the Catholic Emancipation Bill, which also became law in 1829 and which provoked a crisis among the Tories.[47]

There is also good reason to believe that during the 1820s there was some shift in thinking within the ruling élite – both Tory and Whig – about the role of government in the formation and implementation of domestic social policy. Government, which had been seen as a threat to the liberty of 'the freeborn Englishman' unless kept within strict bounds, began to be depicted as the best protection for those who believed that rising crime, indigence, immorality and radicalism were interconnected and that it was these which presented the real danger to liberty.[48] The protection of life and property from the depredations of criminals came to be characterized as a task which only government could perform. For

Wade, 'It is the first duty of Government to protect the persons and properties of the people, and it seems preposterous to have any hesitation about trusting them with the necessary power for the accomplishment of these objects.'[49] Similarly, the Tory *Quarterly Review* claimed that 'police ... is the base on which men's liberties, properties, and social existence repose.'[50]

The London parishes, which might have been expected to oppose the removal of policing from their control, were relatively silent on the bill. Here again attitudes had changed. In spite of the reforms of the previous hundred years and the increased spending, crime seemed to carry on rising. This prompted relentless criticism of the performance of the watch system and the level of expenditure, which must have demoralized not just the watchmen but also the parish officials responsible for the watch. This seems to have reduced the inclination among those officials to resist government involvement.[51]

Parish government in London had also been under attack for its corruption, inefficiency and unaccountability. This criticism had grown with the rapid rise in parish spending since the late eighteenth century. Although much of this increase was the result of rising levels of poor relief, vestries were accused of extravagance and corruption and rate-payers demanded greater accountability. The problem was most acute in those select vestries dominated by a tiny, unelected *élite* who preferred to keep parish affairs, and, in particular, parish accounts, secret. 'Old Corruption', which had scarred eighteenth-century government, lived on not only in the corrupt Parliamentary election system, but also in these self-perpetuating oligarchies.[52] Sir Francis Burdett, who, at the time of the select committee inquiry of 1812, had been an opponent of central government intervention in local affairs, led an attack on the vestry of St. Marylebone in 1828, and, discarding some of his former opinion, argued that, 'The public now saw the ministers acting with and for them'.[53] Reform groups were established in several parishes as ratepayers demanded sight of the accounts; there were even riots at vestry meetings in St. Martin-in-the-Fields in 1822 and the following year in St. Matthew, Bethnal Green. In 1828 a committee was appointed to investigate the select vestries, which eventually led to the Vestry Act 1831. In the meantime, these controversies meant that parishes, like St. Marylebone, which had fairly progressive and efficient policing systems and might have been expected to oppose Peel's police bill, may have had their attention diverted. Such opposition as there was from the parishes was drowned by a combination of approval and silence.[54]

Alongside these developments, some London parishes faced another crisis. In 1826 the Metropolitan Roads Commission took over all the metropolitan turnpikes north of the Thames. To reduce costs, the Commission cut the number of watchmen employed on some of these roads and steadfastly ignored the howls of protest from those parishes served by the roads which had no other watch provisions. Reluctant to call on their own ratepayers, some of these parishes turned to the government for help.[55]

The coming of the Jenny Darbies

The preamble to the Metropolitan Police Act 1829 (10 Geo. IV, c. 44) is almost a summary of the key arguments in Peel's speech:

> Whereas Offences against Property have of late increased in and near the Metropolis; and the local Establishments of Nightly Watch and Nightly Police have been found inadequate to the Prevention and Detection of Crime, by reason of the frequent Unfitness of the Individuals employed, the Insufficiency of their Number, the limited Sphere of their Authority, and their Want of Connection and Co-operation with each other.

Under the act the Home Secretary was given a broad discretion as to the size and deployment of the force, although that discretion was largely delegated to the commissioners appointed to head the police. Constables were instructed to 'obey all such lawful Commands as they may from Time to Time receive from' the commissioners (s. 4), and the commissioners were to make such orders 'as they shall deem expedient' for the management of the force, subject to the approval of the Secretary of State (s. 5). The act also gave officers the powers of constables in the neighbouring counties of Middlesex, Surrey, Hertfordshire, Essex and Kent (s. 4). The constable had powers of arrest without warrant similar to those given to the night watchmen: 'to apprehend all loose, idle, and disorderly Persons whom he shall find disturbing the public Peace, or whom he shall have just Cause to suspect of any evil Designs, and all Persons whom he shall find between Sunset and the Hour of Eight in the Forenoon lying in any Highway, Yard, or other Place, or loitering therein, and not giving a satisfactory Account of themselves' (s. 7). Outlying areas of London fell outside the act to the disappointment of some residents,[56] and the new police were only introduced gradually into those areas to which the act did apply.[57]

The details of the structure of the force, and the methods and objectives of policing were filled in by the *General Instructions* of September 1829. In spite of the reference in the preamble, detection remained primarily the responsibility of the victim, for, while the new police would render assistance in apprehending offenders and searching premises as their predecessors had done, their main objective was set out in a famous declaration:

> the principal object to be attained is the prevention of crime. To this great end every effort of the police is to be directed. The security of the person and property, the preservation of public tranquillity and all the other objects of a Police Establishment will thus be better effected than by the detection and punishment of the offender after he has succeeded in committing crime.

From the outset it was also intended that by creating a single force the new police would be able to deal with public disorder:

> The whole of the police force will be gradually placed under such a degree of discipline as may enable it to act with effect, should any occasion arise for its services, as an united corps – for instance, the late riots in Spitalfields, and tumultuous mobs of any kind.[58]

The *General Instructions* acknowledged that 'something must necessarily be left to the intelligence and discretion of individuals',[59] but the rules to which each constable was subjected ran to several thousand words, thereby restricting this discretion as far as possible: the whole of his life from the pace he walked his beat to his choices of a wife and a place to live were regulated.

Much that has been seen as new about the New Police had been pioneered in the most progressive of the parish watches: the hierarchical system of supervision, the beat system, the uniforms and the minimum age qualifications.[60] The main distinction between the New Police and the watch lay in the severing of the connection with the community police, the parish authorities and the ratepayers. Communities were to be subjected to policing and were expected to co-operate with it. There were no opportunities for people to take part in directing policing strategies or for accountability, other than to the Home Secretary. This became a point of controversy for the parish leaders and for the working classes, who were the objects of the new police: the former disliked their loss of authority, patronage and control, while the latter tended to have an ambivalent relationship with the new police seeing them both as an alien force sent by government to destroy their lifestyles and as a resource.

Reception

There was certainly a good deal of enthusiasm for the New Police. Particularly vocal was *The Times* which had pressed for radical reform for a number of years, particularly after the Queen Caroline Riots.[61] It had originally opposed 'a ministerial police', such as that exemplified by the government-funded police offices, but this criticism disappeared as, seven years later, the newspaper put its full support behind the Metropolitan Police idea in the months leading up to its introduction into Parliament and rejected concerns about the creation of an over-powerful central government: 'A State Police can never be forced upon this country while the Parliament and the press are in existence'.[62] After the introduction of the new police, the Home Office received letters of support from people such as the correspondent from Stepney who wrote:

> Under the Metropolitan force the rabble are defeated … and I hope and trust you will not be induced to change the present system. It is now in its Infancy but working well and will in a short time do wonders both for the State and the man of real Property.[63]

Some, indeed, thought the reform did not go far enough. For instance, one police-office magistrate criticized 'the incompleteness of his Police Reform' in that it left untouched and outside the control of the commissioners 'independent bodies of watchmen, constables and other police officers' and, of course, the City of London police.[64]

But there were also many complaints about the new institution. There was early friction with some police-office magistrates. Within a few days of the new police appearing on the streets, it emerged that senior officers had been discharging arrested people – mainly those who had been picked up for being drunk but also some petty thieves. On learning of this Rogers, a magistrate at Hatton Garden police office, denounced the practice and declared that, once they had made an arrest, the police were obliged to bring the arrested person before a magistrate.[65] The police responded by not arresting drunken people but, instead, taking them home.[66] Around the same time, Sir Richard Birnie of Bow Street police office, having criticized the actions of a police constable, added, 'The fact is, the new policemen have such ridiculous instructions given to them by their superiors, who know nothing whatever of the duties of a police officer, that they are not half so much to blame on these occasions as their superiors.'[67] In July 1830 Swabey, a magistrate at Union Hall police office, having fined two police officers for assaulting a woman, warned that, 'They (the magistrates) were always ready to assist the new police in the performance of their duty, but when they exceeded that and committed outrages on Her Majesty's subjects, it was the magistrates' duty to protect the public against any innovation of that nature.'[68] There were also confrontations between the new and the old police. Parish watchmen were reported to have refused to hand over equipment, and in November 1830 two Metropolitan officers were arrested while on duty and charged with assault by the headborough of All Saints, Poplar, to which the officers countered by claiming the headborough had been drunk.[69]

The police were also characterized by some as a paramilitary government force, even though efforts were made to avoid the accusation. The design of uniform reflected a wish to avoid either military colours or cut, while making the officers distinctive and thereby avoiding the allegation that they were plain-clothes government spies. Yet, there were clear military connections. Peel's determination to provide not just a force to deal with crime but also one capable of coping with disorder seems to have influenced his appointment, as one of the two commissioners in 1829, of Colonel Charles Rowan, who had served in the French Wars and with the army on public order duties in the Midlands and Ireland. Moreover, the separation from the community policed, and the training and structure of the new police did not reassure people. The desire to control the constables led to the adoption of a military model of organization, and drill became virtually the only form of training they received.[70] The denunciation of the police as a military force became a common charge. 'Down with the Raw Lobsters! No Martial Law! No Standing Armies!' shouted one crowd at officers protecting the king during a demonstration in 1830.[71] They were the 'Jenny Darbies', a corruption of the French 'Gens d'armes', a traditional symbol for the English of despotism;[72] they were 'the blue army',[73] the 'Blue Devils',[74] 'the household troops of Sir Robert Peel',[75] and 'a system of repression and coercion, demi civil and demi military, vexatious to men, as well as insulting to the nation. It is an amphibious, ambiguous, hermaphrodite monster',[76] which must have been rather less easy to chant.

The behaviour of individual police officers was denounced:

> 'things of evil gliding through the streets,
> Acting at once the tyrant and the spy,
> Whom gin converteth, and whom bribes can buy!'[77]

Complaints illustrating their abusive behaviour were keenly reported even by newspapers favourable to the police, particularly if the victim was 'respectable'.[78] The newly-founded satirical magazine *Punch* found one of its most consistent targets in the policeman,

'Who, anxious to prove that the peace he maintains,
Sets to work with his staff on an old woman's head,
And silenced her by the loss of her brains.'[79]

Occasionally, such allegations provided focal points for demonstrations against the police, as, for instance, when a large crowd gathered at the Wheat Sheaf in Lower Shadwell where an inquest was being held on John Wood, a waterman, murdered in 1833 by an unidentified officer.[80] Shortly before this case, another coroner's jury pronounced a verdict of justifiable homicide following the death of PC Robert Culley, killed when police charged a political demonstration in Cold Bath Fields.[81]

The general passivity of the parishes during the passage of the legislation turned to active opposition during the late summer and early autumn of 1830 as the Metropolitan Police was gradually introduced across London and as demands for police rates were issued. In parish after parish anger was expressed by meetings of lower middle-class and working-class ratepayers and residents. They complained that the new police was more expensive than the nightly watch, particularly in those parishes which had relied heavily on amateur constables.[82] At some meetings the efficiency of the new police was praised, but the view was also expressed that the problems with the old system had been caused by poor pay and that this had been the fault of corrupt vestries. In other parishes the complaint was that crime had risen because there were fewer police officers on the streets than there had been watchmen, and that this was exacerbated by the removal of officers to police demonstrations, something which would not have occurred under the watch system.[83] Indeed, some parishes covered by the act chose to supplement the new police with private watchmen.[84] At their core, the criticisms were about the removal of parochial control. The watch, including its expenditure, had been under the control of the parish and the watchmen had typically lived in the parish;[85] the police, on the other hand, were 'arbitrary, un-constitutional, and extortionate'.[86]

These protests were enmeshed in broader agitation for the reform of Parliament and of the select vestries. Indeed, it was objected that part of the function of the New Police was to resist reform: 'the New Police were no better than an armed force, who held themselves in readiness at the bidding of the Secretary of State, to crush the Liberties of the people.'[87] When the select vestry of St. Pancras refused to discuss the New Police, an informal meeting was held. It drew 1500 people with several thousand more locked out, and the enthusiasm of its chair, Nathaniel Stallard, was not blunted by having his watch stolen as he pushed his way through the crowd. Motions to present petitions to the king requesting the repeal of the act were passed at meetings throughout London.[88] A committee of householders was formed in St. Martin's-in-the-Fields to try and combine parish opposition, and a meeting for the same purpose was held in October 1830 at the Crown and Anchor in The Strand.[89]

Of course, as was pointed out at the time, while the parishes which held such meetings were newsworthy, those which were satisfied with the new police were not reported. The Middlesex Grand Jury commended the efficiency and intelligence of the officers.[90] Some parishes joined in this approval, but their praise was sometimes subject to caveats, most often to do with the cost. Deptford and St. John's, Hampstead, for instance, approved of the new police but wished for some reduction in its cost.[91] The government did listen to at least some of those parishes that merely wanted modifications in the New Police. A meeting at St. Mary, Stoke Newington welcomed the improved efficiency of the new police and was told that the Home Office had agreed to requests from householders to alter the balance between the day and night patrols. However, the meeting still pressed for the police to be put under parochial control.[92] Even *The Times*, which was largely unsympathetic to the critics and rejected local control, attacked the cost of the police and the diligence of the constables:

> The expense of the New Police is too great, arising from the men being too numerous. That more are employed than is necessary is evident from the frequent instances which every body sees of their loitering about with servant-girls. Still, as a better organized body than the old watchmen, they must be more useful; but their number should be diminished: their pay constitutes a very serious tax on the London householder.[93]

The criticism reached a peak in November 1830 when, as the king returned from opening the new session of Parliament, his coach was met by demonstrators shouting 'Down with the New Police!' and 'No martial law!' As the police moved – supposedly to arrest pickpockets – they were stoned. They retreated to Vine Street police station which was quickly besieged by several thousand people. Meanwhile, officers in Bond Street were attacked and a police clothing shop ransacked. Windows were smashed in the West End and a carriage thought to be carrying the Duke of Wellington, the Prime Minister who had seen the 1829 act through the Lords, was surrounded. The violence may have led some people to drop or soften their criticism. When the demonstrations were renewed, the middle classes flocked to be sworn in as special constables, although when the disorder spilled into the City of London it was claimed that the City constables joined in on the side of the crowd.[94]

Debates on the petitions from the parishes were held in both Houses of Parliament in November 1830. However, Sir Robert Wilson, who introduced the petition from St John, Southwark, set the tone by distancing himself from the opinion it expressed, namely, that the force was 'dangerous … and might be used, by an arbitrary Minister, to crush the liberties of the people.' He did agree that the increase in the cost of the police was excessive. Peel regurgitated the arguments he had put forward in 1829. He was out of government, but spoke in favour of an inquiry, which, he believed, would vindicate the police. He pointed out that people could not expect the police to keep a constant watch on all houses and (apparently forgetting the events of a few days before) claimed that the police had proved remarkably successful in handling large crowds. While acknowledging the need 'to act in concert and cooperate with the parish authorities', he did not clarify what this meant in practice. Others who spoke during the brief debate ignored the broad issues by dismissing criticism of the efficiency of the police and ascribing the objections to the issue of cost.[95]

Criticism from the parishes did not entirely vanish. There was a continuing concern at the cost, although among the more radical parishes the attacks on the police were bound up with their disappointment at what they saw as the failure of the Whig government to press on with constitutional reform and its pursuit of repressive policies as symbolized by its support for the New Police and its enactment of the Poor Law (Amendment) Act 1834. After the vestry of St. Marylebone was taken over by Radicals following the removal of the select vestry and elections in 1832, it complained to the Whig Home Secretary, Lord Melbourne, that the New Police cost three times as much, was less effective than the watch and that, 'a Force such as this must be incompatible with the Liberty of the Subject. It differs from a Military Police only in the name'.[96] Meetings in St George's, Middlesex and All Saints, Poplar in 1833 repeated the demands for reduced cost, greater efficiency and vestry control,[97] and some parishes began to lower the rental value of houses and so reduce the rates they paid.[98]

In 1833 the government attempted to limit opposition by providing a quarter of the funding. The commissioners of the Metropolitan Police acknowledged that they 'were anxious to conciliate public favour',[99] and efforts were made through the Press and Parliament to present positive images of the police, culminating in 1834 when a select committee concluded that the New Police was 'one of the most valuable of modern institutions'.[100] Showing what can be done with a few statistics and some imagination, the report claimed that an increase in committals for assaults and minor thefts showed the success of the police in detecting offenders, while a decrease in committals for burglary and stealing in dwellings was taken as revealing a drop in those offences – in 1829 Peel had used figures showing increases in crime as decisive evidence against the watch. In spite of these efforts the criticism continued into the 1840s and, in the case of St. Marylebone and some others, beyond.[101]

Professional policing outside London

By the early nineteenth century the rural parish constables seemed to have few friends left. From all sides the system was denounced as 'manifestly very defective, and no feeling of security, either for person or property, can be associated with it.'[102] In part this came from a belief, borne out by such evidence as exists, that the office of constable was being filled by poorer people.[103] By the early nineteenth century there was a growth in the practice of householders who had been appointed as constables hiring substitutes or assistants.[104] J.B. Freeland, a lawyer from Chichester and, admittedly, an enthusiast for reform, characterized these deputies as lacking ability and unwilling 'to bestir himself against an offending or suspected neighbour, whose friends may, perhaps, be his own associates'.[105] In the towns there was a greater preponderance of long-serving, semi-professional constables, who were paid by the parish, or from voluntary contributions, or by the local association for the prosecution of felons: Daniel Claridge, who was constable of Banbury between 1823 and 1832, was recalled as 'a very clever thief-catcher, particularly those of stolen horses … his name was in great repute'.[106] There is evidence from Essex of fairly active thief-takers, who also acted as constables and watchmen.[107] Some justices employed professional constables to execute tasks for them: the Whitchurch justices appointed a Metropolitan Police officer as a process server and detective, paying him partly from the county rate and partly from a voluntary subscription.[108]

Critics highlighted the connection between the office of parish constable and the community as a key problem. Yet, this, of course, had been the reason for its creation and its strength: the constable undertook policing functions on behalf of the community and that included, not just chasing offenders, but also maintaining order by utilising internal mechanisms rather than simply relying on prosecution through the courts. The constable had always been, to some extent, trapped between this role within the community and the obligations to the institutions of government which bore down on the community from outside. As has been seen, during the Tudor and early Stuart period there had been an increased tendency for central government to intervene in local affairs and that had placed a greater pressure on the constable. The changing nature of government in the late seventeenth century involved a decentralization of power to the county benches, and this increased the expectations of the justices about – and their disappointment with – the performance of the constables. The justices seemed not to have had a high opinion of the constables in the eighteenth century, but that does not tell us why it was in the early nineteenth century that they began to promote schemes intended to improve the efficiency of rural policing.

The change came with a shift in thinking about policing as something that should be inflicted on communities and should, therefore, not be under their control. This came as a result of the turbulence of the late eighteenth and early nineteenth centuries. Although disorder was a feature of rural life in the eighteenth century,[109] in the early nineteenth century it was seen by the authorities against a broader background of radicalism and labour organization. The Swing disorders of 1830–1 were only the most serious expression of this disorder, rick burning, cattle maiming, machine breaking and rioting became a relatively constant feature of rural life in many parts of the country. Many labourers impoverished by the collapse in agriculture were in revolt against a system which had depended on their deference to authority and which, once that deference had been dissipated by its failure to protect them against poverty, was exposed as bankrupt. Local attempts to reconfigure poor relief at times of crisis had delayed the problems, but had also exacerbated them because they did not halt the declining situation of the rural poor and they increased poor relief expenditure thereby angering ratepayers.

The Whig government, elected in 1830 as the Swing riots exploded, addressed rural poverty through the Poor Law (Amendment) Act 1834. Under this the administration of poor relief was put into the hands of local boards of guardians operating under a national system administered from London. Assistance would only be given within the workhouse, where the conditions were such as to deter the poor from claiming. This ended any pretence of paternalism. Rural disorder continued and in many places the poor tore down the hated workhouses.[110]

The rural gentry could hardly fail to be aware of this fracturing of rural society, but typically ascribed it to the moral degeneration of the labouring classes and this hardened support for the construction of a system which would impose moral discipline through the workhouse system and the greater use of prisons.[111] The rural gentry also became increasingly convinced of the need for a reform of policing. The view emerged that an active system for policing the community was required; one that was, therefore, not imbedded in and dependent upon the community, and did not merely react to the wishes of that community.

This meant not only abandoning the parish constable, but also shifting control from the parish to the justices. Moreover, as the 1830s wore on rural gentry were able to read about the Metropolitan Police in action in the newspapers, to see them during visits to London and to see or hear of their activities when sent to assist authorities outside London. That reputation was increased by the apparent successes of the ex-Metropolitan Police officers hired in some cases to undertake rural policing. If nothing else, the rural gentry were impressed by their detachment from the community – a function of their being brought in from outside – and their apparent intolerance to petty disorder. One gentleman wrote of the impact one officer had in Codicote near Welwyn:

> A regular gang of marauders was established there for some years; the ordinary village police was utterly useless against them; they had become the terror, not only of the parish of Codicote, but of all the surrounding country. By the active exertions of Francis Sapte, Esq. a subscription was collected last spring and a London policeman procured to reside in the village. The results have been most satisfactory; the gang is completely broken up; and though so short a time had elapsed since we commenced operations against them, no less than seven have been transported for various terms of years.... [112]

Such activities were impressive and both improved the reputation of the Metropolitan Police and compared favourably with what were regarded as the inadequacies of the old police.

The politics of this issue were, however, somewhat complex. There was a good deal of support for a national police force.[113] During a debate on the Cheshire Police Regulation Bill, Peel had intimated his intention to 'apply a measure somewhat resembling that contained in the bill to all the counties in England … but it was found, from the nature of the subject, and the number of concurrent jurisdictions, that the previous inquiries must necessarily be very extended, and would occupy a very considerable period.'[114] This got nowhere because the Whigs came into office the next year. However, expectations that they might abolish the Metropolitan Police were soon dashed. Indeed, they worked on a proposal to establish police offices throughout the country each headed by a stipendiary magistrate accountable to the Home Secretary. The proposal foundered on the difficulty of dealing with the likely objections from local authorities, and anyway interest waned as the passage of the Reform Act 1832 was thought to have removed the immediate concerns about public order.[115] Furthermore, supporters of the New Police in

London did not necessarily wish to see a broader application of the idea. John Wade wrote:

> In the smaller towns offenders live as it were in the open champaign, always liable to be observed and detected by the agents of justice. But the metropolis is like an immense forest, in the innumerable avenues of which they may always find retreat and shelter.[116]

In the counties there was recognition among the justices that attacking the parish constables as inefficient and replacing them with professionals might have implications for their own position. Many blamed the rural justices for the policing difficulties,[117] and it was easy to draw parallels with their amateurism, reputation for inefficiency and inactivity. Indeed, some pressed for their replacement by stipendiary magistrates. However, the influence of the rural gentry in Parliament and the power of the justices in the countryside[118] meant that any policing system would have to meet their demands, including an insistence on control being in the hands of the justices. Nevertheless, in their counties the justices, who favoured policing reform, met strong opposition from the middling ratepayers, who, while not necessarily unsympathetic to reform, tended to oppose increases in expenditure or loss of parish control. Doubtless the reporting of the furore in London among ratepayers intensified their anxiety over these issues and cautioned them against accepting any reassurances that were given. Moreover, within all of these groups – commentators, politicians in Parliament, rural justices and ratepayers – there were divisions. The debate was not simply about designing an efficient police system, it was about the protection of vested interests, the desire to extend influence, party politics, and concerns about cost and loss of control. Even so, an impressive number of professional forces was established in rural England in the 1820s and 1830s.[119]

Those who wished to reform the police had a number of options and debates were often not over whether there should be change, but what form it should take. The use of the Improvement Act was, as has been seen, well established and continued to be a popular option in the nineteenth century. In Cheshire the Quarter Sessions obtained a private act (10 Geo. IV, c. 97) in 1829. The justices argued that improved policing in Manchester, Liverpool and Warrington had pushed criminals into neighbouring parts of Cheshire. This explains why the act did not establish a professional police for the whole county and, instead, enabled the justices to appoint officers in particular areas.[120] The problems with such legislation were that obtaining a statute was expensive,[121] and paying for the police fell onto local ratepayers who resented both this burden and the loss of control to commissioners (under an Improvement Act) or justices. The Lighting and Watching Act 1833 (3 & 4 Will. IV, c. 90) met some of these objections.[122] It provided a means of reforming policing within existing structures of parish control and could be adopted by a two-thirds majority of ratepayers in a vestry meeting. Inspectors, appointed for a three-year term, were empowered to hire as many watchmen 'as they shall think sufficient' and regulate their work, hours and wages, subject to overall financial limits set by the ratepayers. The watchmen were to have the same powers as a constable. Once adopted the new scheme could only be abandoned after three years. The difficulty lay in obtaining the necessary majority among ratepayers who were wary of the costs involved.

The other approach adopted to reform was to fund police from the poor rates under the direction of the justices.[123] In Suffolk, for instance, rioting against the Poor Law (Amendment) Act 1834 led two unions in the county to form poor law police forces, as did Swaffham in Norfolk. These forces disappeared after the payment of police from poor law funds was declared unlawful by the Poor Law Commissioners in London, although some became Lighting and Watching Act forces.[124]

The simplest method of reform was to establish a privately-funded police force. Sometimes this was done through an existing association for the prosecution of felons, although often subscribers joined together specifically for the purpose of creating a police force. This put the police under the control of the subscribers and required neither an expensive statute nor the approval of the ratepayers. On the other hand, the cost fell entirely on the subscribers and once the emergency which prompted the creation of the force passed so might the inclination to continue subscribing.[125] In 1789 private night patrols were set up on several of the main thoroughfares in Birmingham, and by 1831 one of these, the Moor Street Patrol Association, was employing eight men.[126] The Barnet General Association had set up a private patrol soon after it was established in 1813, but the Swing Riots led to an increase in its size from two to six men.[127]

The Linton, Hildersham, Bartlow and Hadstock Association, on the border between Cambridgeshire and Essex, set up a rota among its members to patrol the parish (or pay a deputy to do so) in 1820. The following year a paid constable was added and in 1838 a force of three men, paid for by the association, was set up under the Lighting and Watching Act 1833. The Stow-in-the-Wold Police Association was established in 1834 following a murder in the town. Subscribers paid for two Metropolitan Police officers who were accountable to a committee of justices. In Middlesbrough two men were employed in 1836 by the local society for the prosecution of felons.[128] Generally, however, the problems inherent in establishing a subscription force led to the practice of individuals or groups paying the parish constable to give priority to the interests of subscribers.[129]

The borough police after 1835

The formation of a police force was made mandatory in those boroughs which became incorporated under the Municipal Corporations Act 1835 (5 & 6 Will. IV, c. 76, ss. 76–86).[130] The 1835 act was part of the reform of political structures which had already seen the passing of the Vestry Act 1831 and the Reform Act 1832. Not only did many burgeoning northern towns have no adequate government prior to this act, but many old towns were dominated by closed, unaccountable and allegedly corrupt oligarchies. In 1837 the *Birmingham Journal* complained:

> We have our Court Leet and our bailiffs, chosen by themselves; our Street Commissioners, chosen by themselves, our Town Hall Commissioner, chosen by themselves: all working in the dark unseen by the public eye and irresponsible to the public voice, appointing their own officers, levying taxes at their pleasure and distributing them without check or control.[131]

The 1835 act was intended by the Whigs to improve accountability by broadening the principle of election. It also required incorporated boroughs to establish a police force under a watch committee composed of members of the borough council. Emsley has argued that the provision was included simply on the ground that policing had always been in the hands of the boroughs, and certainly this is consistent with the lack of debate on the issue in Parliament and the failure to include mechanisms for ensuring that the forces were efficient.[132] The act did increase the supply of information to the Home Office by requiring quarterly reports regarding the number of constables, equipment, pay and the rules of each force (s. 86). However, the act did not specify a minimum number of officers only that the watch committee 'appoint a sufficient Number of fit Men' (s. 76), leaving the committee to determine whether this require-ment was satisfied. This meant that, while some towns took the op-portunity to reorganize and strengthen existing police, others had tiny forces more like the watch in their functions than the Metropolitan Police. Many appointed separate day and night constables and, as in London, recruited from the pre-incorporation watch.[133]

The decision to adopt the act created problems in those places where the old oligarchies refused to go quietly, particularly if incorporation threatened to shift control between the Tories and the Whigs. Even where incorporation was pushed through, the wrangling sometimes continued and delayed the establishment of a police force: two years after the act only just over half of the boroughs had forces. The new police were in some places bitterly – and even violently – opposed by officers of the old police.[134] Moreover, as the new forces were established familiar accusations were hurled at them: they were 'in effect another standing army – to make the people submit to all the insults and oppressions which government contemplates forcing upon them',[135] and a 'substitute martial force for civil power'.[136] The new watch committees also kept a keen eye on costs, so, for instance, in Salford the force of 44 was cut to 38 in 1849,[137] while in Shrewsbury the original complement of four officers was reduced to three in 1837 and in Bridgnorth a force of thirteen officers in 1836 was reduced to two by 1840.[138] It was often assumed that if more officers were needed then special constables could be drafted in.[139]

Some of these problems were exposed – and the hope that the New Police would reduce the need for military assistance apparently dashed – by the rise of Chartism. The Reform Act 1832 had disappointed those struggling for the extension of political rights. The act was little more than an attempt to prevent a large section of the middle classes from making an alliance with the working classes. The Whigs, who had been seen as the best hope for reform, were denounced for betraying the cause and their support for the New Police merely added salt to the wound.[140] Out of these – and many other – issues arose Chartism. By the late 1830s it seemed to pose a particular threat in Birmingham, Bolton and Manchester where local sympathies and conflicts within the town councils had facilitated its growth. In Birmingham as many as 100,000 were said to have turned out to a Chartist meeting in the summer of 1838 and in the following year the National Convention was relocated there from London. Local magistrates attempted in vain to clamp down on meetings, but lacked the necessary resources because, although Birmingham had become incorporated in 1838, disputes between Tories and Whigs had prevented the establishment of a police force. A large force of Metropolitan Police officers was sent at the request of the mayor, but their appearance sparked a riot which required the intervention of the cavalry.[141]

There were similar problems in Bolton. The old council began a legal challenge to incorporation in 1838 which limited the ability of the new borough authority to raise a police force and meant it had to work alongside the old police in an atmosphere of resentment. A New Police force had been established in Manchester in 1838, but the military leader in the area, Sir Charles Napier, denounced it as inadequate. There were also problems in levying a police tax which made its future uncertain, and the old police had refused to co-operate with the new police and a rival force had been established. In response to the situation in these three places, the government passed emergency legislation in 1839 creating a police force in each town directed by the government. These forces were only turned over to the municipal authorities as Chartism began to wane in 1842 (2 & 3 Vic., c. 87, 88, 95).[142] Elsewhere, the Chartist disturbances led to the reorganization of some borough forces, although often there was a reluctance to increase force size because of the cost involved and the reorganization was restricted to appointing a new chief officer or, as in Newport, obtaining on temporary secondment an officer from the Metropolitan Police.[143]

Criticism of the borough police also came from those on the inside. George Bakewell, who had served as a constable in the Birmingham police during the Chartist period and clearly believed himself a cut above his superior officers, wrote a withering attack on the force: 'It certainly is a frightful reflection, to behold the rapidity with which crime has increased during the last few years notwithstanding the enormous sums which had been paid for the support of the Police'.[144] He claimed that the bulk of the constables and senior officers were either corrupt or in-competent and that good constables were driven out by the mass of petty regulations and the obsession with useless military drill.[145] He was not critical of the principle of a New Police, just its execution in Birmingham. Others, however, leapt to the defence of the borough police. For instance, it was said of the new Liverpool force that its great advantage over the previous arrangements was improved accountability through the watch committee:

> The Police-officers are *now answerable* to the public for their conduct: this was not the case before. If, then, there be any continued want of efficiency in the new Police, *the fault rests entirely with the public:* any well-founded complaints that may now be made are sure to meet with proper attention.[146]

By the 1860s it was not difficult to find general support for the borough police in the local press: in 1862 the *Stockton Gazette and Middlesbrough Times* praised the Middlesbrough police who 'discharge their difficult duties in a highly creditable manner'. But such approval was not un-critical and newspapers were also willing to expose cases of poor conduct, particularly assaults by officers.[147]

The Rural Constabulary Act 1839

When a royal commission was appointed in 1836 to consider extending the New Police to the counties it was the third to look at the issue since 1832.[148] Questionnaires sent out by the commission in 1836 raised some fears that the New Police were about to be forced on reluctant districts and prompted an immediate reaction. For instance, a meeting in Faringdon, Berkshire, declared that 'a police force ... is totally unnecessary'. Others – perhaps forewarned by the London experience – expressed fears about cost and the threat to local control.[149] There were other contentious issues. The game laws, which preserved the exclusive right of the gentry to hunt, had long been a point of conflict in the countryside and there was some resentment at the prospect of landowners shifting the burden of protecting game on to the New Police and, thereby, on to the county's ratepayers, most of whom were prevented by the game laws from hunting.[150] It was also believed that the New Police would be used to force on to a reluctant population the Poor Law (Amendment) Act 1834: 'A Poor-law to drive people mad – a Police-force to keep them in starvation', as one Suffolk grand juror put it.[151] The poor law police forces and the use of police officers as relieving officers showed that the connection was by no means fanciful.[152] Furthermore, even though poor law forces were ruled illegal in 1836, there was concern that the central control model in the Poor Law Act 1834 might be adopted for the county police. Hardly reassuring was the inclusion among the members of the Royal Commission of 1836 of Edwin Chadwick, a well-known supporter of a centralized policing scheme,[153] one of the architects of the 1834 act and Secretary to the Poor Law Commission. One commentator, writing about plans to draw the City of London into the Metropolitan Police, warned that,

> by the New Poor Law the rate-payers and the parishes are deprived, in a great measure, of a due controul and administration of the sums levied for the relief of the poor: by the law respecting the Municipal Police, the rate-payers and parishes of Westminster, and of the suburbs, are also deprived of a proper and wholesome controul over the sums levied for the watch and ward of those districts, and if this law is passed, the same will take place in the City of London; and no doubt shortly all over the kingdom.[154]

Chadwick was principally responsible for writing the Royal Commission's report, which appeared in 1839, although neither his fellow commissioners nor the Home Secretary, Lord John Russell, allowed him to make the sort of proposals he would have liked for a national police under the direction of the Metropolitan Police Commissioners.[155] The report proposed a preventive police for the whole country. It argued: that criminals were migrating from well-policed to poorly-policed areas; that crime was rising faster than even the statistics indicated; that crime arose from the temptation to make easy money not from poverty; that there was a need to establish a police capable of countering industrial action by workers; and that the old police were inefficient.[156] The report recommended: that on a resolution of a quarter sessions such number of constables be appointed as the Metropolitan Police Commissioner (subject to the approval of the Home Secretary) thought sufficient; that a quarter of the costs be met by central government; that the constables be required to report to the magistrates; and that the Commissioner frame the rules for the general management of the force.

The suggestion that government pay for part of the costs was rejected by Russell, not least because there were not the funds to meet such a burden. The government also recognized that a bill would not be carried if it did not give control to the quarter sessions. Nevertheless, Russell seems to have been keen to push ahead with reform, having taken seriously warnings from Sir Charles Napier, the military Commander of the Northern District, about the threat posed by Chartism. At the same time, Russell recognized that Chartism was not regarded as a problem in all counties and that any attempt to impose the New Police might encounter powerful opposition.[157] The Rural Constabulary Act 1839 (2 & 3 Vic., c. 93) was not, therefore, made mandatory. On first glance it appears merely to be 'enlarging' (s. 1) existing powers of the justices of the peace to appoint special constables.[158] This is a deceit. What was being established was a permanent force. Once appointed, the approval of the Home Secretary was required for any increase or reduction in numbers. The Home Secretary made the rules governing the force to ensure uniformity, subject to the county justices applying for amendments (ss. 2 and 3). Unlike the Municipal Corporations Act, there was provision for the appointment of a chief constable (s. 4), and (also unlike the 1835 act under which control was in the hands of the watch committee) while the quarter sessions determined the number of officers, their appointment was left to the chief constable, and he 'at his Pleasure may dismiss all or any of them, and shall have the general Disposition and Government of all the Constables so to be appointed, subject to such lawful Orders as he may receive' from the quarter sessions (ss. 1 and 6).

The 1839 act met with a mixed reception.[159] While rural unrest had diminished since the Swing Riots, it, nevertheless, rumbled on,[160] and in many places exploded again as an expression of resentment at the implementation of the Poor Law (Amendment) Act.[161] Yet opposition to the act was strong. The Reverend Charles Brereton attacked 'this unpatriotic and mischievous measure'.[162] Harking back to 1285, he stridently argued for 'a system of self-government and internal jurisdiction, which the people of this county have always cherished as their inalienable right', at the core of which was the parish constable elected by the parish, not the magistrate appointed by the crown.[163] Although the 1839 act did not place the rural police under central government control, Sir Henry Halford, MP, denounced them as an attack on liberty because they removed 'the interposition of authorities intermediate between the government and the people – of persons and of bodies interested at once to preserve the latter in obedience to the laws, and to protect them from the usurpation of the supreme executive.'[164] Another critic from Suffolk saw a distinction between town and country:

> Policemen, in a town, where perhaps, they may become necessarily tolerated, I look upon with distrust; but a Police, on the contemplated plan, would be so hateful to my feelings as an Englishman, that my blood uplifts every vein at the thought.[165]

There were also objections to control being put in the hands of the quarter sessions. The first was that they were dominated by the larger property owners whose interests were not necessarily in line with the less wealthy householders and farmers, who had a stronger voice in the parish vestry. Secondly, the justices were neither elected by, nor accountable to, the ratepayers.[166] Most rural districts still used unpaid constables, so any permanent force would increase rates. Moreover, it was argued that there was little point in maintaining an expensive, permanent force to meet extraordinary crises, such as the Swing Riots of 1830. If necessary, the military could be called in or special constables appointed under the act of 1835 (5 & 6 Will. IV, c. 43). The other objections came from Chartists who saw the establishment of New Police forces as attempts to suppress reform, and from commissioners appointed under Improvement Acts in towns not incorporated under the 1835 act whose watchmen and powers would vanish if a county force were created.[167]

It is impossible to generalize about the circumstances in which one county established a New Police, while another did not. Decisions often came down to party factionalism or the opinions of influential local figures, and, of course, cost. In Oldham the proposal to adopt the 1839 act was really an attempt to wrest control over the local police from radicals; it failed, but the struggle continued until the town was incorporated as a borough under the 1835 act.[168] In some counties the decision was triggered by a single incident, as in Surrey where a New Police force was established in 1850 following the murder of a clergyman by burglars.[169] In Blofield, Norfolk, enthusiasm for the Rural Constabulary Act 1839 originated in the success of a police force first established by private subscription and later adopted under the Lighting and Watching Act. The 1839 act was seen as a way to reduce the burden to local ratepayers by spreading the cost across the county.[170] Commonly arguments in favour bore some resemblance to those in the report: the migration of criminals, growing crime and so forth. There was no simple connection between rural unrest and the rural police. Essex, which had experienced serious outbreaks of disorder in 1816 and 1830, rapidly established a county force,[171] and other counties dropped their initial reluctance when faced by Chartist disorders; however, others did not.[172]

Once the Chartist crisis passed its peak in 1842 the rate at which new forces were created dropped dramatically.[173] Ratepayers were often active in their opposition to an idea that would increase county spending. The government did apply some pressure on the counties – and, indeed, on boroughs with under-strength forces – by its reluctance to send Metropolitan Police officers or soldiers to places experiencing disorder if they did not have an adequate new police force. This policy was not steadfastly adhered to, but the Home Office could sometimes be resolute, as when it turned down a request from Cardiganshire at the height of the Rebecca Riots in 1843 prompting the county magistrates to establish a rural force.[174]

The establishment of a new county force did not end the debate. Critics accused magistrates who established New Police forces of seeking to extend their patronage, and their tendency to appoint ex-soldiers as chief constables was attacked because, it was claimed, both the chief constables themselves and the military models of organization they adopted were unsuited to the demands of policing. The rural police were condemned for being expensive, inefficient and detached from the communities they served, and ratepayers complained that they rarely saw constables.[175] As in many counties, the enthusiasm of the Essex magistrates for a county force was not necessarily matched by a willingness to spend large amounts of money and this meant that the first chief constable, John McHardy, had to leave parish constables in place.[176] Brereton would have preferred this for he attacked the abandonment a system which had meant that there was 'no place or hamlet without a recognized guardian of the peace, to whom any citizen can at all times, within five minutes, refer. This they have done for a movable rambling police, which no one will ever know where to find.'[177]

The Shropshire County force was criticized by a local newspaper, and, in particular, the Wellington Division under Superintendent William Baxter, who was said to be 'fond of his brandy and pipe', while his officers 'are seen dragging their lazy carcasses about the streets and lanes like so many spies habited in a coarse workhouse livery.'[178] The *Nottingham Journal* complained that the Nottinghamshire force had 'just sufficient number of men … to excite irritation, but by no means a sufficient number to act as a preventive or protective force.'[179]

On the other hand, there were plenty who defended the new police as being more efficient and able to protect all classes of the community alike. The complaint of not seeing the police was rejected on the ground that the method was to target criminals, not guard property. The *Sussex Advertiser* remarked on the new East Sussex police in 1841,

> As the police is now constituted, it is less a direct preventive than a detective force. It is true, after experience proves the improbability of a robbery being effected without detection following, the commission of crime will be checked, but this result cannot be expected yet.[180]

It was also argued that a county force enabled a large body of men to be gathered to quell disorders, which was not possible with a parish-based system.[181] Nevertheless, *The Times* noted in 1842 that 'a strong feeling is gaining ground in different parts of the country, and in most respectable quarters, against the continuance of the rural Police system.'[182] Even a keen supporter candidly acknowledged the problems:

> The system of rural police does not appear to have answered the expectation which was formed as to its utility; it has become unpopular with the ratepayers and also with the magistrates, who in several counties in which it was introduced, proposed to disband the force, on the grounds of its total inefficiency for the purposes for which it was originally established; of its enormous expense, as it considerably increases the present heavy county rates; that it is not sufficiently either a detective or protective force, and because it is a most unconstitutional force.[183]

In places such as Bedfordshire, Northamptonshire, Nottinghamshire, Worcestershire, Norfolk, Lancashire, Isle of Ely, Hertfordshire and East Sussex debates about continuing the county force were conducted fairly soon after they were established.[184] Ratepayers demanded abolition.[185] Thirty Northamptonshire parishes petitioned for abolition on the grounds of expense and inefficiency;[186] in East Sussex, where the police were spread fairly thinly, among other petitions presented, there was one from Portslade ratepayers who complained of having to employ a special constable because of the inefficiency of the New Police;[187] and in Gloucestershire there were complaints that the police rate fell most heavily on farmers whose property it was almost impossible for any number of officers to protect.[188] In Worcestershire the proposal to abolish the force and to use the Parochial Constables Act 1842 instead led to an acrimonious series of debates in the Quarter Sessions in 1842–3.[189] Elsewhere, there were furious debates at any proposal to increase the number of officers,[190] and in Dunstable dissatisfaction with the level of policing provided by the Bedfordshire force led the town to establish its own police in 1865.[191] Nowhere was an existing rural force abolished, although it was a close call in Lancashire in 1842 where the vote fell just short of the two-thirds majority required and it was agreed to reduce the size of the force.[192]

After an initial burst between 1839 and 1841 when the act was adopted for the whole or part of twenty-one counties, the rate slowed to nine more adoptions in the following fifteen years.[193] Yet, to contemporaries the change in policing – in both towns and counties – was dramatic:

> If any individual who had been born and brought up in this country, had been abroad for twenty years, were to return, he would naturally be struck with feelings of astonishment, on finding in almost every district he might visit, the new Police, as if every vestige of English honesty had for ever fled from amongst us[194]

It should be remembered that those who criticized the 1839 act and those counties which did not adopt it often supported some kind of professional police. The Cheshire justices had, for instance, been in the vanguard of innovation in 1829, but declined to adopt the new act because while they favoured reform, they did not like the model put forward. The range of choices open to those who did not wish to adopt the 1839 act opened up even further in the 1840s. Under the Parish Constable Act 1842 (5 & 6 Vic., 109) each county's quarter sessions was required to hold an annual meeting to appoint parish constables. Only those who paid the poor rate and were aged 25 to 55 were eligible for appointment; those appointed were liable to a fine if they refused or failed to provide a suitable substitute. Parishes could decide to have paid constables, whom the justices would appoint and who would be paid from the poor rate. The constable was normally only allowed to operate within the parish to which he had been appointed. If a county force had been established under the 1839 act, he was subject to direction by the chief constable. The right of leet courts to appoint parish constables to undertake functions relating to the preservation of the peace was abolished. Where a lock-up was provided the justices were required to appoint a paid superintending constable who was in charge of both the lock-up and the parish constables. The Superintending Constables Act 1850 (13 Vic., c. 20) allowed the quarter sessions to appoint a superintending constable for any petty sessional division in the county. His function was to direct the constables appointed under the 1842 act as required by the justices. The legislation proved fairly popular and was adopted, partly or wholly, in nine counties.[195]

As with the 1839 act, the power of the justices and the waning importance of the parishes is clear in this alternative system of rural police. Although the parishes retained some influence (they could vote for paid parish constables), most of the key decisions about the adoption of the act, the appointment of constables and so forth were placed in the hands of the justices. One problem was that, in spite of many counties hiring professional policemen to act as superintending constables, the parish constables they commanded were drawn from ratepayers who had shown decreasing enthusiasm for the task: in 1853 the Superintending Constable of Oxfordshire, who had been a member of the Essex County force, asserted that 'half a dozen regular Essex policemen would be equal to the seventy parish constables now under me.'[196]

Concerns about the ability of provincial police forces to contain disorder without relying on the army surfaced again in the 1850s. In 1853 a select committee was appointed with a membership drawn from county members and whose witnesses were mainly county police officers and magistrates supportive of the new police. Almost no evidence was taken from the borough police, and not surprisingly most of the criticism was directed at these forces and counties without police. Captain William Harris, Chief Constable of Hampshire, summed up one theme of the committee's witnesses and its report:[197]

The want of co-operation between boroughs and counties is a great evil; if the forces were consolidated fewer men would be needed. The boroughs are generally the central points from whence criminals issue into the surrounding districts to commit offences, and to which they return with their plunder; the town force having no interest in prevention or detection of offences committed in the county, parties are allowed to pass unquestioned.

The committee also attacked those rural forces established under the Parish Constables Act 1842 and the Superintending Constables Act 1850.

They treated with incredulity the evidence of Andrew Fennick, a land-owner, who seemed fairly content with the efficiency of the twelve 'riding police' appointed under the 1842 act to police rural Northumberland.[198] Sir Robert Sheffield's endorsement of the superintending constable system used in Lincolnshire was trumped by Captain Harris's immediate recall to attack that approach,[199] and the committee clearly preferred the view of William Hamilton, a superintendent at Wendover in Buckinghamshire and a former member of the Essex County force, who said, 'I should prefer four regular paid constables to the 70 parish constables I have got; and certainly eight efficient rural constables would be far preferable to the present force.'[200] Sir William Heathcote, chair of the Hampshire Quarter Sessions, confirmed the committee's opinion of the parish constables and indicated the nature of the shift in the role of the police. When he was asked if they provided an efficient means of regulating beer houses:

> No; they are under the influences of the neighbourhood; it is not fair to call upon them to perform the duty; without there being an actual collusion, they will be slow to interfere with their neighbours[201]

Interestingly, Andrew Fennick agreed that this was a criticism which could be levelled at the parish constable.

The committee proposed that every county be required to establish a force. Just as controversial was the recommendation that small boroughs be merged within their county forces. As a softener the report suggested that the Treasury contribute to the costs of policing. The compulsory merger of the small borough forces proved the sticking point: the boroughs protested against 'this most unjustifiable attack upon the rights and liberties of Municipal Corporations.' The bill based on these proposals was dropped in 1854.[202] However, just two years later the County and Borough Police Act 1856 (19 & 20 Vic. c. 69) made county police forces mandatory.[203] The Home Secretary, Sir George Grey, told the Commons that, while the introduction of a single police for the whole country, 'might theoretically be the best system, [it] would not, I am afraid, meet with much support in the country, from its interfering so largely with the different authorities in counties and boroughs, in whose hands the management of the police is now vested.'[204]

A number of factors increased support for the New Police. The Metropolitan Police had drawn a good deal of approval for its handling of the crowds at the Great Exhibition in 1851 and a demonstration in 1855 against a bill to close shops on Sundays and this contributed to a belief in the ability of the New Police to replace the army in policing civil disorder.[205] Moreover, the army was wearying of this role. Grey was adhering more firmly to the policy of refusing military assistance to those places with inadequate police forces, and affirmed this during the debate on the bill. There were also fears raised by the winding-down of the system of transportation for convicts who, in future, were to be imprisoned. The Penal Servitude Act 1853 provided for early release on a 'ticket-of-leave' to convicts who displayed good behaviour, but this fuelled concerns about the consequences of allowing them to stay in the country which, in turn, led to a crime panic.

Aside from these considerations, the compulsory merging of small borough forces into their counties was withdrawn. But the crucial point was that Treasury funding was promised to all but the smallest forces. The importance of this issue is evident from the debates on the bill. Most of the old objections had vanished. The focus was less on whether this was a good idea and more on how the finance was to be divided between the county and the government.[206] The example of Middlesbrough illustrates some of the financial advantages of the new act. Because of concerns about the size of its force, the watch committee had intended to increase its force from six to nine at a cost of £575, but one of the Inspectors of Constabulary pointed out that nine would not qualify the borough for the grant. However, doubling the force to twelve would and the grant entitlement would mean that this could be achieved at a cost to the borough of only £546.[207]

The act did introduce a government inspection scheme meant to ensure efficiency and uniformity, but there was little inclination among local authorities to concede control over the new police and little desire by the Home Office to intervene. Both sides largely accepted that a force should reflect local needs as interpreted by the ruling *élite* and the chief officer. Even so in 1857 seven of 59 county forces were disqualified from receiving a government grant as inefficient, and as late as 1874 Shropshire magistrates only agreed to an increase in officers under the threat that the grant would be withdrawn.[208] On the other hand, although the Dunstable borough force was criticized by the Inspectors of Constabulary as inefficient, they were powerless to do anything since with a population of 5,000 the town did not qualify for a grant and the borough was determined to maintain its force.[209]

The model of central control in the Metropolitan Police had been rejected. However, that force exercized a strong influence through the common adoption of its regulations, method of working, rank structure and detachment from the community.[210] The appointment of its officers to senior posts was seen as providing the rudiments of a training system: indeed, it was suggested that the Metropolitan Police should 'form a nursery in which to train up policemen'.[211] The Home Office pressed the adoption of uniformity in regulations and methods.[212] Yet, the differences between the county police and the forces in London and other large towns made it impractical for the counties to follow too closely the approach of the latter. Colonel Rowan himself agreed: 'a rural police was rather to prevent crime by detecting offenders than to prevent it by their actual presence in every village'.[213]

Although the Municipal Corporations Act 1835 and the County and Borough Police Act 1856 put the police into the hands of local authorities, this did not end concerns about centralization. These resurfaced in the wake of the nationalization of the local prisons in 1877.[214] The great feminist campaigner, Josephine Butler, believed that centralization of the police was already well advanced by the 1870s as a result of the Home Office's practice of issuing orders to police forces without going through Parliamant. She also argued that the shift of responsibility for performing policing duties from the community to the police had had a detrimental effect: 'inventiveness, self-protection, and manly self-dependence are being gradually driven out of the people by the delegation of the simplest and most primitive duties of citizens to the agents of the Government.'[215] In her view 'police rule … has so established itself as to become a standing menace to liberty, and an embarrassment and even a rival to the Governments which aim at its reform, or at the restriction of its functions.'[216]

There had also been a gradual obliteration of the distinctions between the police and the military: new uniforms, helmets, attempts to arm the police, the Commissioner riding at the head of the mounted police in Hyde Park and the drilling of constables. 'We have in fact a standing army of ten thousand well drilled soldiers, entirely independent of any annual vote of Parliament, not subject to the Mutiny Act, but practically in the pay, and under the control of the Home Secretary.'[217]

The Home Office's level of involvement in policing did increase as its knowledge and expertise improved. It was not just in relation to the Metropolitan Police that the Home Office made its influence felt although, typically, it had no need or wish to use its statutory powers. The controls which Home Secretaries had over the deployment of Metropolitan Police officers or troops in aid of police forces were just some of the tools of influence that could be used to put pressure on county benches and borough watch committees. There was also the threat of the withdrawal of Treasury funding which was rarely made, but ever present. However, perhaps its greatest influence derived from its role in advising police forces on a range of issues and disseminating what it decided was good practice, such as, the instructions issued to constables, the best method of recording footprints, the use of finger-prints for identifying habitual offenders, the use of photographs, the design of police stations, arrangements for mutual aid (that is, the lending of officers between forces).[218] Frequently, such circulars would emerge from discussions held by the Home Office with chief constables.

Quasi-public police

Quasi-public police forces, such as those employed in some dockyards, continued to operate and new ones were created. In 1840 the Canals (Offences) Act enabled canal companies to appoint police officers. Around 1825 the Stockton & Darlington Railway established its Police Department and others followed suit. The main tasks of such forces were the protection of the railway, removal of obstructions from the line and signalling.[219] The problems of jurisdiction where a railway crossed the boundaries of several different police forces were resolved in the case of the London & Birmingham Railway by the company being empowered to appoint special constables in 1833. By 1839 this company had a super-intendent (an ex-Metropolitan Police officer), ten inspectors and 90 constables who were also sworn in as county constables to extend their jurisdiction. In 1838, partly as a result of disturbances caused by railway construction workers, railway companies were required to employ special constables. This provision was criticized by the Royal Com-mission in 1839 as an abrogation of the principle that the police were maintained to protect the whole public and, indeed, criticisms were made that railway police concealed accidents and protected the company rather than its passengers.

Popular reactions to the New Police

Aside from the disputes among the politicians, ratepayers and magistrates, the decision to establish a New Police force sometimes proved difficult to implement against the wishes of local people who saw them as enemies of working-class interests and agents of unpopular government policies, such as the Poor Law (Amendment) Act. When the police were first established in Colne in April 1840 and sought to impose themselves on the town by a strategy of confrontation, they were rapidly driven out. They came back in increased numbers and with the support of the Burnley police and the army, but once the outside assistance had left and the Colne police numbers were reduced, they were again driven out.

This to-and-fro continued until Sir Charles Napier stationed a permanent military presence in the town.

The persistence of the anti-police riots at Colne was unusual, but crowds also rose up against the new police in Middleton, Lancashire in 1840, Ashton-under-Lyne in 1841 and elsewhere. Reliance on military support to impose the New Police could backfire because soldiers sometimes proved to be at the root of anti-police rioting, as was the case in Manchester in 1843 after an attempt had been made to arrest a soldier. The New Police were also an accessible target (in the same way as the workhouse) for the expression of resentment against despised social policies. To many Chartists, for instance, the police were seen as defending a corrupt political system which, in spite of its lack of legitimacy or, rather, because of it, was seeking to repress demands for reform. The Plug Riots of 1842 – when a Staffordshire miners' strike spread into Lancashire, Cheshire, Yorkshire and Wales – linked demands for Chartist reforms to the problems of acute poverty caused by an economic depression, and rioters attacked symbolic targets of repression: workhouses, factories, mines and the new police.[220]

The New Police were, rightly or wrongly, seen by some as an invading force sent by government to impose a moral code which would destroy the recreations, lifestyles and working practices of working people: closing down fairs and markets, preventing cockfights, tightening controls over drinking. This impression seemed to be confirmed by the policy of separating the police from the community, the militarization and the bullying behaviour of some officers and constables.[221]

* * *

The Metropolitan Police Act 1829 did not establish the first New Police force – it came fifteen years after establishment of the Peace Preservation Police in Ireland and seven years after the Irish Constabulary. Nor was it the only viable model of professional policing on offer during the early nineteenth century: there were strands of professional police forces controlled and paid for by private subscribers and businesses, by the parish, by the county and by a combination of these. Many of these forces survived. Businesses continued to employ watchmen and the police forces of the dock, canal and railway companies flourished. While the methods and philosophy of the Metropolitan Police became widely adopted and its officers became eagerly sought after for putting down riots, detecting offenders and heading up police forces, the idea of placing the police in the hands of the Home Secretary was not taken up.

The shape which the police took emerged not in 1856 – as the debates on County and Borough Police Act show, the battle was largely over – but between about 1815 and the early 1850s. The key controversy was over the form of police governance – that is, whether it was to be placed under parish, county or central control – and was part of a broader political debate. The dependence of central government on the justices as administrators and on the rural gentry in Parliament meant that this constituency could not be sidelined. Edwin Chadwick and, perhaps, Sir George Grey may have preferred a single police system, but the nature of British politics meant that this was never likely to be feasible. The main constitutional sufferer was the parish. The legislation of 1835, 1839 and 1856, and even the Parish Constables Act 1842 and Superintending Constables Act 1850, shifted power from the parishes.

However, the shift in opinion which enabled the reforms began in the late eighteenth century – the key moments being the Gordon Riots in 1780 and, for the rural gentry, the Swing Riots in 1830, although the feeling that there was a pervasive climate of disorder among the labouring classes was, perhaps, more important. Towns like London and the rapidly growing cities of the industrial north represented a new and vibrant engine of wealth, but they seemed out of control. That impression appeared to be confirmed by increasing crime and radicalism, both of which seemed also to be spreading into the countryside.

It was not that disorder was new – riot had, after all, long been one of the ways in which political debate was conducted – rather it was that there was a growing lack of tolerance among the ruling classes born of a sense that the old structures of authority, which depended on paternalism and deference, had at last broken down. The ruling classes realized that the connection, which they always assumed (rightly or wrongly) existed between themselves and the labouring classes, had no foundation. The reaction of some was to seek to shore up it, while others assumed that the problem lay in the moral degeneration of the labouring classes and that liberty and property could only be protected from the consequences of this moral decline by intervention from local and central government. At the same time, property owners were not always keen to spend money on reform; this obstructed the creation of new police forces and often meant that cheaper alternatives were set up or new county and borough forces were under-resourced.

Notes

1   Anon (1797) *Regulations of Parochial Police*; Rudé (1964) *The Crowd in History*; Thompson (1968) *The Making of the English Working Class*.

2   Archer (1990) *By a Flash and a Scare*; Booth (1977) 'Food riots in North-West England, 1790–1801'; Booth (1980) 'Popular loyalism and public violence'; Hall (1989) 'Tyranny, work and politics'; Jones (1989) *Rebecca's Children*; Thompson (1968) *The Making of the English Working Class*; Wells (1988) *Wretched Faces*.

3   Evans (1983) *The Forging of the Modern State*, 146.

4   Hobsbawm and Rudé (1973) *Captain Swing*.

5   Eagles (1832) *The Bristol Riots*.

6   Rawlings (1999) *Crime and Power*, 37–8.

7   Rawlings (1999) *Crime and Power*, 39.

8   Gatrell and Hadden (1972) 'Nineteenth-century criminal statistics and their interpretation'.

9   Colquhoun (1797) *A Treatise on the Police*; Radzinowicz (1948–68) *A History of English Criminal Law*, vol IV, 91–112.

10 Paley (1833) *The Works of William Paley*, 161, 165.

11 Rawlings (1999) *Crime and Power*, 43–53.

12 Madan (1785) *Thoughts of Executive Justice*, 133–4.

13 Merewether (1816) *A New System of Police*, 7.

14 Allen (1821) *Brief Considerations on the Present State of the Police*.

15 Reynolds (1998) *Before the Bobbies*, 96–8.

16 Mainwaring (1821) *Observations on the Present State of the Police*, 47.

17 Wade (1829) *A Treatise on the Police*, 78. Also Freeland (1839) *State of the Police*, 7.

18 Reynolds (1998) *Before the Bobbies*, 121.

19 Select Committee on the Police (1822) *Report*, 9. Also Select Committee (1818) *Third Report*, 32–3.

20 Colquhoun (1797) *A Treatise on the Police*. Also Select Committee (1799) *The Report*.

21 Anon (1797) *Regulations of Parochial Police*, 34n.

22 Reynolds (1998) *Before the Bobbies*, 114; Wade (1829) *A Treatise on the Police*, 68–9.

23 Reynolds (1998) *Before the Bobbies*, 116–23.

24 Rudé (1964) *The Crowd in History*; Rudé (1974) *Paris and London in the Eighteenth Century*; Thompson (1993) *Customs in Common*.

25 Castro (1926) *The Gordon Riots*; Hayter (1978) *The Army and the Crowd*; Hibbert (1958) *King Mob*; Linebaugh (1991) *The London Hanged*, 333–60.

26 Rawlings (1999) *Crime and Power*, 36.

27 Palmer (1988) *Police and Protest in England*, 160–2.

28 Cookson (1989) 'The English Volunteer movement'; Eagles (1832) *The Bristol Riots*; Palmer (1988) *Police and Protest in England*, 172–8, 185–90; Reynolds (1998) *Before the Bobbies*, 86–9; Stevenson (1977) 'The Queen Caroline affair'; Vogler (1991) *Reading the Riot Act*; Western (1956) 'The Volunteer movement as an anti-revolutionary force'.

29 Anon (1816) *The Whole Trials of the Thief Takers*.

30 Merewether (1816) *A New System of Police*, 6–7.

31 Avery (1988) 'Patrick Colquhoun'.

32   *The Times*, Sep–Oct 1800. The book was Colquhoun (1800) *A Treatise on the Commerce and Police of the River Thames*.

33   Colquhoun (1797) *A Treatise on the Police*.

34   Linebaugh (1991) *The London Hanged*, 426–35.

35   Gatrell (1994) *The Hanging Tree*.

36   Palmer (1988) *Police and Protest in England*.

37   Select Committee (1822) *Report*.

38   Reynolds, *Before the Bobbies*, 127.

39   Select Committee (1828) *Report*.

40   Emsley (1983) *Policing and its Context*, 61.

41   See also *Parliamentary Debates*, 15 Apr 1829, c 867–84; Select Committee (1828) *Report*.

42   Wade (1829) *A Treatise on the Police*, 97.

43   Chadwick (1829) 'Preventive police', 252.

44   *Parliamentary Debates*, 19 May 1829, c 1488, 1753.

45   *The Times*, 21 Jan 1829; Wade (1829) *A Treatise on the Police*, 72n.

46   Wade (1829) *A Treatise on the Police*, 95–6.

47   Generally Palmer (1988) *Police and Protest in England*, 193–217, 286–94; Reynolds (1998) *Before the Bobbies*, 125–47.

48   Gatrell (1990) 'Crime, authority and the policeman-state'.

49   Wade (1829) *A Treatise on the Police*, 97.

50   Palmer (1988) *Police and Protest in England*, 293. See the views of Peel in Critchley (1978) *A History of Police*, 54. Also Merewether (1816) *A New System of Police*, 5.

51   Reynolds (1998) *Before the Bobbies*, 125, 135–9; Select Committee (1828) *Report*.

52   *Parliamentary Debates*, 22 Nov 1830, c 626–7; 16 Dec 1830, c 1206–8.

53   Reynolds (1998) *Before the Bobbies*, 145.

54   Reynolds (1998) *Before the Bobbies*, 125–47; Wade (1829) *A Treatise on the Police*.

55   Reynolds (1998) *Before the Bobbies*, 137–8.

56   *The Times*, 6 Oct 1829.

57   Reynolds (1998) *Before the Bobbies*, 148–9.

58   *The Times*, 11 Aug 1829.

59   *The Times*, 25 Sep 1829.

60   *The Times*, 11 Aug 1829.

61   For example *The Times*, 3 Oct 1821, 1 Nov, 2 Nov, 3 Nov, 5 Nov, 7 Nov, 8 Nov, 9 Nov 1821.

62   *The Times*, 2 Jan 1829; also 30 Jul 1828, 3 Jan, 13 Jan 1829.

63   Palmer (1988) *Police and Protest in England*, 304.

64   Traill (1839) *A Letter to the Right Hon. Lord Brougham*, 4, 5.

65   *The Times*, 3 Oct 1829.

66   *The Times*, 2 Sep 1833.

67   Fitzgerald (1888) *Chronicles of Bow Street Police-Office*, vol II, 377.

68   *The Times*, 29 Jul 1830. For the reactions of Kent magistrates to local new police forces, see Conley (1991) *The Unwritten Law* 33–4.

69   *The Times*, 11 Nov 1830.

70   See Harris (1858) *A Manual of Drill*.

71   Ignatieff (1979), 'Police and People: the birth of Mr Peel's "Blue Locusts" ', 443.

72   Hypochondriac (1830) *The Blue Devils*, 16.

73   Philips (1980) 'A new engine of authority', 155.

74   Adams (1838) *A Letter to Benjamin Hawes*, 19–20.

75   *The Times*, 12 Oct 1830.

76   Fidget (1838) *A Letter to the Lord Mayor*, 7.

77   Anon (1839b) *Police and Piety*, 10.

78   Cruikshank (1833) *Cruikshank v. The New Police*; Herring (1855) *An Exposition of the Conduct of Police-Serjeant Sterr*; Smethurst (1841) *Conspiracy*; *The Times*, 4 Dec, 31 Dec 1834.

79   *Punch*, 1842, in Pulling (1964) *Mr Punch and the Police*, 40.

80   *The Times*, 15 Jul, 18 Jul, 20 Jul, 23 Jul 1833; Cruikshank (1833) *Cruikshank v. The New Police*.

81   Select Committee (1834) *Report*; Thurston (1967) *The Clerkenwell Riot*.

82   *The Times*, 2 Oct, 9 Oct, 15 Oct 1830; Palmer (1988) *Police and Protest in England*, 304.

83   Reynolds (1998) *Before the Bobbies*, 156–8, 161; Select Committee (1834) *Report*.

84   *Parliamentary Debates*, 7 Dec 1830, c 808–9.

85   Letter from 'Civis', *The Times*, 7 Oct 1830.

86   *The Times*, 2 Oct 1830.

87   *The Times*, 11 Sep 1830. Also letter from 'Civis', *The Times*, 7 Oct 1830. Also *The Times*, 12 Oct 1830, 10 Oct 1833.

88   See, for instance, the petitions from St. Clement Danes, St. George's in the East, St. George-the-Martyr, Southwark, St. John's Horslydown, Mile End Old Town, St. John's, Wapping, St. James, Clerkenwell, St. Leonard's, Shoreditch, St. Luke, Middlesex, St. Pancras: *The Times*, 6 Oct, 7 Oct, 15 Oct, 20 Oct, 21 Oct 1830.

89   *The Times*, 11 Sep, 2 Oct, 15 Oct, 26 Oct 1830.

90   *The Times*, 23 Sep 1830.

91   *Parliamentary Debates*, 13 Dec 1830, c 1046.

92   *The Times*, 22 Oct 1830. See also *The Times*, 12 Nov 1830.

93   *The Times*, 19 Aug. 1830. For other complaints about lazy constables see *The Times*, 19 Aug, 20 Aug, 16 Oct 1830. Thackeray published verses on the romantic experiences of policemen in the kitchens on their beats as 'Loves of the New Police' in *Punch* in 1847; and the joke continued well beyond its sell-by-date into the 1930s: Pulling (1964) *Mr Punch and the Police*, 45, 200.

94   *The Times*, 11 Nov, 12 Nov 1830.

95   *Parliamentary Debates*, 18 Nov, 30 Nov, 7 Dec 1830, c 575–582, 705–6, 807–9.

96   Palmer (1988) *Police and Protest in England*, 307.

97   *The Times*, 10 Oct 1833, 27 Nov 1833.

98   Palmer (1988) *Police and Protest in England*, 308.

99   Anon (1834a) *The Metropolitan Police*.

100 Reynolds (1998) *Before the Bobbies*, 162; Select Committee (1834) *Report*.
101 Committee of the Marylebone Vestry (1843) *Report*.
102 Freeland (1839) *State of the Police*, 6–7.
103 King (2000) *Crime, Justice, and Discretion*, 70.
104 A substitute took on the duties of the constable, while an assistant helped the person appointed as constable.
105 Freeland (1839) *State of the Police*, 7.
106 Herbert (1971) *Shoemaker's Window*, 100. See King (2000) *Crime, Justice, and Discretion*, 70–3.
107 King (2000) *Crime, Justice, and Discretion*, 76–80.
108 Philips and Storch (1999) *Policing Provincial England*, 11–34.
109 Hay (1977) *Albion's Fatal Tree*; Thompson (1977) *Whigs and Hunters*.
110 Archer (1990) *By a Flash and a Scare*; Dunkley (1982) *The Crisis of the Old Poor Law*; Edsall (1971) *The Anti-Poor Law Movement*; Hobsbawm and Rudé (1971) *Captain Swing*; Wells (1990) 'Social protest, class conflict and consciousness'.
111 Harding, Hines, Ireland and Rawlings (1985) *Imprisonment in England and Wales*.
112 Philips and Storch (1999) *Policing Provincial England*, 46; also 36–57.
113 Chadwick (1829) 'Preventive police'; Miles (1836) *Suggestions for the Formation of a General Police*.
114 *Parliamentary Debates*, 13 Apr. 1829, c 741.
115 Phillips and Storch (1994) 'Whigs and coppers'.
116 Wade (1829) *A Treatise on the Police*, 6–7.
117 For example, Peel in *Parliamentary Debates*, 13 Apr 1829, c 741.
118 Landau (1984) *The Justices of the Peace*.
119 Philips and Storch (1999) *Policing Provincial England*, 237–44.
120 James (1957) *To the Best of Our Skill and Knowledge*; Philips and Storch (1999) *Policing Provincial England*, 85–92, 103–10.
121 Prest (1990) *Liberty and Locality*, 5–6.
122 Davey (1983) *Lawless and Immoral*; Philips and Storch (1999) *Policing Provincial England*, 94–7. The 1833 act repealed a similar act, 11 Geo. IV, c. 27 (1830).
123 Freeland (1839) *State of the Police*.
124 Philips and Storch (1999) *Policing Provincial England*, 101–3; Storch (1989) 'Policing in rural Southern England', 233–6.
125 See chapter 4.
126 Reilly (1989) *Policing Birmingham*, 4.
127 Philips (1989) 'Good men to associate and bad men to conspire'; Storch (1989) 'Policing in rural Southern England'.
128 Taylor (1995) *'A Well-Chosen, Effective Body of Men'*, 6.
129 Philips (1989) 'Good men to associate and bad men to conspire'; Philips and Storch (1999) *Policing Provincial England*, 97–101; Storch (1989) 'Policing in rural Southern England'.
130 Hart (1955) 'Reform of the borough police'; Palmer (1988) *Police and Protest in England*, 397–402.
131 Reilly (1989) *Policing Birmingham*, 4–5.

132 Emsley (1983) *Policing and its Context*, 67–8.

133 Bale (1960) *Through Seven Reigns*, 25; Elliott (1984) *Policing Shropshire*; Fairhurst (1996) *Policing Wigan*.

134 For example in Manchester: Hewitt (1979) *A History of Policing in Manchester*, 47–50.

135 Jones (1982) *Crime, Protest, Community and Police*, 174.

136 Bakewell (1842) *Observations on the Construction of the New Police Force*, 34.

137 Neal (1849) *The Chief Constable's Report*.

138 Elliott (1984) *Policing Shropshire*, 4, 23.

139 Elliott (1984) *Policing Shropshire*, 23.

140 Anon (1839b) *Police and Piety*.

141 Birmingham (1840) *Report*.

142 Bakewell (1842) *Observations on the Construction of the New Police Force*; Hart (1955) 'Reform of the borough police'; Joyce (1993) 'The transition from "old" to "new" policing'; Mather (1959) *Public Order in the Age of the Chartists*; Palmer (1988) *Police and Protest in England*, 396–402, 415–20, 440; Sleigh (1844) *A General Police and Constabulary List*; Swift (1988) 'Urban policing in early Victorian England'.

143 Bale (1960) *Through Seven Reigns*, 41–3.

144 Bakewell (1842) *Observations on the Construction of the New Police Force*, 33.

145 Bakewell (1842) *Observations on the Construction of the New Police Force*, 7.

146 Observer (1836) *The Publicans and the Police*, 14–15.

147 Taylor (1995) *'A Well-Chosen, Effective Body of Men'*, 36.

148 The others were the Royal Commission on the Poor Laws and the Royal Commission on the County Rates. See Royal Commission (1839) *First Report*; Anon (1839a) *On the Establishment of a Rural Police*; Brundage (1986) 'Ministers, magistrates and reformers'; Emsley (1996) *The English Police*; Foote (1843) *Suggestions for the Improvement of Portions of the Criminal Law*; Foster (1982) *The Rural Constabulary Act 1839*; Hart (1955) 'Reform of the borough police'; Philips and Storch (1999) *Policing Provincial England*, 111–35.

149 *The Times*, 4 Nov, 28 Nov 1836; Elliott (1984) *Policing Shropshire*, 15–16.

150 Juror (1838) *A Series of Letters, on Rural Police*.

151 Juror (1838) *A Series of Letters, on Rural Police*, 17; *The Times*, 16 Nov 1836.

152 Woodgate (1985) *The Essex Police*, 18.

153 Chadwick (1829) 'Preventive police'.

154 Fidget (1838) *A Letter to the Lord Mayor*, 3–4.

155 Philips and Storch (1999) *Policing Provincial England*, 111–35.

156 Royal Commission (1839) *First Report*.

157 Halford (1840) *Some Remarks on the Report of the Constabulary Force Commissioners*; Palmer (1988) *Police and Protest in England*, 420–7.

158 See 1 & 2 Will. IV, c. 41; 5 & 6 Will. IV, c. 43.

159 Philips and Storch (1999) *Policing Provincial England*, 136–208.

160 *The Times*, 4 Nov 1833; Archer (1990) *By a Flash and a Scare*.

161 Edsall (1971) *The Anti-Poor Law Movement*.

162 Brereton (1839) *A Letter to the Lord Lieutenant*, 67.

163 Brereton (1839) *A Letter to the Lord Lieutenant*, 65. Also Anon (1839a) *On the*

Establishment of a Rural Police, 111.

164 Halford (1840) *Some Remarks on the Report of the Constabulary Force Commissioners*, 57.

165 Juror (1838) *A Series of Letters, on Rural Police*, 6.

166 Brereton (1849) *A Letter to the Lord Lieutenant*; Halford (1840) *Some Remarks on the Report of the Constabulary Force Commissioners*.

167 Waller (1957) *Cuffs and Handcuffs*, 21–2.

168 Foster (1974) *Class Struggle and the Industrial Revolution*.

169 The murder was committed in Hampshire, which had a county force, by burglars from Surrey: Emsley (1996) *The English Police*, 44; Prest (1990) *Liberty and Locality*, 42.

170 Brereton (1839) *A Letter to the Lord Lieutenant*.

171 Woodgate (1985) *The Essex Police*, 4–8.

172 Taylor (1997) *The New Police in Nineteenth-Century England*, 29.

173 Palmer (1988) *Police and Protest in England*, 442–4.

174 Mather (1959) *Public Order in the Age of the Chartists*, 132–3; Radzinowicz (1948–68) *A History of English Criminal Law*, vol IV, 280–3.

175 Foote (1843) *Suggestions for the Improvement of Portions of the Criminal Law*; Halford (1840) *Some Remarks on the Report of the Constabulary Force Commissioners*.

176 Woodgate (1985) *The Essex Police*, 18–19.

177 Brereton (1839) *A Letter to the Lord Lieutenant*, 9

178 Elliott (1984) *Policing Shropshire*, 29–30.

179 Emsley (1983) *Policing and its Context*, 74.

180 Kyrke (1969) *History of East Sussex*, 25.

181 Anon (1841) *Rural Police*.

182 Woodgate (1985) *The Essex Police*, 8.

183 Foote (1843) *Suggestions for the Improvement of Portions of the Criminal Law*, 39.

184 Foote (1843) *Suggestions for the Improvement of Portions of the Criminal Law*, 42.

185 Emsley (1982) 'The Bedfordshire Police, 1840–1856'; Palmer (1988) *Police and Protest in England*, 737; Richter (1990) *Bedfordshire Police 1840–1990*, 21–4.

186 Cowley (1986) *Policing Northamptonshire 1836–1986*, 25.

187 Kyrke (1969) *History of East Sussex*, 24.

188 Thomas (1987) *The History of the Gloucestershire Constabulary*, 6.

189 Smith (1990) 'The establishment and development of the Worcestershire County Constabulary', 19–21.

190 Philips and Storch (1999) *Policing Provincial England*, 220–1.

191 Richter (1990) *Bedfordshire Police 1840–1990*, 36–7.

192 Emsley (1982) 'The Bedfordshire Police, 1840–1856'; Emsley (1996) *The English Police*, 44–6.

193 Philips and Storch (1999) *Policing Provincial England*, 157–63; Sleigh (1844) *A General Police and Constabulary List*.

194 Bakewell (1842) *Observations on the Construction of the New Police Force*, 3.

195 Philips and Storch (1999) *Policing Provincial England*, 213–19.

196 Woodgate (1985) *The Essex Police*, 8. Also, Philips and Storch (1999) *Policing Provincial England*, 215–18.

197 Select Committee (1852–3) *First Report*, 4. See also Conley (1991) *The Unwritten Law*, 29.

198 Select Committee (1852–3) *First Report*, 34–5.

199 Select Committee (1852–3) *First Report*, 37, 45–6.

200 Select Committee (1852–3) *First Report*, 71. Is it simply a coincidence that Hamilton and Harris both mention the figure of seventy parish constables? One does not need to imagine the existence of covert collusion when the report and the conduct of the Commission's hearings provides adequate evidence that it was a reality.

201 Select Committee (1852–3) *First Report*, 19.

202 Palmer (1988) *Police and Protest in England*, 503–7.

203 Brogden (1982) *The Police: Autonomy and Consent*, Emsley (1996) *The English Police*, 48–54; Hart (1955) 'Reform of the borough police'; Hart (1956) 'The County and Borough Police Act, 1856'; Palmer (1988) *Police and Protest in England*, 507–16.

204 *Parliamentary Debates*, 5 Feb 1856, c 230.

205 Harrison (1965) 'The Sunday Trading riots'; see chapter 6.

206 For example, *Parliamentary Debates*, 5 Feb 1856, c 238 (Pakington), c 240 (Hamilton-Nisbet), c 241 (Deedes), c 242 (Palmer), c 243–4 (Stracey).

207 Taylor (1995) *'A Well-Chosen, Effective Body of Men'*, 8–9.

208 Elliott (1984) *Policing Shropshire*, 90.

209 Richter (1990) *Bedfordshire Police 1840–1990*, 36–7.

210 For example, see the instructions to various forces in Anon (1834b) *Instructions for the Police Establishments of His Majesty's Dock Yards*; McHardy (1840) *Essex Constabulary*; Worcester City Police (1861) *City of Worcester*, 3–4.

211 Foote (1843) *Suggestions for the Improvement of Portions of the Criminal Law*, 44. Also Miles (1836) *Suggestions for the Formation of a General Police*. But see the rather different view of the Metropolitan Police in Bakewell (1842) *Observations on the Construction of the New Police Force*.

212 See Home Office Circular A. 54368, 1839 in Home Office (1907) *Home Office Circulars*, 3–4.

213 Emsley (1996) *The English Police*, 43; Steedman (1984) *Policing the Victorian Community*, 6, 31–2, 146–7.

214 Harding, Hines, Ireland, Rawlings (1985) *Imprisonment*.

215 Butler (1879) *Government by Police*, 8.

216 Butler (1879) *Government by Police*, 5.

217 Butler (1879) *Government by Police*, 37. See also Scott (1867) *A Statistical Vindication of the City of London*.

218 Circular A. 54368 of 1839, memorandum, October 1892, Circular A. 63109/16 of 1903, Circular A. 54423/37 of 1905, Circular A. 54032 of 1893, Circular A. 52632 B/18 of 1894 in Home Office (1907) *Home Office Circulars*. These circulars were issued after discussions with chief officers.

219 Appleby (1995) *A Force on the Move*.

220 Palmer (1988) *Police and Protest in England*, 445–7, 455–64; Taylor (1997) *The New Police in Nineteenth-Century England*, 108–11.

221 See chapter 6.

Chapter 6

'In the midst of hordes of starving plunderers': 1850–1939

The terrors of a blue-coat's eye

In 1852 a commentator in *The Edinburgh Review* wrote of the changes in criminal justice over the preceding thirty years and, in particular, the introduction of the Metropolitan Police:

> In London … the arrangements are so good, the security so general, and the complex machinery works so quietly, that the real danger which must always exist where the wealth and luxury of a nation are brought into juxtaposition with its poverty and crime, is too much forgotten; and people begin to think it quite a matter of course, or one of the ordinary operations of Providence, that they sleep and wake in safety in the midst of hordes of starving plunderers.[1]

In the wake of the Reform Bill Riots of 1866, *The Times* commented, 'the quiet and business-like manner in which, at critical moments, the duties of the Force have been discharged, has been frequently noticed by foreigners with surprise and admiration'.[2] The police were praised for their handling of public order, for an apparent fall in crime and for an improvement in 'public tranquillity and decency'.[3] Those who complained seemed concerned about the level of expenditure or the number of officers on the streets, not the issue of whether they should be there at all: the *East London Observer* talked of 'the popular joke about the invisibility of a policeman is a dull and sober reality.'[4] By the early twentieth century, they had become 'the nurse of national morality' and the defence against an invasion of 'vice and crime',[5] while the 'romance of Scotland Yard' involved nothing less than 'the building up, in the face of incredible obstacles, of a vast, ingenious machine which has become one of the greatest instruments of civilisation the world has ever seen'.[6]

The police were claimed to be egalitarian in their methods: 'the police exist to protect the lives and rights of the poor quite as much as the property of the rich'.[7] James Monro, a former commissioner, claimed in 1890, 'The police … are not the representatives of an arbitrary and despotic power, directed against the rights or obtrusively interfering with the pleasures of law-abiding citizens'.[8] Similarly, calling the police 'constables' and so drawing on the ancient tradition of officers who were drawn from the people enabled the Royal Commission on Police Powers in 1929 to claim that the police were merely 'citizens in uniform':

> The Police of this country have never been recognised, either in law or by tradition, as a force distinct from the general body of citizens. Despite the imposition of many extraneous duties on the Police by legislation and administrative action, the principle remains that a Policeman, in the view of the common law, is only 'a person paid to perform, as a matter of duty, acts which if he were so minded he might have done voluntarily.' Indeed, a Policeman possesses few powers not enjoyed by the ordinary citizen, and public opinion, expressed in Parliament and elsewhere, has shown great jealousy of any attempts to give increased authority to the Police. This attitude is due, we believe, not to any distrust of the Police as a body, but to an instinctive feeling that, as a matter of principle, they should have as few powers as possible which are not possessed by the ordinary citizen, and that their authority should rest on the broad basis of the consent and active co-operation of all law-abiding people.[9]

It seemed obvious that since the police were vastly outnumbered by the population, then, to be able to do their work they needed the consent of the people and, because they were doing their work, they must have that consent:

> Weak in numbers as the force is, it would be found in practice altogether inadequate were it not strengthened, to an extent unknown, I believe, elsewhere, by the relations which exist between the police and the public, and by the thorough recognition on the part of the citizens at large of the police as their friends and protectors.[10]

Yet, these truths were not so self-evident to those with direct experience of being policed. The new police had been built on the assumption that crime was committed by the poor, not the rich, and that, therefore, to prevent crime they should concentrate their efforts in those communities. As Colonel Rowan famously put it, 'we look upon it that we are watching St. James's and other places while we are watching St. Giles and bad places in general'.[11] The relationship with the rich was slight and deferential: McHardy, Chief Constable of Essex, told his men to walk on the outside of pavement and 'not shoulder past respectable people, but give way in a mild manner. The *more* respectful and civil the constabulary are, the more they will be supported and respected by the public in the proper execution of their duty.'[12] The experience in the working-class districts on which the police focused was somewhat different.

At its root preventive policing reacted against the implications of 'blood money' (and the detective strategy of Fielding). It was assumed that arresting people for petty offences would stop them from embarking on the inevitable degeneration from misdemeanours and immorality to felonies. In practice this became a street-sweeping strategy in which the police established the authority of the uniform on the streets. In the first weekend of operation of the Metropolitan Police an 'unprecedented number of 46 night charges' was brought at Bow Street, largely as a result of 'the active exertions of the new police, who were busily engaged on Sunday in clearing the streets of drunken and disorderly persons'.[13] This high level of arrest for petty public order offences was an important demonstration of the distinction between the new and the old police which chief officers were keen to emphasize. The Chief Constable of West Suffolk criticized those officers who had 'detected no offenses, in short done nothing ... Persons who can thus pass day after day ... in this unobserving way, are totally unfit for the situation, and may ... very shortly expect their services will be dispensed with without further notice.'[14] Prevention was measured in arrests for incivility offences and those who had been once arrested became easy targets.

This proactive approach to policing engendered an enthusiasm in Parliament and local government – often urged on by temperance or moral purity groups[15] – to create more summary offences attacking not just those working-class activities assumed to lie at the root of crime and poverty, such as drinking and gambling, but also new areas, such as cruelty to children, street selling, street sports and truancy. Some reached apparently absurd levels. It was an offence to drop orange peel on the pavement in Middlesbrough or to shake rugs in the street, other than at particular times, in Huddersfield and Hull.[16] The obsession with orange peel was not confined to the north-east: instructions to Birmingham police officers in 1878 placed the obligation 'to remove all orange peel from the footpath' above the duty to report sudden deaths.[17]

To say that many of these laws were aimed at working-class people is uncontroversial since this was their purpose:[18] the behaviour of the rich might be regarded as scandalous, rarely as criminal. This was carried through into enforcement policies: one chief officer, instructing his men on the enforcement of the Poaching Prevention Act 1862, told them 'not to interfere with anybody whom they knew to be a respectable man'.[19] The borough officer was, therefore, mainly concerned with petty offences committed in the streets – drunkenness, assaults, Sunday leisure activities, kite-flying, street gambling and offences against local bye-laws.[20] In Middlesbrough between the late 1850s and the late 1880s indictable offences never accounted for more than 5 per cent of the total, whereas drunkenness and assaults combined amounted to between 39 per cent and 49 per cent and breaches of the bye-laws between 13 per cent and 24 per cent. In the first decade of the twentieth century, drunkenness alone accounted for 65 per cent of all street offences with gaming at 8 per cent and assaults on the police at 5 per cent.[21] Similarly, the rural constable was almost entirely concerned with offences such as poaching, drunkenness and petty thefts including stealing apples, and with the regulation of alehouses.[22]

The police constable may not have given much thought to the moral values these laws represented, and the high number of early Victorian police officers disciplined for drunkenness suggests they did not necessarily subscribe to them.[23] For them the key issue was to establish their authority. The detective who, in 1909, arrested Arthur Harding, an East End criminal, as a 'suspicious person' under the Vagrancy Act did so 'to teach him a *lesson*'.[24] Yet, while the power of arrest provided the ultimate underpinning of the constable's authority, stop-and-search powers were routinely more valuable because, in practice, they did not open up the officer's decision to external review.[25]

In practice, however, officers and their victims were not concerned about legal authority, the uniform was sufficient to empower almost any action – a house search, an assault, detention in a cell, an order to 'move on'.[26] As one Liverpool officer, who served between the two World Wars, put it, ' Everything we did, we could find justification for. We could always find something in the law to help us.'[27] One man recalled playing in the street in Liverpool as a child in the 1920s: 'All we'd be doing was either playing jumping over backs and playing with a little tennis ball, football and things like that – we didn't have no caseballs … but they still moved you on.'[28] Dealing out summary punishment, such as a thump with a truncheon or the bursting of a precious football, rather than prosecuting someone reinforced the officer's authority by demonstrating his power to choose the form of retribution. For the communities they policed, they symbolized authority. Authority was attached to their uniform: the police constable 'is the most obvious embodiment of the Law that we possess. He is so ubiquitous, so imposing: his uniform and his size mark him out from other men and make him conspicuous. And the rest of the legal machine is so much hidden away with all its apparatus of wigs and robes, counsel and judges and courts.'[29] The police were the Law:

> 'neath the terrors of a blue-coat's eye,
> Hoops must not roll, nor kites presume to fly;
> And the street Orpheus, by compulsion mute,
> Shrinks from the truncheoned, unmelodious brute[30]

The exercise of police authority through arrests for minor offences or stop-and-searches or demands to 'move on' were the constant irritant of daily life for working people. This did not go entirely unnoticed outside working-class communities. Lord Dudley Stuart, MP for Marylebone, claimed in the Commons in 1849 that working people took the view that 'wherever a policeman was found, there was a petty tyrant',[31] and the *Spectator* remarked in 1864 that, 'there are few residents in London who have not at some time or other observed instances of oppression and brutality perpetrated by a policeman against the poor and vicious.'[32] George Holyoake, the journalist, wrote that the Metropolitan Police 'treated the working class as a criminal class, and more frequently attacked them than assisted them.'[33] Even a supporter of the police like Edwin Chadwick admitted that the police were 'reformers of the rich [sent] to act against the labouring classes'.[34]

The relationship between the police and working-class communities was not entirely one-sided. Taylor has estimated that in the 1860s between a half and two-thirds of the Middlesbrough force were assaulted each year,[35] while a report in 1872 claimed that each Metropolitan officer was injured once every two years.[36] Some of these assaults, such as the murders of two officers by armed burglars in London in the 1880s, were the result of criminals seeking to evade capture;[37] others expressed individual or community resentment. An assault might be directed at a despised officer, rather than at the police as such. In 1888 the Chief Constable of Essex tried to remove PC Enoch Raison from Stebbing quietly following threats, but, discovering that there was a plan to sneak him out at night, the villagers came to see him off, and that year it was

Raison's effigy which sat on the bonfire on 5th November.[38] Popular recreations, such as bonfire night celebrations and football matches, became points of confrontation and opportunities for communal expressions of disapproval: on bonfire night at Newport in 1837 the head of the borough force, Superintendent Redman, was assaulted and spent several days in hospital, and in 1875 PC Thomas Turner from the same force died as a result of injuries received after being attacked by a bonfire-night crowd.[39]

Assaults were also part of the resistance to the enforcement of particular laws. In Manchester a rise in assaults on officers in the late 1860s coincided with campaigns against prostitution, vagrancy and street leisure activities,[40] and when the chief officer of Middlesbrough was urged to undertake a campaign against drunkenness by a local temperance lobby, he expressed his concern that such an unpopular policy posed real dangers for his officers.[41] Rural protest rumbled on through much of the nineteenth century and as police officers were brought in to root out offenders and protect farmers' property they were threatened, assaulted and occasionally killed. In some parts of the country there was a state of guerrilla warfare over poaching throughout the nineteenth and twentieth centuries into which the police were drawn, particularly after the Poaching Prevention Act 1862, on the side of the gamekeepers.[42] The enforcement of the Contagious Diseases Acts 1864, 1866 and 1869 provoked resentment because they seemed to be used indiscriminately against working-class women who happened to be alone on the streets.

The Street Gaming Act 1906 also engendered a good deal of conflict in the towns: the law removed a leisure activity, was regarded as hypocritical in that it did not touch the gambling of wealthy people, and threatened the income people derived from betting and acting as runners and bookmakers. As a result, people would allow escape routes for bookies through their houses and refuse to give information to the police. Arrests for gaming on Campbell Road, Islington, prompted at least six collective assaults on the police between 1920 and 1938, and in 1920 a thousand people were said to have attacked the police as they raided a betting house in another part of Islington.[43]

Of course, it is often difficult to uncover the motives behind an assault on an officer and statistics conceal as much as they reveal about general trends. Sometimes a drunk simply lashed out, although that might lead onlookers, for reasons which it is not always easy to discover, to join in the attack rather than to assist the officer. In 1897 PC George Snipe was killed by a crowd in Birmingham after he had attempted to arrest a man for being drunk and disorderly.[44] When PC Hahn and PC Parsons attempted to arrest James Zebedee in the Cross Keys in Cranborne in 1871 for nonpayment of a fine, they were assaulted by James and five other men, during which Parsons was kicked in the head and Hahn badly bitten on the thumb, 'but, although quite a hundred people witnessed the struggle, only one, a man named George Adams, ventured to obey the call.'[45] One London magistrate remarked that he could not understand the reason for people standing by while an officer was attacked,[46] but they often seem to have regarded such a fight as a bit of entertainment; rarely would anyone have dreamed of intervening.[47]

Assaults on officers in the nineteenth century cannot always be explained away as attempts to resist arrest. Sometimes there was a degree of bravado involved in assaulting the police, as Henry Mayhew discovered from interviewing costermongers in the 1850s.[48] In some areas assaulting a police officer was an attempt to limit the intrusion of authority: the police were effectively excluded by some communities, such as the China district of Merthyr Tydfil around the mid-nineteenth century and Jennings' Buildings near Kensington High Street in the late nineteenth century.[49] While such assaults generally declined after the late nineteenth century, there were some streets in which the threat remained such that officers were careful to patrol in pairs, especially at night. The knife-edge existence of many poor communities in the 1920s and 1930s continued to make them resentful of interference with either methods of making a living or leisure activities. Indeed, it was often a crucial part of individual and communal survival to limit the incursions made by the police.[50]

While this hostility limited police action, it also provided them with opportunities. For instance, the resistance encountered among the Irish in Jennings' Buildings and the London costermongers in the nineteenth century made them targets for demonstrations of police power. Only rarely did these tensions come to the attention of the newspaper-reading classes. The campaign against street prostitution in London in the 1880s caused enormous resentment among working-class people for its criminalization of women, but it was only after the prosecution of Elizabeth Cass for soliciting failed in 1887 because her middle-class employer was willing to provide an impeccable character reference that the newspapers took an interest and criticized the police.[51] Normally, any underlying resentment was lost in the reporting: it was simply an assault and, as such, it provided further evidence of the need for firmness in policing.

Yet the relationship between the police and working-class communities was more complex than these assaults might suggest. In general terms, the working class used the police a good deal. The pattern of use depended on the area, the individual officer and the particular circumstances. As a child in the 1880s Arthur Harding used to go along to the police station pretending to be lost because he knew he would be fussed over with bread and jam. Later, as he took up crime as his main profession, his contact with the police became part of his business life: evasion, bribes, arrests (sometimes false), some degree of mutual admiration.[52] On the other side, there was a recognition that full enforcement of the law was unwise and anyway impracticable. The exercise of the discretion not to enforce the law became as important in maintaining authority, as making an arrest.

In 1878 the Liverpool Vigilance Committee persuaded the watch committee to order the Head Constable, Captain Nott Bower, to enforce laws on public houses more strictly both to stamp out drunkenness and to curb their use as brothels. An election in 1880 removed the lobby's majority and the pressure was eased, but in 1889 a petition demanded more vigorous enforcement. The watch committee again pressed Nott Bower, but he resisted. He argued firmly for the police to continue exercising their discretion on the grounds that suppression was impossible in a seaport and that, instead, control should be the aim. He was eventually forced to comply, but petitions from business people later confirmed Nott Bower's initial view by complaining that enforcement had led to brothels springing up across the city.[53] Moreover, enforcing moral laws so clearly aimed at working-class people injured the image of neutrality which, at least in the eyes of the middle classes, the police had tried to maintain.

For their part the constables on the beat were not necessarily un-sympathetic to the pursuits they were being asked to stamp out, although often they found themselves trapped between fulfilling the moral agenda of a watch committee or chief constable and the realities of safely negotiating the streets of a community which resented interference with its way of life. There was also some irony in making constables in the early police forces 'domestic missionaries' in view of the frequency with which they were disciplined for drunkenness.[54] The autonomy con-stables enjoyed on their beats provided plenty of opportunities to boost their meagre pay through blackmail and bribery: extracting services or money out of prostitutes, costermongers, street bookmakers, publicans.[55] Arthur Harding recalled that the relationship between the local police and criminal business-people was based on exchanges. It was common practice for police officers to arrange with bookmakers to arrest them on a sort of rota basis: this provided the officers with evidence for their superiors that they were doing the work and for the bookmakers it spread the arrests around, which meant there was less danger of going to prison. He recalled the regular bribes paid to officers to ensure that street bookmaking was allowed to carry on.[56] Prostitutes were also arrested on a rota basis and publicans paid off police officers to stay open beyond licensing hours.[57] At Liverpool docks in the struggle between employers and employees over the taking of materials from work (defined as theft by the former and as customary supplement to wages by the latter), the police force entered on the side of the employer, but individual officers colluded with workers, sometimes in exchange for a share of the perks.[58]

Only occasionally did people outside working-class communities become aware of such corruption. In 1902 PC Rolls was sentenced to five years in prison for planting a hammer on a man in Hackney and then arresting him.[59] This led to the establishment of the Police and Public Vigilance Society by James Timewell, which was devoted to the exposure of police corruption.[60] Then, in 1906, after the wrongful arrest of Eva d'Angely for street prostitution, the Royal Commission upon the Duties of the Metropolitan Police in Relation to Cases of Drunkenness, Disorder and Solicitation in the Streets was set up.[61] Almost in spite of itself, this inquiry revealed a large number of allegations about officers demanding money or drink from bookmakers, prostitutes and publicans. The Commission suppressed much of the evidence on the ground that publication would be 'detrimental to the administration of the Force generally, and therefore, contrary to the public interest'.[62] Even so it was concluded that, 'The Force cannot, as a whole, be absolved from the charge of receiving money from bookmakers.'[63] In 1928 Sergeant Goddard, who was head of a vice squad at Vine Street in London's West End, was found to have been taking bribes from the night clubs he was meant to be policing, and around the same time corruption in the Liverpool police was exposed.

However, such allegations were never allowed to touch the police as a body. So, for instance, the general verdict of the Commons in 1908 was expressed by one member who incredibly declared that the report of the Royal Commission 'had fully established the high character which many of them attached to the Metropolitan Police – a character above suspicion'.[64] Most allegations were simply dismissed, ignored or never came to light; those that did were characterized as revealing a few bad individuals and even then their behaviour tended to be explained away: Sir John Moylan, Receiver for the Metropolitan Police District, claimed in the 1930s that corruption was 'mainly associated with the enforcement of laws which are out of harmony with public opinion, or in enforcing which the police are compelled (as in the case of night clubs) by lack of adequate powers to have recourse to unsatisfactory methods of detection.'[65]

The police did recognize that some degree of acceptance from the policed was needed and service work was seen as one way of acquiring that support. The Constabulary Commission in 1839 had recommended that officers be given a range of non-crime functions, such as acting as firemen and reporting environmental nuisances.[66] However, government and local authorities tended to regard the constable as a convenient all-purpose official, and this created resentment among the police.[67] In 1868 it was estimated that additional duties had been placed on Metropolitan Police officers by 82 statutes which 'relate to the supervision by the Police of a vast multitude of details of more or less importance connected with vagrancy, public houses, beer houses, sanitary measures, coining, lunatics, street traffic, hackney carriages, and an immense variety of other subjects'.[68]

Some of these tasks – such as acting as poor relief officers or school attendance officers – brought the police into conflict with the community. On the other hand, they undoubtedly did provide tangible assistance to the poor, such as soup kitchens, looking after lost or hungry children, stopping runaway horses and giving assistance at fires or accidents.[69] A glance at the names of those Metropolitan Police officers commemorated (with others) in Postman's Park near St Paul's Cathedral who died saving lives provides one proof of the simple humanity which motivated acts of kindness. Many forces organized charitable assistance for the poor, although genuine aid was often underpinned with a moral purpose. The Birmingham Police Aided Association for Clothing Poor Children was founded in 1893 'to foster friendly and humane relations with the poorest classes of the population'.[70] It was claimed that the moral regulation undertaken by the police was of value to those working-class areas they policed: the police benefited both St Giles and St James because they 'have tended as materially to ameliorate the social condition of the one class of society, by the maintenance of order and decorum, as they have been important to the other class, by the protection of property and the consequent prevention of crime'.[71] The Head Constable of Stockport claimed in 1850 that the police were 'the instrument not only in the promotion of public health and the prevention of crime, but also in promoting the general good of society'.[72] According to one writer in 1852, 'among the poor [the police constable] is considered their protector.'[73]

The police certainly did provide protection, and the poor used them. The view of the police which the poor had was, therefore, equivocal: resenting unwanted interference, welcoming sought-for assistance or an act of kindness. Overall, though, the police were used by the poor because they represented external authority and that was also the reason why they were resented. In 1908 *The Times* commented, 'in many a back street and slum [the policeman] not only stands for law and order; he is the true handyman of our streets, the best friend of a mass of people who have no other counsellor or protector'.[74] The year before, Hugh Gamon, who had been commissioned by the Toynbee Trust to write a report on the East End, compared this view of those who saw the police constable as 'the prosecutor of all wrongdoers; to boot, an exceedingly civil and obliging servant of the community', with the view in the East End where the police 'are no longer the servants of the community. They are masters; at the best kindly champions, at the worst tyrants.'[75]

Riot policing

Peel had largely avoided the subject of the policing of riots and meetings in the debates around the establishment of the Metropolitan Police, but it was certainly in his mind, and, as has been argued,[76] it became of great concern to the Home Office during the Chartist period. At some of the protest meetings in 1830 London ratepayers had deplored the practice of shifting officers from their parishes to deal with public disorder, but by the late 1840s there was plenty of support among the middle classes for the Metropolitan Police in this role. In April 1848 a large number – perhaps around 85,000 people – volunteered as special constables to assist the policing of the enormous Chartist meeting on Kennington Common.[77] The fear of massive disorder never materialized and, although this was perhaps more to do with the strategy of the Chartists' leaders, it provided an opportunity for enormous smugness that, at a time when revolution had flared up across Europe:

> It is a proud thing for England to reflect on the exalted post she has occupied during this marvellous and trying time. While other nations, possessed of far greater military forces, were reeling under the shock, ... she alone has repressed the danger by the constable's baton ... She has conquered the revolutionary spirit, by which so many of the military monarchies of Europe had been prostrated, by moral strength alone; scarce a shot was fired in anger by her troops, and not a drop of blood was shed on the scaffold.[78]

While this was seen as a consequence of the English character – as exemplified by the special constables themselves – it was also regarded as a triumph for the Metropolitan Police. Their handling of the huge crowds attending the Great Exhibition of 1851 drew praise even from *Punch*, which had led the satirical assault on the new police in its early years: 'Every one has been charmed during the Great Exhibition by the mode in which this truly civil power has been rendered effective'.[79] Equally, some were reassured by their willingness to use force during the Sunday

Trading riots in 1855.[80] After the Reform demonstrations in 1866, *The Times* complimented the Metropolitan Police as having been, 'throughout far more calm and forbearing than the police of any country with which we have ever been acquainted'.[81]

Yet although the constables on the ground were praised, some wanted more force to be employed.[82] After the riots in 1855 some blame was placed on the Commissioner of the Metropolitan Police, Mayne; by the time of the 1866–7 disorders there was a strong feeling in government that he had outstayed his usefulness. The *Saturday Review* commented:

> The dangerous classes, in their most dangerous aspect, have been formally assured by authority that authority is impotent to preserve the peace and order of society whenever it suits illegal violence openly to defy and challenge the law.[83]

The view among the crowds was somewhat different. During the 1866 demonstration, the dislike of the police as a body was most clearly demonstrated by the cheering which broke out when the army arrived to restore order: 'the soldiers are men and the others ain't', explained one of the demonstrators, 'The police have no feeling for the working man; they sell themselves for 2s. a day.'[84] This echoed Karl Marx's report that soldiers had, in fact, joined the demonstrators in 1855, shouting 'Long live the army!' and 'Down with the police!'[85]

After 1867 the issue of crowd control did not arise again in London until the late 1880s.[86] An economic depression that lasted longer and was more devastating than the previous slumps of 1866 and 1879 exposed the core of abject poverty among casual workers and the vulnerability of many in the working class. This became more than a matter of humanitarian concern for the propertied classes. They were nervous about the consequences for themselves of the growth of a class of people in London and other major cities with nothing to lose: 'seething in the very centre of our great cities, concealed by the thinnest crust of civilization and decency, is a vast mass of moral corruption, of heart-breaking misery and absolute godlessness'.[87]

Not that this should have been news to the people of London. Edwin Chadwick's *Report on the Sanitary Condition of the Labouring Population of Great Britain*,[88] Henry Mayhew's articles for the *Morning Chronicle* and his book *London Labour and the London Poor* and Charles Dickens's novels – along with a multitude of other books and pamphlets – had all documented the living conditions of the poor. Efforts were made to assist them, but many simply ascribed their difficulties to immorality and idleness. Dickens's readers might weep over the fate of the 'deserving' characters in his novels, but would have been less impressed by the suggestion that their wealth depended on such poverty. However, in the 1880s, as destitution spread beyond the casual poor, to whom the consequences of economic downturns were usually confined, the journalist, G.R. Sims, reminded people of the Paris Commune: 'This mighty mob of famished, diseased and filthy helots is getting dangerous, physically, morally, politically dangerous', and could 'sally forth and give us the taste of the lesson the mob has tried to teach now and again in Paris, when long years of neglect have done their work.'[89] His warning seemed to become a reality in 1886-7 when the East End broke out and threatened to spark a fire that could have burnt the West End down.

Following a particularly severe winter during which large numbers were laid off, a meeting of the unemployed gathered in Trafalgar Square in February 1886.[90] The radical Social Democratic Federation used the occasion to press its political agenda and fighting broke out. A splinter group marched towards Hyde Park only to be insulted by members in their Pall Mall clubs. Rioting ensued: property was attacked, shops looted, carriages mobbed. The police were nowhere to be seen having been ordered to Buckingham Palace by senior officers in the mistaken belief that it was under threat. The people soon returned to the East End, but panic continued to grip the West End as police officers warned of further disturbances, which never materialized. The police were heavily criticized and the Commissioner, Sir Edmund Henderson resigned following a critical inquiry, although many blamed Hugh Erskine Childers, the Home Secretary, for not allowing him a free hand. The *Pall Mall Gazette* called for a commissioner with 'more iron in his blood'. It got its wish.[91]

Henderson's replacement seemed a rather curious choice and yet was not untypical of chief officers in the nineteenth-century police. Sir Charles Warren was a war hero and a noted archaeologist, but he had no experience of policing. This did not trouble the government since the aim was to bring military discipline to the policing of crowds,[92] and Warren proved to be, in the words of one contemporary, 'the iron hand without the velvet glove'.[93]

In autumn 1887 large numbers of the unemployed camped out in Trafalgar Square and St. James's Park. At first, they seem to have been treated as objects of pity, but as their numbers grew so did the alarm of the people living in the West End.[94] The police and the cavalry charged the crowd on 13 November – 'Bloody Sunday'. In the days that followed London remained in a state of tension, which was intensified by the presence on the streets of large numbers of police officers, special constables and soldiers. Warren seems to have celebrated the action, but others criticized him for failing to 'keep his head cool'. Indeed, criticism seemed also to have come from within the police: 'people who previously treated constables with respect and had generally a kind word for them, treated them afterwards with a scowl or contempt.'[95] Ironically, in view of the reason for his appointment, he was condemned as 'this military martinet',[96] and even the *Pall Mall Gazette* turned against this 'soldier in jackboots'.[97] Vogler has recently argued that, 'Warren's handling of the disorders shows the London police, for the first time, able to resist domination by the central state and to exercise independent authority over both the magistracy and the military.'[98] And there lay the problem, for Warren's view of himself as a general in charge of his troops brought him into conflict with the Home Secretary.

The failure of the police to catch the Whitechapel murderer in 1888 added to the criticism of Warren. Hired for his military skills he was being condemned for exercising them and for failing to exercise skills he did not have. His supreme confidence in his own abilities now smacked of arrogance. In October 1888 a placard displayed at a meeting of the unemployed in Hyde Park drew the strands of criticism together, 'The Whitechapel Murders. Where are the Police? Looking after the Unemployed!'[99] Warren seemed determined to stick it out, but was politically naïve and Matthews, who had succeeded Childers as Home Secretary and who had appointed Warren, needed a scapegoat. Matthews disagreed with Warren's opinion of the commissioner's autonomy, and Warren made the mistake of airing some of his views in *Murray's Magazine*. Referring to the public disorder in 1886–7, he

> deplored that successive Governments have not had the courage to make a stand against the more noisy section of the people representing a small minority, and have given way before tumultuous proceedings which have exercised a terrorism over peaceful and law-abiding citizens, and it is still more to be regretted that ex-Ministers, while in opposition, have not hesitated to embarrass those in power by smiling on the insurgent mob.[100]

Rather opaquely he deprecated recent attacks on 'the police administration' which 'if successful ... would effectually cripple the power of the Executive to keep peace'.[101] Matthews demanded his resignation, not, it was claimed, because of the content of the article, but because Warren failed to obtain permission to publish it as he was required to do, although, in truth, the article 'was merely the accident which determined a resignation sooner or later inevitable'.[102] There was little surprise when James Monro, a former Assistant commissioner in charge of CID, who had himself fallen out with Warren and had sided with the Home Office, was appointed as his successor. He did not last long – another casualty of a disagreement with the Home Office – but he and his immediate successors did initiate a policy of strengthening the detective branch.

Outside London, some of the rural and many borough forces had been unable to deal with large-scale disorders in the first half of the nineteenth century and had required assistance from the army or the Metropolitan Police.[103] From the outset the new police were embroiled in industrial disputes. The Royal Commission of 1839 regarded these as issues of public order and, indeed, saw them as another reason for the establishment of the new police.[104] The connection between watch committees and employers was reinforced by the practice in some borough forces of drawing part of their funding from local business: for instance, in the mid-1860s 60% of the officers in the Middlesbrough force were financed by local firms.[105] Nevertheless, the problem of small police forces being unable to cope continued. In 1853 Wigan's police force of ten officers was overwhelmed during riots associated with industrial action by colliers and cotton-workers and the military had to be brought in. This led *The Morning Chronicle* to comment, 'It seems hardly credible that the town maintains ten Policemen … although not fewer than four thousand colliers, described as men of wild character, reside within its precincts'.[106]

In Wigan's case the watch committee quickly decided to more than double the force, but other police authorities were cautious about cost. They resisted increases and preferred to rely on the army where there was a local barracks, as, for instance, happened during the Murphy Riots in Birmingham in 1867,[107] or special constables or a loan of officers from a neighbouring force. When trouble broke out during an election at Llanidloes in 1862, the Montgomeryshire Police obtained assistance from Shropshire, and the following year officers from Shropshire and Denbighshire assisted Flintshire police in support of a colliery owner who was evicting families.[108] The growing reluctance of the Home Office to send out the Metropolitan Police or the army encouraged such 'loans' between forces, but there was doubt about their legality,[109] and the authorities in the 'lending' force were sometimes concerned about the effect of removing officers from the force area.

On a number of occasions rural police brought in to assist a borough force were accused of resorting to excessive violence. Such was the aggression of the Lincolnshire County police drafted into Lincoln during the elections of 1862 that on their withdrawal the mayor's house was attacked and the army had to be called in to restore order.[110] In 1893 following the coal strikes that year, during which the military shot dead two people at Featherstone, a conference at the Home Office formalized a system of mutual aid to avoid the chaos in which magistrates were resorting to the use of troops to intimidate striking miners on behalf of colliery owners.[111]

Problems persisted and in 1908 a select committee urged that the police be organized so as 'to obviate to the utmost possible extent any necessity for resorting to military aid' through, among other things, mutual aid.[112] In 1910 during another miners' strike, Churchill overrode the local magistrates, and imposed his own nominee from the army, General Macready, to head the soldiers in South Wales. A large force of Metropolitan Police officers was also sent into the area.

No proper national system of mutual aid existed until the Desborough Committee considered the matter in 1919–20. The Home Office drew up a formal and more centralized system, which was introduced in 1925 and employed during the General Strike of 1926.[113] By the early twentieth century the growing confidence of chief officers enabled them to call on the support of the Home Office over the heads of a reluctant local police authority, as, for instance, in the 1920s when in places like South Wales there was a good deal of sympathy in the police authorities for the plight of the workers. The army did continue to have a role, but the preference for soldiers over constables in the policing of demonstrations expressed by those present at the Hyde Park demonstrations in 1866 had certainly been reversed by the time of the shootings at Featherstone in 1893, so that rumours of the arrival of the army in the Rhondda in 1910 reignited disturbances.[114]

The detectives

Preventive policing was not enough, the police, like the watch before them, were blamed for crime and expected to have a system of detection. Two days after the murder of Lord William Russell in 1840, *The Times* criticized the failure of the police to make an arrest: 'We are compelled to state, from lamentable experience, our conviction that the means now employed for the detection of those guilty of the foul and horrible crime of murder have proved utterly unavailing.' Worse, the new force was unfavourably compared in this respect with the Bow Street Runners.[115] In 1869 the Home Secretary, Henry Bruce, was lobbied by a delegation of vestrymen drawn from across London complaining about 'the increase of robberies with violence in the streets of London, and reflecting upon the alleged inefficiency of the police'. The spokesperson for the deputation, Professor Marks, revealed how crime had come to be seen as the responsibility of the police alone:

> To deal with crime and criminals we are almost entirely dependent upon the police force, and yet though the police force had been increased to numbers beyond the increase of the population, crime was still gaining ground, and this increase of crime was attributed to the inefficiency of the force, an inefficiency attributed to its organization.

There was, he asserted, 'a perfect organization of criminals' for which the proper response 'should be a corresponding body of criminal police, – a trained body capable of dealing with all the artifices of crime and all its ramifications'.[116] The greater availability of statistics published by police forces encouraged critical scrutiny of their effectiveness.[117]

As designed in 1829 the Metropolitan Police placed their faith in preventive policing and had no detection strategy. The first commissioners were keen to avoid the accusation that officers were government spies and Peel himself had declared, 'God forbid that [I] should mean to countenance a system of espionage.'[118] As a result, although uniform officers were deployed in plain-clothes for particular operations,[119] this remained a politically sensitive issue and, perhaps, accounts for the public humiliation of Sergeant Popay in 1833 for attending political meetings in plain clothes and allegedly acting as an *agent provocateur*.[120] Nevertheless, the Commissioners, Rowan and Mayne, defended their use of these officers by claiming that, with regard to beggars and felons, 'three to one are taken by men in plain clothes'. But both they and the committee of inquiry into the Popay case engaged in a rather bizarre discussion over what amounted to acceptable behaviour. The use of disguises was deplored, which meant that, while it was acceptable to dress in clothes that an officer had worn in a previous, pre-police, life, Popay's mistake had been to dress as a drawing master when he had never been one. He was also criticized for denying that he was a police officer when challenged.[121]

Plain-clothes officers continued to be used for surveillance work: in 1845 each division was instructed to assign at least two constables to maintain surveillance on known offenders and public houses, and during the street-robbery panic of 1862 there was a sharp rise in the use of plain-clothes officers to trap offenders.[122] In addition, it was an unacknowledged but routine practice for the commissioners to pay civilians, such as journalists, for information on political meetings or particular individuals.[123] However, the suspicion of the use of plain-clothes police persisted into the 1930s and beyond. The Macmillan

Committee in 1928 and the Royal Commission in 1929 both disapproved of their use to detect acts of indecency,[124] and the police were always keen to assert that their officers never acted as *agents provocateurs* or spies.[125]

The detection of offenders remained a matter for the victim, although police officers rendered assistance in making arrests, conducting searches and so forth, much as the parish watch and constables had done. The small group of Bow Street Runners was not abolished in 1829 and continued to undertake detection work, and the police-office magistrates (and, in murder cases, the coroners) retained key roles in inquiries.[126] Indeed, the better pay and the prospect of additional fees and rewards available to the Runners apparently attracted men from the Metropolitan Police. Sir Frederick Roe, the chief magistrate at Bow Street, boasted that two officers from the Metropolitan Police had joined the Runners and, while he did not claim men in that force were of poorer quality, he did say, 'I think they [the two officers] have greatly improved under us in their mode of doing their duty.'[127] When the separate police-office forces, including the Bow Street Runners, were abolished in 1839, a detective division of the Metropolitan Police was proposed, although not created until 1842.

However, before this particular Metropolitan Police officers were apparently used for difficult cases. Sergeant James Otway was lent out to assist in a murder inquiry in Uxbridge in 1837 and it became normal to send either Otway or Inspector Nicholas Pearce, who had been with the Bow Street Patrole, on special cases, such as embezzlement at the Post Office, the proposed duel in 1840 involving Prince Louis Napoleon, and the murder of Lord William Russell. Otherwise, investigations were left to the officers in the division where the offence took place. In 1840, following the Russell case, the practice developed of identifying 'an active, intelligent man in each division' to whom various tasks, including detective work, were given.[128] It was from among these officers that some of the detectives whom Dickens later made famous, such as Jonathan Whicher and Stephen Thornton emerged.

The trigger for the establishment of the Detective Department in 1842 was criticism of the police's failure to arrest more rapidly a murderer called Daniel Good.[129] Two inspectors and six sergeants were appointed to work from Scotland Yard under the commissioners. The force was small and the main responsibility for detection continued to rest with the victim and the uniform police. As late as 1869 Sir Edmund Henderson, the Commissioner, remarked, 'the detective system … is viewed with the greatest suspicion … and is, in fact, entirely foreign to the habits and feelings of the nation.'[130] The number of detectives was increased in 1856,

1865 and 1867, but even then there were only fifteen out of a force of roughly 8,000. In 1869 Edmund Henderson, acting on a suggestion made by his predecessor, Mayne, increased the number of central detectives and put full-time detectives in each division. Scotland Yard detectives undertook difficult detection cases, the divisional detectives kept those thought to be criminals as well as habitual offenders under surveillance, and the plain-clothes officers drawn from the uniformed branch were typically detailed to watch property thought to be a target for crime.[131] The willingness of these groups of officers to co-operate with one another was limited.

Forces outside London, also appointed detectives: Birmingham's detective branch was established as early as 1839; Middlesbrough had a detective in 1859 out of a strength of fifteen officers and at that time there were three detectives in Leeds and Bradford and five in Sheffield. Other forces had none: this was the case in Halifax, Huddersfield, Wakefield and York in 1859.[132] Those with inadequate detective resources could obtain assistance from Scotland Yard in difficult cases, as, for instance, happened after the Road-hill House murder,[133] although the reluctance of senior officers to hand control over a case to a detective, especially one from another force, may have reduced the number of occasions on which this occurred.

Public interest in the Metropolitan Police detectives seems to have grown more quickly than their numbers. Stories about the escapades of detectives featured in Tom Taylor's successful play, *The Ticket-of-Leave Man*,[134] in novels,[135] journals,[136] newspaper stories (particularly, *The Illustrated Police News*) and the autobiographies of retired detectives.[137] Charles Dickens was fascinated by them and drew on his nights spent with the detectives for essays in *Household Words* and for the images of the underworld in his novels. Fascinated by the juxtaposition of enormous wealth and grinding poverty in London, Dickens found in the detectives men who seemed able to move easily between these worlds and yet remain apart from both. He based Inspector Bucket in *Bleak House* on Detective Inspector Charles Field, a failed actor and – to the occasional consternation of his superiors – an enthusiastic user of disguises.[138]

However, it was the character of Sergeant Cuff in Wilkie Collins's *The Moonstone* (1868) which really established the police detective in fiction. Cuff was based on Inspector Jonathan Whicher, who had been made famous by Collins's friend Dickens, and, more particularly, by his inquiry into the Road-hill House murder. Of course, the most influential fictional detective was Sherlock Holmes, who first appeared in *Beeton's Christmas Annual* in 1887. He is a private detective whose abilities are in marked contrast to those of the plodding, unimaginative and largely incompetent

Inspector Lestrade – 'that imbecile Lestrade', as Holmes calls him in *The Adventures of Sherlock Holmes*.[139] Lestrade is part of a system that seeks to squash the skills a detective requires: the militaristic discipline of the police and the emphasis on obedience compares with the individualism and scientific skills of Holmes. Yet, in spite of their critical view of Scotland Yard detectives, the novels endorsed the ideas of crime control through detection, of the detective as a breed apart and of detection as a mysterious art which should not be subjected to rules.[140]

John Fielding had made much of the skill involved in detection,[141] and even in the days of the Runners one magistrate had admitted to a select committee that detection was a 'mystery' – in the sense of a secret craft – 'which I can neither understand nor explain'.[142] The distinction between the ordinary officer and the detective lay in this mystery.[143] According to Hughes, who had been a Metropolitan Police detective, 'The province of a detective officer is peculiar, and requires an entire devotion to its duties in order to be successful. Even then, many fail, as is attested by the fact that throughout the whole range of the police few are known as experts in the art of catching thieves.' He continued:

> The detective requires to be possessed of a good memory, a perfect and instant recollection of faces and forms once seen, and an ability to detect instantly the uncertain and wavering expression of the eye and countenance of the thief. He should, moreover, be possessed of the tact of being able to mix to some extent with the criminal classes, and even to conciliate their friendship, whilst at the same time he inspires fear without exciting hatred.[144]

The autobiographies of detectives working outside London confirmed this general description. Richard Jervis, who joined the Lancashire police in 1850 and became a detective soon afterwards recalled how he, 'made a speciality of enlarging my acquaintance with travelling, as well as local, thieves and their haunts', and he insisted on the importance for a detective of 'cultivating the faculty of keen and intelligent observation'.[145] The knowledge, skill and incorruptibility of these detectives was contrasted with the corruption and incompetence which – with one or two exceptions – had become the main hallmark of the literary representation of the Bow Street Runners by the 1840s.[146] Dickens thought the Runners had puffed themselves up beyond their abilities (famously representing them in Blathers and Duff in *Oliver Twist*), whereas 'the Detective Force … is so well chosen and trained, proceeds so systematically and quietly, does its business in such a workman-like manner, and is always so calmly and steadily engaged in the service of the public, that the public really do not know enough of it, to know a tithe of its usefulness.'[147] The ubiquity of the Metropolitan Police detective – dispatched throughout the country to solve crimes – added further to his mystique and power.

Yet, the bulk of arrests (in and outside London) were undertaken by uniformed officers. Some of these came as a result of stopping people or surveillance or acting on information received. In the 1880s PC Thomas Smethurst of Bolton Police stopped a tramp because he had 'something under his coat' and discovered a shirt which turned out to have been stolen.[148] PC Hahn of Dorset Police arrested a deserter in Dawlish in 1864, after having stopped him to ask for his pass, and two months later he arrested Daniel Dennett for stealing apples from a garden that Hahn was watching.[149]

Many forces provided uniform constables with some simple advice on crime detection, such as how to judge whether a burglary had been committed by someone acquainted with premises or a stranger and how to take impressions of footprints.[150] In Dorset officers were instructed in 1859 on 'the necessity of speedy information being sent and quick intelligence forwarded, for the detection and apprehension of offenders'.[151] Constables in plain clothes were assigned to pursue offenders: the burglar and murderer Charles Peace was followed by PC Pearson of the Sheffield Police to Hull, although Peace gave him the slip.[152] When PC Cox of the East Sussex Police went to arrest John Crook in 1860 he travelled from Uckfield to Ealing, then on to Twyford in Berkshire, Acton, Ealing and Brentford, returning to Uckfield after four days; at various points he obtained assistance from a constable, who was probably from the Berkshire Police, and a sergeant from the Metropolitan Police.[153] Sergeant Lear of the Shropshire Police covered about one hundred miles on foot during his pursuit of one suspect in 1871.[154]

Officers might also be required to chase up evidence. In 1842, PC Sheather of the East Sussex police arrested William Ford for horse theft, taking him to Hailsham to be remanded by a magistrate. He then went to Maidstone, Canterbury, Herne Bay and London in a fruitless search for the owner of the horse.[155] The sort of co-operation from uniform officers in other forces which PC Cox experienced was not unusual. Officers from London, Birmingham and Manchester assisted Shrewsbury police in the identification of pickpockets at the Royal Agricultural Show in Shrewsbury in 1846.[156] Inter-force co-operation was also maintained through *The Police Gazette* (formerly *The Hue and Cry and Police Gazette*), published from Bow Street until 1883 when it was taken over by Scotland Yard. In it were published details of crimes and suspects.[157] This central role of Scotland Yard in the dissemination of information was also part of the means of fulfilling the requirements of the Habitual Criminals Act 1869. The act built on the standard technique of keeping those known to have criminal convictions under surveillance by requiring forces to maintain criminal records and to co-ordinate inquiries as to previous convictions through the Metropolitan Police.

In spite of their comparative insignificance in terms of numbers and of arrests, the general fascination with the work of the detectives increased expectations about the ability of the police to solve crime. Individual failures drew adverse comment. Whicher failed to obtain a conviction in his most famous case – the murder at Road-hill House – and this led to his abilities being questioned, with one critic referring to his action in arresting the sister of the victim as 'rash and cruel' and effected without 'even the skeleton of a case made out against her'.[158] He was eventually regarded as vindicated when, five years later, she confessed and was convicted of the murder.[159]

Panics about street robbery in the 1860s drew further criticism on the police as a whole.[160] These had not faded when the Irish Revolutionary Brotherhood bombed Clerkenwell Prison in 1867, killing twelve people and injuring more than 120. The police, who seemed to have received a warning, had failed to look more closely at a barrel placed against one of the prison's walls. In the alarm that followed 50,000 people were sworn in as special constables to guard key buildings and, as government confidence in the Metropolitan Police waned, a secret service operation was established under Lt. Col. W.H.A. Fielding, an army intelligence officer who had led the drive against Fenians in Ireland.[161] Much of the blame was laid on Commissioner Mayne, who was well into his seventies and had been roundly criticized for the policing of the Reform Bill demonstrations in 1866 and 1867. Disraeli wrote to the Prime Minister, the Earl of Derby, urging that, if Mayne failed to resign, he should be dismissed. The government was reluctant to get rid of him after 38 years' service, but Derby did remark,

> It is really lamentable that the peace of the Metropolis, and its immunity from wilful destruction, should depend on a body of Police who, as Detectives, are manifestly incompetent; and under a chief who, whatever may be his other merits, has not the energy, nor, apparently, the skill to find out and employ men fitted for peculiar duties.[162]

Mayne died in 1868 and, following a departmental inquiry into the administration of the police, the detective branch was reorganized in 1869. The central force, which took important cases, was increased and

180 officers were appointed as divisional detectives to undertake surveillance of known criminals.[163] Another reorganization in 1878 was forced by the failure of several murder investigations and the exposure of a betting fraud in which three of the four chief inspectors were implicated.[164] The corruption scandal brought an outcry, but no call for the abolition of the detectives; they were 'a necessary adjunct to every modern police system'.[165] Nevertheless, an inquiry was highly critical of their efficiency and, in particular, the lack of co-operation between central and divisional detectives. Howard Vincent, a young barrister who had written an impressive report on the Paris detective system, was appointed to establish the Criminal Investigation Department in 1878 with 216 officers. However, in 1880, following the prosecution of a chemist called Titley on an abortion charge, there was further criticism, in particular, of the technique of entrapment.[166] There were also allegations that innocent people were being wrongly convicted and that detectives were motivated by the rewards that were still being offered.

> The new department, indeed, has hitherto been an entire failure in every respect. The statistics which you recently noticed made it quite clear that, notwithstanding the great things that were promised on the establishment of the department, there had been an alarming falling-off in the proportion of apprehensions and convictions as compared with those obtained under the old detective system.[167]

In the 1880s the Fenians undertook a bombing campaign: they began with a gas works, a coaling shed and an aqueduct in Glasgow in January 1883, and among their targets in London over the next two years were the House of Commons, the offices of the Local Government Board, Nelson's Column, Scotland Yard, London Bridge and the Tower of London. In the midst of the attacks E.G. Jenkinson, the head of the Secret Service in Ireland, was brought from Dublin to co-ordinate the police response with Robert Anderson, and James Monro, who had been Inspector-General of Police in Bengal where many of the techniques of detection were perfected, took over from Vincent as Assistant Commissioner in charge of the CID. The Special Irish Branch was established in 1884.[168] The Branch's existence was rarely acknowledged, partly, because the nature of its work was believed to require secrecy, and, partly, because of the fear that the existence of a political police force would revive objections about the impact of the police on liberty.[169] Once the bombing campaign tapered off, the nature of the threat to the State from political organizations was seen in broader terms and the Branch later dropped 'Irish' from its title.

The problems of the 1880s combined with anxieties about the threat to Britain's imperial and economic dominance from foreign competitors to drive a reform agenda aimed at improving the moral and physical condition of the working class and turning them away from the attractions of socialist alternatives.[170] At the same time, there was a suspicion of dissent. The relatively open-door policy on immigration had made London something of a base for various anarchist and socialist groups and policing of these was stepped up after the assassination in Russia of Tsar Alexander II in 1881. The fear was that socialists and anarchists were not just organizing revolutions abroad, but might foment them here, and Special Branch was meant to deal with that fear.[171]

Monro enjoyed a close relationship with the Home Office and it seems this irritated Charles Warren, who became Commissioner in 1887, and prompted Monro's resignation. He left office on 31st August, 1888 and, since Anderson, his replacement, was on sick leave, the CID was leaderless on the evening of the murder of Mary ('Polly') Nichols in Whitechapel. Over the next nine weeks a further four women – Annie Chapman, Elizabeth Stride, Kate Eddowes and Mary Kelly – were murdered in the same area apparently by a single person who, some believed at the time, might also have been responsible for a number of other attacks between 1887 and July 1889. While the terror of the people of Whitechapel increased, the Metropolitan Police, who already had a poor record of solving the murders of London prostitutes, seemed baffled. Furthermore, the Whitechapel murders exposed the tension at the heart of the Metropolitan Police between Rowan's project of crime prevention through moral regulation, which involved policing 'bad areas' like Whitechapel, and the idea of crime control through detection. While costermongers were moved on and prostitutes arrested, the Whitechapel murderer was free to butcher poor women. The people of Whitechapel were not denying the need for police, just their aims and methods.[172]

Having held out the notion of protection through detection, the detectives had failed to deliver: *The Times* despaired, 'it is now beginning to be admitted that the detectives are once more at fault.'[173] Even Queen Victoria complained, 'The Queen fears that the detective department is not so efficient as it might be.'[174] It was not just that they failed to identify the murderer, it was also their apparent blundering. Ignoring the laborious house-to-house inquiries that were undertaken, the newspapers focused on the absurdity of some of their methods: officers photographing the eyes of one victim in the hope that an impression of the murderer might be detected upon them and Commissioner Warren allegedly running around Hyde Park to test the tracking ability of bloodhounds.[175]

In part, the newspapers played on this air of incompetence because the detectives adopted a policy of not talking to the press, which was later justified by the claim that copycat murders had been committed in Gateshead, Havant, Bradford and Yeabridge.[176] The embargo merely enraged journalists, made them more critical and added to the confusion as they followed the police, interviewed witnesses and, most infamously, sent the fake Jack-the-Ripper letters. One journalist bitterly complained, 'However much or little they know, the police devote themselves energetically to the task of preventing other people from knowing anything'.[177] Caught in the middle of all this were the people of Whitechapel and they lost patience with the police. Rewards were offered by local business people and vigilance committees formed to patrol the streets.[178] Much of the blame was placed on Commissioner Warren who, as has been seen, was not hired for his detective skills and did not show much interest in this side of police work.[179] When he resigned in 1888, the appointment of Monro indicated a shift in emphasis, and, although he too resigned in 1890, he was succeeded by Edward Bradford and Edward Henry, both of whom supported detective work.[180]

Inside police forces – and, in particular, inside the Metropolitan Police – the detectives were not popular with uniformed officers, who resented their higher pay, superior status and greater working flexibility. There was also a suspicion that the detectives would be used to spy on the uniformed officers. The divisional superintendents disliked not having control over Scotland Yard detectives operating in their areas.[181] The detectives did not fit easily into the idea of preventive policing, in which crime was deterred by arrests for petty offences and by the presence of uniformed officers on the streets. Instead, detectives were secretive and bargained for information by paying informants or ignoring minor breaches of the law. The *Saturday Review* complained in 1884 that there existed 'an informal understanding between the police and the criminal classes' according to which a minor criminal will be indulged 'so long as he does nothing very desperate, and serves the detectives well with hints and suggestions.'[182] Moreover, while, in theory, uniformed officers were meant to be detached from the communities they policed, the reverse was true for detectives. When in 1880 concern was expressed that many uniform officers refused an appointment with the detectives, it was suggested that this was because the work proved 'repugnant to the better class of men in the service, as their duties constantly bring them into contact with the lowest classes, frequently cause unnecessary drinking and compel them at times to resort to trickery [sic] practices which they dislike'.[183]

In 1869 Henderson, the commissioner of the Metropolitan Police expressed concern that the detectives worked 'in secret, away from supervision and control'.[184] This contrasted with the highly-regulated uniform officers, and the fear that the lack of supervision might lead to abuse and corruption was substantiated by the scandal in 1877.[185] However, that secrecy was essential was not doubted by the inquiry which followed, and, indeed, the detectives complained that this was almost impossible to maintain when they worked in the divisions. The 1877 inquiry concluded that the aim of the detectives was 'to render [the] apprehension [of criminals] so probable as to deter them from crime',[186] a view which might have fallen from the mouth of John Fielding.

The reorganisation under Vincent produced neither better supervision nor improved detection and certainly did not end corruption.[187] As Petrow argues, the detectives were able to continue in this way because the official view – from the Home Office, the commissioner and the newspapers – was that as criminals became more calculating so the detectives had to match them.[188] Whether or not this was true hardly mattered once it was believed. Nevertheless, Vincent hoped to reunite the police by switching officers between the detective and uniform branches regularly.[189] This exemplified the view that moral superiority rested in the uniform branch. However, the belief that detection depended on skill and the accumulation of knowledge meant that this strategy would simply make the detectives less efficient. At root the problem was that the uniform and detective branches developed out of two unrelated and irreconcilably different approaches to crime: prevention and detection.

The science of detection in the early twentieth century

The gap between uniform officers and detectives, on which Vincent had remarked in the 1880s, became even more pronounced in the next century. In its discussion of the CID at Scotland Yard, the Royal Commission of 1929, which is so frequently quoted as evidence of uncritical support for the police, criticized 'a tendency among this branch of the service to regard itself as a thing above and apart, to which the restrictions and limitations placed upon the ordinary police do not, or should not, apply.'[190] Five years later, Commissioner Lord Trenchard deplored 'the state of jealous rivalry … between the CID and the uniform branch',[191] and, as Vincent had done before him, he promised to end it by integrating the two, although, unlike Vincent, Trenchard's motivation was, in part, to strengthen discipline by importing military values.

The same elements that separated the detectives from other officers in Dickens's day remained in the twentieth century. Unlike the constable on the beat, whose day was meant to be completely predictable, 'The career of a detective is full of thrills. His life is packed with surprises, and he never knows what a day may bring forth.'[192] But the failures of the Victorian detectives had raised doubts about their competency and, therefore, their methods. As a result, more emphasis was placed on the specialist skills supposedly required: the work 'demands the cultivation of powers of a scope far wider and more far reaching than those required in many other walks of life.'[193] Most important was the way the detective's skills became increasingly wrapped in the mysteries of science. The first goal of creating a workable system for identifying individuals had emerged as a result of requirements in the Habitual Criminals Act 1869 that required police forces to keep records of all habitual offenders.[194] This led to the adoption of photographs, and at Scotland Yard a record combining a photograph, biographical details and physical marks was maintained in the Convict Supervision Office.[195] In 1894 the Bertillon system, which involved measuring people, was adopted, but did not prove particularly successful.

The breakthrough came with fingerprinting. Having developed a means of identifying a person after arrest, the next step was to identify the perpetrator of an offence from fingerprints left on surfaces. In 1902 Henry Jackson was the first person convicted on the basis of fingerprint evidence.[196] The possibilities of science were further opened up by the work of Dr Edmond Locard, Directeur du Laboratoire de Police Technique in Lyon. He held out the possibility of replacing fallible witness evidence with scientific proof through his theory of exchange, that is, the idea 'that every contact leaves traces'.[197] This offered the prospect of discovering criminals 'solely from the imprints or the traces which they have left',[198] and promised a number of significant advantages over proof by witness evidence. The Home Office argued that it made possible the solution of cases where there were no witnesses and that science could supply 'a kind of proof which never lies and never alters its tale'.[199]

> Every person engaged in the administration of justice and every police officer of experience is well acquainted with the frailty and uncertainty of the human element in witnesses and of their contradictory assertions, particularly in those cases where evidence is merely that of observation, whereas in those cases where the evidence is the result of expert examination of matter or material connected with the offence the expert, by reason of his knowledge and technique, may read and interpret evidence which is not the opinion of a fallible mind but is the direct and accurate interpretation of the infallible laws of nature.[200]

This did not mean detectives passed control to the scientists:

> But when every mechanical and scientific aid has been provided the burden still rests with the individual Detective Officer. Guided sometimes by flashes of intuition which even the hero of a detective novel might envy, but more often dependent on the sweat of his brow, he follows the trail to the end, sometimes of success, sometimes the bitter end of failure. The detailed work he may put into a single case is amazing.[201]

This view of the importance of science and the uniqueness of the detective's abilities was accepted by the Departmental Committee on Detective Work, which reported in 1938.[202] Although unable to devise a means of determining the efficiency of the detectives,[203] the report accepted their importance.

At that time the provision of detectives varied enormously, with some smaller forces having only one or two officers or none at all. The 58 county forces had in total only 581 officers employed exclusively on detective duties and the 121 city and borough forces (outside the Metropolitan and City of London) only 1,198. In boroughs the work of detection was generally passed on by the uniform officer to the detectives, whereas in the counties each constable was responsible for all policing on a beat including detection work, although specialist detectives could be called in on difficult cases. In the large forces uniform officers were given 'little or no encouragement to take any part in crime detection'.[204]

The committee noted, as so many had done before, that there was a separation of interest between the two branches and a good deal of resentment and rivalry which interfered with the efficiency of crime work.[205] Yet the committee made recommendations which emphasized the special skills needed for detective work and, therefore, increased the gap between the two branches, although they did bring detectives in different forces closer together. Their proposals included the need for improved training for detectives; the introduction of better record systems and faster communication of information; the application of forensic science to detective work; more systematic co-operation and team working without reference to force boundaries. The inquiry pushed forward the setting up of training programmes for detectives and the establishment of forensic laboratories. In spite of the image of the scientific approach to detection, the Metropolitan Police only established a large-scale laboratory in 1935 with others being constructed under the supervision of the Home Office in Nottingham (1936), Birmingham and

Cardiff (1938). Following the report five more were established in 1939–41.

The committee also recommended the setting-up of a national unit on forensic science to provide advice to police forces and disseminate information. The Home Office had already initiated the Forensic Science Circulars[206] and had sporadically advised forces in the past on matters such as fingerprints and taking impressions of footprints. Finally, the report made suggestions for tightening control over information. The committee believed that since the Judicial Proceedings (Regulation of Reports) Act 1926 had largely closed off 'the publication of unsavoury details of divorce proceedings', newspapers had begun 'to rely for their morbid appeal' on criminal cases and this reporting often proved detrimental to an investigation. The committee encouraged chief officers to bring proceedings for contempt of court and urged an extension of the law to give more protection to the investigation so that the police could control the flow of information to the public.[207]

In spite, then, of identifying the issue of the separation between uniform and detective branches, the report widened the gap between them by reinforcing the mystification of detective work through an emphasis on science and specialist training. This also reduced the internal and external accountability of the detectives. The mysterious nature of fingerprinting and other scientific aids attracted attention and enabled the dramatic presentation of detection successes in high-profile cases, but in truth this provided a highly distorted impression of detection, which, at its heart was – and remains – based on a trade in information between detectives and those involved in, or on the edges of, crime.[208]

Drawing together

For much of the nineteenth century there was a high turnover rate among police officers. This was, partly, because of the rate at which constables were dismissed, mainly for disciplinary offences related to drink. It was also because the police tended not to be considered as anything more than a job, and one which was not particularly attractive at times when other jobs could be found, because of the relatively low pay, the military discipline, the detailed intervention in an officer's entire life and the exhausting demands of beat work.[209]

A constable's choice of accommodation, even his choice of wife might be regulated: in the late nineteenth century Admiral Henry Christian, chief constable of Gloucestershire, required that his officers only use Bryant and May's matches.[210] The rigorous discipline was intended to restrict the opportunity for a constable to exercise discretion, and, although the numbers recruited from agricultural labourers has been exaggerated, such men formed an ideal type for the chief officers in all forces who believed such men to be amenable to discipline.[211]

The impression of beat policing as low-skilled work was reinforced by the lack of any training beyond drilling. So, for instance, in Hull the first sign of police training came in 1883 when each officer was issued with a booklet describing his duties. In many other forces the combination of military drill and reading a manual was still the only formal training at the end of the First World War.[212] The expectation was that skills would be acquired on the job and by following the detailed General Instructions.

In the Metropolitan Police the establishment of the Candidates' Section House in 1886 did not greatly change matters: although there was some specialized training, the Section House was primarily a lodging house and the emphasis remained on military drill, which continued to be taught at Wellington Barracks, St. James's Park.[213] It was only in 1907 with the establishment of Peel House in Hendon that training of recruits in police work was given any real emphasis. Furthermore, the prospect of promotion was limited, especially in the small borough forces, although some attempt was made to offset this by dividing the constable rank into different classes.[214]

During the late nineteenth century there did emerge evidence of cohesion among junior ranks and of a growing sense of pro-fessionalism.[215] The turnover rate had fallen by the last quarter of the nineteenth century and continued to do so. One new recruit to a Northern county force recalled in 1866 having met with agreeable treatment by the older constables and claimed, 'this is the natural consequence of their peculiar social position, which in a great measure isolates them from the rest of the world'.[216] Forty years later, Hugh Gamon observed that, 'The police system is calculated to produce a strong *esprit de corps* … Their life is necessarily a life apart. They are always among the people, but not of the people.'[217] This sense of unity was also promoted in those forces where the constables lived together in section houses and shared sporting and leisure activities.

Forms of group action by police officers appeared in the second half of the nineteenth century. Petitions for pay rises to police authorities from individuals and small groups of officers were common. Large-scale action was unusual, but as early as 1853 there were mass resignations over pay in the Hull and Manchester police,[218] and the dismissal of PC Goodchild for attempting to set up a union led to a strike in the Metropolitan Police in 1872.[219] Elsewhere actions short of these were not uncommon: for instance, in Worcester City Police 'the whole of the sergeants and men' applied for a pay increase in 1865.[220] Campaigning on pay remained important, but other issues emerged, reflecting something of the change in the way constables perceived the job. At meetings in Hyde Park during the summer of 1887, Metropolitan Police officers not only asked for more pay, but also expressed their views on pensions, the severity of internal discipline and the demoralizing nature of police administration.[221] In 1890 there was a strike in the Metropolitan Police over pay and oppressive treatment and an attempt to establish a union.[222] The appearance of journals, such as the *Police Service Advertiser* (established 1866)[223] and the *Police Review and Parade Gossip* (1893), aimed specifically at police constables reinforced the idea of the job as a career: *The Guardian of the Peace, and County and Borough Police Record*, which was first published in Newcastle-on-Tyne in January 1866, expressed its purpose as 'the moral and social elevation of the Force, and to the advocacy – temperately, yet earnestly and firmly – of the interests of its members.'

The peak of this union activity was reached in the period beginning with the formation in 1914 of the National Union of Police and Prison Officers. The union emerged out of the Metropolitan Police Union, which had been formed in the previous year, and claimed to have recruited 1200 members within its first six weeks.[224] Pay remained an issue, but there was growing discontent over other issues: the increasing level of work and hours of duty, especially during the war when the number of officers fell; the failure of many forces to implement the Police Weekly Rest Day Act 1910; the pressure put on Metropolitan constables to make arrests because the sub-divisional inspectors received an allowance based on the number of charges brought; the difficulties of promotion, which virtually ceased during the war; and the tendency to promote from outside forces on grounds unconnected with policing ability.

The focus on the oppressive nature of police discipline was reflected in the union's motto, 'Tyranny is NOT Discipline.' It regarded the practice of appointing military officers to senior ranks in the police as 'an evil custom', both because the union supported the principle of promotion through the ranks and because it opposed militarism, which 'aims at making men creatures of rules and orders, suppresses their individuality, and is inimical to the development of personal initiative, tact, sympathy, and even, in the true sense of the word, of chivalry.' This, the union concluded, damaged police-public relations.[225]

Following the dismissal of a constable for joining the National Union, a strike for higher pay was called in August 1918, which enjoyed strong support in the Metropolitan Police. The constable was reinstated, there were concessions on pay and certain representative organizations were authorized, although not the National Union itself. The Desborough Committee was appointed to consider, among other things, pay and conditions of service in March 1919, but its initial recommendations failed to head off a further strike in July 1919. This was a response to a clause in the Police Bill before Parliament that proposed to make illegal membership of a union other than the non-affiliated Police Federation. The strike attracted strong support in London, Liverpool, Birmingham and Birkenhead, but it failed and the strikers were dismissed the service.[226]

The existence of a large number of separate forces controlled by separate police authorities inhibited the development of a cohesive, national police identity. The relationship between chief officers and their police authorities varied. The Municipal Corporations Act 1835 did not specify the structure of the borough police and the nature of the relationship differed between forces. The background and expertise which came with appointment as chief officer of a large force meant that he was in a better position to resist pressure from the watch committee than the chief officer of a smaller force. Yet, even so he might have to submit because of the watch committee's power under the 1835 act to issue regulations and to dismiss any constable who was negligent or unfit.[227] Even a strong-minded man like Nott Bower was unable to resist the demands of the Liverpool watch committee in the 1890s that he follow a particular approach to policing.[228]

The county chief constables, on the other hand, came mainly from outside the police and many had been military officers.[229] They enjoyed more autonomy than their borough counterparts.[230] This was, partly, because they were often closer in terms of their socio-economic backgrounds to the county magistrates, to whom they were responsible, than the borough chief officers were to members of the watch committees. It was also because under the 1839 and 1856 acts the county chief constables took on many of the functions that the Municipal Corporations Act 1835 had given to the watch committees. Moreover, the magistrates only met quarterly so there were not the opportunities for the sort of detailed control that was possible in the boroughs where watch committees met frequently. The Local Government Act 1888 replaced the committees of magistrates with standing joint committees consisting of magistrates and county councillors, although the fears which the former expressed about this change seemed not to have been realized because, by-and-large, they came from the same backgrounds as the councillors.

Among chief officers there developed some degree of cohesion through the County Chief Constables Club, which was established in

1858, and the Chief Constables Association, formed in 1896 for borough police, although neither body provided a forum for discussing policing matters, and co-operation between the two organisations was limited, largely, it seems, because of the disdain the rural chiefs had for their borough counterparts.

The Home Office

The gradual growth of Home Office influence also provided some pressure on the police to cohere around particular principles. The General Instructions issued to Metropolitan Police officers in 1829 were widely drawn on by other forces and so provided some uniformity of practice, although there were differences in promotion prospects, wages and terms of service. The requirement under the 1856 act that forces be certified by the Inspectors of Constabulary as efficient to qualify for government funding encouraged improvements and some uniformity.[231] The main difficulty seems to have been persuading watch committees to increase borough forces in line with population: indeed, Sheffield briefly lost its grant in 1862–3 on this ground. After 1890 the grant was never withheld; the Home Office preferred to use persuasion and seems to have acquired sufficient authority to be able to do this,[232] although Home Secretaries varied in their willingness to intervene in local government.[233]

Local police authorities were not always believed to have the best interests of police efficiency in mind. One of their main concerns was to control costs, but – and this is some measure of the acceptance of the police – during the second half of the century it was also common for borough authorities to want their own force, either because of a feeling that their town was inadequately policed by the county or because of the status of having borough police. So, whereas before 1850 the Home Office had faced some resistance to the idea of the new police, in the second half of the century it was looking at ways of reducing the number of small forces. Some borough forces had disappeared into their counties as a result of the provisions enabling voluntary amalgamations in the Rural Constabulary Act 1840 (3 & 4 Vic., c. 88): so, for instance, Wenlock's three-man force merged with the Shropshire force in 1841, as did Bridgnorth, which had sunk to one officer by 1850, although the latter withdrew five years later as a result of dissatisfaction with the level of policing in the town.[234]

The government inspection system in the 1856 act led to further amalgamations: for example, the Oswestry force was refused a certificate of efficiency in 1860 and promptly merged with Shropshire police.[235] The Municipal Corporations Act 1877 prevented a new force from being established in a borough with a population of less than 20,000, and the Local Government Act 1888 required all forces in boroughs with a population of under 10,000 to amalgamate with the county. This led to the abolition of 48 forces.[236] Further amalgamations were urged in the twentieth century by the Desborough Committee in 1920 and a select committee in 1932.[237] In 1938 the Departmental Committee on Detective Work argued that an important obstruction to crime detection was 'the degree of disunity created by the existence of so many small units of administration'.[238]

Occasionally, the idea of a national police service was considered, but never with much conviction: for instance, the Desborough Committee in 1920, rejected it as 'foreign to constitutional principle … by which the preservation of law and order in this country is primarily the function of the proper local authorities; it would alter the whole basis of the police system and in particular would prejudice the intimate relations between the Police and the localities where they serve'.[239]

In the early twentieth century there were signs that the Home Office was willing, exceptionally, to override local police authorities, as, for instance, during industrial disputes in 1910 and 1911 and the General Strike of 1926. Discussions on policy issues between chief officers and the Home Office were facilitated in 1918 by the establishment of eight district conferences, each consisting of chief officers from the district and Home Office officials.[240] These conferences fed into the Central Conference of Chief Constables, which was chaired by a senior official from the Home Office. According to one senior civil servant, they enabled the Home Office to act 'as a general clearing-house for the exchange of ideas and experience, and to make its contribution to fostering the well-being and sense of common purpose that invests the whole police service.'[241]

Much of the Desborough Committee's report sought to impose greater uniformity through the medium of the Home Office and to improve co-operation between forces on matters such as training. Desborough also established the Police Council, a body composed of officers drawn from all ranks which advised on police regulations. Following the committee's reports in 1919–20 and the Police Act 1919, government grants to police forces were increased on the ground that the duties of the provincial police had national value rather than purely local value, but this also enabled the imposition of much wider conditions. The Home Office had to be satisfied that the force was properly administered and had to approve rates of pay in all forces, whereas previously the Home Office could not intervene with respect to pay in the borough police.[242]

In 1920 the Home Office acquired the power to deploy a proportion of the police in an emergency and this was used during the General Strike in 1926.[243] Sir Arthur Dixon, a senior civil servant at the Home Office and secretary to the Desborough Committee, believed that,

> as a consequence of these developments, especially the unification of the conditions of service and the establishment of the Home Office as, in effect, a central police authority, it does not seem too much to say that the Police Service became gradually transformed from a collection of separate (sometimes very separate) Forces into what amounted, for most practical purposes, to a single Service.[244]

This overstates the degree of centralization which took place. Dixon himself was forced to admit that the power of the borough watch committee meant that the Home Office did not always pass on certain confidential matters to borough chief officers.[245] Nevertheless, by the 1920s the relationship between the Home Office and the chief officers was squeezing the influence of the police authority.

*　*　*　*

By the 1850s, two images of the police were emerging. The first was of the 'Bobby' who was, depending on your point of view, tough but compassionate, or despised and feared, or a mixture of these. His main function was to prevent crime through the control of the streets and the imposition of a particular moral order. This was to be achieved by the exercise of the authority invested in the blue uniform and was what made the idea of plain-clothes officers so difficult to accept: the whole point of the beat constable was to display the uniform. The second image of the police was of the secretive and dramatic world of the detective, and, in particular, the Scotland Yard detective on whom most publicity was focused. He was entrusted with crime control through detection. Admiring journalists, like Dickens, and detectives in their autobiographies depicted detection as a matter requiring expertise beyond the abilities of ordinary people, so that, although the efficiency of the detectives was challenged, it was accepted, as Professor Marks told the Home Secretary, Henry Bruce, in 1869, that, 'To deal with crime and criminals we are almost entirely dependent upon the police force'.

The functions and methods of these two branches were not just separate, they were opposed. The beat constable represented the idea of preventive policing; the detective's existence demonstrated the failure of that project. The beat constable was meant to be in the public eye, detached from the community and expected to impose a particular set of non-negotiable moral values; even if the practice was often a negotiated accommodation between the officer and the community, there remained a separation that was crucial to the officer's maintenance of authority. The detective, on the other hand, was secretive, his ability to melt into the community was a matter of pride and vital to his collection of the information upon which he depended. The separation between the branches became more pronounced as detection came to be represented as dependent on the acquisition of special skills.

Moreover, from the late nineteenth century, professionalism was working to unpick the attachment between the police and the 'respectable people', represented by the police authorities, and to replace it with a connection to the Home Office. Yet at the same time, while there was a general enthusiasm for ascribing to the police expertise in policing and a willingness among the police to accept that role, the policing work undertaken outside the police continued: victims took direct action or no action, people and businesses employed crime prevention strategies.

Notes

1 *The Edinburgh Review*, Jul 1852, 1. See Clarkson and Richardson (1889) *Police!*, 370.
2 *The Times*, 28 Jul 1866; Custos (1868) *The Police Force of the Metropolis*, 12.
3 *The Edinburgh Review*, Jul 1852, 21–3. On crime figures, see Gatrell (1980) 'The decline of theft and violence'; Jones (1982) *Crime, Protest, Community and Police*, 117–43.
4 Emsley (1996) *The English Police*, 71.
5 Cain (1917) *Address on Policemanship*.
6 Dilnot (1915) *Scotland Yard*, 10.
7 Chapman (1925) *The Poor Man's Court of Justice*, 153. See also the remarks of the Chief Constable of Salford in 1849 in Neal (1849) *The Chief Constable's Report*, 11.
8 Taylor (1997) *The New Police in Nineteenth-Century England*, 162–3.
9 Royal Commission (1929) *Report*, 6. See the commentary in Critchley (1978) *A History of Police*, 201–2.
10 James Monro, 1890, in Taylor (1997) *The New Police in Nineteenth-Century England*, 162.
11 Select Committee (1834) *Report*.
12 McHardy (1840) *Essex Constabulary*, 12.
13 *The Times*, 6 Oct 1829.
14 Storch (1989) 'Policing in rural southern England', 258.
15 Petrow (1994) *Policing Morals*.

16 Taylor (1997) *The New Police in Nineteenth-Century England*, 128.
17 Reilly (1989) *Policing Birmingham*, 30.
18 Dixon (1980) 'Class law: the Street Betting Act of 1906'.
19 Jones (1982) *Crime, Protest, Community and Police*, 78.
20 Smethurst (1983) *Reminiscences of a Bolton and Stalybridge Policeman*.
21 Taylor (1995) *'A Well-Chosen, Effective Body of Men'*, 31–3.
22 Hahn (1989) *Policing Victorian Dorset*.
23 Steedman (1984) *Policing the Victorian Community*, 107–8.
24 Samuel (1981) *East End Underworld*, 189.
25 Parliament provided a plethora of such powers, see, for example, the Metropolitan Police Act 1839 and the Poaching Prevention Act 1862.
26 White (1986) *The Worst Street in North London*, 116.
27 Brogden (1991) *The Police: Autonomy and Consent*, 88.
28 Ayers (1989) *The Liverpool Docklands*, 61.
29 Gamon (1907) *The London Police Court*, 2.
30 Anon (1839b) *Police and Piety*, 13.
31 *Commons Debates*, 3 Jul 1849, c 1260; Smith (1985) *Policing Victorian London*, 52.
32 Smith (1985) *Policing Victorian London*, 52–3.
33 Smith (1985) *Policing Victorian London*, 53.
34 Paley (1989a) 'An imperfect, inadequate and wretched system?', 119.
35 Taylor (1995) *'A Well-Chosen, Effective Body of Men'*, 38.
36 Jones (1982) *Crime, Protest, Community and Police*, 123–4.
37 Jones (1982) *Crime, Protest, Community and Police*, 124.
38 Woodgate (1985) *The Essex Police*, 68.
39 Bale (1960) *Through Seven Reigns*, 24, 54–5. On bonfire night battles in Kent, see Conley (1991) *The Unwritten Law*, 35–7.
40 Davies (1985) 'Classes and police in Manchester 1829–1880'.
41 Taylor (1997) *The New Police in Nineteenth-Century England*, 93–4. See also Humphries (1981) *Hooligans or Rebels?*, 174–208; Jones (1982) *Crime, Protest, Community and Police*, 162–3.
42 Archer (1990) *By a Flash and a Scare*; Hopkins (1986) *The Long Affray*; Jones (1982) *Crime, Protest, Community and Police*, 33–84.
43 Ayers (1989) *The Liverpool Docklands*, 62–4; White (1986) *The Worst Street in North London*, 118–19, 121.
44 Reilly (1989) *Policing Birmingham*, 42–3.
45 Hahn (1989) *Policing Victorian Dorset*, 55.
46 Chapman (1925) *The Poor Man's Court of Justice*, 153.
47 Samuel (1981) *East End Underworld*.
48 Cohen (1979) 'Policing the working-class city'.
49 Cohen (1979) 'Policing the working-class city'; Davis (1989) 'From "rookeries" to "communities"'; Jones (1982) *Crime, Protest, Community and Police*, 85-116; Samuel (1981) *East End Underworld*; Storch (1975) 'The plague of the blue locusts'; Storch (1976) 'The policeman as domestic missionary'.
50 Cohen (1979) 'Policing the working-class city'; White (1986) *The Worst Street in North London*, 113–21.

51 Petrow (1994) *Policing Morals*; Storch (1977) 'Police control of street prostitution'.
52 Samuel (1981) *East End Underworld*.
53 Brogden (1991) *The Police: Autonomy and Consent*, 68–9. For a similar dispute in Birmingham in 1880, see Critchley (1978) *A History of Police*, 131–2.
54 Storch (1976) 'The policeman as domestic missionary'.
55 Gamon (1907) *The London Police Court*, 28–36.
56 Samuel (1981) *East End Underworld*, 180, 182, 184. Harding claimed the police fixed a murder charge for £16,000: ibid, 186.
57 Chapman (1925) *The Poor Man's Court of Justice*, 154–5.
58 Ayers (1989) *The Liverpool Docklands*, 65.
59 Kempster (1904) *The Dalston Perjury Case*.
60 Timewell (1911) *Royal Commission*.
61 Royal Commission (1908) *Royal Commission upon the Duties of the Metropolitan Police*; Samuel (1981) *East End Underworld*, 190–4.
62 Timewell (1911) *Royal Commission*, 6.
63 *Commons Debates*, 29 Jul 1908, c 1593.
64 *Commons Debates*, 29 Jul 1908, c 1598.
65 Moylan (1934) *Scotland Yard and the Metropolitan Police*, vii.
66 Royal Commission (1839) *First Report*, 149–50.
67 Steedman (1984) *Policing the Victorian Community*, 159.
68 Custos (1868) *The Police Force of the Metropolis*, 8–9.
69 Samuel (1981) *East End Underworld*; Smethurst (1983) *Reminiscences of a Bolton and Stalybridge Policeman*; White (1986) *The Worst Street in North London*.
70 Reilly (1989) *Policing Birmingham*, 42.
71 Sleigh (1844) *A General Police and Constabulary List*, viii.
72 Steedman (1984) *Policing the Victorian Community*, 140.
73 *The Edinburgh Review*, Jul 1852, 33.
74 Taylor (1997) *The New Police in Nineteenth-Century England*, 89.
75 Gamon (1907) *The London Police Court*, 28.
76 Chapter 5.
77 Goodway (1982) *London Chartism*; Palmer (1988) *Police and Protest in England*, 483–90; Thompson (1984) *The Chartists*. On the problems this brought, see Metropolitan Police Office (1848) *Memorandum*.
78 *Blackwood's Magazine*, Oct 1848 in Palmer (1988) *Police and Protest in England*, 484.
79 Emsley (1996) *The English Police*, 63.
80 Bowes (1966) *The Police and Civil Liberties*, 79–82; Richter (1981) *Riotous Victorians*; Smith (1985) *Policing Victorian London*; Vogler (1991) *Reading the Riot Act*, 39–43.
81 *The Times*, 28 Jul 1866; also 25 Jul 1866; Custos (1868) *The Police Force of the Metropolis*.
82 Royal Commission (1856) *Report*; Smith (1985) *Policing Victorian London*, 127–49.
83 Smith (1985) *Policing Victorian London*, 171, 175.

84 *The Times*, cited in Smith (1985) *Policing Victorian London*, 166, also 161–82.

85 Smith (1985) *Policing Victorian London*, 134.

86 Although Jones (1982) *Crime, Protest, Community and Police*, 123.

87 Mearns and Powell (1883) *The Bitter Cry of Outcast London*, 3–4.

88 Home Department (1842) *Report*.

89 Jones (1984) *Outcast London*, 224–5.

90 Jones (1984) *Outcast London*; Richter (1981) *Riotous Victorians*.

91 Williams (1967) *Keeping the Peace*, 76.

92 Clarkson and Richardson (1889) *Police!*, 93–4.

93 Pulling (1964) *Mr Punch and the Police*, 111.

94 Bailey (1981) 'The Metropolitan Police, the Home Office and the threat of outcast London'; Jones (1984) *Outcast London*; Richter (1981) *Riotous Victorians*; Vogler (1991) *Reading the Riot Act*, 60–9.

95 Police Constable (1888) *The Metropolitan Police and Its Management*, 1, 3.

96 Police Constable (1888) *The Metropolitan Police and Its Management*, 16.

97 Williams (1967) *Keeping the Peace*, 78.

98 Vogler (1991) *Reading the Riot Act*, 68–9.

99 Sugden (1995) *The Complete History of Jack the Ripper*, 134–5, 286.

100 Warren (1888) 'The police of the Metropolis', 578.

101 Warren (1888) 'The police of the Metropolis', 579.

102 *The Times*, 13 Nov 1888.

103 Morgan (1987) *Conflict and Order*; Weinberger (1991b) *Keeping the Peace*; see also chapter 5.

104 Royal Commission (1839) *First Report*, 68–88.

105 Taylor (1995) *'A Well-Chosen, Effective Body of Men'*, 6. Also Jones (1982) *Crime, Protest, Community and Police*, 92.

106 Fairhurst (1996) *Policing Wigan*, 8.

107 Reilly (1989) *Policing Birmingham*, 21–2.

108 Elliott (1984) *Policing Shropshire*, 79–80.

109 But see Police Act 1890, s. 25 and Home Office circular A.52632 B/18 of 1894.

110 Emsley (1996) *The English Police*, 68. Also Bale (1960) *Through Seven Reigns*, 51–4; Palmer (1988) *Police and Protest in England*, 534.

111 Select Committee (1893) *Report*; Vogler (1991) *Reading the Riot Act*, 69–74.

112 Select Committee (1908) *Report*; Dixon (1963) *The Emergency Work of the Police*, 16.

113 Dixon (1963) *The Emergency Work of the Police*, 27.

114 Vogler (1991) *Reading the Riot Act*, 78.

115 Cobb (1957) *The First Detectives*, 170–1.

116 *The Times*, 1869, in collection of cuttings, British Library at C.T. 482.

117 Aspland (1868) *Crime in Manchester*. See Birmingham Police Office (1847–50) *Number of Persons Taken into Custody*; Doncaster (1863) *Criminal and Miscellaneous Statistical Returns*; Manchester Police (1841–2) *Number of Persons Taken into Custody*; Manchester Police (1844) *Criminal Statistical Returns*.

118 Smith (1985) *Policing Victorian London*, 61.

119   *The Times*, 11 Nov 1830.
120   Select Committee (1833) *Report*.
121   Select Committee (1833) *Report*, 3, 78–80.
122   For the use of plain-clothes officers outside London, see Elliott (1984) *Policing Shropshire*, 127–8.
123   Smith (1985) *Policing Victorian London*, 66–8, 72–7.
124   Moylan (1934) *Scotland Yard and the Metropolitan Police*, 191–2.
125   But see Hannington (1936) *Unemployed Struggles*, 1919–1936.
126   Anon (1844) *A Full Report of the Evidence Taken at the Thames Police Court*.
127   Select Committee (1837) *Report*, 23.
128   Cobb (1957) *The First Detectives*, 172–4.
129   Anon (1842) *The Life, Trial, and Sentence of Daniel Good*; Moylan (1934) *Scotland Yard and the Metropolitan Police*, 181; Smith (1985) *Policing Victorian London*, 65.
130   Moylan (1934) *Scotland Yard and the Metropolitan Police*, 185.
131   Smith (1985) *Policing Victorian London*, 62–3, 65, 68.
132   Taylor (1995) *'A Well-Chosen, Effective Body of Men'*, 30, 51 n69.
133   Barrister-at-Law (1860) *The Road Murder*; Bridges (1954) *Saint – With Red Hands?*; Ware (1866) *The Road Murder*.
134   Taylor (1863) *The Ticket-of-Leave Man*.
135   Forrester (1863) *The Private Detective*.
136   For example, *The Edinburgh Review*, Jul 1852, 12–20.
137   Hughes (1864) *Leaves from the Note-Book of a Chief of Police*.
138   Collins (1965) *Dickens and Crime*.
139   Doyle (1892) *The Adventures of Sherlock Holmes*.
140   Although see Barnett (1888) *Police Sergeant C 21*. See Wiener (1990) *Reconstructing the Criminal*, 215–24.
141   Rawlings (1995) 'The idea of policing'.
142   Chadwick (1829) 'Preventive police', 264.
143   *Household Words*, 13 Jul 1850.
144   Hughes (1864) *Leaves from the Note-Book of a Chief of Police*, 6, 7.
145   Jervis (1995) *Chronicles of a Victorian Detective*, 19, 26. Also Caminada (1895) *Twenty-five Years of Detective Life*.
146   Richmond (1976) *Scenes in the Life of a Bow Street Runner*, ix.
147   Dickens (1861) *The Lamplighter's Story*, 35.
148   Smethurst (1983) *Reminiscences of a Bolton and Stalybridge Policeman*, 12–13.
149   Hahn (1989) *Policing Victorian Dorset*, 42, 43.
150   Harris (1868) *Questions and Answers Framed for the Instruction of Constables*, 25–6; Kyrke (1969) *History of East Sussex Police*, 103–5.
151   Hahn (1989) *Policing Victorian Dorset*, 29.
152   Anon (1878) *Life and Examination of Charles Peace*, 6.
153   Kyrke (1969) *History of East Sussex Police*, 70.
154   Elliott (1984) *Policing Shropshire*, 94.
155   Kyrke (1969) *History of East Sussex Police*, 69.
156   Elliott (1984) *Policing Shropshire*, 44.
157   Waters (1994) *The Police Gazette*.

158 Barrister-at-Law (1860) *The Road Murder*, 2.

159 Adam (1914) *Police Work from Within*, 9n; Bridges (1954) *Saint – With Red Hands?*.

160 Bartrip (1981) 'Public opinion and law enforcement'; Davis (1980) 'The London garotting panic of 1862'; Sindall (1990) *Street Violence in the Nineteenth Century*.

161 Short (1979) *The Dynamite War*; Smith (1985) *Policing Victorian London*, 193–5.

162 Smith (1985) *Policing Victorian London*, 192.

163 Petrow (1993) 'The rise of the detective in London', 92–3.

164 Dilnot (1928) *The Trial of the Detectives*.

165 *The Times* in Petrow (1993) 'The rise of the detective in London', 94.

166 Moylan (1934) *Scotland Yard and the Metropolitan Police*, 188–9.

167 Letter from X.Y.Z. to *The Pall Mall Gazette*, 29 Jan 1880.

168 Allason (1983) *The Branch*; Porter (1985) *The Origins of Britain's Political Police*; Porter (1987) *The Origins of the Vigilant State*; Short (1979) *The Dynamite War*.

169 This secrecy fell away, to some extent, as retired officers began publishing their memoirs: Burst (1935) *"I Guarded Kings"*; Burst (1937) *In Plain Clothes*; Woodhall (1934) *Guardians of the Great*.

170 Rawlings (1999) *Crime and Power*, 119–20.

171 Later they expanded their interest to suffragettes and, in the run up to the First World War, to rooting out possible spies.

172 Adam (1914) *Police Work from Within*, 241, 245; Anon (1888b) *Ghastly Murder in the East End*; Anon (1888c) *Horrible Mutilation*; Anon (1888d) *The Whitechapel Horrors*; Rawlings (1999) *Crime and Power*; Sugden (1995) *The Complete History of Jack the Ripper*; Walkowitz (1992) *City of Dreadful Delight*.

173 *The Times*, 13 Sep 1888.

174 Critchley (1978) *A History of Police*, 161.

175 *The Times*, Sep–Nov 1888 *passim*.

176 Clarkson and Richardson (1889) *Police!*, 273, 277–86.

177 Sugden (1995) *The Complete History of Jack the Ripper*, 4.

178 Sugden (1995) *The Complete History of Jack the Ripper*, 2, 19; *The Times*, 3 Sep, 12 Sep, 19 Oct 1888.

179 For his view of detectives, see Warren (1888) 'The police of the Metropolis', 587.

180 Petrow (1993) 'The rise of the detective in London', 97. For some notable detective successes in the years after the Whitechapel murders, see McLaren (1993) *A Prescription for Murder*; Shore (1923) *Trial of Thomas Neil Cream*. When Henry was forced out by the Home Office following the Police Strike of 1918, he was succeeded by General Macready, who had gained reputation by his handling of the military during the miners' strike of 1910 in South Wales. Macready was more in the model of Warren, declaring his wish 'to bring the discipline of the Metropolitan Police up to the standard of a Guards' Regiment': Vogler (1991) *Reading the Riot Act*, 97.

181 Moylan (1934) *Scotland Yard and the Metropolitan Police*, 187.

182 Petrow (1993) 'The rise of the detective in London', 100. See the denunciation of police-office constables for using this technique: Select Committee (1834) *Report*, 21.
183 Petrow (1993) 'The rise of the detective in London', 98.
184 Petrow (1993) 'The rise of the detective in London', 93.
185 Dilnot (1928) *The Trial of the Detectives*.
186 Petrow (1993) 'The rise of the detective in London', 94.
187 Petrow (1994) *Policing Morals*.
188 Petrow (1993) 'The rise of the detective in London', 104.
189 Clarkson and Hall (1889) *Police!*.
190 Evans (1974) *The Police Revolution*, 108.
191 Ascoli (1979) *The Queen's Peace*, 239–40.
192 Morrish (1955) *The Police and Crime-Detection Today*, 15.
193 Else and Garrow (1934) *The Detection of Crime*, 2.
194 Petrow (1994) *Policing Morals*, 49–113.
195 Bonomi (1872) *Project for an Instrument for the Identification of Persons*; Monro (1886) *A Report on the History of the Department of the Metropolitan Police*; Petrow (1994) *Policing Morals*, 87–101.
196 Lambourne (1986) 'A brief history of fingerprint identification', 8.
197 Morrish (1955) *The Police and Crime-Detection Today*, 74. See Locard (1920) *L'Enquête Criminelle et Les Méthodes Scientifiques*, 295.
198 Locard (1920) *L'Enquête Criminelle et Les Méthodes Scientifiques*, 19.
199 Home Office (1936) *Scientific Aids to Criminal Investigation*, 3, 4.
200 Else and Garrow (1934) *The Detection of Crime*, xii.
201 Scott (1949) *Police Problems of Today*, 21.
202 Home Office (1938) *Report of the Departmental Committee*.
203 Home Office (1938) *Report of the Departmental Committee*, vol I, 20–39.
204 Home Office (1938) *Report of the Departmental Committee*, vol I, 53.
205 Home Office (1938) *Report of the Departmental Committee*, vol I, 54–7.
206 For example, Home Office (1936) *Scientific Aids to Criminal Investigation*.
207 Home Office (1938) *Report of the Departmental Committee*, vol I, 27–8.
208 Hobbs (1992) *Doing the Business*.
209 Bakewell (1842) *Observations on the Construction of the New Police Force*.
210 Thomas (1987) *The History of Gloucestershire Constabulary*, 27.
211 Shpayer-Makov (1991) 'The appeal of country workers'. On the socio-economic background of recruits, see Emsley (1996) *The English Police*, 191–206; Emsley and Clapson (1994) 'Recruiting the English policeman'; Shpayer-Makov (1990) 'The making of a police labor force'; Steedman (1984) *Policing the Victorian Community*, 69–105.
212 Clarke (1992) *The Policemen of Hull*, 62; Martin and Wilson (1969) *The Police*, 24.
213 Clarkson and Richardson (1889) *Police!*, 88–96.
214 Taylor (1995) *'A Well-Chosen, Effective Body of Men'*.
215 But Weinberger (1991a) 'Are the police professionals?'.
216 *The Guardian of the Peace, and County and Borough Police Record*, 1866, 2.
217 Gamon (1907) *The London Police Court*, 15.

218 Clarke (1992) *The Policemen of Hull*, 54–6; Emsley (1996) *The English Police*, 96.

219 Anon (1872) *The Revolution in the Police*; Reynolds and Judge (1968) *The Night the Police Went on Strike*, 202–12; *Daily News*, 31 Oct 1872.

220 Worcester City Police (1865) *City of Worcester*, 3.

221 Police Constable (1888) *The Metropolitan Police and Its Management*. Also Hunt (1863) *The Policeman's Struggle*; Trafford (1848) *Trafford (Late Police Constable)*.

222 Emsley (1996) *The English Police*, 97–9; Reynolds and Judge (1968) *The Night the Police Went on Strike*, 213–25.

223 It became *Police Guardian* in 1872.

224 *Police & Prison Officers' Journal*, 30 Jan 1914, 6 Feb 1914.

225 *Police & Prison Officers' Journal*, 2 Oct 1914.

226 Emsley (1996) *The English Police*, 97–103, 121–7, 132–6; Martin and Wilson (1969) *The Police*, 29–31, 36–7; Reynolds and Judge (1968) *The Night the Police Went on Strike*.

227 Reiner (1991) *Chief Constables*, 12–13.

228 Brogden (1991) *The Police: Autonomy and Consent*, 69.

229 Wall (1998) *The Chief Constables of England and Wales*, 243. Such appointments were not always welcomed: see Anon (1957) *The Kent Police Centenary*, 41.

230 Emsley (1996) *The English Police*, 84–93.

231 Critchley (1978) *A History of Police*, 118–23; Hart (1956) 'The County and Borough Police Act'; Steedman (1984) *Policing the Victorian Community*, 38–41.

232 Hart (1956) 'The County and Borough Police Act', 410; Martin and Wilson (1969) *The Police*, 34.

233 See the views of Harcourt when Home Secretary in 1880–5 in Critchley (1978) *A History of Police*, 130.

234 Elliott (1984) *Policing Shropshire*, 24, 50, 57–9.

235 Elliott (1984) *Policing Shropshire*, 76–7.

236 Hart (1951) *The British Police*, 35.

237 Select Committee (1932) *Report*.

238 Home Office (1938) *Report of the Departmental Committee*, vol I, 43.

239 Home Office (1938) *Report of the Departmental Committee*, vol I, 41. See Emsley (1996) *The English Police*, 161–3.

240 Dixon (1963) *The Emergency Work of the Police*, 7.

241 Critchley (1978) *A History of Police*, 183.

242 Police Act 1919; Dixon (1963) *The Emergency Work of the Police*, 7.

243 Emsley (1996) *The English Police*, 137–8.

244 Dixon (1963) *The Emergency Work of the Police*, 8.

245 Emsley (1996) *The English Police*, 160.

Chapter 7

'The foundations of law and order'

Post-war blues

At the end of the Second World War the Home Secretary, Chuter Ede, praised the efforts of the police in terms which had, by that time, become very familiar:

> The civilian police force of this country is an object of universal admiration ... and undoubtedly some of the more recent phases of their activities have given them an even higher standing with the ordinary citizen than they ever had before.[1]

To *The Times* the police provided 'the foundations of law and order'.[2] However, there were two main problems: a rising crime rate and a shortage of officers.

The *Police Review* claimed in 1944 that there was 'substantial evidence of a serious increase in crime in many parts of the country'.[3] However, it was believed that this increase was the result of the dislocation caused by the war and that the figures would fall.[4] There was a good deal of confidence that the programme of social reconstruction initiated by the Beveridge Report would eradicate poverty and, thereby, largely eliminate crime.[5] Indeed, the figures seemed to peak in 1948.[6] Unfortunately, this was just a temporary dip, and they rose again from the mid-1950s to such an extent that by 1960 the Inspectors of Constabulary were warning of the danger of crime getting out of control.[7] The Royal Commission on the Police (1960–2) was rather dumbfounded. Noting that between 1949 and 1959 national wealth had risen by over a quarter and average earnings by 35 per cent in real terms, yet crime had increased by 45 per cent:

> This is a distressing accompaniment to the benefits of the welfare state, the virtual elimination from our society of poverty and widespread unemployment, the increased leisure now enjoyed by all classes and the educational opportunities open to all.[8]

Many forces had been below strength at the outset of the war. The HM Inspectors of Constabulary reported:

> The view was expressed by prominent members of some police authorities either that they did not believe in war, or that war could not come to them. They had in some instances the sole idea of avoiding added cost to the rates![9]

Emergency measures filled the gap during the war,[10] but by the late 1940s the shortage had become acute. This was the result of a combination of factors: the retirement of those who had been kept on for the duration of the war; the loss of reserve officers and special constables; the high wastage rates; the difficulty of recruiting caused by a buoyant job market and the discouragements of low police pay and quasi-military discipline. The Oaksey Committee found that by 1948 there was a shortage of just under 12,000 officers in England and Wales,[11] and the Home Office admitted that in London and some other large cities recruitment is 'dangerously low'.[12]

While Oaksey thought the main problem was that the police were underpaid relative to other workers, other changes were also recommended, such as the reorganization of the mechanisms for pay negotiations, improved prospects for promotion, the civilianization of some clerical tasks, and, in what can now be identified as something of a Wallace-and-Gromett moment, extra rations of cheese.[13] Although chief officers hoped Oaksey would encourage recruits,[14] the problems remained. A year later Birmingham reported a shortfall of 538 officers, which amounted to a quarter of the authorized establishment, and over the next decade recruitment barely kept pace with wastage. In 1960 119 officers resigned, nine more than joined that year, and, although the shortfall had by then dropped to 292 officers, it rose again to a peak of 619 in 1965, which was still about a quarter of the authorized establishment.[15]

Other forces reported similar problems: there were 346 vacancies in Liverpool in December 1949,[16] and the Metropolitan Police was 20 per cent under-strength in 1954.[17] An inquiry by the Police Advisory Board in 1967 reported a deficiency of just under 16,000 in England and Wales, which was about 16 per cent of the total authorized establishment.[18] Among policewomen the numbers had risen to 3,108, but this still represented a shortage of 806. The report proposed abolishing minimum height standards, modifying the eye-sight requirement, increasing the upper age for recruitment and measures to attract graduates and students with 'A' levels. There were also proposals to increase civilianization, particularly the use of traffic wardens (who could be appointed by a police authority under the Road Traffic and Roads Improvement Act 1960, s. 2(1)), and the use of special constables.

By 1971 Tom Critchley, who had been secretary to the Royal Commission on Police in 1960–2, was expressing the concern that a shortage of police officers had forced police to concentrate on law enforcement to the detriment of their social service roles, many of which had passed to other agencies, such as the probation and child care services: 'The balance has tilted towards a more oppressive role'.[19] By the end of 1974 there were still almost 14,000 vacancies in England and Wales, about 12 per cent of the authorized establishment, with the worst hit being the City of London, which was nearly 24 per cent below strength, the Metropolitan Police nearly 22 per cent and the West Midlands 18 per cent.[20] Indeed, it was not until the early 1980s that recruitment improved markedly as a result of an extremely generous pay award, increasing unemployment and a new government eager to impress the country with its commitment to law and order.

Several solutions were adopted by individual forces to tackle the shortage of officers. Existing officers were required to work longer hours, and many forces attempted to broaden their appeal by, for instance, relaxing the military-discipline of the section houses for single officers and, in the 1960s, accepting recruits who wore glasses.[21] The other strategy was to recruit women. The wives of police officers had played a role since well before the arrival of the new police and police matrons had engaged in the supervision, searching and escorting of women and children in custody since the late nineteenth century, but it was the First World War which provided the impetus for the recruitment of women police.

Initially there were two entirely separate forces:[22] the Voluntary Women Patrols were formed by the National Union of Women Workers (later the National Council of Women); the Women Police Volunteers (later the Women Police Service) were formed by Margaret Damer-Dawson and drawn mainly from suffragettes who had dropped their campaign at the outbreak of war. In essence, the origin of the women police lay in concerns to limit the autonomy which employment and an absence of men gave to women during the war. Their role was seen as to protect the moral and physical health of those women in spite of themselves.[23] In Leeds, for instance, their objective was, 'to define and assist in promoting a higher moral code among girls, and so to guide and encourage them that they will have every hope of becoming self-respecting citizens.'[24] Part of the work was to watch out for 'workless or unstable girls' who gathered around soldiers. These women, according to Mary Allen, who succeeded Damer-Dawson in 1920, were 'simply carried away in an hysteria of patriotism, and wished to give something – anything, even themselves – to the men who were so shortly going to fight for England, and who perhaps in many cases might never taste happiness again.'[25]

Women police were also used for air raid duty in the First World War, training munitions workers, anti-espionage work and trying to control drug trafficking to soldiers. After the war the Metropolitan Police established a small force drawn from the Voluntary Women Patrols, deliberately choosing not to use the ex-suffragettes of the Women Police Service, and, indeed, when the WPS continued to patrol, they were prosecuted for impersonating police officers. By 1921 a private tuition college, the Bristol Training School for Policewomen and Patrols, had been established offering 'to prepare suitable women' for policework and 'to pass them on to the appointing authorities wherever required.'[26]

However, while a few forces kept on small numbers of women police, most had none in the inter-war years and the Police Federation remained implacably opposed to policewomen. The enthusiastic endorsements of their abilities given during the 1920s and 1930s by the Home Office and various committees fell on deaf ears.[27] The Committee on the Employment of Women on Police Duties in 1920 found that of 241 police forces in England, Wales and Scotland, 142 believed 'the circumstances of their own areas are not such as to call for the employment of policewomen'; many witnesses argued that there was no scope for full-time policewomen outside large towns; and the general view (including that of the committee) was 'that women cannot be regarded as substitutes for men in a police force'.[28]

In 1936 there were just 175 women police officers in England and Wales.[29] Newport was not untypical. It appointed its first woman constable in 1940 and it was another 19 years before a woman reached the exalted rank of sergeant.[30] Their work continued to be fairly restricted. Even the chief constable of Birmingham, who was unusual in his enthusiasm for the employment of women police, wrote in 1927 that their role was to 'patrol the streets, parks, and public places, to get in touch with and assist females in distress, out of work, or in bad company.'[31] Only a handful of forces had women detectives: the Department

Committee on Detective Work concluded that there was no 'special need for the employment of police women as detective officers' and no evidence 'of their special aptitude for this work'.[32]

By 1939 there was still only a minority of forces using policewomen and only 226 officers in total, of whom 127 were in the Metropolitan Police. The Second World War meant that police forces not only had to open their doors to both regular policewomen and the Women's Auxiliary Police Service, they also had to give them what had previously been seen as men's work. By 1942 there were 2,800 full-time policewomen (regular and auxiliary) and 844 part-time.[33] By the end of the war HM Inspectors of Constabulary were signalling a new era for policewomen: 'it is now recognised that no force can be regarded as complete unless it has an appropriate number of police women'.[34] In 1947 even the Police Federation relented and agreed to admit women as members.[35] Government recruitment campaigns began in earnest, but, although these emphasized that they had 'the same powers and responsibilities as a policeman', they added 'though policewomen naturally specialize in work with women, children and young people.'[36] Some forces held out: Liverpool City Police only appointed policewomen in 1948.[37] However, between 1939 and 1949 the number of policewomen rose from 246 to 1,148, and, whereas in 1939 138 out of 183 forces employed no policewomen, by 1949 all forces did. Yet, progress towards full equality remained painfully slow.

Many forces sought to tackle the twin problems of a shortage of officers and a rise in crime through greater specialization. For instance, Birmingham police identified certain types of shops, particularly those selling electrical goods, as targets and set up a Night Crime Patrol in 1961 to keep them under surveillance, although the work was hampered by the shortage of officers. Soon after a Special Crime and Accident Prevention Squad was formed which focused primarily on vehicle theft and traffic enforcement at high accident spots. A regional crime squad had been created in 1956 with detectives drawn from Staffordshire, Warwickshire and Worcestershire and this worked with the Birmingham Crime Squad. In 1966 Birmingham established its Drugs Squad and Stolen Car Squad, and in 1969 a Criminal Intelligence Section was created to improve the collection and dissemination of data.[38]

More fundamental changes were in the air. The beat system had survived largely unchanged since the establishment of the new police, but after the war it came under challenge: its efficiency was questioned in the light of changing patterns of crime and, in particular, the rise in car crime; there was a problem in maintaining the beat patrols in view of the shortage of officers; and there was the concern about the effect that the grinding nature of beat patrolling was having on recruitment.[39] In the late 1940s the Police Post-war Committee suggested that beat officers might be supplemented by radio cars,[40] and, indeed, some forces had been experimenting with them since the 1920s.[41] The Oaksey Committee commended the Aberdeen system of team policing in which these new technologies were built into the organization of policing.[42]

A dizzying array of other experiments were put in train during the 1950s by different forces,[43] but it was the unit beat policing scheme that became favoured in the 1960s after initial trials in Kirkby, Widnes and Bury. Its fame was guaranteed by the television series Z Cars. While prompted by the shortage of officers, the idea was also meant to deal with inner-city crime more effectively, and, crucially, to improve contact between police and public, thereby dealing with concerns expressed by the Association of Chief Police Officers in 1962 that 'the post-war tendency to offset dwindling manpower by mechanizing beats has led to a loss of communication between the public and the police'.[44] The force area was divided into beats and each beat was policed by a group of officers on foot and in cars supported by radio communications and detectives. By 1968 60 per cent of the population was covered by a unit beat scheme. However, the hope that officers would routinely leave their cars to patrol on foot and so maintain contact with the public 'became more honoured in the breach than in the observance', and complaints about the lack of foot patrols became common. One explanation for this was that the system led to greater demand, but Robert Reiner offers the equally plausible suggestion that, 'The constables' action-packed perspective on policing was accentuated by the technology of fast cars, sirens and flashing blue lights.'[45]

The Royal Commission on the Police 1960

In the midst of all this, the Royal Commission on the Police was appointed in 1960.[46] This followed fierce criticism of the Home Secretary's decision to pay £300 to settle litigation brought against a police officer for an alleged assault. One of the issues that arose from the case was the allegation that complaints against the police were not being properly investigated.[47] However, the influence of a broader background can be felt in the decision to set up the Royal Commission. There had been a series of scandals stretching back to 1956 when disciplinary action was taken against the Chief Constable of Cardiganshire which alleged that the force was not properly administered and led to its compulsory amalgamation with Carmarthenshire.[48] In the following year there were allegations of corruption in Brighton, where the Chief Constable was acquitted after a criminal trial but dismissed the force, two senior officers were imprisoned and it became clear that there had been a cover-up in the force since 1951. That same year the Chief Constable of Worcester was imprisoned for fraud, and there was an inquiry into allegations that police officers in Thurso had assaulted a boy and that the complaint had not been properly investigated.[49] In 1959 there was a serious dispute between the Chief Constable of Nottingham and the watch committee, and a row broke out over an allegation that a man called Guenther Fritz Podola had been assaulted while in police custody.

There were also complaints about the use of police horses to charge crowds demonstrating at the time of the Suez crisis in 1956 in London, police aggression at a demonstration in 1960 outside the South African Embassy in Trafalgar Square following the Sharpeville massacre, and the brutality shown towards council tenants demonstrating in St. Pancras.[50] Moreover, mass protests against nuclear weapons began in earnest in the late 1950s and, together with a general climate of fear created by the Cold War, made the police and the government nervous about dissent.[51]

For their part, the police saw the relationship with the public as having deteriorated. In part, this was ascribed to an 'increasingly critical outlook by a more widely and highly educated public'.[52] The National Council for Civil Liberties agreed, declaring that, 'The post-war public is not pre-pared to be prevented from exercising their democratic rights by arbitrary police action.'[53] This was not an entirely new issue. There had been some long-term concern about the deterioration of the relationship between the police and the middle classes. The policing of the suf-fragettes in the early part of the century, and, in particular, allegations of assaults by police officers at a demonstration around Parliament in 1910, brought strong criticism,[54] although some took the view that it was the suffragettes who had committed brutal assaults on the police and who had, thereby, proved conclusively that women were not fit for the vote.[55] In 1929 the *Saturday Review* remarked on 'the coldness between police and people' and put it down to the 'multiplication of the occasions of collision between the police and decent honest citizens' as a result of the increase in the regulation of ordinary life.[56]

The key point of conflict was, however, the motor car. The *Punch* cartoon of a child asking, 'Mother, what *did* policemen do when there weren't any motors?' gives some idea of the change in the relationship between the police and the middle classes brought about by the car, as does another slightly later *Punch* cartoon of a young county woman who, having been stopped for speeding, says to a police officer, 'Don't you know who I am?', to which he replies, 'No, and I'll want your address as well.'[57] The car was a potential target for thieves and a means of committing crime, but, more importantly in this context, it was a point of confrontation over road safety between motorists, who did not regard themselves as criminals, and the police.[58]

There was also the relationship between the police and the growing black community. While the question of racist policing had been familiar in the American academic literature and in American police forces since the Second World War,[59] recognition outside black communities that there was a problem came much later in Britain.[60] In its evidence to the Commission the National Council for Civil Liberties argued that black people lacked confidence in the police because of the treatment they received. The failure to solve the case of Kelso Cochrane, who was murdered in Notting Hill in 1959, seemed to demonstrate to the black community that the police took racist murders less seriously and confirmed the belief that racist attacks were not investigated.[61]

The notion that the state could protect liberty and property had ushered in the new police and this idea had developed into an increasingly interventionist form of welfare provision from the late nineteenth century, culminating in the implementation of the Beveridge report in the late 1940s. Yet, within ten years the welfare state was under severe scrutiny. Increasing numbers of people, convinced that it was simply a matter of time before The Bomb was dropped, were growing sceptical about the idea that the State could, indeed, be trusted to provide for the welfare of the individual and the protection of liberty, and, of course, this questioning of the State involved a challenge to the instruments of its power, including the police.

The Royal Commission on the Police considered two main problems. The first was recruitment. This was assumed to be primarily a question of pay and was treated as a matter of urgency with a report appearing in 1960.[62] The second was a general belief that relations between the police and the public had deteriorated. The Commission drew three inferences from recent incidents: 'it was suggested by many that the police were not subject to adequate accountability; that their constitutional position in the state was ill-defined; and that the method of dealing with complaints against them was ineffective and not always fair to the complainant.'[63] The Commission's final report on these matters proved a disappointment to some. *The Spectator* commented:

A glance at the list of witnesses makes instructive reading; the overwhelming majority were policemen, Home Office spokesmen (there were four former Home Secretaries ...), magistrates, local police authorities, and the like. This being so, it is not surprising that the

Report, with the exception of the dissent by Professor Goodhart, recommends little but continuing complacency – little of substance at any rate.[64]

The nature of the report is suggested by the assertion that 'the uniformed man on the beat ... provides the most effective deterrent to crime'. This was unsupported by any research and had been regarded as unrealistic and even untrue for at least ten years.[65] The report also lacked adequate research on complaints, efficiency, or the relationships between the police and young people and the police and black people. One commentator remarked that the report 'seems permeated with a fear of worrying the morale of the force.'[66] The problem, as the limited evidence which the Commission collected showed, was that morale was already low and mere words were unlikely to reassure.

In terms of police-public relations the simple answer from the Commission was, what crisis? Everyone had simply got it wrong. It was claimed that an opinion poll showed 'an overwhelming vote of confidence in the police' and, indeed, 'that such change as there has been in public opinion in recent years has been mainly in favour of the police.'[67] As for the police, their misguided view was the result of their alienation from the community which means 'that the police are continually in a defensive position and any real or imagined criticism ... is liable to produce in the police mind a distorted impression of what the public in general feel about them.'[68] Blame for such worsening of relations as had occurred was placed on young people who 'had grown increasingly resentful of authority', and on the fact that 'the public in general were more knowledgeable about the law and their rights'.[69]

The Royal Commission rejected a proposal for independent inquiries into complaints in a statement which gives an insight into their cockeyed reasoning: 'the appearance of greater justice to the public is liable to be bought at the expense of the police'.[70] Although some changes to the complaints system were recommended,[71] no major reform was required because relations between the police and the public were good, complaints were being properly dealt with under the existing system, and 'this system could not be adapted in such a way as to claim public confidence in a greater measure than has been possible hitherto'.[72] Nevertheless, pressure for a greater independent element continued, and, indeed, gained some support within the Police Federation, not because they believed the system to be unsatisfactory, but to gain public confidence.[73] Although a Joint Working Party of the Police Advisory Boards, whose report in 1971 was not published, again rejected the idea, police authorities were encouraged to increase their supervision and chief constables urged to use officers from other forces to investigate serious complaints.[74] Following the claim by the Select Committee on Race Relations and Immigration that the complaints procedure was damaging police relations with the black community and a private member's bill on the issue in 1973, another inquiry was launched by a Home Office working group.[75]

Eventually the Police Act 1976 reached what proved something of an unsatisfactory compromise in the form of the Police Complaints Board. Subject to certain conditions, the Board was able to review decisions by chief officers with respect to the initiation of disciplinary proceedings following a complaint, although the investigation of complaints remained with the police. Criticisms continued: for instance, the Police Complaints Board proposed more independence in the investigation of complaints and expressed concern about the level of withdrawn complaints;[76] while Scarman's report on the Brixton Riots in 1981 recommended that racism be made a disciplinary offence.[77] Further inquiries and legislation continued to refine this area, although two key problems remained: the first was whether the public could have confidence in a system in which the police investigated complaints made against them, and the second was whether the police would have confidence in a system in which they did not investigate complaints.[78]

The major outcome of the 1960–2 Commission was its confirmation of the change in the relationship between the Home Office, the local police authority and the chief officer in the Police Act 1964.[79] Different witnesses played out the familiar local *versus* central control debate. Although the weight of the Commission's report favoured greater centralization, the outcome was a compromise, but one which, nevertheless, took account of the shift of power away from the local police authorities towards the chief officers and the Home Office that had been underway for most of the twentieth century. Reiner argues that the Commission in effect concluded, 'it would be better to provide the means of *de facto* centralization while maintaining a semblance of local accountability'.[80] The vague wording of the Police Act enabled the Association of Chief Police Officers and the Home Office to continue to acquire power by excluding, or at least limiting, the ability of the police authorities to intervene. Aside from the general public (whose interests, one assumes, are supposedly represented by the Home Office), the other group that was left out of this division of the spoils was the Police Federation, the representative organization of the junior ranks of the police force.[81]

Under the Police Act 1964 the local police authority was to be composed of elected councillors and justices of the peace and charged with maintaining 'an adequate and efficient police force'. Subject to the approval of the Home Secretary, it determined the size of the force and appointed the chief constable; it could dismiss the chief constable (as well as the deputy and assistant chief constables) 'in the interests of efficiency'. The authority also controlled expenditure, but could be required to undertake such expenditure as was necessary to implement regulations made by the Home Secretary. While the powers and responsibilities of the police authority are given in some detail, those of the chief constable and the Home Office are vague, so, for instance, the police are 'under the direction and control of the chief constable'.

This has to be read alongside the pronouncements of senior judges which, in spite of their dubious basis in precedent, strongly support the idea that operational policing should be left in the hands of the police because they possess 'neutral professional expertise' and will not give themselves up to 'ideological' or 'irrelevant' considerations.[82] The judges supported the notion of 'constabulary independence' and took the view that the chief officer is not obliged to follow the instructions of the police authority.[83] The chief officer, according to Lord Denning MR in the Court of Appeal, is required 'to enforce the law of the land …but in all these things he is not the servant of anyone, save of the law itself'.[84] So, for instance, one court overruled the refusal of a police authority to pay for officers 'borrowed' by its chief officer from another force to police a strike even though the authority had expressly disapproved of him taking this action.

This judicial attitude coincided with the approach of the Home Office since the late nineteenth century in favouring the chief officer over the local police authority where the two were in dispute. The power enjoyed by individual chief officers was increased by their collective strength. By the late 1960s the Association of Chief Police Officers (ACPO) had become an important means by which chief officers extended their involvement in policy-making, but it also contributed to the process of unifying the voice of chief officers and making the connection with central government more important than that with local government.

The Home Secretary was given various powers by the Police Act 1964, including: to issue regulations on the administration of the police, the terms of service of officers and the equipment to be used by the police; to arbitrate between a chief officer and police authority; to require the retirement of a chief officer; to appoint Her Majesty's Inspectors; to set up inquiries into policing in particular areas. These powers were to be used in a way 'best calculated to promote the efficiency of the police', and, where there is a difference of opinion between the police authority and the Home Secretary as to the best means of promoting the efficiency of the force, the latter's view prevails. Robert Reiner summed up the tripartite relationship:

In the operational sphere the chief constable is clearly said to reign supreme. However, in the administrative and regulative functions of maintaining, providing, and equipping the police, ascertaining their requirements, and monitoring their efficiency, the role of local police authorities is entirely subordinate to and overdetermined by, central government. The Inspectorate which is relied upon to supply the neutral expertise for the proper conduct of this function is constituted as part of one leg of the tripartite structure (the Home Office) and selected by them from a second leg (the chief constables). It is hard to see where the third leg, the police authorities, is supposed to figure in this scheme of things.[85]

The position of the Home Office was enhanced further by the recommendations of the Royal Commission for the establishment of a central unit for planning police methods, developing new equipment and researching new techniques 'so as to enable the police service to deal promptly and effectively with changes in the pattern of crime and the behaviour of criminals'.[86] This led to the creation by the Home Office of a police scientific research branch staffed by police and scientists in 1963 to undertake research and its publication. In 1969 research was integrated into the Police Department of the Home Office and three research groups were created: Police Research Services Branch under an Assistant Chief Constable to determine the needs of the police service in terms of research and to disseminate research to the police, Police Scientific Development Branch under a senior scientist to develop scientific knowledge, and Police Management and Planning Group under the Economic Adviser to the Home Office to develop a planning-programming-budgeting system, including performance indicators. The Local Government Act 1985 further enhanced the authority of the Home Office: following the abolition of the six metropolitan county councils, the Home Office was, in effect, given the power to set the budget and staffing levels of the police forces in the old metropolitan county councils, which amounted to about half of the total police strength in England and Wales.[87]

The Police Act 1964 also included provisions for the amalgamation of police forces. The compulsory abolition of small forces had begun in the nineteenth century,[88] but, although suggestions had been made during the twentieth century for further rationalization, no further progress was made until the Second World War. In 1942 the Home Office acquired powers under the Defence (Amalgamation of Police Forces) Regulations to make compulsory amalgamations which were justified on military grounds. The regulations brought strong protests and reassurances appeared to have been given that the mergers would be reversed after the war. In the event, however, while some forces, such as those in East and West Sussex, were demerged,[89] the government decided to put through the Police Act 1946 (9 & 10 Geo. VI, c. 46). Under this all non-county borough forces were merged with county forces in addition to the thirteen already amalgamated under the regulations and another three which had disappeared in mergers (s. 1).[90] The act also allowed the Home Secretary to compulsorily amalgamate other forces and allowed voluntary amalgamations (ss. 3, 4). The compulsory power was used sparingly because the Home Office expressed reluctance to act against local wishes:

> Local authorities are naturally jealous of their independence, and the view has been taken, I think rightly, that their police forces should not be amalgamated against their wishes unless there is a clear case for doing so on the grounds of public interest.[91]

Indeed, by a quirk of the Police Act 1946 new county borough forces were allowed if none had existed before. This led to the establishment of Bournemouth police in 1948 and, when Luton, whose non-county borough force had been amalgamated with Bedfordshire in 1947 by virtue of the act, became a county borough in 1964, it established its own force against the advice of the Home Office and the Police Federation.

After the 1964 act, the Home Secretary, Roy Jenkins, acted decisively with the support of the Conservatives and the various police associations, to cut the number of forces in England and Wales from 117 to 46 in 1966 (five more were lost in 1972). There was opposition from some of the police authorities. For instance, Alderman Langfeld, chair of the Southport Watch Committee, prefaced a history of the recently abolished borough force with his view that it was one of the best of the county borough forces and that he feared that handing policing over to 'an elephantine force' – the Lancashire Police – 'may well preclude Southport enjoying better police cover in the future' and that on this ground the amalgamation had been 'fought every inch of the way'.[92]

The continuing problems

The Royal Commission did not put an end to the problems that had confronted the police in the 1950s. In 1963 there was the 'rhino whip' case involving the Sheffield Crime Squad, which had been formed in 1963 as a response to increasing crime and declining detection rates. Two officers, Derek Millicheap and Derek Streets, were dismissed from the force following their convictions for assaulting prisoners and it was their decision to appeal against the dismissals which forced an inquiry.[93] The squad saw itself as an *élite* 'which could use tough methods to deal with tough criminals and take risks to achieve speedy results'. Streets told the inquiry,

> that criminals are treated far too softly by the Courts, that because criminals break rules, police may and must do so to be a jump ahead, that force is justified as a last resort as a method of detection when normal methods fail, and that a beating is the only answer to turn a hardened criminal from a life of crime.

That same year, following the arrest of a demonstrator during the visit of the King and Queen of Greece, allegations were made that Detective-Sergeant Harry Challenor of the Metropolitan Police had engaged in corrupt practices to secure convictions, including planting evidence. Subsequently, ten convictions were quashed, seven prosecutions withdrawn and one defendant was acquitted. There followed three official reports on the case, only one of which was published.[94] It was concluded that Challenor had been mentally ill and that his illness had escaped notice because it was difficult to diagnose.

The James inquiry into the case followed a familiar pattern in which the terms of reference were restricted, so that the general practices at West End Central, where Challenor was stationed, were not investigated, and, therefore, it was a foregone conclusion that the inquiry would lay the blame on Challenor without trying to see if his behaviour was exceptional. In 1964 there was another inquiry following the death in custody of Herman Woolf.[95] In 1969 allegations about corruption in *The Times* led to an inquiry and the subsequent trial of three detectives suggested there had been systematic corruption through the 1950s and 1960s.[96] This seemed to be confirmed by investigations into the Drugs and Obscene Publications Squads a few years later.[97] It probably came as no surprise when a report for the Metropolitan Police in 1975 suggested that a majority of people believed that police officers had lost touch with the people, were corrupt (although 'not very often') and were often rude or bullying.[98]

During this period, there were also flare-ups between police and demonstrators: for instance, at a demonstration in support of the Campaign for Nuclear Disarmament in Trafalgar Square in 1961, when the *Daily Telegraph* reported that people 'were thrown to the pavements, dragged forcibly to the vans and coaches, and manhandled';[99] at demonstrations during the Cuban Missile crisis in 1962 and during the visit of the King and Queen of Greece in 1963; and at demonstrations in the late

1960s against the Vietnam War and throughout the 1960s and 1970s over apartheid in South Africa.[100] In 1974 a student was killed in Red Lion Square during a clash between anti-fascists, fascists and police.[101]

There was also growing evidence of conflict between the police and black people.[102] Lambert's study in Birmingham, carried out in 1966–7, urged 'a sensitive awareness of the different policing needs of various communities'.[103] Meanwhile, black people were trying to make their voices heard: anger at the policing of the Mangrove café in London led to a demonstration in 1970 that clashed with the police.[104] Two years later the Select Committee on Race Relations and Immigration published a report on what it referred to as police-immigrant relations. This used stereotypes in ways which remained commonplace into the 1980s: 'Asians … retained much of their closely-knit community life, family discipline and organizations with recognized leaders … Their view of the police, conditioned to some extent by police customs in their homelands, varies from submissive awe through positive appreciation to suspicious passivity', and generally Asian crime rates were lower than those of the rest of the population; 'West Indians were variously described to us as exuberant, happy-go-lucky, volatile' and were 'not as closely knit'.

The committee did identify a problem in the relationship between young black people and the police, although the tendency was to excuse the police and to lay blame on the black community itself – the result of things such as a lack of parental control and family tensions, which, combined with 'the discrimination they feel is practised against them, tend to give them a sense of insecurity and frustration which make them resentful of society. This resentment is naturally turned against an obvious, recognizable target, the police.'[105] The committee rejected suggestions that black youths were more involved in crime or were stopped by the police more frequently than whites.

The Home Office took the view that the police often 'find themselves held in some sense responsible' for social deprivation, and that the main issue for the police was simply a matter of more training to reduce 'misunderstandings [which] arise through difficulties of communication with new immigrants'.[106] Similarly, Tom Critchley from the Home Office told a Police Federation seminar in 1971 that the police and 'the indigenous population have grown up each understanding the traditions of policing in this country, an understanding that coloured people cannot possibly have.'[107]

This explanation of problems as coming from misunderstandings had been a commonplace of Home Office attitudes since the 1960s,[108] and its presence in the Scarman report on the Brixton riots meant it remained influential in the 1980s.[109] This meant the issue was not seen as any deep-rooted or conscious racism, it was just about the communication of information about black people to the police, the recruitment of black officers,[110] and 'the need for immigrants themselves to make their contribution'.[111] Some efforts to improve recruitment of black officers and relations with the black community were made. In 1960 there seems to have been no black police officers in England and Wales, by 1966 there were only three and by 1974 there were only 101 black police officers, including just 16 women.[112] The problem of recruitment was explained away as a problem with black people who were too short, or hostile to the police because of attitudes brought from their (or their parents') country of birth, or unable to make themselves understood.[113] Some police forces had also appointed community liaison officers by the early 1970s and training in community relations was being introduced for new recruits.

Dealing with 'The Department'

By the mid-1970s senior police officers around the country were firmly in the public eye and willing to air their opinions. During an interview with *The Times* in 1971, Peter Brodie, one of the candidates to succeed Sir John Waldron as Commissioner of the Metropolitan Police, declared a general exasperation in the police with the lack of tough action against criminals and government support for the police and with 'do-gooders', such as the National Council for Civil Liberties:

> They do all the thumping and get all the publicity. The majority, the other 98 per cent, are silent, but we believe we have their support. The trouble is that we can't climb on a soap box at Marble Arch on a Sunday afternoon and say so. We also know that no government will change its policy and risk losing votes, unless it is pushed by public opinion.[114]

Robert Mark, Brodie's rival for the post – and the eventual successor – presented a less aggressive approach, but at the core there was agreement about the issues. His view was that, 'The police are… very much on their own in attempting to preserve order in an increasingly turbulent society'.[115] For Mark the criminal justice system protected the professional criminal from conviction and he consistently argued for a shift away from rules which, to him, enabled the guilty to keep silent: 'the system of justice is weighted so heavily in favour of the criminal and defence lawyer that it can only be made to work by bending the rules.'[116]

However, on becoming Commissioner, one of Mark's most immediate concerns was the CID. Scotland Yard detectives still regarded themselves as the *élite* of the police. This image was reinforced by the continued practice of smaller forces occasionally resorting to calling on them for assistance,[117] and by a series of dramatic cases in the 1960s. Increasing the number of specialist squads had been regarded as a key strategy for dealing with rising crime. These squads were able to boast of successes, such as the arrest of the Great Train Robbers and the Richardson and Kray gangs, and the secrecy with which they worked enabled them to conceal the rather questionable (but, as has been seen, long-standing) nature of the relationship between detectives and those involved in crime on whom they depend for information. These successes both supported the idea that the detectives were an *élite* and enabled them to ride out a difficult period: the CID in London emerged from the 1960s with an image of efficiency 'unmatched in any comparable period in the history of the detective branch.'[118]

However, by the time Mark became commissioner, that image was becoming tarnished. In his opinion there was evidence of widespread corruption among the CID. He was also alarmed at what he also saw as the widening rift between the detectives and the uniformed branch: 'There was no interchange between CID and the uniformed branch and the force had no sense of corporate identity.'[119]

> The uniformed policeman in London bears the brunt of violence, whether political, industrial, criminal or from hooliganism and he had long resented the airs and graces of the CID, generally known as 'the department'. The CID regarded itself as an élite body, higher paid by way of allowances and factually, fictionally and journal-istically more glamorous[120]

He told the CID 'they represented what had long been the most routinely corrupt organization in London, that nothing and no one would prevent me from putting an end to it and that if necessary I would put the whole of the CID back into uniform and make a fresh start'.[121] This, he later claimed, was applauded by uniform colleagues: 'the uniform branch were only too pleased to see someone deal with a department which had long brought the force as a whole into disgrace.'[122] He forced out 478 officers. For him – as for Vincent and, particularly, Trenchard – the uniform officers represented the moral core of the police and he, therefore, sought to return to an emphasis on them. In this he was facilitated by a number of high-level incidents, such as the Balcombe Street and Spaghetti House sieges in 1975. These enabled him to demonstrate the military efficiency of the uniform branch.[123]

In 1976 the Chief Constable of Kent, Barry Pain, undertook another inquiry into the Metropolitan Police which purportedly showed (it was never published) that senior detectives had assisted in criminal frauds. In 1978 Operation Countryman was set up to inquire into these issues, but it was soon being alleged that it was being obstructed and, as it dragged on, this claim was renewed by Granada Television's *World in Action* programme in 1982. Although these claims were consistently denied, during that programme John Alderson, a former assistant commissioner, expressed the opinion that corruption was still widespread. Between 1979 and 1981 224 officers left the force for disciplinary reasons, although it is impossible to know how many left following allegations of corruption.[124]

In spite of the best efforts of Dixon of Dock Green,[125] the events of the 1960s and 1970s did undermine the traditional images of the bobby on the beat, although senior officers like Robert Mark undoubtedly took the view that, while Dixon's moral values were worth pursuing, the world had moved on and so should policing. The move towards patrolling in cars and the shift away from walking the beat was not universally welcomed. The idea of minimum force became less tenable as the virtues of a strong, disciplined response was promoted by Mark and as the Special Patrol Group – a specialist squad of uniform officers – shot dead two Pakistani demonstrators inside the Indian Embassy in 1973 and demonstrators were killed in clashes with the police in Red Lion Square in 1974 and at Southall in 1979. At the same time, the successes enjoyed by the detectives in the 1960s (boosted by television dramatisations of investigations) were being somewhat undermined by the corruption scandals that had followed them. Then, an inquiry into the interrogation of suspects in the murder of Maxwell Confait raised questions about the methods used in the investigation of crime and led to the appointment of the Royal Commission on Criminal Procedure in 1977.[126]

The police and the politics of the 1980s and 1990s

Paradoxically, as the 1970s came to a close, there was much for the police to feel optimistic about. As problems over recruitment continued, the Police Federation began a public campaign over pay which bore fruit in the appointment of an inquiry. More importantly, the leader of the Conservative opposition, Margaret Thatcher, conflated the issues of rising crime and shortages in the police with criticism of the Labour government's economic policies and its relationship with the trade unions, which reached its nadir during the industrial unrest in 'the Winter of Discontent' in 1978–9: 'the vandals on the picket lines and the muggers in our streets have got the same confused message – "we want our demands met or else" and "get out of the way give us your handbag" '.[127] The Conservatives promised to get tough on criminals and to 'spend more on fighting crime even while we economize elsewhere'.[128] Perhaps it was mere coincidence that as Thatcher made a major speech advancing these policies, the Police Federation organized a campaign calling for all the political parties to address the issue of law-and-order.[129]

After victory in the General Election of 1979, the Conservative government sought to put into effect its simple approach to crime by increasing the prison population and giving greater resources to the police. Their intentions were signalled by the decision to implement in full – rather than in stages, as the previous administration had intended – the proposals on police pay recommended by Edmund Davies[130] and by continuing to make promises on resources: 'If they need more men, more equipment, they shall have them'.[131] Senior police officers were now sought out for their views on policy and some were willing to pronounce on a wide-range of social policy issues, not all of them connected to policing. Many would have agreed with the general thrust, although not the extreme language, used in 1982 by the Chief Constable of Greater Manchester, James Anderton, when he claimed that the police protected society from 'dangerous, insidious and ruthless … [enemies] … in our midst' and in 1984–5 during the Miners' strike when he referred to picketing as 'terrorism without the bullet and the bomb'.[132]

Anderton also argued that the greatest danger for Britain lay, not in the problem of crime, but in the subversion of the basic institutions of government, including the police. The idea that the police were prevented from doing the job of catching criminals, which only they properly understood, by do-gooders who were allowing criminals to escape unpunished proved very popular, if the themes of much of the film and television drama of the period are anything to go by. Britain's television Flying Squad detectives, Carter and Regan, fought not just criminals in *The Sweeney*, but also senior officers and rules which prevented them from doing 'real' policework.

However, the honeymoon period with the Thatcher government drew to a close as it completed its first term. The simple approach of pumping resources into the police and expecting crime to drop had not worked. Not only were the official statistics showing increasing crime and falling detection rates, but also the British Crime Survey, commissioned by the Home Office, showed that large amounts of crime did not appear in the statistics because they were not reported to the police.[133] In addition, a combination of rising unemployment, which had increased welfare expenditure, and the cuts in public spending implemented by the previous government had made it difficult to reduce spending and, therefore, to introduce tax reductions promised by the Conservatives. The government needed to look more widely for cuts in spending and the police became a target. Personnel costs comprised the bulk of police expenditure and these had risen because of the Edmund Davies pay award.

In practice the government was unable to cut back on existing commitments without this being interpreted as a weakening of law-and-order policy. Nevertheless, a change in emphasis became evident. This was summed up by Douglas Hurd, when he was Home Secretary in 1986:

> The truth is that, however many laws we change, however much equipment we provide, however many police officers we put on the streets, these measures will not alone turn back the rise in crime.[134]

This excused slow progress on crime rates and enabled cuts in expenditure on the police. It also fitted in with a general premise of Thatcherism that governments could not resolve social problems through intervention: 'Combating crime is everybody's business, everybody's responsibility. It cannot be left solely to the police.'[135] The government extended its crime prevention agenda, involving the Departments of Education and Science and of Environment as well as the Home Office in projects which emphasized the responsibility of individuals to protect themselves, their children and their property, of architects to build in crime prevention, of schools to provide alarms and closed-circuit television, and so forth.

The Home Office launched a major initiative in the mid-1980s involving, amongst other things, a fictional couple called Steve and Sally, who were 'the crime spotters'.[136] The title for the principal campaign, 'Let's crack crime together', was, perhaps, unfortunate since it came just as crack cocaine emerged as an issue in this country.[137] Much of the advice was sensible, but some of it was problematic, such as, the tendency to depict the danger for women in terms of public space and so implicitly present the home as safe.[138] These campaigns tapped into and reinforced the rapidly expanding private security industry of locks, alarms, closed-circuit television and guards.[139] Security firms guarded shops, shopping centres, warehouses and even Bramshill Police College. Pubs and clubs routinely employed bouncers. The policing of city centres became the work of the private operators whose objectives and methods of working were set in accordance with the needs of their employer. The police, meanwhile, were slipping into the role of providing the emergency reserves.

Ministers were careful not to claim that the police made no difference and continued to express their support, but, as had been the case since the foundation of the new police, the Home Office was able to press through changes without having to go through the tedious and potentially embarrassing process of Parliamentary debate. In 1983 the Home Office issued to chief officers circular 114/1983 in which they were warned that 'the constraints on public expenditure … make it impossible to continue with the sort of expansion which has occurred in recent years' and counselling them to make effective use of existing resources. This began a flow of circulars which addressed particular aspects of police resources, all backed up by a tougher auditing and inspection regime. The drip-drip nature of the change, the relatively high level of wages and resources that the police had compared with other public services, the expressions of support from government ministers and the continued increase in crime made it difficult to raise public outrage at the change in government policy, although the police did argue that both rising crime figures and low detection rates were the result of obstructions at various points in the criminal justice system. In particular, they highlighted the protections for suspects introduced by the Police and Criminal Evidence Act 1984 and the shifting of responsibility for decisions on prosecution to the Crown Prosecution Service which, it was argued, was too cautious in its approach.[140]

Pressure on the police was growing from other sources. In the years just before the Brixton Riot of 1981, the problematic nature of the relationship between the police and the black community had become more evident. One campaigning organization claimed, 'The police in Lambeth have several functions. Among them, undoubtedly, is to control the young black population of Brixton. This has little to do with fighting crime but a lot to do with racism.'[141] A concerted attack on the 'sus' law (that is, arrest under the Vagrancy Act) had drawn support from the Home Affairs Select Committee, which claimed it was having a detrimental effect on race relations, and the power was repealed.[142] This left stop-and-search and there was plenty of evidence that it was being used more frequently against black people.[143] To the police the justification was simple, the power assisted in crime control. One delegate to the Police Federation's Annual Conference in 1982 declared:

in every urban area there's a large minority of people who are not fit to salvage. The only way in which the police can protect society is quite frankly by harassing these people[144]

The stop-and-search tactic provided a spark that was to ignite into the

Brixton riots in 1981. The Special Patrol Group had undertaken a number of raids and there followed a large-scale stop-and-search campaign Operation Swamp. The aim was to reduce mugging, but, while mugging might be prevented by high level police presence, this did not need the stop-and-search element, and, in any case, such operations could not be sustained indefinitely.[145] The other side was that by identifying black people as muggers and mugging as the target crime, no attention was being given to black people as victims of crime and, in particular, racist crimes were neglected. This led to anger after a fire in New Cross, London killed 13 young people attending a party in 1981 and the belief spread that the police were not properly investigating the possibility of arson by racists.[146]

The police still tended to marginalize community relations or else shift the blame. Superintendent Roach of the Community Relations Branch in the Metropolitan Police in 1978 referred to those who, 'did not readily recognize or accept the traditional English way of policing.'[147] The police clung to the traditional aim of street policing, that is, establishing authority and black youths were regarded as defying that authority.[148] The riots in Bristol in 1980 and the more widespread riots of 1981 presented just such a challenge to the authority of the police. As one officer put it, 'Nobody rules the streets of London, Brixton, or even Railton Road, except the Metropolitan Police.'[149] The instant responses of the police to the riots were to re-examine their weaponry and, in London, to undermine Lord Scarman's inquiry into the Brixton riots by publishing figures purporting to show that black people committed more mugging – figures which the Lord Chief Justice, Lord Lane, denounced as 'most misleading and very largely unintelligible'.[150] The appearance of these statistics was made even more curious by the government twice declaring in 1981 that such statistics could not be collected 'as the identity of the offender is often not known'.[151]

The issues did not go away. Opinion poll evidence suggested growing suspicion about the behaviour of the police and falling satisfaction with their work.[152] In 1983 a report by the Policy Studies Institute, which had been commissioned by the Metropolitan Police, supplied apparently damning evidence of widespread racism in the force.[153] Research studies continued to suggest that black people were disproportionately targeted by the police and further rioting broke out in inner-city areas, most notably in 1985 in Handsworth and in Tottenham where PC Blakelock was murdered on the Broadwater Farm Estate.[154]

There was also criticism of the police from other groups, such as victims of rape and domestic violence, and organizations and campaigns developed. Some of these organizations, such as Rape Crisis Centres,

Women's Aid, Southall Black Sisters in London and Saheli in Manchester, were, primarily (but not exclusively), concerned to offer support and advice to victims. Others focused more on campaigning to draw attention to alleged police abuses,[155] to encourage the police to take action,[156] and/ or to develop responses to crime which took more account of the wishes of those most directly affected.[157] Local councils became involved. Some had become increasingly resentful at being sidelined (or, in London, never involved) by chief constables and the Home Office, while still being required to pay part of the costs of policing. This became a particular source of annoyance in some areas during the Miners' strike in 1984–5 as police authorities clashed with chief constables about the deployment of their officers in mining areas or about the borrowing of officers from other forces: George Moores claimed that mutual aid 'is destroying something that we have worked hard for in South Yorkshire – full consultation, policing by consent'.[158]

Some local authorities set up police monitoring groups, commissioned research and encouraged debate on policing issues. The Greater London Council fought for local accountability,[159] established a Police Committee and Police Monitoring and Research Group after the Brixton riots, published a regular newspaper,[160] and provided funds for various groups, including Inquest. On a more local level, some of the London boroughs had their own monitoring groups, such as the Wandsworth Policing Campaign. Fulham and Hammersmith's Community and Police Committee was particularly active, researching and publishing information on subjects such as domestic violence, victimization and closed circuit television.[161]

Special research studies were commissioned.[162] The police took part in some of the initiatives or allowed access for some research projects. Gradually, the campaigns and research had some impact on policing, although to what degree is a matter of debate: for instance, special facilities for interviewing the victims of rape were set up and policies on domestic violence and racist attacks formulated, as police forces sought to show that they were taking these issues seriously.

The Scarman report on the Brixton riots exposed some divisions within the police.[163] His relatively mild criticism and his endorsement of community policing schemes amounted to an allegation that the police were out of touch with the community. The Metropolitan Police did initiate a strategy to integrate home beat officers into the mainstream of operational policing and to improve the status of those who were often derided by colleagues as 'Hobby Bobbies'.[164] But after Sir Kenneth Newman was appointed Commissioner he was heckled at a meeting of the Police Federation when he talked about the need for consultative groups and for more 'sensitive policing' in inner city areas.[165] The Police Federation had dismissed the rioters as muggers aggrieved at the efficiency of saturation policing in Brixton – a view with which Scarman, to some extent, agreed[166] – and, on this basis, Scarman's Report was criticized for introducing a more timid approach to policing.[167] James Jardine of the Federation declared, 'Genuine consultation is all to the good, providing the people you consult with are on the same side and there is goodwill and a willingness in maintaining the rule of law.'[168]

Among government ministers, while there was approval for a more aggressive response to the riots in the form of authorizing the purchase of defensive and offensive equipment, even in the face of opposition from the local police authority,[169] there was also support for Scarman's ideas and the Home Office issued a circular in 1982 directing chief officers to set up community policing schemes involving consultation. The idea did not attract universal support, but in the end a requirement of consultation was put in the Police and Criminal Evidence Act (PACE) 1984 (s. 106). Significantly, those regarded as key figures in community policing, such as Alderson, Chief Constable of Devon and Cornwall and Webb, whose scheme in Handsworth had been particularly praised, did not last long in the police.[170]

Nevertheless, police forces did seek to take account of the wishes of the community. As has been seen, in the wake of the Scarman Report and the focus of Home Office Circular 114/1983 on operational efficiency, some forces commissioned research studies and were more prepared to facilitate and to co-operate with research projects to determine policing needs and the effectiveness of policing strategies.[171] The Metropolitan Police looked to public relations consultants to improve its image. Neighbourhood watch schemes and consultative committees were introduced, which focused around crime prevention and regular meetings between residents and the police. Notably, these schemes did not encourage intervention by the community in the police, and typically did not reflect the diversity of the local population.

For the police, community policing schemes did offer the prospect of further weakening the local police authority by building direct links with communities, and there was, perhaps, some hope of influencing the government by showing a willingness to consult and by constructing popular support. Yet, these initiatives also exposed a divergence of opinion over what the police were supposed to be doing. The police had built a self-image as a crime-fighting organization, yet the bulk of calls to the police were found to relate to non-crime work: Hough found that only 36 per cent of the incidents attended by patrols in his study related to crime.[172] Moreover, the police found themselves out of touch with public opinion on policing styles. For instance, while research suggested that the public favoured beat policing because they measured their feeling of security according to their perceptions as to the presence of police, Kinsey's *Survey of Merseyside Police Officers* revealed that,

> while patrol officers are relatively interested in their work most would prefer other jobs within the force ... Morale among foot patrol officers is lower than in the force at large ... Throughout the force at large patrol work is not sought after and would not appear to be a particularly high status job.[173]

There was also pressure building in the 1980s for policing resources to be put into other areas diametrically opposed to even the limited notion of inclusion in community policing schemes. There had been a growing belief that crime could not be tackled by police forces confined to particular geographical boundaries. As a result, regional, national and international agreements and police squads were established to deal with offences such as terrorism, drug trafficking, football hooliganism, art theft and money laundering.[174] The nature of these crimes, the expertize which it was presumed was needed to tackle them and the broad geographical scope of the work precluded the sort of local accountability envisaged by community policing. In other areas the police also drifted away from this idea of accountability. The technological and logistical developments brought by public order policing in Northern Ireland and the inner cities of England and Wales were refined for industrial disputes, most notably the policing of the Miners' strike in 1984–5 and the Wapping newspaper strike of 1986–7: the use of roadblocks, denying access to particular areas, identity checks, snatch squads.[175]

From the Conservative government's point of view there were dangers in imposing financial constraints on the police since it threatened to undermine its efforts to present itself as the party of law-and-order, and, indeed, there was almost a three-fold increase in expenditure on the police in the ten years after 1983, causing a former head of the Audit Commission to remark that the police was the public service least affected by Thatcherism.[176] Nevertheless, within the police there was growing dissatisfaction. Home Secretaries from the late 1980s had to face increasingly hostile audiences when they went to address the Annual Conference of the Police Federation. There was criticism from the police that the Police and Criminal Evidence Act 1984 provided too much protection for suspects and that the Crown Prosecution Service was too cautious when making decisions about prosecution. Many police had enjoyed the large amounts of overtime earned during the Miners' Strike of 1984–5, but afterwards expressed concern at the criticism that had been levelled at them and complained at being used 'by the Coal Board to do their dirty work'.[177] In 1990 one senior officer claimed that 'within the service there is a depressing lack of confidence in the ability of central government to recognize and provide for the need and efficiency of the service', and it was alleged that a think-tank in Scotland Yard viewed the prospect of a Conservative victory in the 1992 election with 'undisguised pessimism'.[178]

In 1993 John Major's Conservative government produced a White Paper on the police. This argued that, 'While the police service has grown in strength and efficiency, levels of crime have also risen significantly ... The police service alone cannot tackle the problem of crime. They need the active support and involvement of the communities they serve.'[179] In some ways this appeared to be a good time to squeeze expenditure on the police: crime had continued to rise and detection rates had fallen, and there were scandals about miscarriages of justice, such as the Guildford Four, Birmingham Six and Maguire cases concerning terrorist bombings, and the practices of the West Midlands Serious Crime Squad which led to its disbandment.[180] The White Paper's proposals were supposedly aimed at devolving more authority to the police and the local police authorities and, within police forces, placing more power in the hands of local police managers.

A bill based on these ideas was the subject of a vigorous debate in Parliament, particularly over the power of the Home Secretary to appoint members of the police authority, which led to various amendments. The Police and Magistrates' Courts Act 1994 emerged, shorn of some of the more extreme centralist measures contained in the original bill, but still, in effect, enabling the Home Secretary to select five of the nineteen members of the authority. The Home Secretary sets national objectives for the police which the authority and the chief officer incorporate into an annual local plan, and this plan contains targets so that police efficiency can be measured. The aim has been to make policing and the work of the police authority more 'businesslike', although, as Reiner pointed out, it seemed that 'the business they will be doing is that of central government rather than the local electorate'.[181] Nevertheless, the police authority's role has been changed from maintaining an 'adequate' force (Police Act 1964) to ensuring that it is 'efficient and effective', and these words might, with its part in forming the policing plan, enable the police authority to claw back some of the power it has lost in the last hundred years.

At the same time as the White Paper was introduced, the government sought to tackle the expenditure on police pay in 1993 through the Sheehy inquiry.[182] The proposals provoked a storm of protest from the police. Since this came just as the government was facing a revitalized Opposition, which seemed to be making incursions into its claim to be the party of law-and-order, the more controversial proposals were dropped.[183]

Police protection

The pressure on the police that had built up in the 1980s from various sections of the community continued in the next decade. What emerged was a notion that the police were responsible for providing protection to the community, but what that meant became controversial. The black community's anger at both the lack of protection from racist assaults and the use of stop and search came to a head again over the murder in London in 1993 of Stephen Lawrence by racists. Following accusations that the case was mishandled, there was an inquiry by the Kent police into the conduct of the investigation and a failed private prosecution by the Lawrence family, angry at what they saw as the failures of the police. Then, in 1997 Sir William Macpherson was commissioned by the incoming Labour government to hold a public inquiry. His report focused on the investigation of Mr Lawrence's murder by the Metropolitan Police, but also looked more broadly into the issues raised and, as a result, saw it, not simply as a bungled case, but as evidence of a deeper problem. The inquiry concluded that there was evidence of 'institutional racism':

> upon all the facts we assert that the conclusion that racism played its part in this case is fully justified. Mere incompetence cannot of itself account for the catalogue of failures, mistakes, misjudgements, and lack of control which bedevilled the Stephen Lawrence investigation.

This was based on a number of observations. The first was the conduct of the investigation, the treatment of the family and of the principal witness, the failure to see it as a racist murder, and 'the lack of urgency and commitment in some areas of the investigation'. The second was that the disparity across the country in stop and search meant that, in spite of other explanations, 'there remains, in our judgment, a clear core conclusion of racist stereotyping'. The third was 'the significant under-reporting of "racial incidents" occasioned largely by a lack of confidence in the police and their perceived unwillingness to take such incidents seriously.' Again, while recognizing that there were other factors involved, the report concluded, 'we find irresistible the conclusion that a core cause of under-reporting is the inadequate response of the Police

221

Service which generates a lack of confidence in victims to report incidents'. Finally, the report 'identified failure of police training', as evidenced both by various studies and by the fact that 'not a single officer questioned before us in 1998 had received any training of significance in racism awareness and race relations throughout the course of his or her career.'[184]

The controversy did not end with the report. The cross-party consensus, which had been apparent on its publication in 1999, seemed to break down as both major parties began to wind up their law-and-order policies in preparation for the next General Election. The debate threw the meaning of protection back into the cauldron of party politics. In a speech in December 2000 the Leader of the Opposition, William Hague, while deploring Mr Lawrence's murder, linked a decline in stop and search both to an apparent increase in street crime and to the Macpherson report. He attacked what he called a 'liberal *élite*' for branding all police officers as racist and announced,

> I say to the law-abiding majority: I will give you back your country
> – I will give you back your streets, and your town centres, and your
> homes, and your shops … We will wage war against crime like no
> other Government in the history of our country has ever done.

He acknowledged that the investigation of Mr Lawrence's murder had been bungled, but declared that his government would put more officers on the streets and support rather than criticize the police: 'Political correctness will not be allowed to get in the way of law enforcement.'[185]

Around the time of the Macpherson inquiry another issue concerning the definition of protection emerged as the police were confronted by people angry at the release into the community of people convicted of pædophile offences. In 1998 Robert Oliver was released from prison after serving a sentence for the manslaughter of a teenager. There followed demonstrations in East Sussex, Milton Keynes and Rutland and it was alleged that it had cost Thames Valley Police £5,000 to provide protection for him. Oliver appeared to have settled in Wiltshire, but was chased out and was reported to have moved to Dublin.[186] That same year Oliver's associate Sydney Cooke was also released and concerns that he would be attacked led the police to persuade him to enter voluntary custody at a police station in the West Country. Rumours circulated about where he was living. There were demonstrations at police stations in Yeovil, Bristol, Bridgewater and Minehead, and at one of these there was rioting, the stoning of police and the use of petrol bombs. Similarly, after the murder of Sarah Payne in 2000 and, particularly after the release by *The News of the World* of information about the location of pædophiles, there were various demonstrations outside the homes of those identified (and those wrongly identified), at one of which, in Portsmouth, a police officer was injured.[187]

Meanwhile, the ability of the detectives to provide protection had been placed in doubt by the miscarriages of justice that seemed to flood out with frightening regularity from the late 1980s. However, in the midst of allegations that seemed so damning, science, which had borne some of the blame for the miscarriages, came to the rescue through discoveries concerning DNA evidence. Suddenly, a number of dramatic break-throughs were made in cases thought incapable of solution. In January 2000 Duncan Jackson was convicted of the murder in 1985 of Avril Dunn,[188] and nine months later Ian Lowther was imprisoned for life after having admitted the murder of Mary Gregson in 1977. The judge at Gregson's trial remarked, 'Thank goodness for advances in DNA profiling, thank goodness for the determination of the police and thank goodness that the arm of the law is long.'[189]

Paradoxically, in spite of the miscarriages of justice and the Lawrence case, the detectives may have emerged into the new century in a better state than officers in the uniform branch. The public image of the detectives depends on the dramatic solution of major crimes, not their prevention. The detectives work is, therefore, discussed in terms of breakthroughs in particular cases. It matters less that detection rates may have fallen so long as the big cases come along, and, in particular, cases with an element of Sherlock Holmes, that is, cases which required some skills beyond the comprehension of non-detectives.

Uniform officers, on the other hand, are generally involved in work which produces little in the way of dramatic results that can be made into a good news story, unless something goes wrong. Criticism about rising crime or the fear of crime tends to be criticism about the level of pro-tection provided by the uniform police.[190] This is not necessarily blamed on the police themselves, nevertheless, the pessimism about the ability of the police to provide routine protection has fuelled an enormous growth in the private security industry and self-policing through, for instance, informally organized neighbourhood patrols or vigilante responses to crime. These other forms of policing did not vanish on the establishment of the new police, but the promise that the new police would eradicate crime made them seem less important, less noteworthy. Their re-discovery suggests more about the problems of the police than about shifts in the nature of policing.

Notes

1 Bottoms and Stevenson (1992) 'What went wrong?', 7.
2 *The Times*, 13 Feb 1948.
3 Smithies (1982) *Crime in Wartime*, 188.
4 *The Times*, 23 Jan, 3 Jun 1948.
5 For the optimism which followed Beveridge, see Rowntree and Lavers (1951) *Poverty and the Welfare State*; for the critique, see Abel-Smith and Townsend (1965) *The Poor and Poorest*.
6 Smithies (1982) *Crime in Wartime*, 201.
7 *The Times*, 28 Jul 1960; McClintock and Avison (1968) *Crime in England and Wales*.
8 Royal Commission (1960) *Royal Commission on the Police*, 4.
9 Dixon (1963) *The Emergency Work of the Police Forces*, 139.
10 Dixon (1963) *The Emergency Work of the Police Forces*, 17–24; Howgrave-Graham (1947) *The Metropolitan Police at War*. On the wartime police, see also Critchley (1978) *A History of Police*, 223–36; Ingleton (1994) *Gentlemen at War*.
11 Home Office (1949b) *Report*, pt I, 2–3.
12 Home Office (1949c) *Statement on Pay and Conditions*, 4. See also Home Office (1949b) *Report*, pt I, 2–3.
13 Home Office (1949b), *Report*, pt II.
14 Scott (1949) *Police Problems of Today*.
15 Reilly (1989) *Policing Birmingham*.
16 Liverpool City Police (1950) *Report on the Police Establishment*, 11.
17 *Commons Debates*, 18 Feb 1954, wa 224.
18 Police Advisory Board (1967) *Police Manpower, Equipment and Efficiency*; Fowler (1966) *The Police State*. Generally Martin and Wilson (1969) *The Police*.
19 Critchley (1971) 'The developing role of the police', 2.
20 Home Office (1975) *Police Recruitment and Wastage*.
21 Fairhurst (1996) *Policing Wigan*, 63; Reilly (1989) *Policing Birmingham*, 113, 133; Woodgate (1985) *The Essex Police*, 150.
22 Lock (1979) *The British Policewoman*.
23 Bland (1985) 'In the name of protection'; Levine (1994) 'Walking the streets in a way no decent woman should'.
24 Clay (1974) *The Leeds Police 1836–1974*, 71.
25 Allen (1936) : 29–30; Wyles (1952) *A Woman at Scotland Yard*.
26 Anon (1921) *A Handy Guide to the Police Forces*, ii.
27 Home Office (1949a) *Committee on Police Conditions of Service*, appendix I; Royal Commission (1929) *Report*. But see Birmingham Police (1927) *Report of the Police Establishment*, 1927, 5; Reilly (1989) *Policing Birmingham*.
28 Home Office (1949a) *Committee on Police Conditions of Service*, 119.
29 Allen (1936) *Lady in Blue*, 263–4.
30 Bale (1960) *Through Seven Reigns*, 93.
31 Birmingham Police (1927) *Report of the Police Establishment*, 1927, 7; Reilly

(1989) *Policing Birmingham*, 64–5.

32 Home Office (1938) *Report of the Departmental Committee*, vol II, 8.
33 Dixon (1963) *The Emergency Work of the Police Forces*, 151–4.
34 Dixon (1963) *The Emergency Work of the Police Forces*, 223.
35 Hart (1951) *The British Police*, 145.
36 Central Office of Information (c1950) *A Career for Women*.
37 Liverpool City Police (1950) *Report on the Police Establishment*, 7.
38 Reilly (1989) *Policing Birmingham*, 149–51. Generally Critchley (1978) *A History of Police*, 256–7.
39 Police Advisory Board (1967) *Police Manpower, Equipment and Efficiency*, 115–21.
40 Police Advisory Board (1967) *Police Manpower, Equipment and Efficiency*, 132.
41 Critchley (1978) *A History of Police*, 211–12; Fairhurst (1996) *Policing Wigan*, 45; Woodgate (1985) *The Essex Police*, 147.
42 Home Office (1949b) *Report*, pt II, appendix V.
43 Police Advisory Board (1967) *Police Manpower, Equipment and Efficiency*, 133–8.
44 Police Advisory Board (1967) *Police Manpower, Equipment and Efficiency*. Also *The Times*, 18 Nov 1960; Lambert (1970) *Crime, Police, and Race Relations*, 148.
45 Bottoms and Stevenson (1992) 'What went wrong?', 28–32; Critchley (1978) *A History of Police*, 307–8; Jones (1990–1) 'Where did it all go wrong?'; Police Advisory Board (1967) *Police Manpower, Equipment and Efficiency*, 139–41; Reilly (1989) *Policing Birmingham*, 164–5.
46 Critchley (1978) *A History of Police*, 267–95.
47 *Commons Debate*, 18 Nov 1959, c 1239–1303; *Lords Debates*, 8 Dec 1959, c 4–55; *The Times*, 27 Oct 1959; *Daily Herald*, 18 Dec 1959; National Council for Civil Liberties (1960) *Submission to the Royal Commission*, 13.
48 Home Office (1957) *Report of Enquiry*.
49 Report of the Tribunal (1958) *Report of the Tribunal*.
50 Bowes (1966) *The Police and Civil Liberties*, 84–7; National Council for Civil Liberties (1960) *Submission to the Royal Commission*, 18–22.
51 Campaign for the Limitation of Secret Police Powers (1956) *The Secret Police and You*; National Council for Civil Liberties (1960) *Submission to the Royal Commission*, 41–3.
52 National Council for Civil Liberties (1960) *Submission to the Royal Commission*, 8; Ward and Benn (1987) 'Were the police ever innocent?'.
53 National Council for Civil Liberties (1960) *Submission to the Royal Commission*, 32.
54 Conciliation Committee for Woman Suffrage (1911) *Treatment of the Women's Deputations*; Morrell (1981) *'Black Friday' and Violence against Women in the Suffragette Movement*.
55 Latham (1911) *Is the British Empire Ripe for Government by Disorderly Women*.
56 Wright (1929) *Police and Public*, 9.
57 Pulling (1964) *Mr Punch and the Police*, 19; Critchley (1971) 'The developing role of the police', 2. Also Emsley (1993) '"Mother, what did policemen do when there weren't any motors?"'.

58 Birmingham Police (1927–30) *Report of the Police Establishment*.
59 For example, Lohman (1947) *The Police and Minority Groups*; Curry and King (1962) *Race Tensions and the Police*.
60 Although see Richmond (1954) *Colour Prejudice in Britain*.
61 National Council for Civil Liberties (1960) *Submission to the Royal Commission*, 36–9.
62 *The Times*, 13 Oct, 15 Oct, 18 Nov 1960; *Commons Debate*, 16 Dec 1959, c 1452–3.
63 Royal Commission (1962) *Royal Commission on the Police: Final Report*, 5.
64 *The Spectator*, 8 Jun 1962; Bowes (1966) *The Police and Civil Liberties*, 153.
65 Royal Commission (1960) *Royal Commission on the Police*, 21.
66 Whittaker (1964) *The Police*, 17.
67 Royal Commission (1962) *Royal Commission on the Police: Final Report*, 102, 103.
68 Evans (1974) *The Police Revolution*, 84.
69 Royal Commission (1962) *Royal Commission on the Police: Final Report*, 104, 108.
70 Quoted in Whittaker (1964) *The Police*, 17.
71 Later implemented by the Police Act 1964, 12 & 13 Eliz. II, c. 48.
72 Royal Commission (1962) *Royal Commission on the Police: Final Report*, 138.
73 Smith (1972) *An Examination of the Procedure for Dealing with Complaints*.
74 *Commons Debates*, 2 Dec 1971, c 652–7. Also Police Advisory Board (1971) *The Handling of Complaints*.
75 Select Committee (1972) *Select Committee on Race Relations and Immigration*; Home Office (1974) *The Handling of Complaints*.
76 For example, Police Complaints Board (1980) *Triennial Review Board*, but see Home Office (1981) *The Establishment of an Independent Element in the Investigation of Complaints*.
77 Scarman (1981) *The Brixton Disorder 10–12 April 1981*.
78 Home Office (1983) *Complaints and Discipline Procedures*; Police and Criminal Evidence Act 1984.
79 Jefferson and Grimshaw (1984) *Controlling the Constable*; Reiner (1991) *Chief Constables*, 10–38.
80 Reiner (1991) *Chief Constables*, 23.
81 Easton and Rawlings (1996) 'The Citizen's Charter and the police'; Rawlings (1991) 'Creeping privatisation?'; Rawlings (1992b) 'Who needs a royal commission?'.
82 Reiner (1991) *Chief Constables*, 27.
83 *Fisher* v. *Oldham Corporation* [1930] 2 KB 364.
84 *ex parte Blackburn* [1968] 2 QB 118 at 135–6.
85 Reiner (1991) *Chief Constables*, 28.
86 Royal Commission (1962) *Royal Commission on the Police: Final Report*, 76.
87 Lustgarten (1986) *The Governance of the Police*; Reiner (1991) *Chief Constables*, 16–28.
88 See chapter 6.
89 Kyrke (1969) *History of East Sussex Police*, 128, 130.

90 Critchley (1978) *A History of Police*, 239–45; Dixon (1963) *The Emergency Work of the Police Forces*, 191–6. But the act did allow new borough forces, see Madigan (1993) *'The Men Who Wore Straw Helmets'*; Whittaker (1964) *The Police*, 87–8.

91 Lord Chesham, *Lords Debates*, 8 Dec 1958, c 37. For an example of a compulsory amalgamation, see Home Office (1948) *In the Matter of the Police Act, 1946*.

92 Darwin (1969) *Southport County Borough Police*, vii; Home Office (1968) *Police Act 1964: Report of Inquiry*; *Commons Debates*, 18 May 1966, c 1341–7.

93 Home Office (1963) *Sheffield Police Appeal Inquiry*.

94 Grigg (1965) *The Challenor Case*; Home Office (1965) *Report of Inquiry by Mr A.E. James, Q.C.*; National Council for Civil Liberties (1966) : 14)

95 Home Office (1964) *Report of Inquiry into the Action of the Metropolitan Police*.

96 *The Times*, 29 Nov 1969.

97 Cox, Shirley and Short (1977) *The Fall of Scotland Yard*; Evans (1974) *The Police Revolution*, 109–10; Whittaker (1979) *The Police*.

98 Belson (1975) *The Public and the Police*.

99 Bowes (1966) *The Police and Civil Liberties*, 92; National Council for Civil Liberties (1961) *Public Order and the Police*.

100 Bowes (1966) *The Police and Civil Liberties*, 95–105.

101 Scarman (1975) *The Red Lion Square Disorders*.

102 Belson (1975) *The Public and the Police*.

103 Lambert (1970) *Crime, Police, and Race Relations*, 289. This study also took in the Irish community.

104 Evans (1974) *The Police Revolution*, 85–7.

105 Select Committee (1972) *Select Committee on Race Relations and Immigration*, 67–9.

106 Home Office (1973) *Police/Immigrant Relations*, 3, 4.

107 Critchley (1971) 'The developing role of the police', 7.

108 See Select Committee (1971) *Select Committee on Race Relations and Immigration*, 1–5.

109 Scarman (1981) *The Brixton Disorder 10–12 April 1981*.

110 Home Office (1982) *Report of a Study Group*.

111 Home Office (1973) *Police/Immigrant Relations*, 5.

112 Evans (1974) *The Police Revolution*, 73–4; Home Office (1975) *Police Recruitment and Wastage*, 14; National Council for Civil Liberties (1960) *Submission to the Royal Commission*, 39.

113 Friedlander and Mitchell (1974) *The Police*, 136–9.

114 Evans (1974) *The Police Revolution*, 111.

115 Hain (1984) *Political Trials in Britain*, 61.

116 Mark (1978) *In the Office of Constable*, 123.

117 For example, in connection with a murder in Wigan in 1954: Fairhurst (1996) *Policing Wigan*, 64.

118 Hobbs (1992) *Doing the Business*, 61 and *passim*.

119 Mark (1978) *In the Office of Constable*, 123.

120 Mark, 1978, in Hobbs (1992) *Doing the Business*, 72.

121 Mark, 1978, in Hobbs (1992) *Doing the Business*, 73.

122 Mark (1978) *In the Office of Constable*, 97.

123 Hobbs (1992) *Doing the Business*, 77–83; Mark (1978) *In the Office of Constable*.

124 *Policing London*, Sep, Nov 1982.

125 George Dixon was the avuncular police officer in a long-running television series, which originated in the film *The Blue Lamp* (Dixon had actually been murdered in the film) and which depicted uniform officers – specifically, Dixon – as maintaining the solid moral core of policing.

126 Price and Caplan (1977) *The Confait Confessions*; Royal Commission (1981) *Royal Commission on Criminal Procedure*.

127 Bake and Hale (1992) *Public Order and Private Lives*, 15.

128 Rawlings (1991) 'Creeping privatisation?'.

129 Clarke and Taylor (1980) 'Vandals, pickets and muggers'.

130 Home Office (1978) *Committee on Inquiry on the Police*.

131 Thatcher in *Police Review*, 23 May 1985.

132 Rawlings (1985) 'Bobbies, aliens and subversives', 83–4.

133 Hough and Mayhew (1983) *The British Crime Survey*.

134 *Police*, Jun 1986.

135 Thatcher in *The Times*, 26 May 1988. See also Brake and Hale (1992) *Public Order and Private Lives*; Taylor (1987) 'Law and order, moral order'.

136 Home Office (1986) *Neighbourhood Watch*.

137 Home Office (1988–91) *Practical Ways to Crack Crime*.

138 Home Office (1987) *Violent Crime*.

139 Johnston (1992) *The Rebirth of Private Policing*; Shearing and Stenning (1981) 'Modern private security'.

140 Rawlings (1991) 'Creeping privatisation?'; Saunders and Young (1994) *Criminal Justice*.

141 All Lambeth Anti-Racist Movement (1982) *A Cause for Alarm*, 28.

142 Home Affairs Select Committee (1980) *Race Relations and the 'Sus' Law*.

143 Bishton and Homer (1978) *Talking Blues*; Brown (1977) *Shades of Grey*; Smith and Gray (1983) *Police and People in London*.

144 *Guardian*, 22 Oct 1982.

145 On an earlier mugging panic, see Hall et al (1978) *Policing the Crisis*.

146 Metropolitan Police (1982) *The Report of the Commissioner of the Police*; *Policing London*, Oct 1982.

147 Roach (1978) 'The Metropolitan Police Community Relations Branch', 18.

148 Southgate (1982) *Police Probationer Training*, 6.

149 *Daily Mirror*, 13 Apr 1981. On the riots, see Joshua, Wallace and Booth (1983) *To Ride the Storm*; Kettle and Hodges (1982) *Uprising!*; Scarman (1981) *The Brixton Disorder 10–12 April 1981*; Vogler (1991) *Reading the Riot Act*, 112–62.

150 *Lords Debates*, 24 Mar 1982, c 987; Greater London Council (1982) *Policing London*; *Policing London*, Jul/Aug 1982; Easton (1981) 24; Sim (1982) 'Scarman: the police counter-attack'.

151 *Commons Debates*, 14 Apr 1981, wa 84; 27 Nov 1981, c 478.

152 *Policing London*, Oct, Nov 1982.

153 Smith and Gray (1983) *Police and People in London*.

154 Cashmore and McLaughlin (1991) *Out of Order? Policing Black People*; Gaffney (1987) *Interpretations of Violence*; Gifford (1986) *The Broadwater Farm Enquiry*.

155 For example, Inquest (1982/3–99) *Annual Reports*. See also Amnesty International (2000) *United Kingdom: Deaths in Custody*.

156 For instance, to treat domestic, sexual or racist violence in the same way as other crimes: London Rape Crisis Centre (1984) *Sexual Violence*; Hensman and London Rape Crisis Centre (1999) *Sexual Violence*.

157 Manchester Police Monitoring Unit (1987) *Breaking the Silence*.

158 Reiner (1986) 'A watershed in policing', 21.

159 See now the Metropolitan Police Authority: Greater London Authority Act 1999, ss. 310–25.

160 *Policing London*, Jul/Aug 1982.

161 Hammersmith and Fulham Council (1988) *Subways: Closed Circuit Television and Safety from Crime*; Hammersmith and Fulham Council (1989) *What Support? Domestic Violence Project*; Plotnikoff (1989) *Hammersmith and Fulham Services to Victims of Crime*.

162 Edwards (1989) *Policing 'Domestic' Violence*; Hall (1985) *Ask Any Woman*; Hamner and Saunders (1984) *Well-Founded Fear*.

163 Scarman (1981) *The Brixton Disorder 10–12 April 1981*.

164 Metropolitan Police (1982) *Report of the Commissioner*.

165 *Policing London*, Nov 1982.

166 Kettle and Hodges (1982) *Uprising!*, 185; Scarman (1981) *The Brixton Disorder 10–12 April 1981*, para 5.53.

167 *The Times*, 18 May 1982.

168 *Guardian*, 18 Mar 1982.

169 Mainwaring-White (1983) *The Policing Revolution*.

170 Alderson (1979) *Policing Freedom*; Alderson (1984) *Law and Disorder*; Brown (1977) *Shades of Grey*; Brown (1982) *Policing by Multi-Racial Consent*; Kettle and Hodges (1982) *Uprising!*, 237–9; Rawlings (1985) 'Bobbies, aliens and subversives'.

171 For example, Baker and Waddon (1991) *It Speaks for Itself*; Kinsey (1985) *Survey of Merseyside Police Officers*.

172 Hough (1985) 'Organization and resource management in the uniformed police'.

173 Kinsey (1985) *Survey of Merseyside Police Officers*, 104.

174 Sheptycki (1995) 'Transnational policing'; Sheptycki (1996) 'Law enforcement, justice and democracy in the transnational arena'.

175 National Council for Civil Liberties (1986) *No Way in Wapping*; Northam (1988) *Shooting in the Dark*; Police Monitoring and Research Group (1987) *Policing Wapping*.

176 Johnston (2000) *Policing Britain*, 25–6; McLaughlin and Murji (1993) 'Controlling the bill', 95.

177 *Police Review*, 24 May 1985. Generally Rawlings (1991) 'Creeping privatisation?'; Rawlings (1992b) 'Who needs a royal commission?'.

178 Newing (1990) 'Policing'; *The Observer*, 16 Jun 1991.

179   Home Office (1993a) *Police Reform*, 1.
180   Rose (1996) *In the Name of the Law*.
181   In Johnston (2000) *Policing Britain*, 78.
182   Home Office (1993b) *Inquiry into Police Responsibilities*.
183   Easton and Rawlings (1996) 'The Citizen's Charter and the police'.
184   Macpherson (1999) paras 6.44–.45.
185   Hague (2000) 'Speech to the Centre for Policy Studies'.
186   *The Daily Telegraph*, 10 Mar 1998; *The Independent*, 5 Mar 1998; *The Irish Times*, 3 Jan 1998; *The Observer*, 6 Feb 1998; *The Times*, 10 Jan 1998.
187   *The Independent*, 5 Aug 2000.
188   *The Times*, 28 Jan 2000.
189   *The Times*, 30 Sep 2000.
190   The uniform police has also suffered criticism over public order, most notably, the damage during the May Day demonstrations in London in 2000. This, it might be claimed, prompted the police to set up the demonstrations in 2001 as something of a re-match: a cynical commentator might think that in the run up to May Day the police presented the demonstrators as posing an enormous threat to civil order in order to ensure that they emerged with their reputation restored by manifestly preventing that disorder in the full glare of the media.

Chapter 8

The long history of policing

In its long history policing has passed through three stages. The first was the blood-feud, where the victim – perhaps, in concert with her or his kin – took direct action against the offender: the stolen property was snatched back, compensation was extracted, or the thief was physically attacked. The desire to prevent direct action from degenerating into a lengthy and bloody private war that could destroy the social order prompted the broader community of the village or town to establish processes and institutions which encouraged settlements or took on the role of adjudicating between parties.

The second stage brought the village within the larger nation state. The desire of a sovereign to establish authority (and to boost revenue) found expression in, among other things, the imposition of a system of royal justice. The sovereign promised to deliver justice, maintain order and protect from invasion in exchange for allegiance. That, in turn, involved placing restraints on the ability of the individual to take direct action. The victim was expected to bring any accusation before the courts, and the crown constructed procedures to ensure this happened. Obligations were placed on the community: so, for instance, the community had to present offenders, provide a watch and produce members of the tithing who committed crimes, and it would be fined for failing to do these things.

The practical problem of bringing the whole community to account led to the emergence of representatives – the chief pledge and later the parish constable – who answered on its behalf. The constable became a medium (although never an entirely passive medium) through which the state pressed in upon the community, and this sometimes placed him in a difficult position where the wishes of the community conflicted with those of the state.

The increased institutionalization of policing and criminal justice did not remove the role of the victim. While the right of direct action was lost, the victim was expected to engage in the detection of offenders who would be brought before a court. However, victims did not necessarily believe their best interests were served by prosecution and they continued to engage in actions outside the formal policing and justice structures. The victim of theft might, for instance, prefer to secure the return of stolen property by entering an agreement with the thief, rather than seeing the goods forfeited to the state and the thief hanged.

The growing reluctance to undertake odious policing duties led to the third stage of policing in which certain roles were professionalized. Many householders hired substitutes to undertake, on their behalf, the duties of the watch or the parish constable. While eighteenth-century property owners were no less interested in policing than their medieval ancestors, they did not necessarily regard the performance of these tasks to be part of their civic duty. By the eighteenth century many places formalized this practice of substitution to ensure the quality of the watchmen and to remove the obligation on the householders to serve. Parish vestries took on the responsibilities of hiring and directing the watch, while the householders exchanged their duty to serve for a duty to pay a rate.

In detection as well there was some professionalization as common informers and thief-takers were encouraged to undertake some of this work by the rewards offered. The only controls were judicial rules about the admission of evidence, but John Fielding did attempt to impose a structure on the thief-takers. His view was that crime could be reduced by improving the likelihood that offenders would be detected. However, detection was too difficult to be left in the hands of the victims. Therefore, Fielding argued, it was necessary to construct a bureaucracy, which would control the flow of information on crime and put detection into the hands of skilled officers, with the whole under the direction of Fielding himself. So, while the street patrolling of the watch and the detective work of the thief-takers were, for the most part, separate, by the end of the eighteenth century both were emerging as tasks which required professional expertise and, therefore, detachment from the community and the victim.

These features were at the core of the development of the police forces of the nineteenth and twentieth centuries. At first, the police rejected Fielding's idea of crime control through detection and, instead, undertook a project of crime prevention through the regulation of working-class communities. This built on a tradition stretching back to the late medieval period in which the state sought to minimize the consequences of inequality and ensure the reproduction of the labour force by regulating the poor. However, the modern police were anxious to present themselves as having a monopoly over all aspects of crime control and this led them to establish specialist detective branches. Although these developments marginalized and de-legitimized the policing activities of those who were not police officers, it did not mean such activities ceased. Alongside the history of the formation of the state police there is a broader and largely hidden history of policing: the victims who fought back, who settled with offenders or who just tried to forget; the people who took preventive action by installing alarms and locks, or who organized with their neighbours to respond to crime by vigilante action.[1]

The creation of a policing system which did not necessarily reflect the wishes of those on whom it depended (victims, witnesses) was bound to encounter difficulties in maintaining its claim to have a monopoly over policing. Added to which there were internal divisions in the police: uniform officers were deployed like an army of occupation (although beat constables never quite worked in this way), while detectives depended on establishing a relationship with the communities they policed.

The idea of combining patrolling, detection and public order policing was a curious one. In drawing these disparate functions together they have all come to be seen as merely aspects of crime control. This has had profound implications for the way in which the performance of these tasks is approached and has created a disparity between the expectations the public have of the police (and the public's own role in policing) and the expectations the police have of the public. The truth is that the term policing hides a range of activities and the only reason we have tended to view them as a single activity is because they were, apparently, taken over by the modern police. In truth, however, the police have never enjoyed a real monopoly and recognizing the diversity in policing allows us also to recognize that it has more potential for popular involvement than might be supposed.

Notes

1 See, for example, the discussions in Johnston (1992) *The Rebirth of Private Policing* and Shapland and Vagg (1988) *Policing by the Public.*

Bibliography

Government publications and parliamentary papers

Central Office of Information (c. 1950) *A Career for Women*, London: Central Office of Information.

Committee of the Marylebone Vestry (1843) *Report of a Committee of the Marylebone Vestry on the Expenses of the Metropolitan Police Borne by that Parish since its Establishment*, Parliamentary Papers, (248), Vol. XLII.

Home Affairs Select Committee (1980) *Race Relations and the 'Sus' Law*, HC 599, London: HMSO.

Home Department (1842) *Report to Her Majesty's Principal Secretary of State for the Home Department, from the Poor Law Commissioners, on an Inquiry into the Sanitary Condition of the Labouring Population of Great Britain*, London: HMSO.

Home Office (1907) *Home Office Circulars Issued to Police Authorities, 1884–1907*, London.

Home Office (1936) *Scientific Aids to Criminal Investigation: Instructional Pamphlet for the Use of Police Officers*, London: HMSO.

Home Office (1938) *Report of the Departmental Committee on Detective Work and Procedure*, London: HMSO.

Home Office (1948) *In the Matter of the Police Act, 1946. Enquiry into the Proposed Compulsory Amalgamation of the County Police Forces of Breconshire, Montgomeryshire and Radnorshire*, London: HMSO.

Home Office (1949a) *Committee on Police Conditions of Service. Home Office Memorandum of Evidence*, London: HMSO.

Home Office (1949b) *Report of the Committee on Police Conditions of Service*, Part I, cmnd 7674, and Part II, cmnd 7831, London: HMSO.

Home Office (1949c) *Statement on Pay and Conditions of Service of Police*, cmnd 7707, London: HMSO.

Home Office (1957) *Report of Enquiry into the Administration and Efficiency of the Cardiganshire Constabulary and the State of Discipline in the Force*, cmnd 251, London: HMSO.

Home Office (1963) *Sheffield Police Appeal Inquiry*, cmnd 2176, London: HMSO.

Home Office (1964) *Report of Inquiry into the Action of the Metropolitan Police in Relation to the Case of Mr. Herman Woolf*, cmnd 2319, London: HMSO.

Home Office (1965) *Report of Inquiry by Mr. A.E. James, Q.C. Into the Circumstances in Which It Was Possible for Detective Sergeant Harold Gordon Challenor of the Metropolitan Police to Continue on Duty at a Time When He Appears to Have Been Affected by the Onset of Mental Illness*, cmnd 2735, London: HMSO.

Home Office (1968) *Police Act, 1964: Report of Inquiry In Respect of the Objections to the Proposed Compulsory Amalgamation of the Police Areas of the County of Lancaster and Thirteen County Boroughs*, cmnd 3538, London: HMSO.

Home Office (1973) *Police/Immigrant Relations in England and Wales: Observations on the Report of the Select Committee on Race Relations and Immigration*, cmnd 5438, London: HMSO.

Home Office (1974) *The Handling of Complaints. Report of the Working Group for England and Wales*, cmnd 5582, London: HMSO.

Home Office (1975) *Police Recruitment and Wastage: Observations on the Seventh Report from the Expenditure Committee*, cmnd 6016, London: HMSO.

Home Office (1978) *Committee on Inquiry on the Police*, cmnd 7283, London: HMSO.

Home Office (1981) *The Establishment of an Independent Element in the Investigation of Complaints against the Police: Report of a Working Party Appointed by the Home Secretary*, cmnd 8193, London: HMSO.

Home Office (1982) *Report of a Study Group: Recruitment into the Police Service of Members of the Ethnic Minorities*, mimeograph.

Home Office (1983) *Police Complaints and Discipline Procedures*, cmnd 9072, London: HMSO.

Home Office (1986) *Neighbourhood Watch: Steve and Sally: Crime Spotters*, London: HMSO.

Home Office (1987) *Violent Crime: Police Advice to Women on How to Reduce the Risks*, London: Central Office of Information, HMSO

Home Offfice (1988–91) *Practical Ways to Crack Crime*, London: HMSO.

Home Office (1993a) *Police Reform: A Police Service for the Twenty-First Century*, London: HMSO.

Home Office (1993b) *Inquiry into Police Responsibilities and Rewards*, London: HMSO.

Macpherson, Sir William (1999) *The Stephen Lawrence Inquiry*, cmnd 4262, London: HMSO.

Police Advisory Board (1967) *Police Manpower, Equipment and Efficiency*, London: HMSO.

Police Advisory Board (1971) *The Handling of Complaints against the Police. Report of the Working Group*, cmnd 5582, London: HMSO.

Police Complaints Board (1980) *Triennial Review Report*, cmnd 7966, London: HMSO.

Report of the Tribunal (1958) *Report of the Tribunal Appointed to Inquire into the Allegation of Assault on John Waters*, cmnd 718, London: HMSO.

Royal Commission (1839) *First Report of the Commissioners Appointed to Inquire as to the Best Means of Establishing an Efficient Constabulary Force in the Counties of England and Wales*, Parliamentary Papers, (169), Vol. XIX.

Royal Commission (1856), *Report of Her Majesty's Commissioners Appointed to Inquire into the Alleged Disturbances of the Public Peace in Hyde Park on Sunday July 1st 1855*, Parliamentary Papers, (2016), Vol. XXIII.

Royal Commission (1908) *Royal Commission upon the Duties of the Metropolitan Police*, cmnd 4156, London: HMSO.

Royal Commission (1929) *Report of the Royal Commission on Police Powers and Procedure*, cmnd 3297, London: HMSO.

Royal Commission (1960) *Royal Commission on the Police: Interim Report*, cmnd 1222, London: HMSO.

Royal Commission (1962) *Royal Commission on the Police: Final Report*, cmnd 1728, London: HMSO.

Royal Commission (1981) *Royal Commission on Criminal Procedure: Report*, cmnd 8092, London: HMSO.

Scarman, Sir Leslie (1975) *The Red Lion Square Disorders of 15 June 1974*, London: HMSO.

Scarman, Lord (1981) *The Brixton Disorder 10–12 April 1981: Report of an Inquiry by the Rt. Hon. The Lord Scarman, OBE*, cmnd 8427, London: HMSO.

Select Committee (1772) *Report from the Committee Who Were Appointed to Enquire into the State of the Nightly Watch within the City and Liberty of Westminster*, London.

Select Committee (1799) *The Report of the Select Committee Appointed by the House of Commons, Relative to the Establishment of a New Police in the Metropolis, &c.*, London.

Select Committee (1818) *Third Report from the Committee on the State of the Police of the Metropolis*, Parliamentary Papers, (423) Vol. VIII.

Select Committee (1822) *Report from the Select Committee on the Police of the Metropolis*, Parliamentary Papers, (440) Vol. IV.

Select Committee (1828) *Report from the Select Committee on the Police of the Metropolis*, Parliamentary Papers, (533) Vol. VI.

Select Committee (1833) *Report from the Select Committee on the Petition of Frederick Young and Others (Police)*, Parliamentary Papers, (627) Vol. XIII.

Select Committee (1834) *Report from the Select Committee on the Police of the*

Metropolis, Parliamentary Papers, (600) Vol. XVI.

Select Committee (1837) *Report from the Select Committee on Metropolis Police Offices*, Parliamentary Papers, (451), Vol. XII.

Select Committee (1852–3) *First Report from the Select Committee on Police*, Parliamentary Papers, (603), Vol. XXXVI.

Select Committee (1893) *Report of the Committee Appointed to Inquire into the Circumstances Connected with the Disturbances at Featherstone on 7th September 1893*, cmnd 7234.

Select Committee (1908) *Report of the Select Committee on the Employment of Military in Cases of Disturbances*, H.C. 236.

Select Committee (1932) *Report from the Select Committee of the House of Commons on Police Forces (Amalgamation)*, H.C. 106.

Select Committee (1971) *Select Committee on Race Relations and Immigration. Session 1971–72. Police Immigrant Relations. Minutes of Evidence Wednesday, 1st December, 1971*, HC 45–I, London: HMSO.

Select Committee (1972) *Select Committee on Race Relations and Immigration. Session 1971–72. Police/Immigrant Relations* cmnd 471, London: HMSO.

Trial series

Home Circuit, *The Genuine Proceedings at the Assizes on the Home Circuit*.

OBSP, *Old Bailey Sessions Paper*.

Surrey Assizes, *The Proceedings on the King's Common of the Peace, and Oyer and Terminer, and Gaol-Delivery of the County Gaol, held for the County of Surry*. (Also entitled *The Proceedings of the Assizes for the County of Surry*).

Books, essays and theses

Abel-Smith, B. and Townsend, P. (1965) *The Poor and the Poorest*, London: Bell.

Aberth, J. 'Crime and justice under Edward III: the case of Thomas De Lisle', *English Historical Review*, 107: 283–301.

Adam, H.L. (1914) *Police Work from Within. With Some Reflections upon Women, the Law and Lawyers*, London.

Adams, H. (1962) *Policemen and the Police Force*, Oxford: Basil Blackwell.

Adams, J. (1838) *A Letter to Benjamin Hawes, Esq. M.P.*, London.

Alderson, J. (1979) *Policing Freedom: a Commentary on the Dilemmas of Policing in Western Democracies*, Estover: Macdonald and Evans.

Alderson, J. (1984) *Law and Disorder*, London: Hamilton.

Allason, R. (1983) *The Branch: A History of the Metropolitan Police Special Branch*, London: Secker & Warburg.

Allen, L.B. (1821) *Brief Considerations on the Present State of the Police of the Metropolis: with a Few Suggestions Towards its Improvement*, London.

Allen, M.S. (1936) *Lady in Blue*, London: Stanley Paul.

All Lambeth Anti-Racist Movement (1982) *A Cause for Alarm: a Study of Policing in Lambeth*, London.

Amnesty International (2000) *United Kingdom: Deaths in Custody: Lack of Police Accountability*, Report EU 45/42/00, London: Amnesty International.

Anon. (1700) *Proposals for Making Provisions for Setting the Poor on Work*, London.

Anon. (1722a) *Tyburn's Worthies, or, the Robberies and Enterprizes of John Hawkins, and George Simpson, Lately Executed for Robbing the Bristol-Mail*, London: T. Warner.

Anon. (1722b) *The Form of a Petition Submitted to the Consideration and Correction of Those Noblemen and Gentlemen who Desire to Subscribe What Sums Shall Be Necessary for Relieving, Reforming and Employing the Poor*, London.

Anon. (1725) *The True and Genuine Account of the Life and Actions of the Late Jonathan Wild*, London.

Anon. (1732a) *The Life and Infamous Actions of that Perjur'd Villain John Waller, Who Made His Exit in the Pillory, at the Seven-Dials, on Tuesday, the 13th Day of this Instant June*, London.

Anon. (1732b) *The Tryals of Jeremy Tooley, William Arch, and John Clawson*, London.

Anon. (1748) *Memoirs of the Life and Times, of Sir Thomas Deveil, Knight, one of His Majesty's Justices of the Peace*, London.

Anon. (1751a) *Serious Thoughts In Regard to the Publick Disorders*, London.

Anon. (1751b) *The Vices of the Cities of London and Westminster*, London.

Anon. (1754) *The Right Method of Maintaining Security in Persons and Property to all the Subjects of Great-Britain*, London.

Anon. (1755a) *Case of the Petitioners against the Bill, for Establishing a Nightly-Watch within the City of Bristol* (no place of publication).

Anon. (1755b) *Reasons in Support of the Bristol Watch Bill* (no place of publication).

Anon. (1755c) *The Bristol Watch-Bill: A Dialogue between Two Brothers; or, the Dismal Story of Jack and the Tory*, Bristol.

Anon. (1765a) *An Account of John Westcote, late Porter to the Right Honourable The Earl of Harrington. In Which is Laid Down an Effectual Method for Preventing Theft and Robbery*, London.

Anon. (1765b) *Considerations on Taxes, As They are Supposed to Affect the Price of Labour in Our Manufactures*, London.

Anon. (1773) *Observations on the Present State of the Parochial and Vagrant Poor*, London.

Anon. (1786) *Outlines of a Plan for Patrolling and Watching the City of London, Borough of Southwark, and their Environs*, London.

Anon. (1787a) 'A letter to the citizens of Glasgow, containing a short view of the management of the poor's funds', in T. Gilbert (ed) *A Collection of Pamphlets Concerning the Poor*, London.

Anon. (1787b) *A Letter to Thomas Gilbert, Esq; On His Intended Reform of the Poor Laws*, London.

Anon. (1797) *Regulations of Parochial Police, Combined with the Military and Naval Armaments*, London, 1797.

Anon. (1816), *The Whole Trials of the Thief Takers, and Their Confederates*, G. Vaughan,

R. Mackay, G. Brown, J. Dannelly, T. Brock, J. Pelham, M. Power, and B. Johnson, London.

Anon. (1834a) *The Metropolitan Police: Its Expenses Examined; Its Efficiency Questioned; and Several Objections Discussed*, London.

Anon. (1834b) *Instructions for the Police Establishments of His Majesty's Dock Yards*, London.

Anon. (1839a) *On the Establishment of a Rural Police*, London.

Anon. (1839b) *Police and Piety; or The Agnews of Downing Street. A Satire*, London.

Anon. (1841) *Rural Police. An Address to the Rate-payers of the County of Hertford*, London.

Anon. (1842) *The Life, Trial, and Sentence of Daniel Good, with His Confessionn of the Murder of J. Jones*, London.

Anon. (1844) *A Full Report of the Evidence Taken at the Thames Police Court, and the Coroner's Inquest, before Mr. Baker, and a Respectable Jury, at Stepney, on the 10th of June, 1844; on the Alleged Poisoning Case, also the Trial of J.C. Belany for the Murder of His Wife, at the Central Criminal Court, On August the 21st & 22nd, 1844*, Alnwick.

Anon. (1872) *The Revolution in the Police, and the Coming Revolution of the Army and Navy*, London.

Anon. (1878) *Life and Examination of Charles Peace, charged with the Bannercross Murder*, London.

Anon. (1888a) *Capture of Leather Apron* (no place of publication).

Anon. (1888b) *Ghastly Murder in the East-End. Dreadful Mutilation of a Woman. Capture of Leather Apron* (no place of publication).

Anon. (1888c) *Horrible Mutilation in the East End* (no place of publication).

Anon. (1888d) *The Whitechapel Horrors* (no place of publication).

Anon. (1895) *The Walsall Anarchists. Trapped by the Police*, London.

Anon. (1920) *A Handy Guide to the Police Forces of the United Kingdom*, London: Police Review Publishing.

Anon. (1938) *A Handy Guide to the Police Forces At Home and Overseas*, London: Police Review Publishing.

Anon. (1940) *The Book of Orders of 1630/1 Reprinted at the University of Reading, in the Year 1940*, Reading: The University of Reading.

Anon. (1957) *The Kent Police Centenary: Recollections of a Hundred Years* (no place of publication).

Appleby, P. (1995) *A Force on the Move: The Story of the British Transport Police 1825–1995*, Malvern: Images.

Archer, J.E. (1990) *By a Flash and a Scare: Incendiarism, Animal Maiming, and Poaching in East Anglia 1815–1870*, Oxford: Clarendon Press.

Ascoli, D. (1979) *The Queen's Peace: The Origins and Development of the Metropolitan Police 1829–1979*, London: Hamish Hamilton.

Ashcroft, M. (ed.) *Scarborough Records 1600–1640: A Calendar*, North Yorkshire County Record Office Publications, no. 47.

Aspland, A. (1868) *Crime in Manchester, and Police Administration*, London,

Atkinson, Rev. J.C. (ed.) (1884) *The North Riding Record Society Volume I. Quarter Sessions Records*, London.

Attreed, L.C. (ed.) (1991) *The York House Books 1461–1490*, Stroud: Alan Sutton.

Avery, M.E. (1988) 'Patrick Colquhoun (1745–1820): "A being clothed with divinity"', *Journal of the Police History Society*, 3: 24–34.

Ayers, P. (1989) *The Liverpool Docklands: Life and Work in Athol Street*, Docklands History Project: Liverpool.

Bailey, S.H. Harris, D.J. and Jones, B.L. (1980) *Civil Liberties: Cases and Materials*, London: Butterworths.

Bailey, V. (1981) 'The Metropolitan Police, the Home Office and the threat of outcast London', in V. Bailey (ed.) *Policing and Punishment in Nineteenth-Century Britain*, London: Croom Helm.

Baker, C. and Waddon, A. (1991) *It Speaks for Itself: An Independent Opinion Survey of the Members of the North Wales Police Service*, Bangor: University of Wales.

Baker, J.H. (1990) *An Introduction to English Legal History*, London: Butterworths.

Bakewell, G. (1842) *Observations on the Construction of the New Police Force with a Variety of Useful Information*, London.

Bale, I. (1960) *Through Seven Reigns: A History of the Newport Borough Police*, Pontypool: The Griffin Press.

Banton, M. (1964) *The Policeman in the Community*, London: Tavistock.

Barnes, T.G. (1955) 'Examination before a justice in the seventeenth century', *Somerset and Dorset Notes and Queries*, 27: 39–42.

Barnes, T.G. (ed.) (1959) *Somerset Assize Orders 1629–1640*, Somerset Record Society, vol. 65.

Barnes, T.G. (ed.) (1961) *Somerset 1625–1640: A County's Government During the "Personal Rule"*, London: Oxford University Press.

Barnett, R. (1888) *Police Sergeant C 21*, London: Walter Scott.

Barrett, G. (1786) *An Essay Towards Establishing a System of Police, on Constitutional Principles*, London.

Barrister-at-Law (1860) *The Road Murder*, London.

Bartrip, P.W.J. (1981) 'Public opinion and law enforcement: the ticket-of-leave scares in mid-Victorian Britain', in V. Bailey (ed.) *Policing and Punishment in Nineteenth Century Britain*, London: Croom Helm.

Bates Harbin, The Rev. E.H. (ed.) (1907–08) *Quarter Sessions Records for the County of Somerset*, 2 vols, Somerset Record Society, vols 23 and 24.

Battestin, M.C. with Battestin, R.R. (1989) *Henry Fielding: A Life*, London: Routledge.

Beattie, J.M. (1986) *Crime and the Courts in England 1660–1800*, Oxford: Oxford University Press.

Bee, J. (1828) *(pseud. Baldock, J.) A Living Picture of London, for 1828 and Stranger's Guide Through the Streets of the Metropolis*, London.

Beer, B.L. (1982) *Rebellion and Riot: Popular Disorder in England during the Reign of Edward VI*, Kent State University Press.

Beier, A.L. (1985) *Masterless Men: The Vagrancy Problem in England 1560–1640*, London: Methuen.

Bellamy, J.G. (1964) 'The Coterel Gang: an anatomy of a band of fourteenth-century criminals', *English Historical Review*, 79: 698–717.

Bellamy, J.G. (1973) *Crime and Public Order in England in the Later Middle Ages*, London: Routledge & Kegan Paul.

Belson, W.A. (1975) *The Public and the Police*, London: Harper & Row.

Beresford, M.W. (1957–8) 'The common informer: the penal statutes and economic regulation', *Economic History Review* (2nd ser.), 10: 221–38.

Bettey, J.H. (1982) *Calendar of the Correspondence of the Smyth Family of Ashton Court 1548–1642*, Bristol Record Society, vol 35.

Bevell, J. (1765) *An Authentic Narrative of the Methods by which the Robbery Committed in the House of the Right Honourable the Earl of Harrington, in the Stable-Yard, St. James's, was Discovered. With Some Remarkable Anecdotes, and Original Letters Sent to Sir John Fielding on the Occasion*, London.

Birmingham (1840) *Report of the Committee Appointed by the Town Council, September 3rd, 1839, to Investigate the Causes of the Late Riots*, Birmingham.

Birmingham Police (1927–30), *Report of the Police Establishment and the State of Crime in the City of Birmingham*, Birmingham.

Birmingham Police Office (1847–50), *Number of Persons Taken into Custody by the Birmingham Police, and the Results*, Birmingham.

Bishton, D. and Homer, B. (1978) *Talking Blues: The Black Community Speaks about its Relationship with the Police*, Birmingham: AFFOR.

Bland, L. (1985) 'In the name of protection: the policing of women in the First World War', in C. Smart (ed.) *Women-in-Law*, London: Routledge.

Blizzard, W. (1785) *Desultory Reflections on Police*, London.

Blything Association (1830) *The Association for the Protection of Property, and Punishment of Offenders, Entered into and Agreed upon by the Proprietors and Occupiers of Land, Tradesmen and Others, in the Hundred of Blything, and Parishes Adjacent*, Halesworth.

Bohannan, P. (1968) *Justice and Judgment Among the Tiv*, London: Oxford University Press.

Bolton, J.L. and Maslen, M. (eds) (1985) *Calendar of the Court Books of the Borough of Witney 1538–1610*, Oxfordshire Record Society, vol. 54.

Bonomi, J. (1872) *Project for an Instrument for the Identification of Persons for use in Military Establishments, Police Offices, &c. and for Physiological and Artistic Research*, London.

Booth, A. (1977) 'Food riots in North-West England, 1790–1801', *Past and Present*, 77: 84–101.

Booth, A. (1983) 'Popular loyalism and public violence in the North-West of England, 1790–1800', *Social History*, 8: 295–313.

Bottoms, A.E. and Stevenson, S. (1992) '"What went wrong?": criminal justice policy in England and Wales, 1945–70', in D. Downes (ed.) *Unravelling Criminal Justice: Eleven British Studies*, London: Macmillan.

Bowes, S. (1966) *The Police and Civil Liberties*, London: Lawrence & Wishart.

Bradford, G. (ed.) (1911) *Proceedings in the Court of the Star Chamber in the Reigns of Henry VII. and Henry VIII*, Somerset Record Society, vol. 27.

Brake, M. and Hale, C. (1991) *Public Order and Private Lives: The Politics of Law and Order*, London: Routledge.

Brand, P. (1992) *The Making of the Common Law*, London: Hambledon Press.

Brereton, the Rev. C.D. (1839) *A Letter to the Lord Lieutenant and Magistrates of the County of Norfolk on the Proposed Innovation in the Rural Police*, Swaffham.

Brewer, J. (1989) *The Sinews of Power: War, Money and the English State, 1688–1783*, London: Unwin Hyman.

Bridges, Y. (1954) *Saint – With Red Hands? The Chronicle of a Great Crime*, London: Jarrolds.

Brinkworth, E.R. (ed.) (1942) *The Archdeacon's Court: Liber Actorum, 1584*, Oxfordshire Record Society, vols. 23–24.

Brogden, M. (1982) *The Police: Autonomy and Consent*, London: Academic Press.

Brogden, M. (1991) *On the Mersey Beat: Policing Liverpool Between the Wars*, Oxford: Oxford University Press.

Brown, J. (1977) *Shades of Grey: a Report on Police-West Indian Relations in Handsworth*, Bedford: Cranfield Institute of Technology.

Brown, J. (1982) *Policing by Multi-Racial Consent: the Handsworth Experience*, London: Bedford Square Press.

Brownlow, Detective and Tuevoleur, Monsieur (1866) *The Dance of Death: or The Hangman's Plot. A Tale of London and Paris*, London.

Brundage, A. (1986) 'Ministers, magistrates and reformers: the genesis of the Rural Constabulary Act of 1839', *Parliamentary History*, 5: 55–64.

Brust, H. (1935) *"I Guarded Kings": The Memoirs of a Political Police Officer*, London: Stanley Paul.

Brust, H. (1937) *In Plain Clothes: Further Memoirs of a Political Police Officer*, London: Stanley Paul.

Burne, S.A.H. (ed.) (1932) *The Staffordshire Quarter Sessions Rolls, Vol. II, 1590–1593*, Kendal: The William Salt Archæological Society.

Butler, J.E. (1879) *Government by Police*, London.

Butler, T. (1992) 'Police and the Citizen's Charter', *Policing*, 8: 40–50.

Cain, H. (1917) *Address on Policemanship*, London.

Cam, H.M. (1921) *Studies in the Hundred Rolls: Some Aspects of Thirteenth-Century Administration*, Oxford Studies in Social and Legal History, vol. 6, Oxford: Clarendon Press.

Cam, H.M. (1924) 'The general eyres of 1329–30', *English Historical Review*, 39: 241–52.

Cam, H.M. (1930) *The Hundred and the Hundred Rolls: An Outline of Local Government in Medieval England*, New York: Burt Franklin.

Cam, H.M. (1944) *Liberties and Communities in Medieval England: Collected Studies in Local Administration and Topography*, Cambridge: Cambridge University Press.

Cam, H.M. (1950) 'Shire officials: coroners, constables, and bailiffs', in Willard, Morris and Dunham (1950).

Cam, H.M. (ed.) (1968) *The Eyre of London 14 Edward II A.D. 1321*, Selden Society, vol. 85.

Caminada, J. (1895) *Twenty-five Years of Detective Life*, Manchester: John Heywood.

Campaign for the Limitation of Secret Police Powers (1956) *The Secret Police and*

You, London: Campaign for the Limitation of Secret Police Powers.

Campbell, B.M.S. (ed.) (1991) *Before the Black Death: Studies in the 'Crisis' of the Early Fourteenth Century*, Manchester: Manchester University Press.

Campbell, G.A. (1943) *Our Police Force*, London: Oxford University Press.

Cary, J. (1696) *A Proposal Offered to the Committee of the Honourable House of Commons, Appointed to Consider Ways for the Better Provising, For the Poor, and Setting Them on Work* (no place of publication).

Cashmore, E.E. and McLaughlin, E. (1991) *Out of Order? Policing Black People*, London: Routledge.

Castro, J.P. de (1926) *The Gordon Riots*, London.

Chadwick, E. (1829) 'Preventive police', *London Review*, 1: 252–308.

Chapman, B. (1970) *Police State*, London: Pall Mall.

Chapman, C. (1925) *The Poor Man's Court of Justice: Twenty-Five Years as a Metropolitan Magistrate*, London: Hodder and Stoughton.

Clanchy, M.T. (1974) 'Law, government, and society in medieval England', *History*, 59: 73–8.

Clanchy, M.T. (1978) 'Highway robbery and trial by battle in the Hampshire eyre of 1249', in Hunnisett and Post (1978), 26–61.

Clark, P. (1983) *The English Alehouse: A Social History 1200–1830*, London: Longman.

Clarke, A. and Taylor, I. (1980) 'Vandals, pickets and muggers: television coverage of law and order in the 1979 election', *Screen Education*, 38: 99–111.

Clarke, A.A. (1992) *The Policemen of Hull: The Story of Hull Police Force 1836 to 1974*, Beverley.

Clarkson, C.T. and Richardson, J.H. (1889) *Police!*, London.

Clay, E.W. (ed.) (1974) *The Leeds Police 1836–1974*, Leeds.

Cobb, B. (1957) *The First Detectives and the Early Career of Richard Mayne Commissioner of Police*, London: Faber and Faber.

Cockburn, J.S. (1972) *A History of English Assizes 1558–1714*, Cambridge: Cambridge University Press.

Cockcroft, T. (2001) 'Police culture', unpublished paper.

Cohen, P. (1979) 'Policing the working-class city', in M. Fitzgerald, G. McLennan and J. Pawson (eds) *Crime and Society: Readings in History and Theory*, London: Routledge & Kegan Paul.

Cohen, S. (1985) *Visions of Social Control: Crime, Punishment and Classification*, Cambridge: Polity Press.

Collins, P. (1965) *Dickens and Crime*, London: Macmillan.

Colquhoun, P. (1797) *A Treatise on the Police of the Metropolis of London*, London.

Colquhoun, P. (1800) *A Treatise on the Commerce and Police of the River Thames*, London.

Conciliation Committee for Woman Suffrage (1911) *Treatment of the Women's Deputations of November 18th, 22nd and 23rd, 1910, by the Police*, London.

Conley, C.A. (1991) *The Unwritten Law: Criminal Justice in Victorian Kent*, Oxford: Oxford University Press.

Cookson, J.D. (1989) 'The English Volunteer movement of the French wars, 1793–1815: Some contexts', *The Historical Journal*, vol 32.

Coombes, B.L. (1939) *These Poor Hands: The Autobiography of a Miner Working in South Wales*, London: Victor Gollancz.

Coulon, A. (1892) *Anarchy is Too True a Doctrine to Suffer Because of Some Miscreants Sneaking Amongst Us* (no place of publication).

Cowan, S. (2001) *Identity, Community, and Difference: feminist and queer perspectives on the regulation of sexuality*, PhD thesis, Brunel University.

Cowley, R. (1986) *Policing Northamptonshire 1836–1986*, Studley: KAF Brewin Books.

Cox, B., Shirley, J. and Short, M. (1977) *The Fall of Scotland Yard*, Harmondsworth: Penguin.

Cox, D.C. (1975–6) 'Peace-keeping without frankpledge: Shropshire's claims in 1307', *Transactions of the Shropshire Archaeological Society*, 40: 81–95.

Cox, J. (1756) *A Faithful Narrative of the Most Wicked and Inhuman Transactions of the Bloody-minded Gang of Thief-takers, alias Thief-makers, Macdaniel, Berry, Salmon, Eagan, alias Gahagan; (with a Curious Print of Macdaniel) as also that Notorious Accomplice of Theirs, Mary Jones, and Others*, London.

Critchley, T.A. (1967) *A History of Police in England and Wales, 900–1966*, London: Constable.

Critchley, T.A. (1971) 'The developing role of the police in a changing society' in R.F. Gale (ed.) *The Police in Society: Proceedings of The Police Federation Seminar on "The Developing Role of the Police in a Changing Society" June 1971*, Surbiton: The Police Federation.

Critchley, T.A. (1978) *A History of Police in England and Wales*, London: Constable.

Crook, D. (1982a) *Records of the General Eyre*, P.R.O. Handbooks No. 20, London: HMSO.

Crook, D. (1982b) 'The latter eyres', *English Historical Review*, 97: 241–68.

Crowley, D.A. (1975) 'The later history of frankpledge', *Bulletin of the Institute of Historical Research*, 48: 1–15.

Cruikshank, I.R. (1833) *Cruikshank v. The New Police; Showing the Great Utility of that Military Body, Their Employment, &c*, London.

Cubin, J. (1832) *Sketch of A New National Police Bill*, London.

Cunnington, B.H. (ed.) (1925) *Some Annals of the Borough of Devizes. Being a Series of Extracts from the Corporation Records, 1555 to 1791*, Devizes: George Simpson.

Cunnington, B.H. (ed.) (1932) *Records of the County of Wilts Being Extracts from the Quarter Sessions Great Rolls of the Seventeenth Century*, Devizes: George Simpson.

Curry, J.E. and King, G.D. (1962) *Race Tensions and the Police*, Springfield: Charles C. Thomas.

Custos (1868) *The Police Force of the Metropolis in 1868*, London.

Dance, E.M. (ed.) (1958) *Guildford Borough Records 1514–1546*, Surrey Record Society, vol. 24.

Darwin, C.A. (1969) *Southport County Borough Police 1870–1969*, Southport.

Davenant, C. (1695) *An Essay Upon Ways and Means of Supplying the War*, London.

Davey, B.J. (1983) *Lawless and Immoral: Policing a County Town 1838–1847*, Leicester: Leicester University Press.

Davies, S.J. (1985) 'Classes and police in Manchester 1829–1880', in A.J. Kidd and K.W. Roberts (eds) *City, Class and Culture: Studies of Social Policy and Cultural Production in Victorian Manchester*, Manchester: Manchester University Press.

Davis, J. (1980) 'The London garotting panic of 1862: a moral panic and the creation of a criminal class in mid-Victorian England', in V.A.C. Gatrell and B. Lenman and G. Parker (eds) *Crime and the Law: The Social History of Crime in Western Europe since 1500*, London: Europa.

Davis, J. (1989) 'From "rookeries" to "communities": race, poverty and policing in London, 1850–1985', *History Workshop Journal*, 27: 66–85.

Defoe, D. (1709) *Review* (Edinburgh edition), 7 Apr.

Defoe, D. (1725) *A True and Genuine Account of the Life and Actions of the late Jonathan Wild*, London.

Dennett,, J. (ed.) (1933) *Beverley Borough Records, 1575–1821*, Yorkshire Archæological Society Record Series, vol. 84.

Dickens, C. (1861) *The Lamplighter's Story; Hunted Down; The Detective Police; and Other Nouvellettes*, Philadelphia.

Dilnot, G. (1915) *Scotland Yard: the Methods and Organisation of the Metropolitan Police*, London: Percival Marshall.

Dilnot, G. (ed.) (1928) *The Trial of the Detectives*, London: Geoffrey Bles.

Dixon, Sir Arthur L. (1963) *The Emergency Work of the Police Forces in the Second World War*, mimeograph.

Dixon, D. (1980) '"Class law": the Street Betting Act of 1906', *International Journal of the Sociology of Law*, 8: 101–28.

Doncaster Police (1863) *Criminal and Miscellaneous Statistical Returns of the Doncaster Police*, Doncaster.

Douglas, D.C. and Greenaway, G.W. (1981) *English Historical Documents Volume II: 1042–1189*, London: Eyre Methuen.

Downer, L.J. (ed.) (1996) *Leges Henrici Primi*, Oxford: Oxford University Press.

Doyle, A.C. (1892) *The Adventures of Sherlock Holmes*, London.

Dunkley, P. (1982) *The Crisis of the Old Poor Law in England, 1795–1834*, New York: Garland.

Eagles, J. (1832) *The Bristol Riots: Their Causes, Progress, and Consequences*, London.

Earwaker, J.P. (ed.) (1891–2) *The Constables' Accounts of the Manor of Manchester*, 2 vols., Manchester.

Easton, S. and Rawlings, P.J. (1996) 'The Citizen's Charter and the police', in C. Willett (ed.) *Public Sector Reform and the Citizen's Charter*, London: Blackstone Press.

Eastwood, D. (1997) *Government and Community in the English Provinces 1700–1870*, Basingstoke.

Edsall, N. (1971) *The Anti-Poor Law Movement, 1834–44*, Manchester: Manchester University Press.

Edwards, S.S.M. (1989) *Policing 'Domestic' Violence: Women, the Law and the State*, London: Sage.

Elliott, D.J. (1984) *Policing Shropshire 1836–1967*, Studley: KAF Brewin.

Else, W.M. and Garrow, J.M. (1934) *The Detection of Crime: An Introduction to Some*

Methods of Scientific Aid in Criminal Investigation, London: The Police Journal.

Emmison, F.G. (1970) *Elizabethan Life: Disorder*, Chelmsford: Essex County Council.

Emsley, C. (1982) 'The Bedfordshire Police, 1840–1856: a case study in the working of the Rural Constabulary Act', *Midland History*, 7: 73–92.

Emsley, C. (1983) *Policing and its Context 1750–1870*, London: Basingstoke.

Emsley, C. (1985) '"The thump of wood on a swede turnip": police violence in nineteenth-century England', *Criminal Justice History*, 6: 125–49.

Emsley, C. (1993) '"Mother, what *did* policemen do when there weren't any motors?" The law, the police and the regulation of motor traffic in England, 1900–1939', *Historical Journal*, vol 36.

Emsley, C. (1996) *The English Police: A Political and Social History*, London: Longman.

Emsley, C. and Clapson, M. (1994) 'Recruiting the English policeman, c. 1840–1940', *Policing and Society*, 3: 269–86.

Evans, E.J. (1983) *The Forging of the Modern State: Early Industrial Britain 1783–1870*, London: Longman.

Evans, P. (1974) *The Police Revolution*, London: George Allen & Unwin.

Evans-Pritchard, E.E. (1940) *The Nuer: A Descripton of the Modes of Livelihood and Political Institutions of a Nilotic People*, Oxford: Clarendon Press.

Fairhurst, J. (1996) *Policing Wigan: The Wigan Borough Police Force 1836–1969*, Blackpool: Landy Publishing.

Fidget (1838) *A Letter to the Lord Mayor, and Citizens of London, respecting the Introduction of the New Police*, London.

Fielding, H. (1754) *The Journal of a Voyage to Lisbon*, London.

Fielding, H. (1988) *An Enquiry into the Causes of the Late Increase of Robbers*, Oxford: Oxford University Press.

Fielding, J. (1755) *A Plan for Preventing Robberies within Twenty Miles of London. With an Account of the Rise and Establishment of the Real Thieftakers*, London.

Fielding, J. (1758) *An Account of the Origin and Effects of a Police Set Upon Foot by His Grace the Duke of Newcastle in the Year 1753, Upon a Plan Presented to His Grace by the Late Henry Fielding, Esq.*, London.

Fielding, J. (1768) *Extracts from Such of the Penal Laws, as Particularly Relate to the Peace and Good Order of this Metropolis*, London.

Fielding, J. (1769) *Extracts from Such of the Penal Laws, as Particularly Relate to the Peace and Good Order of this Metropolis*, London.

Fitzgerald, P. (1888) *Chronicles of Bow Street Police-Office*, London.

Foote, W. (1843) *Suggestions for the Improvement of Portions of the Criminal Law, Cognizable before Justices Out of Sessions, and for the Reorganization of the Rural Police Force*, London.

Forrester, A. (1863) *The Private Detective*, London.

Foster, D. (1982) *The Rural Constabulary Act 1839*, London: Bedford Square Press.

Foster, D. (1985) 'The East Riding Constabulary in the nineteenth century', *Northern History*, 21: 193–211.

Foster, J. (1974) *Class Struggle and the Industrial Revolution: Early Industrial*

Capitalism in Three English Towns, London: Methuen.

Fowler, N. (1966) *The Police State*, London: Bow Publications.

Fraser, C.M. (ed.) (1996) *The Court Rolls of the Manor of Wakefield for 1608/9*, The Wakefield Court Rolls Series of the Yorkshire Archaelogical Society, vol. 11.

Freeland, J.B. (1839) *State of the Police in the Rural Districts with Some Suggestions for its Improvement*, Chichester.

Friedlander, C.P. and Mitchell, E. (1974) *The Police: Servants or Masters?*, London: Hart-Davis.

Fryde, N. (1978) 'A medieval robber baron: Sir John Molyns of Stoke Poges, Buckinghamshire', in Hunnisett and Post (1978).

Gaffney, J. (1987) *Interpretations of Violence: the Handsworth Riots of 1985*, Coventry: Centre for Research in Ethnic Relations.

Gamon, H. (1907) *The London Police Court To-day & To-morrow*, London.

Gardiner, R. (1724) *The Complete Constable. Directing Constables, Headboroughs, Tithingmen, Church-wardens, Overseers of the Poor, Surveyors of the Highways, and Scavengers, In the Duty of their Offices, According to the Power Allowed Them By the Laws*, London.

Gaskill, M. (2000) *Crime and Mentalities in Early Modern England*, Cambridge: Cambridge University Press.

Gatrell, V.A.C. (1980) 'The decline of theft and violence in Victorian and Edwardian England', in V.A.C. Gatrell, B. Lenman and G. Parker (eds) *Crime and the Law: The Social History of Crime in Western Europe since 1500*, London: Europa.

Gatrell, V.A.C. (1990) 'Crime, authority and the policeman-state', in Thompson, F.M.L. (eds) *The Cambridge Social History of Britain 1750–1950: Volume 3*, Cambridge: Cambridge University Press.

Gatrell, V.A.C. (1994) *The Hanging Tree: Execution and the English People 1770–1868*, Oxford: Oxford University Press.

Gatrell, V.A.C. and Hadden, T. (1972) 'Nineteenth-century criminal statistics and their interpretation' in E.A. Wrigley (ed.) *Nineteenth-Century Society*, Cambridge: Cambridge University Press.

Gifford, Lord (1986) *The Broadwater Farm Enquiry. Report of the Independent Enquiry into Disturbances of October 1985 at the Broadwater Farm Estate, Tottenham*, London: Karia.

Gikes, R.K. (ed.) (1997) *The 'Bawdy Court' of Banbury: The Act Book of the Peculiar Court of Banbury, Oxfordshire and Northamptonshire 1625–1638*, Banbury Historical Society, vol. 26.

Gilbert, T. (1786) *A Plan of Police*, London.

Given, J.B. (1977) *Society and Homicide in Thirteenth-Century England*, Stanford: Stanford University Press.

Gleason, J.H. (1969) *The Justices of the Peace in England 1558 to 1640: A Later Eirenarcha*, Oxford: Clarendon Press.

Gluckman, M. (1970) *Custom and Conflict in Africa*, Oxford: Basil Blackwell.

Goddard, H. (1956) *Memoirs of a Bow Street Runner*, London: Museum Press.

Goldie, M. (1997) 'The Hilton gang: terrorising dissent in 1680s London', *History*

Today, 47: 26–33.

Goodway, D. (1982) *London Chartism, 1838–1848*, Cambridge: Cambridge University Press.

Goring, J. and Wake, J. (eds) *Northamptonshire Lieutenancy Papers and Other Documents 1580–1614*, Northamptonshire Record Society, vol. 27.

Greater London Council (1982) *Policing London: The Policing Aspects of Lord Scarman's Report on the Brixton Disorders*, London: GLC.

Green, M.A.E. (ed.) (1867) *Calendar of State Papers, Domestic Series, of the Reign of Elizabeth 1591–1594*, London: Longman, Green, Reader, Dyer.

Green, M.A.E. (ed.) (1869) *Calendar of State Papers, Domestic Series, of the Reign of Elizabeth 1595–1597*, London: Longman, Green.

Green, T. (1985) *Verdict According to Conscience: Perspectives on the English Criminal Trial Jury 1200–1800*, Chicago: University of Chicago Press.

Grigg, M. (1965) *The Challenor Case*, Harmondsworth: Penguin.

Gurney, J. (1775) *An Account of the Arguments of Counsel with the Opinions at Large of the Honourable Mr. Justice Gould, Mr. Justice Ashhurst, and Mr. Baron Hotham*, London.

Guy, J.A. and Beale, H.G. (eds) (1984) *Law and Social Change in British History: Papers Presented to the Bristol Legal History Conference, 14–17 July 1981*, London: Royal Historical Society.

H.D. (1725) *The Life of Jonathan Wild, from His Birth to His Death*, London.

Hague, W. (2000) 'Speech to the Centre for Policy Studies', 14 Dec. http//www.conservatives.com.

Hahn, M. (1989) *Policing Victorian Dorset*, Wincanton: Dorset Publishing.

Hain, P. (1984) *Political Trials in Britain*, London.

Halford, Sir Henry (1840) *Some Remarks on the Report of the Constabulary Force Commissioners, and Upon the Acts Founded on that Report*, Leicester.

Hall, R. (1985) *Ask Any Woman: a London Inquiry into Rape and Sexual Assault*, Bristol: Fallingwall Press.

Hall, R.G. (1989) 'Tyranny, work and politics: the 1818 strike wave in the English cotton district', *International Review of Social History*, 34: 433–70.

Hall, S., Critcher, C., Jefferson, T., Clarke, J. and Roberts, B. (1978) *Policing the Crisis: Mugging, the State, and Law and Order*, London: Macmillan.

Hammersmith and Fulham Council (1988) *Subways: Closed Circuit Television and Safety from Crime*, London: Hammersmith and Fulham, Community and Police Committee.

Hammersmith and Fulham Council (1989) *What Support? Domestic Violence Project: An Exploratory Study of Council Policy and Practice, and Local Support Services in the Area of Domestic Violence within Hammersmith and Fulham*, London: Hammersmith and Fulham, Community and Police Committee.

Hamner, J. and Saunders, S. (1984) *Well-Founded Fear: a Community Study of Violence to Women*, London: Hutchinson.

Hanawalt, B.A. (1974–5) 'Fur collar crime: the pattern of crime among the fourteenth-century English nobility', *Journal of Social History*, vol 8.

Hanawalt, B.A. (1979) *Crime and Conflict in English Communities 1300–1348*,

Cambridge, Mass.: Harvard University Press.

Hanawalt, B.A. and Wallace, D. (1999) 'Introduction', in B.A. Hanawalt and D. Wallace (eds) *Medieval Crime and Social Control*, London: University of Minnesota Press.

Hannington, W. (1936) *Unemployed Struggles, 1919–1936: My Life and Struggles Amongst the Unemployed*, London: Lawrence and Wishart.

Harding, A. (1960) 'The origins and early history of the keeper of the peace', *Transactions of the Royal Historical Society*, (5th series), 10: 85–109.

Harding, A. (1978) 'Early trailbaston proceedings from the Lincoln roll of 1305', in Hunnisett and Post (1978).

Harding, A. (1981) *The Roll of the Shropshire Eyre of 256*, Selden Society, vol. 96.

Harding, A. (1984) 'The revolt against the justices' in R.H. Hilton and T.H. Ashton (eds) *The English Rising of 1381*, Cambridge: Cambridge University Press.

Harding, C., Hines, W., Ireland, R. and Rawlings, P.J. (1985) *Imprisonment in England and Wales: A Concise History*, London: Croom Helm.

Hardwicke, G. (1980) *Keepers of the Door: The History of the Port of London Authority Police*, London: Peel Press.

Hardy, E. (1859) *How to Repel Invasion. The Rural Police of England an Auxiliary To Rifle Corps, in Two Letters to Arthur Kinglake, Esq., Justice of the Peace for Somerset*, London.

Harris, W.C. (1858) *A Manual of Drill, Prepared for the Use of the County and District Constables*, London.

Harris, W.C. (1868) *Questions and Answers Framed for the Instruction of Constables, on Joining the Police*, London.

Harrison, B. (1965) 'The Sunday Trading riots of 1855', *Historical Journal*, 8: 219–45.

Hart, J. (1951) *The British Police*, London: George Allen & Unwin.

Hart, J. (1955) 'Reform of the borough police, 1835–1856', *English Historical Review*, 70: 411–27.

Hart, J. (1956) 'The County and Borough Police Act, 1856', *Public Administration*, vol 34.

Hassell Smith, A. and Baker, G.M. (eds) (1984) *The Papers of Nathaniel Baker of Stiffkey Volume II 1578–1585*, Norfolk Record Society.

Hassell Smith, A., Baker, G.M., and Kenny, R.W. (eds) (1979) *The Papers of Nathaniel Baker of Stiffkey Volume I 1556–1577*, Norfolk Record Society, vol. 46.

Hay, D. (1977) 'Property, authority and the criminal law' in D. Hay *et al* (eds) *Albion's Fatal Tree: Crime and Society in Eighteenth-century England*, Harmondsworth: Penguin.

Hayter, T. (1978) *The Army and the Crowd in Mid-Georgian England*, London: Macmillan.

Henderson, T. (1999) *Disorderly Women in Eighteenth-Century London: Prostitution and Control in the Metropolis 1730–1830*, London: Longman.

Hensman, S and London Rape Crisis Centre (1999) *Sexual Violence: The Reality for Women*, 3rd edn, London: Women's Press.

Herbert, G. (1971) *Shoemaker's Window: Recollections of Banbury in Oxfordshire before the Railway Age* (ed. C.S. Cheney and B.S. Trinder), London: Phillimore for Banbury Historical Society.

Herring, P. (1855) *An Exposition of the Conduct of Police-Serjeant Sterr, with Reference to the Late Charge of "Attempted Murder and Suicide," Heard at the Police Court, Marylebone, Against Philip Herring. With the Correspondence Between Sir Richard Mayne & Mr Herring*, London.

Herrup, C. (1987) *The Common Peace: Participation and the Criminal Law in Seventeenth-Century England*, Cambridge: Cambridge University Press.

Hewitt, E.J. (1979) *A History of Policing in Manchester*, Didsbury: E.J. Morten (Publishers).

Hewitt, J. (1783) *The Proceedings of J. Hewitt, Alderman*, Birmingham.

Hewitt, J. (1790) *A Journal of the Proceedings of J. Hewitt, Senior Alderman, of the City of Coventry, And One of His Majesty's Justices of the Peace for the said City and County, In His Duty as a Magistrate, during a Period of Thirty Years, and Upwards*, 2nd edn (no place of publication).

Hibbert, C. (1958) *King Mob: The Story of Lord George Gordon and the Riots of 1780*, London: Longmans, Green & Co.

Hindle, S. (1996) 'The keeping of the public peace' in P. Griffiths, A. Fox and S. Hindle (eds) *The Experience of Authority in Early Modern England*, Basingstoke: Macmillan.

Hobbs, D. (1992) *Doing the Business: Entreprenuership, the Working Class, and Detectives in the East End of London*, Oxford: Oxford University Press.

Hobsbawm, E.J. and Rudé, G. (1973) *Captain Swing*, Harmondsworth: Penguin.

Holdsworth, W.S. (1923) *A History of English Law*, vol. II, London: Methuen.

Holloway, R. (1773) *The Rat-Trap: Dedicated to the Rt. Hon. Lord Mansfield, Chief Justice of England: Addressed to Sir John Fielding*, London.

Hopkins, H. (1986) *The Long Affray: The Poaching Wars 1760–1914*, London: Macmillan.

Hopkinson, A.M. (2000) *The Rolls of the 1281 Derbyshire Eyre*, Derbyshire Record Society, vol. 27.

Hough, M. (1985) 'Organization and resource management in the uniformed police', in K. Heal, R. Tarling and J. Burrows (eds) *Policing Today*, London: HMSO.

Hough, M. and Mayhew, P. (1983) *The British Crime Survey*, Home Office Research Study, 76, London: HMSO.

Howgrave-Graham, H.M. (1947) *The Metropolitan Police at War*, London: HMSO.

Howson, G. (1987) *It Takes a Thief: The Life and Times of Jonathan Wild*, London: Cresset Library.

Hudson, J. (1996) *The Formation of the English Common Law: Law and Society in England from the Norman Conquest to Magna Carta*, London: Longman.

Hughes, A. (1864) *Leaves from the Note-Book of a Chief of Police*, London.

Humphries, S. (1981) *Hooligans or Rebels? An Oral History of Working-Class Childhood and Youth 1889–1939*, Oxford: Basil Blackwell.

Hunnisett, R.F. (1961) *The Medieval Coroner*, Cambridge: Cambridge University Press.

Hunnisett, R.F. and Post, J.B. (eds) (1978) *Medieval Legal Records: Edited in Memory of C.A.F. Meekings*, London: HMSO.

Hunt, J. (1863) *The Policeman's Struggle; Addressed to the Inhabitants of the Metropolitan Police District*, London

Hurnard, N.D. (1941) 'The jury of presentment and the Assize of Clarendon', *English Historical Review*, 56: 374–410.

Hurnard, N.D. (1969) *The King's Pardon for Homicide Before A.D. 1307*, Oxford: Clarendon Press.

Hutchings, W.J. (1957) *Out of the Blue: History of Devon Constabulary*, Torquay.

Hyams, P.R. (1996) 'What Did Edwardian Villagers Understand by 'Law'?', in Z. Ravi and R. Smith (eds) *Medieval Society and the Manor Court*, Oxford: Clarendon Press.

Hypochondriac, A (1830) *The Blue Devils; or, New Police. A Poem: in Three Cantos*, London.

Ignatieff, M. (1979) 'Police and people: the birth of Mr Peel's "Blue Locusts"', *New Society*, 30 Aug, 443–4.

Ingleton, R.D. (1994) *Gentlemen at War: Policing Britain 1939–45*, Maidstone: Cranborne.

Ingram, M. (1996) 'Reformation of manners in early modern England', in P. Griffiths, A. Fox and S. Hindle (eds) *The Experience of Authority in Early Modern England*, Basingstoke: Macmillan.

Innes, J. (1990) 'Politics and morals: the reformation of manners movement in late eighteenth-century England', in E. Hellmuth (ed.) *The Transformation of Political Culture: England and Germany in the Late Eighteenth Century*, Oxford: Oxford University Press.

Inquest (1982/3–99), *Annual Reports*, London.

Ireland, R.W. (1986) 'The presumption of guilt in the history of English criminal procedure', *Journal of Legal History*, 7: 243–55.

James, R.W. (1957) *To the Best of Our Skill and Knowledge: A Short History of the Cheshire Constabulary*, Chester: Cheshire Constabulary.

Jefferson, T. and Grimshaw, R. (1984) *Controlling the Constable: Police Accountability in England and Wales*, London: Frederick Muller.

Jervis, R. (1995) *Chronicles of a Victorian Detective*, Runcorn: P & D Riley.

Jewell, H.M. (1972) *English Local Administration in the Middle Ages*, Newton Abbot: David & Charles.

Johnston, L. (1992) *The Rebirth of Private Policing*, London: Routledge.

Johnston, L. (2000) *Policing Britain: Risk, Security and Governance*, London: Longman.

Jones, D.J.V. (1982) *Crime, Protest, Community and Police in Nineteenth-Century Britain*, London: Routledge & Kegan Paul.

Jones, D.J.V. (1989) *Rebecca's Children: A Study of Rural Society, Crime and Protest*, Oxford: Clarendon Press.

Jones, D.J.V. (1990–1) '"Where did it all go wrong?": crime in Swansea, 1938–68', *Welsh History Review*, 15: 240–74.

Jones, G.S. (1984) *Outcast London: A Study of the Relationship between Classes in Victorian Society*, Harmondsworth: Penguin.

251

Joshua, H., Wallace, T. and Booth, H. (1983) *To Ride the Storm*, London: Heinemann.

Joyce, P. (1993) 'The transition from "old" to "new" policing in early 19th century Manchester', *Police Journal*, Apr., 197–210.

Juror, A (1838) *A Series of Letters, on Rural Police and the Poor Law Amendment Act, Proving Their Intimate Connexion*, Ipswich.

Kaeuper, R.W. (1979) 'Law and order in fourteenth-century England: the evidence of special commissions of oyer and terminer', *Speculum*, 54: 734–84.

Kempster, J. (1904) *The Dalston Perjury Case*, London: Police Review Office.

Kent, J.R. (1986) *The English Village Constable 1580–1642: A Social and Administrative Study*, Oxford: Clarendon Press.

Kerr, M.H. (1995) 'Angevin reform of the appeal of felony', *Law and History Review*, 13: 351–91.

Kettle, M. and Hodges, L. (1982) *Uprising! The Police, the People and the Riots in Britain's Cities*, London: Pan Books.

Kimball, E.G. (ed.) (1959) *The Shropshire Peace Roll 1400–1414*, Shrewsbury: Salop County Council.

Kimball, E.G. (ed.) (1983) *Oxfordshire Sessions of the Peace in the Reign of Richard II*, Oxfordshire Record Society, vol. 53.

King, E.J. (1984) 'The anarchy of King Stephen's reign', *Transactions of the Royal Historical Society*, (5th series), 34: 133–53.

King, P. (1989) 'Prosecution associations and their impact on eighteenth-century Essex', in D. Hay and H. Snyder (eds) *Policing and Prosecution in Britain 1750–1850*, Oxford: Oxford University Press.

King, P. (2000) *Crime, Justice, and Discretion in England 1740–1820*, Oxford: Oxford University Press.

Kinsey, R. (1985) *Survey of Merseyside Police Officers: First Report, June 1985*, Merseyside County Council.

Kinsey, R., Lea, J. and Young, J. (1986) *Losing the Fight Against Crime*, Oxford: Basil Blackwell.

Kyrke, R.V. (1969) *History of East Sussex Police, 1840–1967*, Kenilworth.

Lambert, J.R. (1970) *Crime, Police, and Race Relations: A Study in Birmingham*, London: Oxford University Press.

Lambourne, G. (1986) 'A brief history of fingerprint identification', *Journal of the Police History Society*, 1: 1–9.

Landau, N. (1984) *The Justices of the Peace, 1679–1760*, Berkeley: University of California Press.

Langbein, J.H. (1974) *Prosecuting Crime in the Renaissance: England, Germany, France*, Cambridge, Mass.: Harvard University Press.

Langbein, J.H. (1983) 'Shaping the eighteenth-century trial: a view from the Ryder sources', *University of Chicago Law Review*, 50: 1–136.

Latham, F. (1911) *Is the British Empire Ripe for Government by Disorderly Women Who Smash Windows and Assault the Police?*, London.

Latham, R.E. and Timings, E.K. (1950) 'Six letters concerning the eyres of 1226–8',

English Historical Review, 65: 492–504.

Lee, W.L. Melville (1901) *A History of Police in England*, London: Methuen.

Lemon, R. (ed.) (1865) *Calendar of State Papers, Domestic Series, of the Reign of Elizabeth 1581–1590*, London: Longman, Green, Longman.

Leslie-Melville, R. (1934) *The Life and Work of Sir John Fielding*, London: Lincoln Williams.

Levine, P. (1994) '"Walking the streets in a way no decent woman should". Women police in World War One', *Journal of Modern History*, 66: 34–78.

Linebaugh, P. (1977) 'The Tyburn riot against the surgeons', in D. Hay *et al* (eds) *Albion's Fatal Tree: Crime and Society in Eighteenth-Century England*, Harmondsworth: Penguin.

Linebaugh, P. (1991) *The London Hanged: Crime and Civil Society in the Eighteenth Century*, London.

Lister, J. (ed.) (1888–1915) *West Riding Sessions Rolls*, Yorkshire Archæological and Topographical Association Record Series, vols. 3 and 54.

Liverpool City Police (1950) *Report on the Police Establishment and the State of Crime for the Year ending 31st December, 1949*, Liverpool.

Locard, E. (1920) *L'Enquête Criminelle et Les Méthodes Scientiques*, Paris: Ernest Flammarion.

Lock, J. (1979) *The British Policewoman: Her Story*, London: Robert Hale.

Lohman, J.D. (1947) *The Police and Minority Groups*, Chicago.

London Rape Crisis Centre (1984) *Sexual Violence: The Reality for Women*, London: Women Press.

Lowe, W.J. (1983) 'The Lancashire Constabulary, 1845–1870: the social and occupational function of a Victorian police force', *Criminal Justice History*, 4: 41–62.

Loyn, H.R. (1984) *The Governance of Anglo-Saxon England 500–1087*, London: Edward Arnold.

Lugard, C.E. (ed.) (1933) *Trailbaston*, 3 vols, Ashover: The Dirty Duck Press.

Lustgarten, L. (1986) *The Governance of the Police*, London: Sweet & Maxwell.

McClintock, F.H. and Avison, N.H. (1968) *Crime in England and Wales*, London: Heinemann.

McConville, S. (1981) *A History of English Prison Administration: Volume I 1750–1877*, London: Routledge.

McCrea, B. (1981) *Henry Fielding and the Politics of Mid-Eighteenth-Century England*, Athens: The University of Georgia Press.

McHardy, Captain J.B.B. (1840) *Essex Constabulary. Orders & Instructions Framed and Issued for the Superintendents and Constables of the Essex Constabulary*, Chelmsford.

McIntosh, M.K. (1998) *Controlling Misbehaviour in England, 1370–1600*, Cambridge: Cambridge University Press.

McLaren, A. (1993) *A Prescription for Murder: The Victorian Serial Killings of Dr Thomas Neil Cream*, London: University of Chicago Press.

McLaughlin, E. and Murji, K. (1995) 'Controlling the bill: restructuring the police in the 1990s', *Critical Social Policy*, May–Jun., 95–103.

McMullan, J.L. (1996) 'The new improved monied police: reform, crime control, and the commodification of policing in London', *British Journal of Criminology*, 36: 85–108.

Madan, M. (1785) *Thoughts on Executive Justice &c.*, London.

Maddern, P.C. (1992) *Violence and Social Order: East Anglia 1422–1442*, Oxford: Clarendon Press.

Madigan, T.J. (1993) *'The Men Who Wore Straw Helmets': Policing Luton 1840–1974*, Dunstable: The Book Castle.

Mainwaring, G.B. (1821) *Observations on the Present State of the Police of the Metropolis*, London.

Mainwaring-White, S. (1983) *The Policing Revolution: Police, Technology, Democracy and Liberty in Britain*, Brighton: Harvester Press.

Maitland, F.W. (ed.) (1884) *Pleas of the Crown for the County of Gloucester 1221*, London: Macmillan.

Maitland, F.W. (ed.) (1888) *Select Pleas of the Crown Volume I. A.D. 1200–1225*, Selden Society, vol. 1.

Maitland, F.W. (ed.) (1889) *Select Pleas in Manorial and Other Seignorial Courts: Volume I. Reigns of Henry III and Edward I*, Selden Society, vol. 2.

Maitland, F.W. and Baildon, W.P. (eds) (1891) *The Court Baron: Being Precedents for Use in Seignorial and Other Local Courts*, Selden Society, vol. 5.

Malthus, T. (1798) *An Essay on the Principles of Population*, London.

Manchester, A.H. (1984) *Sources of English Legal History, 1750–1950*, London: Butterworths.

Manchester Committee (1772) *For the More Effectual Security of this Town*, Manchester.

Manchester Police (1841–2) *Number of Persons Taken into Custody by the Manchester Police*, Manchester.

Manchester Police (1844) *Criminal Statistical Returns of the Manchester Police*, Manchester.

Manchester Police Monitoring Unit (1987) *Breaking the Silence: Manchester Women Speak Out: Women & Violence Survey Report*, Manchester: Police Monitoring Unit.

Mark, Sir Robert (1978) *In the Office of Constable*, London: Collins.

Marshall, D. (1926) *The English Poor in the Eighteenth Century: A Study in Social and Administrative Theory*, London.

Marshall, R. (1981) 'Police, media, and the policy of disclosure', *Bramshill Journal*, 1 (3): 39–42.

Martin, J.P. and Wilson, G. (1969) *The Police: A Study in Manpower: The Evolution of the Service in England and Wales 1829–1965*, London: Heinemann.

Mather, F.C. (1959) *Public Order in the Age of the Chartists*, Manchester: Manchester University Press.

Matthews, G. (1986) 'The search for a cure for vagrancy in Worcestershire, 1870–1920', *Midland History*, 11: 100–16.

Mayhew, H. (1967) *London Labour and the London Poor*, London: Frank Cass.

Mearns, A. and Preston, W.C. (1883) *The Bitter Cry of Outcast London*, London.

Meekings, C.A.F. (1961) *Crown Pleas of the Wiltshire Eyre, 1249*, vol. 16.

Mercier, C.A. (1918) *Crime and Criminals: Being the Jurisprudence of Crime, Medica, Biological, and Psychological*, London: University of London Press.

Merewether, H.A. (1816) *A New System of Police, with references to the Evidence Given Before the Police Committee of the House of Commons*, London.

Meriton, G. (1669) *A Guide for Constables, Churchwarden, Overseers of the Poor, Surveyors of the Highways, Treasurers of the County Stock, Masters of the House of Correction, Bayliffs of the Mannours, Toll-Takers in Fairs, &c*, London.

Metropolitan Police (1982) *The Report of the Commissioner of the Police of the Metropolis 1981*, London: HMSO.

Metropolitan Police Office (1848) *Memorandum of Suggestions for the Use of Special Constables*, London.

Metropolitan Police Service (1993) *Our Performance*, London: Metropolitan Police, News Branch.

Meyer, E.T. (1950) 'Boroughs', in Willard, Morris and Dunham (1950).

Mildmay, W. (1763) *The Police of France*, London.

Mildmay, W. (1765) *The Laws and Policy of England*, London.

Miles, W.A. (1773) *A Letter to Sir John Fielding, Knt. Occasioned by His Extraordinary Request to Mr. Garrick for the Suppression of the Beggar's Opera*, London.

Miles, W.A. (1836) *Suggestions for the Formation of a General Police: In a Letter to the Right Hon. Lord John Russell*, London.

Monro, J. (1886) *A Report on the History of the Department of the Metropolitan Police, known as the Convict Supervision Office: Detailing System, and Showing Results and Effects Generally on the Habitual Criminal Population*, London.

Morgan, J. (1987) *Conflict and Order: The Police and Labour Disputes in England and Wales, 1900–1939*, Oxford: Oxford University Press.

Morrell, C. (1981) *'Black Friday' and Violence against Women in the Suffragette Movement*, Explorations in Feminism No. 9, London: Women's Research and Resources Centre.

Morris, W.A. (1910) *The Frankpledge System*, London: Longmans, Green & Co.

Morrish, R. (1955) *The Police and Crime-Detection Today*, London: Oxford University Press.

Moylan, Sir John (1934) *Scotland Yard and the Metropolitan Police*, London: Putnam.

Musson, A. (1995) *Public Order and Law Enforcement: The Local Administration of Criminal Justice, 1294–1350*, Woodbridge: The Boydell Press.

Musson, A. and Ormrod, W.M. (1999) *The Evolution of English Justice: Law, Politics and Society in the Fourteenth Century*, London: Macmillan.

National Council for Civil Liberties (1960) *Submission to the Royal Commission on Police*, London: NCCL.

National Council for Civil Liberties (1961) *Public Order and the Police: A Report on the Events in Trafalgar Square Sunday 17th to Monday 18th September, 1961*, London: NCCL.

National Council for Civil Liberties (1966) *The James Report: Comment on the 'Report of Inquiry' by Mr A.E. James, Q.C.*, London: NCCL.

National Council for Civil Liberties (1986) *No Way in Wapping*, London: NCCL.

Neal, S. (1849) *The Chief Constable's Report to the Watch Committee, Comprising the Criminal and Statistical Returns in Connection with the Police Force*, Salford.

Newing, J. (1990) 'Policing: a crisis in confidence', paper delivered to the Crime and Policing Conference, Islington.

Northam, J. (1988) *Shooting in the Dark: Riot Police in Britain*, London: Faber and Faber.

O'Brien, B.R. (1990) *Studies of the "Leges Edwardi Confessoris" and their milieu*, PhD thesis, Yale University.

Observer, An (1836) *The Publicans and the Police, with some Observations on the Contemplated Borough-Rate*, Liverpool.

Page, W. (ed.) (1891) *Three Early Assize Rolls for the County of Northumberland*, Surtees Society, vol. 88.

Paley, R. (1989a) '"An imperfect, inadequate and wretched system?" Policing London before Peel', *Criminal Justice History*, 10: 95–130.

Paley, R. (1989b) 'Thief-takers in London in the age of the McDaniel gang, *c.* 1745–1754', in D. Hay and F. Snyder (eds) *Policing and Prosecution in Britain 1750–1850*, Oxford: Oxford University Press.

Paley, W. (1833) *The Works of William Paley, D.D. Archdeacon of Carlisle. With a Life of the Author*, London.

Palmer, R.C. (1993) *English Law in the Age of the Black Death, 1348–1381: A Transformation of Governance and Law*, London: The University of North Carolina Press.

Palmer, S. (1988) *Police and Protest in England and Ireland, 1788–1850*, Cambridge: Cambridge University Press.

Parris, H. (1961) 'The Home Office and the provincial police in England and Wales, 1856–1870', *Public Law*, vol 20.

Payling, S.J. (1989) 'The Ampthill dispute: a study in aristocratic lawlessness and the breakdown of Lancastrian government', *English Historical Review*, 104: 881–907.

Petrow, S. (1993) 'The rise of the detective in London, 1869–1914', *Criminal Justice History*, 14: 91–108.

Petrow, S. (1994) *Policing Morals: The Metropolitan Police and the Home Office, 1870–1914*, Oxford: Oxford University Press.

Philips, D. (1980) '"A new engine of authority": the institutionalization of law enforcement in England 1780–1830', in V.A.C. Gatrell, B. Lenman and G. Parker (eds) *Crime and the Law: the Social History of Crime in Western Europe since 1500*, London: Europa.

Philips, D. (1989) 'Good men to associate and bad men to conspire: associations for the prosecution of felons in England 1768–1860', in D. Hay and F. Snyder (eds) *Policing and Prosecution in Britain 1750–1850*, Oxford; Oxford University Press.

Philips, D. and Storch, R.D. (1994) 'Whigs and coppers: the Grey ministry's national police scheme, 1832', *Historical Research*, 67: 75–90.

Philips, D. and Storch, R.D. (1999) *Policing Provincial England, 1829–1856: The*

Politics of Reform, London: Leicester University Press.

Police Constable, A (1888) *The Metropolitan Police and Its Management. A Reply to Sir Charles Warren's Article in "Murray's Magazine"*, London.

Police Monitoring and Research Group (1987) *Policing Wapping: An Account of the Dispute 1986/7*, Briefing Paper No. 3, London: London Strategic Policy Unit.

Pollock, Sir F. and Maitland, F.W. (1968) *The History of the English Law Before the Time of Edward I*, 2 vols, Cambridge: Cambridge University Press.

Plotnikoff, J. (1989) *Hammersmith and Fulham Services to Victims of Crime*, London: Hammersmith and Fulham, Community and Police Committee.

Porter, B. (1985) *The Origins of Britain's Political Police*, Warwick Working Papers in Social History, No. 3.

Porter, B. (1987) *The Origins of the Vigilant State: The London Metropolitan Police Special Branch before the First World War*, London: Weidenfeld & Nicolson.

Post, J.B. (1976) *Criminals and the Law in the Reign of Richard II*, D.Phil. thesis, University of Oxford.

Post, J.B. (1983) 'Local jurisdictions and judgment of death in later medieval England', *Criminal Justice History*, 4: 1–21.

Potter, R. (1775) *Observations on the Poor Laws, on the Present State of the Poor, and on the Houses of Industry*, London.

Pound, J.F. (ed.) (1971) *The Norwich Census of the Poor 1570*, Norfolk Record Society, vol. 40.

Powell, D.L. and Jenkinson, H. (eds) (1934) *Surrey Quarter Sessions Records: Order Book and Sessions Rolls 1659–1661*, Surrey Record Society, no. 35.

Powell, D.L. and Jenkinson, H. (eds) (1938) *Surrey Quarter Sessions Records: Order Book and Sessions Rolls Easter 1663– Epiphany 1666*, Surrey Record Society, no. 39.

Powell, E. (1984) 'Settlement of disputes by arbitration in fifteenth-century England', *Law and History Review*, 2: 21–43.

Powell, E. (1987) 'The administration of criminal justice in late-medieval England: peace sessions and assizes', in R. Eales and D. Sullivan (eds) (1987) *The Political Context of Law*, London: The Hambledon Press.

Powell, E. (1989) *Kingship, Law, and Society: Criminal Justice in the Reign of Henry V*, Oxford: Clarendon Press.

Poynter, J.R. (1969) *Society and Pauperism: English Ideas on Poor Relief, 1795–1834*, London.

Pratt, J.T. (1891) *The Lighting and Watching Act* (ed. S. Wright), London.

Prest, J. (1990) *Liberty and Locality: Parliament, Permissive Legislation, and Ratepayers' Democracies in the Nineteenth Century*, Oxford: Clarendon Press.

Prestwich, M. (1988) *Edward I*, London: Methuen.

Price, C. and Caplan, J. (1977) *The Confait Confessions*, London: Marion Boyars.

Pugh, R.B. (1967) *Itinerant Justices in English History*, Exeter: University of Exeter.

Pugh, R.B. (ed.) (1975) *Calendar of London Trailbaston Trials under Commissions of 1305 and 1306*, London: HMSO.

Pugh, R.B. (ed.) (1978) *Wiltshire Gaol Delivery and Trailbaston Trials 1275–1306*, vol. 30.

Pulling, C. (1964) *Mr Punch and the Police*, London: Butterworths.

Putnam, B.H. (1908) *The Enforcement of the Statute of Labourers During the First Decade After the Black Death 1349–59*, New York: Columbia University.

Putnam, B.H. (1929) 'The transformation of the keepers of the peace 1327–80', *Transactions of the Royal Historical Society*, (4th series), 12: 19–48.

Putnam, B.H. (ed.) (1938) *Proceedings before the Justices of the Peace in the Fourteenth and Fifteenth Centures: Edward III to Richard III*, Ames Foundation, London: Spottiswoode, Ballantyne & Co.

Radzinowicz, L. (1948–68) *A History of English Criminal Law and Its Administration since 1750*, 4 vols, London: Stevens.

Raine, A. (ed.) (1939–53) *York Civic Records*, 8 vols, Yorkshire Archæological Society Records Series.

Rawcliffe, C. (1984) 'The great lord as peacekeeper: arbitration by English noblemen and their councils in the later middle ages', in Guy and Beale (1984).

Rawlings, P.J. (1983) 'Defoe and street robberies: an undiscovered text', *Notes and Queries*, (n.s.), 30: 23–6.

Rawlings, P.J. (1985) 'Bobbies, aliens and subversives: the relationship between community policing and coercive policing', in J. Baxter and L. Koffman (eds) *The Police, the Constitution and the Community*, Abingdon: Professional Books.

Rawlings, P.J. (1991) 'Creeping privatisation? The police, the Conservative government and policing in the late 1980s', in R. Reiner and M. Cross (eds) *Beyond Law and Order: Criminal Justice Policy and Politics into the 1990s*, London: Macmillan.

Rawlings, P.J. (1992a) *Drunks, Whores and Idle Apprentices: Criminal Biographies of the Eighteenth Century*, London: Routledge.

Rawlings, P.J. (1992b) 'Who needs a royal commission?', *Policing*, 8: 15–25.

Rawlings, P.J. (1995) 'The idea of policing: a history', *Policing and Society*, 5: 129–49.

Rawlings, P.J. (1999) *Crime and Power: A History of Criminal Justice 1688–1998*, Longman: London.

Read, C. (ed.) (1962) *William Lambarde and Local Government: His "Ephemeris" and Twenty-nine Charges to Juries and Commissions*. Ithaca, New York: Cornell University Press.

Reay, B. (1998) *Popular Cultures in England 1550–1750*, London: Longman.

Reilly, J.W. (1989) *Policing Birmingham: An Account of 150 Years of Police in Birmingham*, Birmingham: West Midlands Police.

Reiner, R. (1986) 'A watershed in policing', *Journal of the Police History Society*, 1: 10–21.

Reiner, R. (1991) *Chief Constables: Bobbies, Bosses, or Bureaucrats?*, Oxford: Oxford University Press.

Reiner, R. (1992) *The Politics of Police*, Hemel Hempstead: Wheatsheaf.

Reiner, R. (1997) 'Policing and the police', in M. Maguire, R. Morgan and R. Reiner (eds) *The Oxford Handbook of Criminology*, Clarendon Press: Oxford.

Reith, C. (1956) *A New Study of Police History*, Edinburgh: Oliver and Boyd.

Reynolds, E.A. (1998) *Before the Bobbies: The Night Watch and Police Reform in Metropolitan London, 1720–1830*, Stanford University Press: Stanford.

Reynolds, G.W. and Judge, A. (1968) *The Night the Police Went on Strike*, London: Wedenfeld and Nicolson.

Richardson, H. (ed.) (1969–78) *Court Rolls of the Manor of Acomb*, 2 vols, Yorkshire Archæological Society Records Series, vols. 131 and 137.

Richardson, H.G. and Sayles, G.O. (eds) (1955) *Fleta Volume II*, Selden Society, vol. 55.

Richardson, H.G. and Sayles, G.O. (1963) *The Governance of Mediaeval England from the Conquest to Magna Carta*, Edinburgh: University of Edinburgh Press.

Richardson, H.G. and Sayles, G.O. (1966) *Law and Legislation from Æthelberht to Magna Carta*, Edinburgh: University of Edinburgh.

Richardson, S. (1734) *The Apprentice's Vade Mecum: or, Young Man's Pocket Companion*, London.

Richmond (1976), *Scenes in the Life of a Bow Street Runner Drawn From His Private Memoranda* (1827), (introduction by E.F. Beiler), New York: Dover Publications.

Richmond, A. (1954) *Colour Prejudice in Britain: A Study of West Indian Workers in Liverpool, 1941–54*, London: Routledge & Kegan Paul.

Richter, A.F. (1990) *Bedfordshire Police 1840–1990*, Bedford: Paul Hooley and Associates.

Richter, D.C. (1981) *Riotous Victorians*, London: Ohio University Press.

Riggs, C.H. (1963) *Criminal Asylum in Anglo-Saxon Law*, University of Florida Monographs in Social Studies No. 18, Gainesville, Florida: University of Florida Press.

Ritchie-Noakes, N. (1984) *Liverpool's Historic Waterfront: The World's First Mercantile Dock System*, Merseyside County Museums and Royal Commission on Historical Monuments Supplementary Series, no. 7, London: HMSO.

Roach, L. (1978) 'The Metropolitan Police Community Relations Branch', *Police Studies*, 3: 17–23.

Roberts, M.J.D. (1983) 'The Society for the Suppression of Vice and its early critics, 1802–1812', *The Historical Journal*, vol 26.

Roberts, M.J.D. (1984) 'Making Victorian morals? The Society for the Suppression of Vice and its critics, 1802–1886', *The Historical Studies*, vol 21.

Robertson, A.J. (1925) *The Laws of the Kings of England from Edmund to Henry I*, Cambridge: Cambridge University Press.

Robinson, C.D. (1979) 'Ideology as history: a look at the way some English police historians look at the police', *Police Studies*, 2: 35–49.

Robinson, C.D., Scaglion, R. with Olivero, J.M. (1994) *Police in Contradiction: The Evolution of the Police Function in Society*, Westport: Greenwood Press.

Robison, W.B. (1988) 'Murder at Crowhurst: a case study in early Tudor law enforcement', *Criminal Justice History*, 9: 31–62.

Rose, D. (1996) *In the Name of the Law: The Collapse of Criminal Justice*, London: Jonathan Cape.

Rosenheim, J.M. (ed.) (1991) *The Notebook of Robert Doughty 1662–1665*, Norfolk Record Series, vol. 54.

Rothwell, H. (1975) *English Historical Documents Volume III: 1189–1327*, London: Routledge.

Rowntree, B.S. and Lavers, G.R. (1951) *Poverty and the Welfare State: A Third Social*

Survey of York Dealing Only with Economic Questions, London: Longmans, Green & Co.

Rubin, S. (1996) 'The *bot*, or composition in Anglo-Saxon law: a reassessment', *Journal of Legal History*, 17: 144–54.

Rudé, G. (1964) *The Crowd in History: A Study of Popular Disturbances in France and England, 1730–1848*, New York.

Rudé, G. (1974) *Paris and London in the Eighteenth Century: Studies in Popular Protest*, London: Fontana.

Rule, J. (1992) *Albion's People: English Society, 1714–1815*, London: Longman.

Rumbelow, D. (1971) *I Spy Blue: The Police and Crime in the City of London from Elizabeth I to Victoria*, London: Macmillan.

Rumbelow, D. (1988) *The Houndsditch Murders and the Seige of Sydney Street*, London: W.H. Allen.

Salgado, G. (ed.) (1972) *Cony-Catchers and Bawdy Baskets: an Anthology of Elizabethan Low Life*, Harmondsworth: Penguin.

Samuel, R. (1981) *East End Underworld: Chapters from the Life of Arthur Harding*, London: Routledge & Kegan Paul.

Saunders, A. and Young, R. (1994) *Criminal Justice*, London: Butterworths.

Sayles, G.O. (1939) *Select Cases*, Selden Society, vol 58.

Schofield, P.R. (1996) 'The late medieval view of frankpledge and the tithing system: an Essex case study', in Z. Ravi and R. Smith (eds) *Medieval Society and the Manor Court*, Oxford: Clarendon Press.

Schwartz, R.D. and Miller, J.C. (1964) ' Legal evolution and societal complexity', *The American Journal of Sociology*, 70: 159–69.

Scott, Sir B. (1867) *A Statistical Vindication of the City of London; or, Fallacies Exposed and Figures Explained*, London.

Scott, Sir Harold (1949) *Police Problems of Today*, London: Stevens.

Shapland, J. and Vagg, J. (1988) *Policing by the Public*, London: Routledge.

Sharpe, J.A. (1977) 'Crime and delinquency in an Essex parish 1600–1640', in J.S. Cockburn (ed.) *Crime In England 1550–1800*, London: Macmillan.

Sharpe, J.A. (1980) 'Enforcing the law in the seventeenth-century English village', in V.A.C. Gatrell and B. Lenman and G. Parker (eds) *Crime and the Law: The Social History of Crime in Western Europe since 1500*, London: Europa.

Sharpe, J. (1999) *Crime in Early Modern England 1550–1750*, London: Longman.

Shearing, C.D. and Stenning, P. (1981) 'Modern private security: its growth and implications', in M. Tonry and N. Norris (eds) *Crime and Justice: An Annual Review of Research*, Chicago: University of Chicago Press.

Sheptycki, J. (1995) 'Transnational policing and the makings of a modern state', *British Journal of Criminology*, 35: 613–35.

Sheptycki, J. (1996) 'Law enforcement, justice and democracy in the transnational arena: reflections on the war on drugs', *International Journal of the Sociology of Law*, 24: 61–75.

Shoemaker, R.B. (1991) *Prosecution and Punishment: Petty Crime and the Law in London and Rural Middlesex, c. 1660–1725*, Cambridge: Cambridge University Press.

Shore, W. Teignmouth (ed.) (1923) *Trial of Thomas Neil Cream*, London: William Hodge.

Short, K.R.M. (1979) *The Dynamite War: Irish-American Bombers in Victorian Britain*, Dublin: Gill and Macmillan.

Short, T. (1750) *New Observations on the Bills of Mortality*, London.

Shpayer-Makov, H. (1990) 'The making of a police labour force', *Journal of Social History*, 24: 109–34.

Shpayer-Makov, H. (1991) 'The appeal of country workers: the case of the Metropolitan Police', *Historical Research*, 64: 186–203.

Silver, A. (1967) 'The demand for order in civil society: a review of some themes in the history of urban crime, police, and riot', in D.J. Bordua (ed.) *The Police: Six Sociological Essays*, New York: John Wiley.

Silverthorne, E. (ed.) (1978) *Deposition Book of Richard Wyatt, JP, 1767–1776*, Surrey Record Society, vol. 30.

Sim, J. (1982) 'Scarman: the police counter-attack', *Socialist Register*, 57–77.

Simpson, A.W.B. (1981) 'The laws of Ethelbert', in M.S. Arnold, T.A. Green, S.A. Scully and S.D. White (eds) *On the Law and Customs of England: Essays in Honor of Samuel E. Thorne*, Chapel Hill: The University of North Carolina Press.

Sindall, R. (1990) *Street Violence in the Nineteenth Century: Media Panic or Real Danger?*, Leicester: Leicester University Press.

Slack, P.A. (1972) 'Poverty and politics in Salisbury 1597–1666', in P. Clark and P. Slack (eds) *Crisis and Order in English Towns 1500–1700: Essays in Urban History*, London: Routledge & Kegan Paul.

Slack, P.A. (1974) 'Vagrants and vagrancy in England, 1598–1664', *Economic History Review*, (2nd series), 27: 360–79.

Slack, P.A. (ed.) (1975) *Poverty in Early Stuart Salisbury*, Wiltshire Record Society, vol. 31.

Slack, P.A. (1988) *Poverty and Policy in Tudor and Stuart England*, London: Longman.

Slack, P.A. (1990) *The Impact of Plague in Tudor and Stuart England*, Oxford: Clarendon Press.

Slack, P.A. (1999) *From Reformation to Improvement: Public Welfare in Early Modern England*, Oxford: Clarendon Press.

Sleigh, Capt. A.W. (1844) *A General Police and Constabulary List and Analysis of Criminal and Police Statistics. For the Quarter Ending September, 1844*, London, 1844.

Smethurst, J. (1841) *Conspiracy. A Petition to Parliament*, London.

Smethurst, T. (1983) *Reminiscences of a Bolton and Stalybridge Policeman 1888–1922*, Swinton: Neil Richardson.

Smethurst, T. (1993) *A Policeman's Notebook*, Bolton: Aurora Enterprises.

Smith, C.R. (1972) *An Examination of the Procedure for Dealing with Complaints against the Police*, Police Federation Occasional Papers, Surbiton: Police Federation.

Smith, D. and Gray, J. (1983) *Police and People in London*, London: Policy Studies Institute.

Smith, D.J. (1990) 'The establishment and development of the Worcestershire

County Constabulary 1839–1843', *Journal of the Police History Society*, 5: 3–23.

Smith, P.T. (1985) *Policing Victorian London: Political Policing, Public Order, and the London Metropolitan Police*, Westport: Greenwood Press.

Smith, Sir Thomas (1982) *De Republica Anglorum* (ed. M. Dewar), Cambridge: Cambridge University Press.

Smithies, E. (1982) *Crime in Wartime: A Social History of Crime in World War II*, London: George Allen and Unwin.

Soderlund, R.J. (1998) ' "Intended as a terror to the idle and profligate": embezzlement and the origins of policing in the Yorkshire worsted industry, *c.* 1750–1777', *Journal of Social History*, 31: 647–70.

Southgate, P. (1982) *Police Probationer Training in Race Relations*, Home Office Research and Planning Unit, no. 8, London: HMSO.

Spufford, M. (1985) 'Puritanism and social control?', in A. Fletcher and J. Stevenson (eds) *Order and Disorder in Early Modern England*, Cambridge: Cambridge University Press.

Steedman, C. (1984) *Policing the Victorian Community: The Formation of English Provincial Police Forces, 1856–80*, London: Routledge & Kegan Paul.

Stenton, D.M. (ed.) (1937) *Rolls of the Justices in Eyre being the Rolls of Pleas and Assizes for Yorkshire in 3 Henry III (1218–19)*, Selden Society, vol. 56.

Stenton, D.M. (ed.) (1953–67) *Pleas before the King or His Justices 1198–1202*, 4 volumes, Selden Society, vols. 67, 68, 83 and 84.

Stephen, G. (1829) *Practical Suggestions for the Improvement of the Police*, London.

Stevens, P. and Willis, C. (1979) *Race, Crime and Arrests*, Home Office Research Study, no. 58, London: HMSO.

Stevenson, J. (1977) 'The Queen Caroline affair', in J. Stevenson (ed.) *London in the Age of Reform*, Oxford: Basil Blackwell.

Stevenson, J. (1979) *Popular Disturbances in England 1700–1870*, London: Longman.

Stewart-Brown, R. (1936) *The Serjeants of the Peace in Medieval England and Wales*, Manchester: University of Manchester Press.

Stones, E.L.G. (1957) 'The Folvilles of Ashby Folville, Leicestershire, and their associates in crime, 1326–1347', *Transactions of the Royal Historical Society*, (5th series), 7: 117–36.

Storch, R.D. (1975) 'The plague of the blue locusts: police reform and popular resistance in northern England, 1840–1857', *International Review of Social History*, 20: 61–90.

Storch, R.D. (1976) 'The policeman as domestic missionary: urban discipline and popular culture in northern England, 1850–80', *Journal of Social History*, 9: 481–509.

Storch, R.D. (1977) 'Police control of street prostitution in Victorian London', in D. Bayley (ed.) *Police and Society*, London: Sage.

Storch, R.D. (1989) 'Policing in rural southern England before the police: opinion and practice, 1830–1856', in D. Hay and F. Snyder (eds) *Policing and Prosecution in Britain 1750–1850*, Oxford: Oxford University Press.

Styles, J. (1983) 'Sir John Fielding and the problem of crime investigation in eighteenth-century England', *Transactions of the Royal Historical Society*, (5th series), 33: 127–49.

Styles, J. (1989) 'Print and policing: crime advertising in eighteenth-century provincial England', in D. Hay and F. Snyder (eds) *Policing and Prosecution in Britain 1758–1850*, Oxford: Oxford University Press.

Sugden, P. (1995) *The Complete History of Jack the Ripper*, New York: Carroll & Graf.

Summerson, H.R.T. (1979) 'The structure of law enforcement in thirteenth century England', *American Journal of Legal History*, 23: 313–27.

Summerson, H. (1986) 'Maitland and the criminal law in the age of *Bracton'*, *Proceedings of the British Academy*, 89: 115–43.

Summerson, H. (1992) 'The enforcement of the Statute of Winchester, 1285–1327', *Journal of Legal History*, 13: 232–50.

Summerson, H. (1996) 'The criminal underworld of medieval England', *Journal of Legal History*, 17: 197–224.

Sutherland, D.W. (1973) *The Assize of Novel Disseisin*, Oxford: Clarendon Press.

Sutherland, D.W. (ed.) (1983) *The Eyre of Northampton 3–4 Edward III A.D. 1329–1330*, Selden Society, vols. 97–8.

Sutton, D. (ed.) (1978) *York Civic Records Volume IX*, Yorkshire Archæological Society Rolls Series, vol. 138.

Swift, R. (1988) 'Urban policing in early Victorian England, 1835–56: a reappraisal', *History*, 73: 211–37.

Tawney, R.H. and Power, E. (1951) *Tudor Economic Documents Being Selected Documents Illustrating the Economic and Social History of Tudor England*, 3 vols, London: Longmans, Green and Co.

Taylor, D. (1991) 'Crime and policing in early Victorian Middlesborough, 1835–55', *Journal of Local and Regional Studies*, vol 11.

Taylor, D. (1995) *'A Well-Chosen, Effective Body of Men': The Middlesborough Police Force, 1841–1914*, Teeside Paper in North Eastern History, no. 6, Cleveland: University of Teeside.

Taylor, D. (1997) *The New Police in Nineteenth-Century England: Crime, Conflict and Control*, Manchester: Manchester University Press.

Taylor, I. (1987) 'Law and order, moral order: the changing rhetoric of the Thatcher government', *Socialist Register*, 297–331.

Taylor, M.M. (1950) 'The justices of assize', in Willard, Morris and Dunham (1950).

Taylor, T. (1863) *The Ticket-of-Leave Man*, London.

Thomas, H. (1987) *The History of the Gloucestershire Constabulary 1839–1985*, Gloucester: Alan Sutton for Gloucestershire Constabulary.

Thomas, K. (1978) *Religion and the Decline of Magic: Studies in Popular Beliefs in Sixteenth- and Seventeenth-Century England*, Harmondsworth: Peregrine Books.

Thomas, S. (1974) *The Bristol Riots*, Bristol: Bristol Historical Association.

Thompson, D. (1984) *The Chartists: Popular Politics in the Industrial Revolution*, New York: Pantheon.

Thompson, E.P. (1968) *The Making of the English Working Class*, Harmondsworth: Pelican.

Thompson, E.P. (1977) *Whigs and Hunters: The Origin of the Black Act*, Harmondsworth: Penguin.

Thompson, E.P. (1993) *Customs in Common*, Harmondsworth: Penguin.

Thorpe, B. (1840) *Ancient Laws and Institutions of England*, London.

Thurston, G. (1967) *The Clerkenwell Riot: The Killing of Constable Culley*, London: George Allen & Unwin.

Timewell, J. (1911) *Royal Commission upon the Duties of the Metropolitan Police. Suppressed Evidence*, London: James Timewell, Police & Public Vigilance Society.

Tomlin, M. (1936) *Police and Public*, London: John Long.

Tout, T.F. and Johnstone, H. (1906), *State Trials of the Reign of Edward the First 1289–1293*, London.

Torrington, F.W. (1972–8) *House of Lords Sessional Papers*, Dobbs Ferry, NY: Oceana.

Trafford, W. (1848) *Trafford (Late Police Constable 344, S. Division) Who Saved 7 Lives from Fire*, London.

Traill, J. (1839) *A Letter to the Right Hon. Lord Brougham and Vaux, on the Police Reports and the Police Bills*, London.

Trustees of the Liverpool Docks (1810) *A Statement of the Grounds Upon Which the Trustees of the Liverpool Docks Propose Applying to Parliament, Next Session, For Authority to Provide Additional Dock Space, &c. &c.*, Liverpool.

Turner, R.V. (1985) *The English Judiciary in the Age of Glanvill and Bracton, c. 1176–1239*, Cambridge: Cambridge University Press.

Underdown, D. (1987) *Revel, Riot and Rebellion: Popular Politics and Culture in England 1603–1660*, Oxford: Oxford University Press.

Underdown, D. (1992) *Fire from Heaven: The Life of an English Town in the Seventeenth Century*, London: HarperCollins.

Van Caenegem, R.C. (ed.) (1990–91) *English Lawsuits from William I to Richard I*, 2 volumes, Selden Society, vols. 106–7.

Vinogradoff, Sir Paul (1920) *Outlines of Historical Jurisprudence*, 2 vols, London: Oxford University Press.

Vogler, R. (1991) *Reading the Riot Act: the Magistracy, the Police and the Army in Civil Disorder*, Milton Keynes: Open University.

Wade, J. (1829) *A Treatise on the Police and Crimes of the Metropolis*, London.

Wake, J. (ed.) (1924) *Quarter Sessions Records of the County of Northampton. Files for 6 Charles I and Commonwealth (A.D. 1630, 1657, 1657–8)*, Northamptonshire Record Society.

Walker, S.K. (1989) 'Lordship and lawlessness in the palitinate of Lancaster, 1370–1400', *Journal of British Studies*, 28: 325–48.

Walkowitz, J.R. (1992) *City of Dreadful Delight: Narratives of Sexual Danger in Late-Victorian London*, London: Virago.

Walker, T. (1728) *The Quaker's Opera*, London.

Wall, D. (1987) 'Chief constables: a changing élite', in R. Mawby (ed.) *Policing*

Britain, Plymouth: Plymouth Polytechnic, Department of Political and Social Sciences.

Wall, D. (1998) *The Chief Constables of England and Wales: The Socio-Legal History of a Criminal Justice Elite*, Aldershot: Ashgate/Darmouth.

Wallace-Hadrill, J.M. (1958–9) 'The bloodfeud of the Franks', *The Bulletin of the John Rylands Library*, 41: 459–87.

Wallace-Hadrill, J.M. (1971) *Early Germanic Kingship in England and on the Continent: The Ford Lectures Delivered in the University of Oxford in Hilary Term 1970*, Oxford: Clarendon Press.

Waller, S. (1957) *Cuffs and Handcuffs: The Story of Rochdale Police Through the Years 1252–1957*, Rochdale: Rochdale Borough Police Watch Committee.

Wandsworth Policing Campaign, Working Party (1986) *Racism in the Police Force is Now a Disciplinary Offence*, London: Wandsworth Policing Campaign

Ward, T. and Benn, M. (1987) 'Were the police ever innocent?', *New Society*, 80 (no. 1277), 19 June: 14–17.

Ware, J.R. (1866) *The Road Murder*, London.

Warren, C. (1888) 'The police of the Metropolis', *Murray's Magazine*, 4 (22): 577–94

Warren, W.L. (1987) *The Governance of Norman and Angevin England 1086–1272*, London: Edward Arnold.

Waters, L. (1994) *The Police Gazette: Part 1*, Marlborough: Adam Matthew Publications.

Watson, E.J. (1902) *Pleas of the Crown for the Hundred of Swineshead and the Township of Bristol*, Bristol: W. Crofton Hemmons.

Weikel, A. (ed.) *The Court Rolls of the Manor of Wakefield from 1537 to 1539*, The Wakefield Court Rolls Series of the Yorkshire Archaeological Society, vol. 9.

Weinberger, B. (1981) 'The police and the public in mid-nineteenth century Warwickshire', in V. Bailey (ed.) *Policing and Punishment in the Nineteenth Century*, London: Croom Helm.

Weinberger, B. (1991a) 'Are the police professionals? An historical account of the British police institution', in C. Emsley and B. Weinberger (eds) *Policing Western Europe: Politics, Professionalism, and Public Order, 1850–1940*, London: Greenwood Press.

Weinberger, B. (1991b) *Keeping the Peace: Policing Strikes in Britain*, Oxford: Oxford University Press.

Wells, R. (1988) *Wretched Faces: Famine in Wartime England, 1793–1803*, Gloucester: Alan Sutton.

Wells, R. (1990) 'Social protest, class conflict and consciousness in the English countryside 1700–1880', in M. Reed and R. Wells (eds) *Class, Conflict and Protest in the English Countryside 1700–1880*, London: Cass.

Western, J.R. (1956) 'The Volunteer movement as an anti-revolutionary force, 1793–1801', *English Historical Review*, vol 4.

White, J. (1986) *The Worst Street in North London: Campbell Bunk, Islington, Between the Wars*, London: Routledge & Kegan Paul.

Whittaker, B. (1964) *The Police*, Harmondsworth: Penguin.

Whittaker, B. (1979) *The Police in Society*, London: Eyre Methuen.

Whittaker, W.J. (ed.) (1895) *The Mirror of Justices*, Selden Society, vol. 7.

Whitworth, Sir Charles (1773) *The Draught of an Intended Act, for the Better Regulation of the Nightly Watch and Beadles within the City and Liberty of Westminster*, London.

Wiener, M.J. (1990) *Reconstructing the Criminal: Culture, Law and Policy in England, 1830–1914*, Cambridge: Cambridge University Press.

Willard, J.F., Morris, W.A., and Dunnard, W.H. (eds) (1950) *The English Government at Work, 1327–1336: Volume III*, Cambridge, Mass.: The Medieval Academy of America.

Williams, D. (1967) *Keeping the Peace: The Police and Public Order*, London: Hutchinson.

Wilson, R. (1722) *A Full and Impartial Account of the all the Robberies Committed by John Hawkins, George Sympson, (Lately Executed for Robbing the Bristol Mails) and Their Companions*, London: J. Peele.

Wilson, Rev. (1743) *A Genuine Account of the Behaviour, Confessions, and Dying Words of the Malefactors … Who were Executed at Kennington-Common, on Thursday the 25th of August, 1743*, London.

Winslow, C. (1977) 'Sussex smugglers', in D. Hay *et al* (eds) *Albion's Fatal Tree: Crime and Society in Eighteenth-Century England*, Harmondsworth: Penguin.

Wise, E. (1751) *The Remarkable Tryal of Thomas Chandler*, Reading.

Wood, I. (1795) *Some Account of the Shrewsbury House of Industry, Its Establishment and Regulations*, Shrewsbury.

Woodbridge Select Committee (1827) *Report of the Select Committee, Appointed at a Public Meeting of the Inhabitants of Woodbridge*, Woodbridge.

Woodgate, J. (1985) *The Essex Police*, Lavenham: Terence Dalton.

Woodhall, E.T. (1934) *Guardians of the Great*, London: Blandford Press.

Woodward, J. (1697) *Sodom's Vices Destructive to Other Cities and States*, London.

Woodward, J. (1702) *A Sermon Preach'd at the Parish-Church of St. James's, Westminster, on the 21st of May, 1702. At the Funeral of Mr. John Cooper, a Constable*, London.

Worcester City Police (1861) *City of Worcester. General Regulations, Instructions, & Orders for the Government and Guidance of the Worcester Police Force, As Framed by the Watch Committee, and Approved by the Town Council*, Worcester.

Worcester City Police (1865) *City of Worcester. Annual Reports of the Committees of the Council and Local Board of Health*, Worcester.

Wormald, P. (1997) 'Frederic William Maitland and the earliest English law', *Law and History*, 16: 1–25.

Wormald, P. (1999) *The Making of English Law: King Alfred to the Twelfth Century*, Oxford: Blackwell.

Wright, S. Fowler (1929) *Police and Public*, London: Fowler Wright.

Wrightson, K. (1980) 'Two concepts of order: justices, constables and jurymen in seventeenth-century England', in J. Brewer and J. Styles (eds) *An Ungovernable People: The English and Their Law in the Seventeenth and Eighteenth Centuries*, London: Hutchinson.

Wrightson, K. and Levine, D. (1995) *Poverty and Piety in an English Village: Terling, 1525–1700*, Oxford: Clarendon Press.

Wyles, L. (1952) *A Woman at Scotland Yard: Reflections on the Struggles and Achievements of Thirty Years in the Metropolitan Police*, London: Faber and Faber.

Young, A. (1770) *A Six Months' Tour through the North of England*, London.

Zirker, M.R. (1966) *Enquiry into Fielding's Social Pamphlets*, Berkeley and Los Angeles: University of California Press.

Index